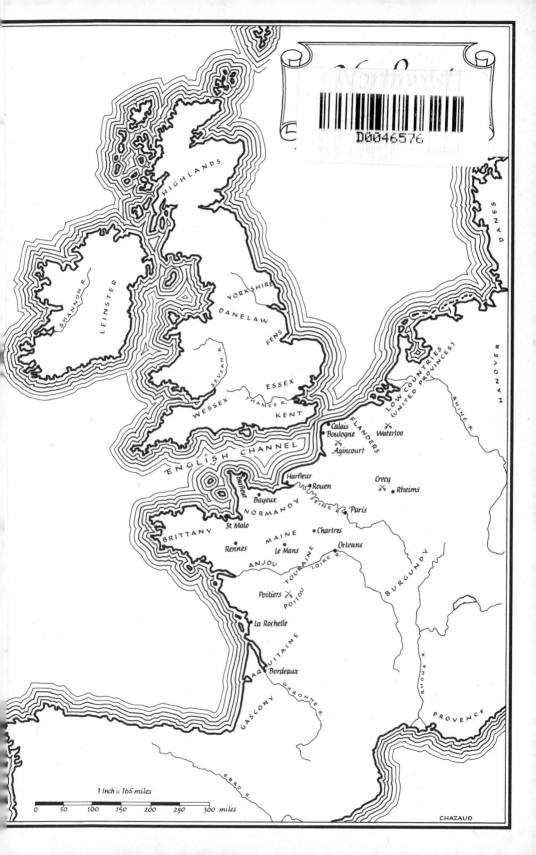

HIGHLANDS

LEINSTER

SHANNON R.

YORKSHIRE

DANELAW

FENS

SEVERN R.

WESSEX

THAMES R.

ESSEX

KENT

ENGLISH CHANNEL

Calais
Boulogne

Agincourt

FLANDERS

LOW COUNTRIES
(UNITED PROVINCES)

Waterloo

DANES

HANOVER

RHINE R.

Barfleur

Harfleur

Rouen

SEINE R.

Paris

Crecy

Rheims

Bayeux

NORMANDY

St. Malo

BRITTANY

MAINE

Chartres

Rennes

Le Mans

Orleans

ANJOU

TOURAINE

LOIRE R.

Poitiers

POITOU

BURGUNDY

La Rochelle

AQUITAINE

Bordeaux

GASCONY

GARONNE R.

RHONE R.

PROVENCE

EBRO R.

1 Inch = 165 miles

0   50   100   150   200   250   300 miles

CHAZAUD

THE
MONARCHS
OF
ENGLAND

HONI SOIT MALY PENSE

DIEU ET MON DROIT

THE
MONARCHS
OF
ENGLAND

by JEAN MORRIS

CHARTERHOUSE

New York

The Monarchs of England
COPYRIGHT © 1975 BY Jean Morris

LIBRARY OF CONGRESS CATALOG CARD NUMBER: 74–82977
ISBN 0–88327–043–9
MANUFACTURED IN THE UNITED STATES OF AMERICA
DESIGNED BY JACQUES CHAZAUD

Dedicated with great affection
to my Father,
E. C. Morris,
and to my Daughter,
Mercy.

Contents

Introduction

This book attempts the history of a relationship.

It is not a history of England, nor of the English monarchy, nor of the English constitution. It began as a history of the men who have been Kings of England, trying to discover, from their acts and from the words of their contemporaries, what sort of men they were and how they looked on their position. But there are two sides to that position, and, if we ask what the English Kings did to England, we must also wonder what England did to its Kings.

For a thousand years the English people have had Kings reigning over them. This is more than curious when you consider that they were, by a good many centuries, the first European people to resist successfully the principle that the common man lives, works, and dies for the benefit of his rulers. Like the rest of Europe, and of those countries which stem from Europe, England experienced centuries of government that left her convinced that no series of single men could safely be trusted with supreme power. Why, then, through many periods when the monarchy could easily have been cast off, has she stubbornly insisted on keeping it?

The English people, as we understand the term today, did not exist before the Conquest of 1066, when William I brought in the Norman blood that was to mix with the native Anglo-Saxon and emerge as English. All through the years of Norman rule there persisted in the common people much of the spirit, more of the traditions, and all of the local laws. Perhaps because these laws and traditions were those of the people, concerned not with power and prestige but with the vital business of everyday living, their continuance bred in the people an embryo of unity, an embryo of perception that life exists to be best lived in peace with neighbors.

So the Kings, the unfortunate men who by accident of birth or conquest came to rule over this people, found themselves with this incradicable instinct to contend with. One or two of them, whose names are honored, understood it and worked with it; one or two understood it and fought it; most of them, alas, had not the least idea of what was going on. Good Kings molded the people, little Kings were molded by the people, and the great Kings lived in a relationship with their people that made them both the better for it. It is sad to record that bad Kings made their people the worse for it.

Vast areas of history are missing from this book, and even vaster areas have been reduced to summary, since it concerns only the Kings. Henry II was a Continental prince, Richard I a Crusader, William III a Protestant general, Victoria a politician. For those who want it, there is a list of books for further reading in the Appendix. In particular, the history of the sister Kingdoms has been included only where it has a bearing upon the history of England. For the personalities of the Kings, I have used the evidence of their contemporaries. In general outlines, I have been guided by those distinguished historians whose works are mentioned in the Appendix, but the interpretation is my own responsibility. I have been very much helped in the research by Michael Bakewell, Isabel Maskell, and E. C. Morris, and my daughter Mercy assisted in the drawing of the genealogical chart and maps. I must express my gratitude to Charterhouse Books, and in particular to Carol Eisen Rinzler, for their patience and helpfulness.

"Ahem!" said the Mouse with an important air, "are you all ready? This is the driest thing I know. Silence all round if you please! William the Conqueror, whose cause was favoured by the Pope—"

—Alice in Wonderland.

THE MONARCHS
FROM ALFRED THE GREAT

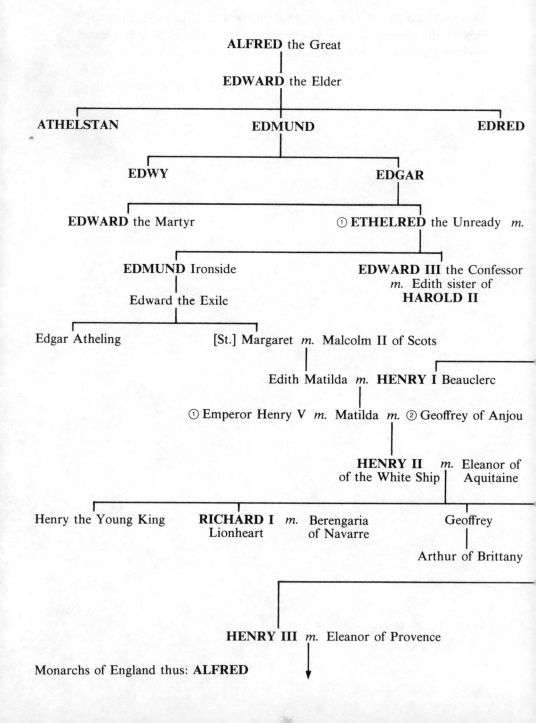

ALFRED the Great

EDWARD the Elder

ATHELSTAN   **EDMUND**   **EDRED**

EDWY   **EDGAR**

EDWARD the Martyr   ① **ETHELRED** the Unready *m.*

EDMUND Ironside   **EDWARD III** the Confessor
                             m. Edith sister of
                             HAROLD II

Edward the Exile

Edgar Atheling   [St.] Margaret *m.* Malcolm II of Scots

Edith Matilda *m.* **HENRY I** Beauclerc

① Emperor Henry V *m.* Matilda *m.* ② Geoffrey of Anjou

HENRY II   *m.* Eleanor of
of the White Ship | Aquitaine

Henry the Young King   **RICHARD I** *m.* Berengaria   Geoffrey
                              Lionheart   of Navarre

Arthur of Brittany

HENRY III *m.* Eleanor of Provence

Monarchs of England thus: **ALFRED**

OF ENGLAND
TO ELIZABETH II

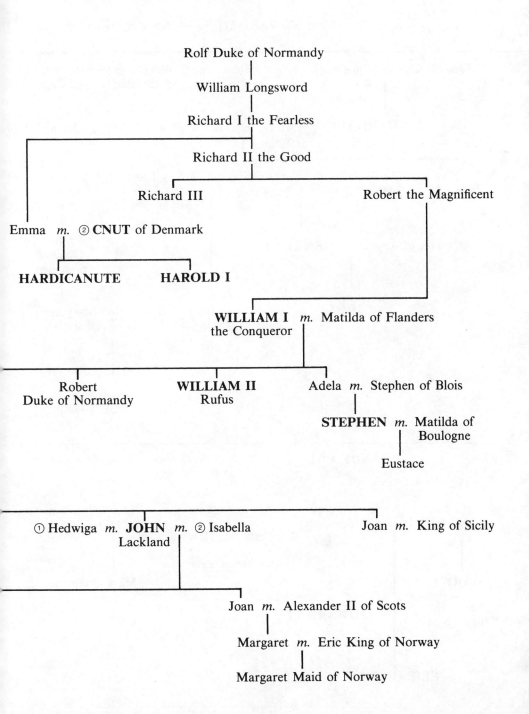

Rolf Duke of Normandy

William Longsword

Richard I the Fearless

Richard II the Good

Richard III

Robert the Magnificent

Emma *m.* ② **CNUT** of Denmark

HARDICANUTE   **HAROLD I**

WILLIAM I *m.* Matilda of Flanders
the Conqueror

Robert
Duke of Normandy

WILLIAM II
Rufus

Adela *m.* Stephen of Blois

STEPHEN *m.* Matilda of
Boulogne

Eustace

① Hedwiga *m.* **JOHN** *m.* ② Isabella
Lackland

Joan *m.* King of Sicily

Joan *m.* Alexander II of Scots

Margaret *m.* Eric King of Norway

Margaret Maid of Norway

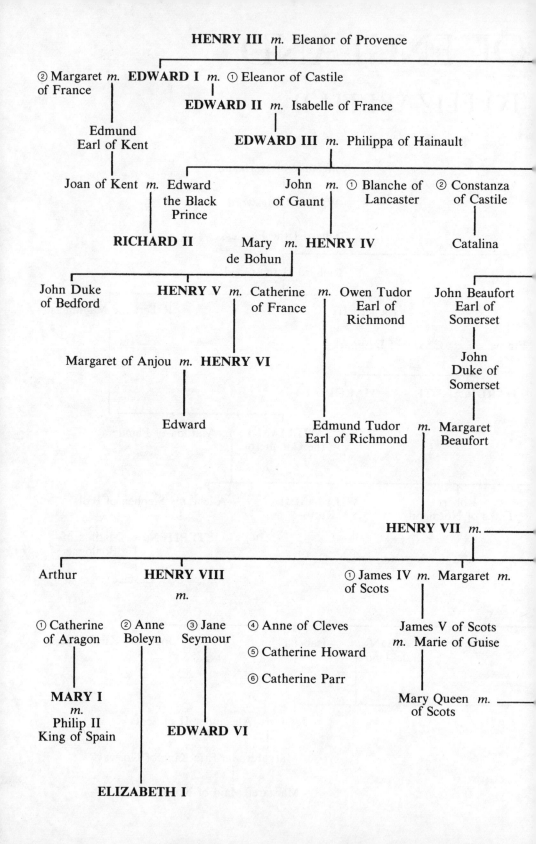

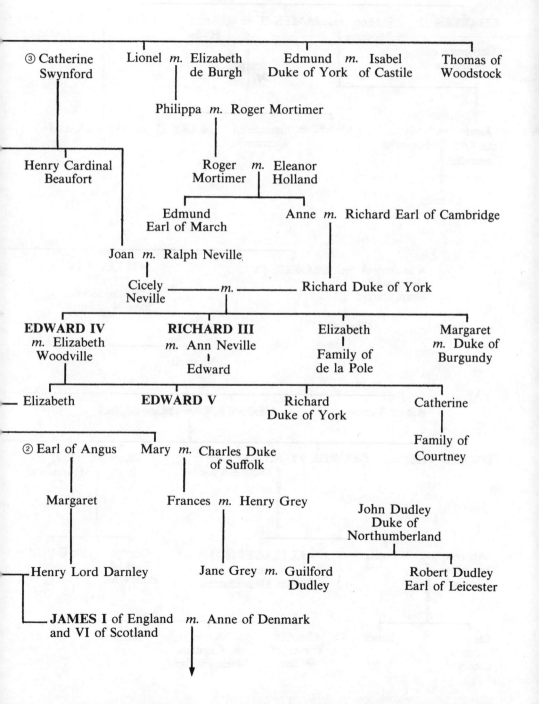

Margaret *m.* Alexander III of Scots

③ Catherine Swynford

Lionel *m.* Elizabeth de Burgh

Edmund *m.* Isabel Duke of York of Castile

Thomas of Woodstock

Philippa *m.* Roger Mortimer

Henry Cardinal Beaufort

Roger Mortimer *m.* Eleanor Holland

Edmund Earl of March

Anne *m.* Richard Earl of Cambridge

Joan *m.* Ralph Neville

Cicely Neville ———— *m.* ———— Richard Duke of York

EDWARD IV *m.* Elizabeth Woodville

RICHARD III *m.* Ann Neville

Edward

Elizabeth

Family of de la Pole

Margaret *m.* Duke of Burgundy

Elizabeth

EDWARD V

Richard Duke of York

Catherine

Family of Courtney

② Earl of Angus

Mary *m.* Charles Duke of Suffolk

Margaret

Frances *m.* Henry Grey

John Dudley Duke of Northumberland

Henry Lord Darnley

Jane Grey *m.* Guilford Dudley

Robert Dudley Earl of Leicester

JAMES I of England and VI of Scotland *m.* Anne of Denmark

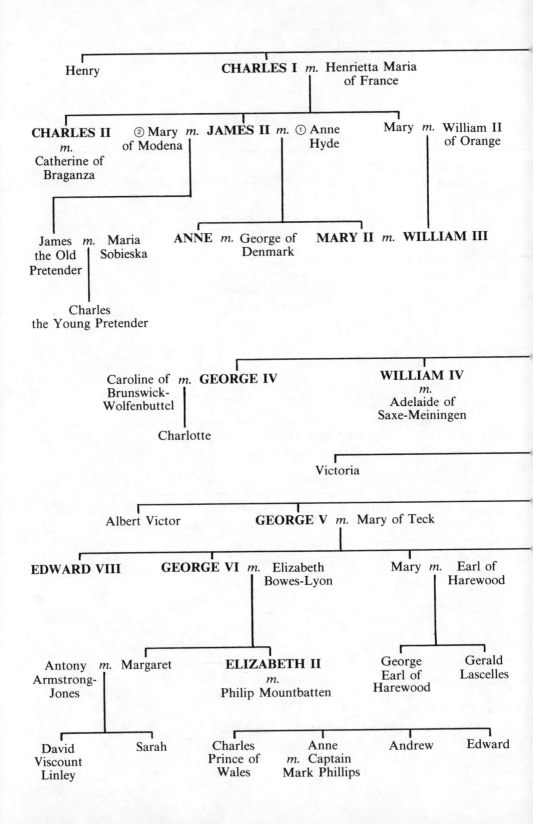

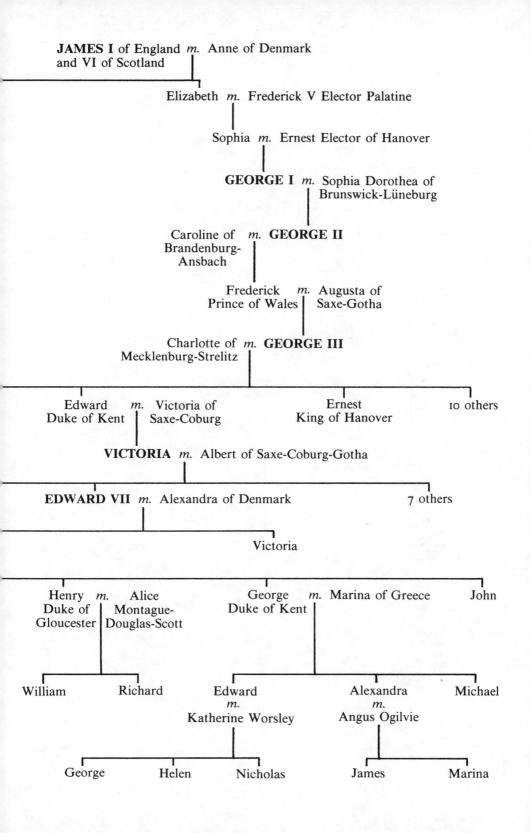

JAMES I of England *m.* Anne of Denmark
and VI of Scotland

Elizabeth *m.* Frederick V Elector Palatine

Sophia *m.* Ernest Elector of Hanover

GEORGE I *m.* Sophia Dorothea of
Brunswick-Lüneburg

Caroline of *m.* **GEORGE II**
Brandenburg-
Ansbach

Frederick *m.* Augusta of
Prince of Wales Saxe-Gotha

Charlotte of *m.* **GEORGE III**
Mecklenburg-Strelitz

Edward *m.* Victoria of   Ernest   10 others
Duke of Kent Saxe-Coburg   King of Hanover

VICTORIA *m.* Albert of Saxe-Coburg-Gotha

EDWARD VII *m.* Alexandra of Denmark   7 others

Victoria

Henry *m.* Alice   George *m.* Marina of Greece   John
Duke of Montague-   Duke of Kent
Gloucester Douglas-Scott

William   Richard   Edward   Alexandra   Michael
m.   *m.*
Katherine Worsley   Angus Ogilvie

George   Helen   Nicholas   James   Marina

THE
MONARCHS
OF
ENGLAND

ANGLO-SAXON KINGS

❁

ALFRED, known as The Great	871–901
EDWARD, known as The Elder	
son of Alfred	901–925
ATHELSTAN	
son of Edward	925–942
EDMUND I	
brother of Athelstan	942–948
EDRED	
brother of Athelstan	948–955
EDWY	
son of Edmund	955–959
EDGAR	
brother of Edwy	959–975
EDWARD, known as The Martyr	
son of Edgar	975–979
ETHELRED II, known as Unready	
brother of Edward	979–1016
EDMUND II, known as Ironside	
son of Ethelred	1016
CANUTE (Cnut) of Denmark	1016–1036
HAROLD I, known as Harefoot	
bastard son of Canute	1036–1040
HARDICANUTE	
son of Canute	1040–1042
EDWARD, known as the Confessor	
son of Ethelred	1042–1066
HAROLD II Godwinson	
brother-in-law of Edward	1066

Note: Anglo-Saxon names are given in modern form. Some dates are uncertain or disputed.

KING ARTHUR AND ALFRED THE GREAT

In the year A.D. 462 the last Roman legions abandoned Britain and the Dark Ages began.

We know little of the history of those long centuries. While the broad Roman roads fell into disrepair and the handsome Roman villas quietly crumbled under bramble and nettle, invaders swarmed in from the neighboring shores. Some plundered and went, some killed and settled. In an overgrown and marshy island, the people lived in tiny villages cleared from the surrounding forest, people of dozens of different Celtic and Norse tribes, lawless, disunited, and always in fear of their neighbors. Peace, justice, religion, and art slowly vanished.

We can only guess (a guess partially supported by modern archaeological research) that somewhere in England, probably in the South, there lived for a time a local warrior chieftain whose name was perhaps something like Arthur. He had some local successes in battle against his neighbors, and some local fame because when he had established his position as chieftain, he spent his time and wealth on the well-being of his people. Then he was killed in battle, and to this day we are still looking for firm evidence that he ever lived. But somewhere in the collective consciousness of the miserable people who lived in the island, the garbled memory of this inconsiderable soldier lived on, and in the course of centuries brought forth a remarkable legend.

It was an imperative legend, a people's dream of what it wanted of its national life. Even as early as this, the people of the island had discovered that those whom they called their chieftains, worked for,

· 3 ·

fought for, paid their tribute to, could do very little to make their lives tolerable. They needed something more, and that something they imagined they had in the life of Arthur. Arthur was the first, and is still the most dearly loved, of the folk-heroes.

His legend spread so far beyond England that he became one of the great champions of Christendom (even though it was three hundred years after the departure of the Romans that Saint Augustine converted the island to Christianity). He was said to have conquered the Roman Emperor; the French invented a great romantic history for him; later heroes were glorified by being given seats at his Round Table. So we do not know now what was the first and purely island version of this story. But even today, when we have long forgotten the belief that one man alone can be trusted with power, everyone in England knows what Arthur stands for. He was the ideal ruler: the King we have never had.

He was a powerful King, but only humanly so; his battles were won with human flesh and blood. He was a moral King, bound by the laws of God even when they were against him. He was a merciful King; he punished justly, accepted penitence, and forgave after punishment. And, above all, he was the King of the common people. Any man or woman wronged had only to come to him, and the whole strength of the Round Table was at his service.

In the end, of course, Arthur was defeated. But he did not die; he was taken away to the lake-island of Avalon, where he lies sleeping until England needs him again. This is the eternal human dream of rescue waiting round the corner. It is also the eternal human knowledge that things are bound to get worse; for, if they were as bad as they could be, Arthur would be awake. But the Arthurian dream has had remarkable power in England. Few Kings have been able altogether to ignore it, a surprising number have shared it, and never in seven centuries did the people quite forget it. It was only at the end of those seven centuries that they realized that Arthur was dead at last, and that they must start the new struggle of learning to rule themselves.

In the ninth century there appeared a man who might have been the reincarnation of Arthur: Alfred the Great, King not of all England but of Wessex, and one among the great Kings in England.

As the invasions of the Dark Ages had proceeded, the people had come together in ever larger agglomerations of tribes, ruled by chieftains who called themselves Kings; there were as many as seven of them at one time. We call these people the Anglo-Saxons, and contemporary chroniclers called them the *Angli*. By the eighth century they were thoroughly Christianized and had reached a fair level of peace and civilization, and thus became the target of the raiding Vikings in force. Of all the merciless energetic pagan Norsemen who regarded unprotected shores and peaceful lands their rightful prize, the Danes had emerged as the most powerful, and they were not now content merely to raid; they settled. By Alfred's time they were securely established in the Danelaw, a great triangle of land with its base along two hundred and fifty miles of the northeastern coast and its tip reaching to the northwestern coast. To stop their moving south, the Anglo-Saxons paid them, an expensive and often useless expedient; for in five terrible years, from 866 to 871, the Danish host conquered all England north of the Thames. Against them stood only Alfred of Wessex, King of one of the little southern kingdoms, a boy of twenty, frail in health and gentle in temperament. Somehow he gained the loyalty of the men of the south, and at the great battle of Ethandune in 878, one of the decisive battles of English history, he drove the Danes back.

Perhaps the old legend of the cakes tells us how he gained that loyalty. It was not written down until three hundred years later, but it may have stayed in the folk-memory for a good reason. At the depth of his fortunes, the story says, he took refuge in a peasant's hut in the marshes, and the housewife, not knowing who he was, told him to watch the cakes of bread baking by the fire. His head full of cares, he let the bread burn, and when she scolded him for it took the scolding meekly. Did his people preserve that story because, with a kingdom to save, he could still understand the disaster of one family's spoiled meal?

Alfred reigned for twenty years after Ethandune, undisputed King, though never of all England, for he never had the strength to conquer the Danelaw. In those years all his endeavours were toward restoring peace and law and learning. He wrote regretfully of

the learned men there used to be in England, and how foreigners would come here for knowledge and teaching; and now we have to get our knowledge and teaching from abroad.

Characteristically, he took a personal hand in the work, bringing young men to court and teaching them himself, and adding to the store of books in the vernacular. In one translation he gives us a charming glimpse of his way of working:

When I realized that although knowledge of Latin had decayed in England many could still read English, I began to turn *The Shepherd-Book* into English, even among all the cares of the kingdom. Sometimes I translated it word for word; sometimes I had to consult my teachers for a paraphrase, and when I had the meaning clear I put it into English as best I could understand and express it.

He died in 901, and the historian Ethelward wrote:

In this year there passed from this world Alfred King of the Saxons: unshakeable pillar of the people, a man full of justice, active in war, learned in speech, and full of the knowledge of sacred literature. The King died on the seventh day before the Festival of All Saints, and his body rests in peace in the City of Winchester.

Winchester was Alfred's capital city. We do not now know where his grave is, but his statue stands high above the traffic in Winchester, a step through quiet alleys from the great cathedral that has replaced the small church of his day. Ethelward's description of him could very well have been applied to Arthur, and his life must considerably have strengthened his people's conviction that Arthur would come again when he was needed. They were soon to be in desperate need of such help, and Arthur was not to appear to them.

HAROLD
GODWINSON

But still the Norse invaders came, in ever greater numbers, and a hundred years after Alfred's death the great Danish soldier Cnut, or Canute the Great, ruled in England. (England was not alone in this affliction from the north, for round about the time of Alfred the Great's death, France had had to resign herself to a smaller Danelaw in the parts we now call Normandy.) The Anglo-Saxons of those years could not have found conquest very disagreeable. The Danes were near kin to them, with similar language and traditions, and were rapidly becoming Christianized. And Canute was a remarkable man, who ruled not as a conqueror but as an Englishman. It seemed that England was to be part of the Scandinavian corner of Europe, separated from the remains of the old Roman Empire of which she had once been part.

But Canute's heirs were weak, and in 1042, five years after his death, the great landowners of the kingdom, the earls, brought back the heir of the line of Alfred, King Edward the Confessor, to rule over what were to be the last years of old England.

Old England was then still a country of villages, though the villages had grown bigger and more prosperous. The people worked land cleared from forest and marsh, clearing a little more when they could, and, as far as we can tell, making a peaceful and law-abiding life of it. There were cities—London was already powerful—and there was external and internal trade; but in general the people were farmers. They fought the Welsh and the Scots when the land was invaded, but on the whole they were unaggressive and contented. The great religious houses throughout the land were centers of art and learning as well as of religion; the people spoke a rich and flexible language that had some remarkable poetry and a prose that was far in advance of that of any other European country. And, in the loosest sense of the word, they were democratic in their daily life.

They did not elect representatives; that is a very modern idea. But their government at village level was based on a tangle of ancient local laws in which both lord and laborer had inalienable rights. These laws were enforced by nothing but public opinion, formed by long centuries of experience, that in small communities the best security is the good will of your neighbors. Nor was it a static society socially; a clever village boy could rise to be a great man, usually by having a church education and becoming a clerk (as lettered men were called).

Matters were less good on the higher levels of law. The great earls, though as far as we can tell they respected local laws, were no less greedy for power than other great lords in all times and all countries. There was nothing to restrain them but the law of the King, and this did not always run without power to back it up. Nevertheless, it did run to a growing extent; earls rebelled, but were defeated; even in what had once been the Danelaw the central authority was increasingly accepted. After some years of Edward the Confessor's reign England was already beginning to look like an ordered kingdom.

This was in no sense thanks to Edward himself. His one indisputable personal achievement was the foundation of Westminster Abbey, and he went down in history as the Virgin King, too holy to take on cares of state. He may very well have been saintly, but on worldly evidence he was a weak, stubborn, cunning, mildly homosexual man in a position whose responsibilities he would not assume. The dusty work of ruling fell by default into the hands of the most capable of the earls: Harold, eldest son of that Earl Godwin who had led the movement to bring Edward back to England. By the end of Edward's long and comparatively peaceful reign Harold was known as the Vice-King, and, since Edward had no children, was a reasonable candidate for the succession.

Succession to the throne of Anglo-Saxon England was by election, a sensible system when a strong military leader was a necessity. The electing body was the Witenagemot, or Council of Elders, which included the great earls and other men of influence, and they could legally pass over even a son of the late King if they judged him unsuitable. There was, in fact, an heir of Alfred's line in England who was undeniably unsuitable; he was Edgar the Atheling (or prince), who was a child in his teens. (He had a sister, Margaret, who much later was to have more influence than her brother on the throne of England.) But Edward the Confessor seems to have disliked Harold, perhaps from an ancestral enmity, and it was possibly this that led him to a wholly illegal step. It may have been as early as 1052 that he promised the crown—which was not his to give—to a distant cousin, the bastard grandson of his French mother Emma. This young man, a product of the feudal French society in which Edward had grown up, was Duke William of Normandy, at that time very precarious in his own duchy. He grew more powerful as the years went by, so that it became plain that the greedy Normans to the south were as dangerous to the freedom of England as the greedy Norsemen to the east.

Many years later, it was probably a certain Norman named Odo, half-brother of Duke William, who commissioned a great tapestry to celebrate the events of the years 1065 and 1066. It is unlikely that he was pleased with what he got, for the Bayeux Tapestry is no glorification of the Normans, but a detached and factual account that gives due value to both sides. (Internal evidence suggests that it was designed by a Norman and executed by English workers; perhaps that is why.) It is one of the most valuable sources of evidence about the Conquest, but it leaves too much unexplained. In 1065 something— we can only guess that it was King Edward's order—sent Harold, the possible heir of England, into the power of Normandy, the possible invader of England. Oddly enough, they made friends—you can see it on the tapestry; but before Harold left he took an oath to William: VBI HAROLD SACRAMENTVM FECIT VVILELMO DUCI. The likelihood is that it was an oath of loyalty, and the old story tells that Harold took it only under threat of imprisonment. Whatever the truth, the designer of the tapestry is confident that it was an oath that Harold broke when he fought William the next year, and that his defeat was divine vengeance. The curious thing is that there are hints that Harold himself felt some guilt; he had been used to fight under the banner of Holy Cross, but in his last year abandoned it for the Fighting Man, as if he were no longer worthy of the Cross.

But whatever the oath it was a matter personal to Harold, without effect on the deliberations of the Witenagemot after the death of Edward the Confessor on January 5, 1066. On his deathbed Edward had given Harold his royal ring, and in all legality, on January 6, 1066

Harold Godwinson was elected, crowned, and hallowed King of England.

About Harold personally we do not know much. He was fair like his Danish mother, and his weapon was the two-handed axe, which demands broad shoulders. As a young man he had married a girl of the people, Edith Swan-Neck, and they had at least six children, though in 1066, to ensure the loyalty of the northern earls, Edwin and Morcar, he married their sister, Aldyth.

Duke William published his story of Harold's oath-breaking and sent to Rome to buy the Pope's support for his claim to England; but while the Norman forces were assembling on the French coast, another danger was imminent from the east. Harold had a brother, Tostig, whom he had (quite justly) exiled, and Tostig joined Harald Hardrada King of Norway in another attempted invasion, sailing in mid-1066 with 240 ships.

England had no standing army. The King had a professional corps, perhaps two thousand strong, called the King's Thanes, and his own House-Carles, and for the rest he had to rely on the *fyrd,* the men of England in arms. The trouble was that he had the right to call out the *fyrd* for only forty days, and after that only the most obvious danger would keep the men from their fields. William's army was largely professional; he had only to keep Harold waiting until the *fyrd* had melted away to the harvest and then the Channel coast would be unprotected but by the Thanes and House-Carles. On the eighth of September Harold gave up the struggle with his dwindling army and let the *fyrd* disband. Luckily for him, William also needed a fair wind, which he did not get; for within days came the news that Hardrada and Tostig had sailed into the mouth of the Humber in Yorkshire.

Harold took his Thanes and House-Carles and marched north, knowing that at his back the Channel wind might change at any moment. York was 250 miles away, and when he reached the city he found it surrendered. Hardrada, thinking himself safe, had withdrawn his army to rest. On September 20, Harold rode down on him from the hills above Stamford Bridge.

It is said he tried to make peace with his brother, offering him his earldom if he would desert Hardrada. Tostig refused, and Hardrada asked what Harold had to offer him. He was a giant of a man, and Harold said, "Six feet of English earth, or so much more as so big a man needs." Hardrada got his English earth, and Tostig, too, and the Norsemen were so utterly defeated that when Harold let the survivors sail home in peace they needed only twenty-four ships out of the 240 they had brought with them. On the twenty-seventh of September the wind went into the south, and Duke William landed at Pevensey on the south coast.

With a tired army Harold made his great march again from north to south, and by the eleventh of October, with the remainder of his Thanes and House-Carles and the newly summoned *fyrd* of the south, he was starting on the fifty-eight miles from London to the coast. He had left the northern earls, Edwin and Morcar, to bring the northern *fyrd* after him; but the loyalty of the Earls was suspect, and it seems that Harold was hoping to cut William off from his ships. He miscalculated; on the morning of the fourteenth of October, with a worn-out army, he was suprised by Duke William of Normandy on the shallow ridges north of Hastings.

By our standards the armies were small, probably only a few thousand on either side. The Anglo-Saxons fought in the old fashion of the shield-wall, forming up in a solid circle around their banners on a small ridge that then had no name (it is called Battle now). Both sides had archers; but William's strength was in his trained and mounted knights. And also in his own presence; the only moment when the Normans wavered was when word went round that the Duke had fallen. William lifted the visor of his helm (there is a picture of it in the tapestry), and his men rallied. The shield-wall would not break, and he resorted to a tactic impossible to any but highly trained men. He had them feign retreat; the English broke ranks to pursue, and the Normans swarmed in through the gap. Harold and his brothers died on the ridge, but even after the banners had gone down the Anglo-Saxons fought on; after darkness one group set up so fierce a resistance that the Normans thought the field was lost. But it was not; that night William pitched his tent and slept on the spot where Harold had planted his banner and died.

On that same spot now stands the high altar of the Abbey of Battle, built by William as thanksgiving for his victory. The Norman chroniclers never gave this battle a name; to them it was simply The Battle. And quite rightly; it changed the history and the people of England, it changed the history of Normandy, it took England out of Scandinavia and back into the old Roman Europe, and in doing that it altered the history of Europe.

So mangled were the bodies on the field that they had to send for

Edith Swan-Neck to find Harold among them. William refused him Christian burial, saying he was an oath-breaker and usurper and under the ban of the Church, and he was buried by night on the battlefield. It was not until he himself was safely crowned that William let them take the body to Harold's own Abbey of Waltham Holy Cross in Essex. It still lies there, though the exact spot was lost in the Reformation, and only a tablet in what is now Waltham Parish Church records the grave. His people said that King Harold was not dead, and would come again to drive out the invaders. They were wrong. England now had the Normans for good, and would only be rid of them by the long, slow process of absorbing them into herself.

House of

NORMANDY

WILLIAM I
The Conqueror
1066–1087

✿

Born in Falaise, Normandy, in 1025.
Bastard son of Duke Robert the Magnificent of Nor-
mandy and Herleve of Falaise.
Recognized as Duke of Normandy in 1032, in the absence
of his father, who died in 1035.
Married in 1053 Matilda, daughter of Baldwin V Count of
Flanders; their children were:

> Robert known as Curthose, later Duke of Normandy,
> who died a prisoner in Cardiff Castle in 1135, having
> had a son,
> > William Clito, who died in Flanders in 1128;
>
> William known as Rufus, later William II; Henry
> known as Beauclerc, later Henry I; Adela, who mar-
> ried Stephen Count of Blois and died in 1137, having
> had a son,
> > Stephen of Blois, later King Stephen.

Took the throne of England after the Battle of Hastings,
October 14, 1066.
Died at Rouen in 1087 and was buried in the Abbaye-des-
Hommes, Caen.

WILLIAM I
The Conqueror

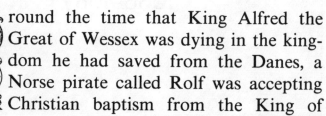round the time that King Alfred the
Great of Wessex was dying in the king-
dom he had saved from the Danes, a
Norse pirate called Rolf was accepting
Christian baptism from the King of
France, who had defeated him outside Chartres. In reward (or, more
likely, to keep him quiet) he was given some lands in the valley of
the lower Seine. A century and a half later, Rolf's descendants, a
heady mixture of Norse and French, had taken England and Sicily,
terrorized Italy, and were moving out through Greece toward
Byzantium and the Holy Land.

The Normans were not altogether an attractive people. Contemporary chroniclers record their faithlessness, their greed, their passion
for conquest, their disregard for the common people. These are
common by-products of a military system with a weak central authority, but the Normans specialized in disloyalty and broken oaths.
Yet even their enemies admitted to their personal virtues; they were
admirably austere in their lives, temperate in food and drink, chaste
in sexual matters, and of a dry, discriminating taste in art; they built
some of the most magnificent buildings in Europe. No one ever
questioned their courage in battle, and when they were under the
control of a worthy leader they were formidable. Above all, they had
immense energy.

William was born in 1025, the illegitimate great-great-great-grand-
son of Rolf. It was said that his mother, Herleve of Falaise, was the
daughter of a tanner, and that his father, Duke Robert, first saw her
dancing in the street. In 1032 Duke Robert announced his intention
of going on pilgrimage to the Holy Land, and somehow induced his

barons to swear fealty for the time of his absence to this bastard boy. He departed then for the east and soon died there, and the forlorn boy was thereafter Duke William Bastard.

The Normans being what they were, their oath of fealty was meaningless, and William's duchy was open to whomever was strong enough to take it. The devotion of Herleve's brothers saved his life, and it was his good luck that at one critical point his overlord the King of France found it politic to support him. A little later he found it politic to abandon him; if William was to have few endearing qualities throughout his life, he had been given little opportunity to develop them. By the time he was sixteen he had taken charge of his own affairs, and by 1062 he was secure in Normandy. These were the years of the Normans' expansion south, so it was hardly likely that the greatest of them should remain quietly within his own borders.

Duke William was a strong man, as one who fought mounted in armor had to be, broad-shouldered and hard; he grew stout when he was old, but never soft; his recreation was hunting. He was secretive, cunning, avaricious, and much feared in his anger, but trusted and respected by his men. The only odd thing about him was his marriage. He not only claimed to be a God-fearing man, but also knew the value of the Church's support; yet in 1053 he married, against the ban of the Church (because they were too nearly akin), Matilda of Flanders. They had a large family, Matilda often acted capably and loyally as his regent, and as far as we know he was impeccably faithful to her; yet this lady was a dwarf, hardly four feet tall. What is odder is that this fact was discovered only when her tomb was opened long after her death; no contemporary sources made note of it.

It does not much matter whether the story is true that Edward the Confessor promised his throne to William. England was there for the taking, and in deciding to take her William was following the values of his society (one which had not yet come to England), the feudal society.

Feudalism has come to mean no more than the village boy touching his cap to his betters: "God bless the squire and his relations/ And keep us in our proper stations." We have forgotten nowadays that to be kept in your proper station has its good side as well as its bad. Feudalism, in fact, was a social system of great complexity, and in William's day a sound and tolerably successful system, based on values and necessities that were everywhere accepted.

The basis of the system was land. The land provided the wealth, the landowner protected it from intruders. So, strictly, the King owned the land, and he granted great tracts of it to his greatest men, and they in turn granted smaller tracts to their men, and so on down to the small knight who got a single manor with a few acres. The land was granted on condition that the vassal, as the tenant was called, swore fealty to his lord and promised him loyalty and knight-service —that is, the service of a certain number of fighting men when the lord had need of them. It was, or it should have been, an important feature of the system that, although the lesser men were vassals of the greater, the overriding fealty of them all was to the King. The power of the King was thus in the number of fighting men he could call on in need, and his own personal wealth was the exchequer of the country. With its reliance on the honour and fealty of the individual knight, it could be a very noble system; it could also be a very cruel and constricting one, for it was tailored exclusively and inflexibly for the benefit of one class, the land-owning knights.

It did not prove wholly efficient, and became less and less so as time went on and society grew more complex. Landowners did not always prove to be soldiers; nor was the King always strong enough to prevent his tenants-in-chief setting up as rulers on their own. Wives did not always provide the necessary male heirs, and no single law of inheritance through the female branch was accepted in all countries. And, most fatally to the throne of England, royal inheritance, even through the male line, was not fixed. All the sons of a King expected great inheritances, and the less the inheritance the more their discontent, and the greater the inheritance the more chance they had of stealing from the others. The Normans had no reverence, least of all for their own sworn oaths; it was not until they had absorbed some of the Anglo-Saxon reverence for a crowned and hallowed king that the method of succession was settled to that of male primogeniture.

Duke William, then, descended on England, swearing that it was his by legal right, to turn it into a feudal country. The Anglo-Saxons did not stop fighting him for ten years after The Battle, but they were opposed to better organization and stronger leadership. William had his own method of subduing cities; he burned their neighbors. By the time he had marched east to west south of the Thames, and west to east north of the Thames, killing and pillaging as he went, London was ready to submit, and with London he had the south of England

and at least the nominal submission of the northern earls (the treacherous Edwin and Morcar, who had deserted Harold Godwinson). William was crowned in Westminster Abbey on Christmas Day, 1066.

Norman conquest did not lie as easily as Danish. William had knights to reward and a kingdom to secure, and for both purposes he needed land and money. The money came from crippling taxation, the legal fiction that Harold had been a usurper providing the excuse for confiscations from his supporters, and Norman arms and the building of Norman castles soon did the rest.

By 1068 the south was quiet, but the Norsemen had by no means given up their own hopes of conquest, and in 1069 the men of northern England, who had much Danish blood in them, rose to welcome an invasion by the Danish King Sweyn Estrithson (who was Harold Godwinson's cousin and heir), and the Welsh crossed their border of Offa's Dyke to support them. In perhaps his greatest campaign, and certainly his most cruel, William drove out the Danes, drove back the Welsh, and inflicted a terrible punishment on the English. His treatment of Yorkshire has been called genocide by modern historians, and even the Norman chroniclers, usually favorable to him and inured to the habits of the age, could not excuse him, condemning him for an act which "levelled both the bad and the good in one common ruin." They tell of starvation, plague, putrefying corpses blocking the roads, cannibalism, men selling themselves and their families into slavery to escape their atrocious King. Even twenty years later, when William undertook his great survey of the kingdom, the Domesday Book, his treatment of his people is revealed; Yorkshire was still largely desert.

The Harrowing of the North achieved its purpose. The knights took over their lands, the castles rose, the taxes had to be paid. The common man had now, all over the land, mostly sunk to the wretched position of villein, forbidden to change his position, working for a foreign lord, and tied for life to land that was no longer his. England was held in a net of Norman castles, Norman taxation, Norman law.

The Norman law imposed by William differed considerably, however, from that which ran in the duchy. In the duchy he had been hampered by ambitious vassals and fiefs grown too large, but in England he intended to be master. It was ten years or so before the barons fully understood how effectively he had curtailed their powers, and they turned on him, then and at odd times later, but that was too late. William had his power, and what William had he held.

His governmental organization was complex, derived in its upper ranks from his experience in Normandy, though he retained the old Anglo-Saxon division of the country into shires, as well as the Anglo-Saxon office of shire-reeve or sheriff. The center of all authority was in himself. To advise him, he had the King's Council, a body that was appointed by himself and had no powers beyond what he allowed it. Its members varied according to their availability and the questions on which it was advising, but essentially it included the great vassals and other leading officers of church and state (where these were not in themselves the great vassals).

This King's Council was to continue throughout the centuries but would vary widely according to circumstances and personalities. Where the King was strong, it was merely advisory; where he was weak, it tried to take over his powers. Where he was popular, it carried out his orders, where he was disliked, took on the task of representing to him the feeling of his people. It was sometimes a mere wrangling mob, sometimes dominated by one great man, and when, three hundred years after William I's reign, it found a rival power in the emergent Parliament, it still retained its identity and usefulness.

In pursuance of his own policies, William made a significant concession to his new subjects: he left them their local laws. The old Anglo-Saxon traditions became manor law, administered in thousands of tiny manor courts, and in the course of the succeeding reigns were integrated with the King's law. There is no doubt that this preservation of the accustomed background of their lives encouraged the people to accept the Conquest; but, centuries later, the tradition of law among and for the common people was to give those people an immense power of their own, and many a king had to learn that no power of arms could force the cooperation of thousands of local justices of the peace.

Throughout his reign William was never free of threats to his domains. In 1072 he defeated Malcolm III of Scotland, who had an interest in the throne of England because he had given refuge to Edgar Atheling, the heir of Alfred's line, and had married his sister Margaret. Philip I of France, too, made trouble where he could, preferring to keep a too-powerful vassal engaged; and, unhappily for William—for his family affections seem to have been strong—his eldest son Robert proved ungrateful.

As early as 1069, when he was hardly twenty, Robert rebelled, apparently because William, to secure Normandy during the campaign in 1066, had had the barons swear fealty to his son and then deprived him of any real power. Robert was forgiven, but remained restive; he was a typical young Norman, but seems also to have had a streak of irresponsibility in him. By 1083 he was deep in a more serious rebellion, and at a time when William was hard-pressed. Odo Earl of Kent was in revolt, Cnut of Denmark was preparing an invasion, and, to cap it all, the faithful Matilda died. William was nearing sixty now and grown corpulent, but he went as steadily as ever about his wars. By good luck Cnut died before he could sail, and in Kent the common people themselves, faced with the choice between Willham and the unpleasant Odo, preferred to fight for William. In Normandy he was, as always, victorious, though all his neighbors were, as always, pressing upon his frontiers; his particular enemies there were the Angevins, the counts of Anjou, further south. Late in 1087 he sacked Mantes. It was a cruel sack, in accord with his lifelong principle that the cruel sack of one city quickly opens the gates of the next. But as he rode into the ruined city in the evening, the timbers falling from a burning building startled his mount, and he was thrown heavily against the high saddle-pommel that heavily armored knights used. The fall injured him internally; slowly and in great pain he had himself carried to Rouen, and there he died.

His deathbed dispositions were made carefully. He wanted to disinherit the rebellious Robert, but was finally persuaded to name him Duke of Normandy; Robert promptly rode off to secure his duchy. Henry, the third son, was left no land but five thousand pounds (then a very large sum), and he, too, rode off to secure his money. When it came to England, we must assume that William was genuinely in fear for the well-being of his soul. He acknowledged that he had had no legal claim to England, but had taken her by force. For this reason, he said, he could only leave the kingdom to God, but he trusted that God would be good enough to give it back to his second son William. To help God's goodness, William Rufus was already on his way to the Channel ports. William the Conqueror died lonely and abandoned.

The fate of his body is curiously horrible. None of his men would stay to watch it, and the servants took the opportunity to plunder the house, so it was left entirely alone. When they came later to enclose it, the coffin was too small, so the leg-bones had to be broken; and it was already putrefying, so that when the coffin was carried into the church it burst open with a thunderous crack and a horrible stench. William was buried in the Abbaye-des-Hommes in Caen, which he himself had founded, next to the Abbaye-des-Femmes, which his wife Matilda had founded and in which she lay. In the French Revolution, 700 years later, the French, as an earnest of irreligion, dug up the grave and scattered the bones.

That deathbed fit of fear of the wrath of God is perhaps the only endearing thing ever recorded about the Conqueror. But the standards of William's time were so far from ours that we have no way of judging him. We can only acknowledge that he was born into lawlessness, and out of it he made law. Bad or good, he made the Kingdom of England, and we have no right to say that without him England would have been either a better or a worse place.

WILLIAM II
Rufus
1087–1100

✿

Born in Normandy 1056
Second son of William I and his wife Matilda of Flanders.
Unmarried.
Killed by a hand unknown in the New Forest, buried at
   Winchester.

WILLIAM II
Rufus

t must be put to the credit of William the Conqueror that he had got, and kept, the loyalty of one of the good and great men of his time, Lanfranc of Bec. In 1087 Lanfranc was Archbishop of Canterbury, the chief ecclesiastical authority in England, and it was to Lanfranc in England that William Rufus went at the end of his hasty journey from his father's deathbed in Rouen. By Lanfranc's good offices Rufus was crowned and hallowed King William II of England.

William Rufus was the poor son of a great father. He was a capable soldier, and enough of an administrator to recognize the worth of the massive organization of state that his father had left him, though he strained it to its limits whenever it suited him. But he was a ruffian nonetheless, greedy, brutal, and seeing kingship as no more than an extension of feudal lordship: broader lands to defend, more vassals to defend them with, better forests to hunt in, and fewer men to deny him his pleasures. He was also homosexual, indifferent to who was to succeed him on the throne. His younger brother, Henry Beauclerc, professed himself shocked by Rufus's sexual morals. Henry himself was safe from similar accusations; he had a wife and an array of mistresses, and children both legitimate and bastard.

England had suffered in Edward's time from a royal family with no strong heir; now she was to suffer from a royal family with too many strong heirs. It was the Norman ethos to fight over spoils. In 1088 Robert attacked Rufus, and they fought in England. In 1090 Rufus attacked Robert, and they fought in Normandy. They fought in Normandy for five years, varying the situation now and again by attacking their prudent brother Henry, who with his inheritance of five thousand pounds and his cool brain was quietly building up a fief for himself. To make the situation worse, there was a rebellion in 1090 in the north of England, which was supported by the King of Scots, while Philip of France, always nervous of this dangerous vassal, tried to weaken Normandy by fomenting her quarrel with England. Rufus proved himself the best soldier in these sterile battles; he had a stable land to govern, but not a happy one. The rulers, from the King down to the petty knight who was lord of the manor, were a different people from the ruled; they spoke a different language, lived a different life, regarded the common people as slave labor. In many cases the Norman lord had other lands in Normandy, so that his English holdings were no more than extra sources of income. To the common people of the time their lives must have appeared an endless, hopeless servitude.

In 1089 the loved and respected Archbishop Lanfranc died. The Pope had to confirm a new archbishop but the King had to nominate him, and while the see was vacant the revenues were paid to the Crown. Rufus refused to nominate a new Archbishop, and for the next five years enjoyed the considerable revenues of Canterbury. At the end of the time he fell ill, and thought himself dying; like his father, but with infinitely less dignity, he fell into a fit of panic. To Canterbury he nominated the holiest man he knew, the pious Anselm (later to be canonized). At the proposal, the chronicler Edmer tells us, Anselm grew pale, and resisted with all his might, begging them to let him live in peace. The scene at the bedside of the supposedly dying King was uproarious: Rufus, weeping with misery, reproached Anselm for condemning him to die in sin and go to everlasting torment, while the bishops and clergy held the poor old man still and forced the pastoral staff against his clenched fist. Afterward he said to them, "Do you understand what you have done? You have yoked to the plough an untamed bull and an old feeble sheep, and what good will come of that?"

It was a comic scene, but a stupid one, because the King who provoked it was thinking of no more than money. He was soon to learn that there was more to the Church than its revenues, and that the holy Anselm, far from being an old, feeble sheep, was a powerful political mind and strong in defense of Church against King. He disputed William's claim to invest his own bishops (a matter of great importance in the days when bishops had political as well as ecclesiastical power) and finally took his case to Rome. The Conqueror had been at great pains to keep on good terms with the Church while carefully limiting its powers in his kingdom. Rufus's foolishness ruined this relationship, and he expected excommuncation, which was then a powerful weapon. Anselm saved him from that, for he trusted the institutions of the Conqueror to outlive the stupidity of his son.

During all these years, great and terrible things had been happening in the East. Byzantium, the last capital of the old Roman Empire, besides whose wealth, culture, and sophistication the Westerners were overawed barbarians, was so closely pressed by the Muslims that the Emperor Alexius Comnenus appealed to Western Christendom for help. The religious saw the freeing of Jerusalem from the infidel; the ambitious saw wealthy lordships to be won in the East. The Pope proclaimed a Crusade, and the armies gathered, happy in the thought that the highest call of religion was to lead them to loot. (Christians associated worldly success with divine approval more easily than we can do nowadays.)

Among these Crusaders was Duke Robert of Normandy. Able neither to conquer England nor to control his own duchy, he very coolly pawned that duchy to the King of England for enough money to take him to the East. Yet Robert was not wholly inconsiderable, for he was to be one of the Christian commanders at the capture of the Holy City of Jerusalem in 1099. Rufus now possessed the double realm of his father, and no doubt hoped that Robert would never come back.

He did, but not in Rufus's lifetime. One of the great complaints of the common people against the Norman Kings was their love of hunting, for to indulge it they took over great tracts of the countryside, evicting those who lived there. It has been calculated that at one time almost a third of the acreage of the kingdom was enclosed for hunting and ruled only by the savage forest laws.

The Anglo-Saxon Chronicle, a history of great antiquity, was kept in several religious houses, and thus was both unusually frank about Kings and unusually close to the feelings of the common people; of the Conqueror it wrote

He made a great forest for deer, and enacted laws therein, so that whoever killed a hart or hind should be blinded. As he forbad killing the deer, so also the boars and hares. And he loved the tall stags as if he were their father [a perhaps unconscious illustration of the chroniclers' views of William's tenderer feelings]. The rich complained and the poor murmured, but he was so strong he recked nothing of them.

Later, the penalty for killing a stag was increased to death. Rufus loved hunting as much as his father had, and by the time he had reigned thirteen years he had such a reputation for brutality that he was heartily hated, and not only by the common people. Perhaps this hatred is the reason for the mystery that has gathered around his death in the New Forest in Hampshire in August, 1100.

The story as we have it from William of Malmesbury is this: After dinner Rufus went hunting with a small band of attendants, among them a certain Walter Tirel, who was said to have come from France attracted by the liberality of the King. Because it was late in the day, with the sun already low, the hunters went out on foot, with bows, waiting for beaters to drive the deer past them. The King, at his stand, shot at a stag and wounded it, and, holding up one hand to keep the rays of the sinking sun from his eyes, started after it. At the same moment Tirel, who alone had stayed with him, loosed an arrow at another stag, and Rufus, running into his line of fire, received the arrow in his chest. Tirel then got on his horse and bolted, a perfectly reasonable thing to do when you have killed a much-hated King in the middle of a band of his followers, and the King's body was left to lie until a countryman carried it to Winchester on his cart. Very much the same thing had happened at the death of Rufus's father, for at the end of a reign sensible men looked after themselves before any dead body.

Nevertheless there remains an air of mystery about Rufus's death. Most certainly, if the common people could have killed him they would gladly have done so, and the hint of revenge about his death was increased by the fact that two more of the Conqueror's family, a son and a grandson, both died in the New Forest (to make which two thousand people had been deprived of their homes and livelihoods). But in the accounts we have, there is no shadow of suggestion that there were any of the common people in the vicinity. It has been pointed out that when the King was hunting, the one man who had to stay at his side was his Chief Huntsman, and that he could have loosed the fatal arrow, with Tirel fleeing in the realization that he himself would be blamed. It has even been suggested that Rufus was the Witch-King, an adherent of the Old Religion, and being at the end of his appointed time went willingly to his death at the hands of the appointed executioner.

What seems not to have been said at the time, and very wisely, too, was that if anyone was a hired assassin, his brother Henry was the obvious man to have hired him. It is worth noting that, on the whole, the Normans did not use assassination as a weapon in their game of political power. On the whole Henry was an honorable man; but he was also a thoroughly sensible one, and Rufus's life was doing no good at all to his kingdom.

William of Malmesbury said of Rufus (neatly hiding his disloyal opinions behind God):

He was a man much to be pitied by the clergy for throwing away a soul which they could not save.

The Anglo-Saxon Chronicle, much more to the worldly point, says:

All that was hateful to God and to just men was usual in the land at his time, and therefore he was hateful to his people and odious to God; as his end showed, because he departed this life in the midst of his injustices without repentance or reparation.

HENRY I
Beauclerc
1100–1135

✿

Born at Selby, Yorkshire, in 1070.
Third son of William I and his wife Matilda of Flanders.
Married in 1100 Edith Matilda, daughter of Malcolm III
King of Scots and his wife (Saint) Margaret, who was
a descendant of Alfred the Great. Their only surviving
child was

> Matilda (or Maud), born 1103, who in 1114 married the
> Holy Roman Emperor Henry V. They had no chil-
> dren, and he died in 1125. In 1127 Matilda married
> Geoffrey Plantagenet Count of Anjou, and they had
> one son,
> Henry, later Henry II.

In 1118 Edith Matilda died, and in 1121 Henry I married
Adela of Brabant, by whom he had no children.
Died at Angers in 1135 and was buried in Reading Abbey.

Henry I was the last King of the House of Normandy.

HENRY I
Beauclerc

Henry I was born in 1070, and was thus thirty-one at the time of his brother's death. He was black haired and brawny, William of Malmesbury tells us, with a manner that was always easy and pleasant and at the right times merry, though he had the Norman austerity in food and drink, and hated drunkenness. He was not personally aggressive, and preferred to work by diplomacy rather than force, a preference that can perhaps be explained by his thirty-one years of being younger brother to Duke Robert and King William. He was the best son of his great father.

Henry's claim to the throne when Rufus's body came back to Winchester in a countryman's cart was an immediate one: he was on the spot. But his expressed claim was original and unique: it was the right of porphyrogeniture, one acknowledged in some periods of Byzantine history, but never before or after urged in England. He was, he said, the only son of the Conqueror to be "born in the purple" —born, that is, while his father was King. It was an impudent claim, made by a man who could for the moment afford impudence, but there was a little truth in it.

For one thing, Henry was nearer to an Englishman than either his father or his brothers, since he had been born and mostly brought up in England. He was the first Norman King to speak English (the Conqueror had made one attempt to learn the language and had quickly given it up), to know anything of England, to feel himself English before Norman. For another and more important thing, he knew that his tenure of the crown was in the end insecure, because nothing but their own interest would keep the loyalty of the barons.

Henry was the clever one among the Conqueror's sons, and he could see even more clearly than his father the way kingship would be obliged to take in the future. To establish his crown, he appealed to the common people.

At his coronation he issued a "charter of liberties," addressed not to the barons but to the people. He promised them to rule "by the laws of King Edward (the Confessor)," with such amendments as his father had made. Within three months he had made another gesture to them, by marrying a wife they held dear. She was Edith Matilda, daughter of Malcolm III King of Scots and his wife Margaret, and thus fourth granddaughter of Alfred the Great, so that in Henry's children the ancient legitimate line of the Anglo-Saxon Kings would be restored to their throne. Henry's instinct was a sure one, for he had seen the basic danger of feudalism as it was understood by Norman knights. As William of Malmesbury tells us of them:

The Normans are so inured to war that they can scarcely live without it; they weigh treason by its chances of success and will change their opinions for the sake of gain. They envy their equals and wish to outshine their superiors.

Henry had need of support, for back from the First Crusade there now came the Conqueror's eldest son, Duke Robert of Normandy, much enhanced in both wealth and reputation.

With him on this famous First Crusade had gone his brother-in-law Stephen Count of Blois, husband of the Conqueror's domineering daughter Adela. It was Adela who had sent her husband crusading, and he wrote her some charming letters describing his travels; the Eastern Emperor Alexius Comnenus, he told her, was even more lavish with his gifts than her father had been (Alexius knew how to deal with Westerners). But at the siege of Antioch, Stephen's courage had failed him; seeing the size of the vast infidel army, he had escaped through a window and made full speed for home. Adela promptly sent him back again, and he died a respectable death in battle, but it was too late to save his reputation. It was a reputation that in later years was to harry their son Stephen, and England with him.

Duke Robert attacked Henry, but was not strong enough to displace him. Four years later Henry attacked in his turn, and at the battle of Tinchebrai in 1106 decisively defeated Robert. Robert was taken prisoner and kept in Cardiff Castle until he died in 1134, an old man in his eighties.

Henry was now undisputed ruler of both England and Normandy. The union with Normandy brought its problems, since, as its Duke, Henry was in fealty to the King of France; but it was of value to England, bringing her into closer contact with what was now the center of political power, the northwest of Europe. Europeans then had no sense of nationality. In one sense they all belonged to the same state, which was Christendom; in another, to the tiny changing states of any feudal lord who happened to be the strongest in the neighborhood. Feudalism unchecked by a central power was disrupting Europe; feudalism controlled by a strong King was making a stable country out of England.

Henry I's great work was in the law. Like his father, he was determined that the highest law should be not that of the barons but of the King (even when it had to be administered by barons, since his own courts could not handle cases of small national importance). He achieved this in the simplest possible way: he made the King's law the fastest, the justest, and the strongest.

He left untouched the system of manor law, only ensuring its regular running by visitations from his own men, and he widened and strengthened the Conqueror's administration by shires. From these courts the appeal upward to the King's court was easy, but a more difficult matter was the ecclesiastical courts. The Church claimed what were called its liberties, which were in theory the rights of jurisdiction over matters ecclesiastical, but the separation between ecclesiastical and civil was not always possible. Since the Pope had a significant amount of political power, and claimed to have much more, and archbishops and bishops ranked and behaved as feudal magnates, religion could seldom be divided from politics. The Archbishop of Canterbury—who was still the Anselm who was Rufus's enemy—stood as firmly for the rights of the Church as Henry for the rights of the King. In the end they compromised; the Pope was to invest bishops and archbishops (with their spiritual power, that is), but the King was to receive their homage as temporal lords. Since this left the King with the useful power of nominating bishops favorable to him, the compromise worked satisfactorily for the time being. But it had not solved the real problem, and that battle was to be fought through many centuries.

Henry is best remembered in England as the King of the White Ship, after the tragedy that saddened his last years and all but ruined his kingdom. He had several illegitimate children, but only two by his wife: Matilda, who in 1114 had married the German Emperor Henry V, and William, born in 1103, whom in his long-sighted way Henry had prepared for the succession by associating his son with himself in the ruling of the kingdom. In November, 1120, Henry was returning from Barfleur to England when William and a party of friends, not quite sober, hit on the idea of racing him in their new White Ship. It was dusk, and the crew, too, were a little drunk, and in the darkness they ran the ship on a rock. The young prince got clear in a small boat, but heard his half-sister calling to him for help. He turned back for her, and his boat was swamped by the press of drowning men trying to scramble aboard. "One countryman alone", said William of Malmesbury, "floating all night on a spar," survived until the morning to describe the unhappy accident.

"No ship," he adds with truth, "ever brought so much misery to England." It is said that after his son's death Henry never smiled again. His wife Edith Matilda had died two years before, so it seemed that the return of the line of Alfred was to remain another English dream. Henry married again, but his hopes of another son were disappointed, and his next male heir remained William Clito, son of the long-suffering Robert of Normandy, a young man wholly French and supported by the King of France. Henry fell back on what he must have known was a desperate expedient. He called home from Germany his daughter the Empress Matilda, now a childless widow, and at Christmas, 1126, persuaded the barons of both England and Normandy to swear fealty to her.

Matilda came reluctantly, and the barons swore reluctantly (though not under duress, as was to be alleged later). Louis VI of France strengthened his support of William Clito by giving him his half-sister in marriage, and in retaliation Henry married Matilda to Geoffrey the Fair of Anjou. The Angevins had long been enemies of the Normans, but Henry liked Geoffrey (though he was eleven years younger than Matilda), and hoped that a soldierly husband would make her more acceptable to a baronage whose chief demand of a King was to be a leader in battle. It did not; and, unfortunately, Matilda united an ungovernable temper with an apparent lack of interest in her own inheritance.

But her marriage had one good result. In 1134 she bore Geoffrey a son, whom we call Henry Plantagenet, from the sprig of broom or *planta genista* the Angevins bore as a badge. Perhaps Henry I took this birth as a good omen; but he was an old man by then, and a dying one, and must have suspected that his death was to be his kingdom's ruin. He died on December 1, 1135, and left his people to years of anarchy: a sad death for the best of the sons of the Conqueror.

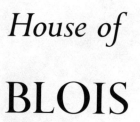

House of

BLOIS

STEPHEN
1135-1154

✲

Born at Blois in 1104.
Son of Stephen Count of Blois and his wife Adela, daughter of William I.
Married Matilda of Boulogne; their only surviving son, Eustace, died in 1153.
Died at Dover in 1154 and was buried at Faversham, Kent.

STEPHEN

A t the death of Henry I in December, 1135, it seemed that chaos was averted by a miracle.

Two possible heirs had claims on the throne that were unacceptable to the barons. Henry's own choice, his daughter Matilda, was disliked by the barons, and descent through the female line was not admitted in feudal society; the next heir in the male line, William Clito, was the son of one enemy, Robert of Normandy, and the dependent of another, Louis of France. In the face of this situation, decisive action by a strong man with a fair claim in blood and strong support in England was more than welcome. Count Stephen of Blois disembarked on the South Coast, and within a short time was acclaimed and crowned.

Stephen of Blois was the son of the Conqueror's daughter Adela and her husband, the elder Stephen of Blois. He had been brought up in Henry's court, and was courageous, affable, and generous. He also seemed energetic and decisive, for on hearing in Boulogne of Henry I's death, he had taken his opponents by surprise with the speed of his arrival in England. He also had an able and powerful brother, Henry Bishop of Winchester, who brought to his support (in spite of his oath of allegiance to Matilda) William of Corbeil Archbishop of Canterbury. The support of Canterbury was essential to a King because no coronation could take place without him. The citizens of London (already a powerful body) accepted Stephen with enthusiasm. "They believed," says the chronicler of Stephen's life, "that the kingdom was exposed to danger when the source of order and justice failed, and that it was therefore of the utmost importance to choose at once a king who could establish peace for the common good."

They had mistaken their man; Stephen was incapable of becoming the source of order and justice. As far as we can judge, he had nothing of Henry I's view of kingship, seeing the King in Continental fashion as the most powerful of the barons. He was of the stuff of knights, not of Kings, and his vigorous action in claiming the throne was no more than an unhappy spark of self-assertion. His father had been a charming and chivalrous knight whose one act of cowardice had made him the scorn of Europe, and his mother a domineering woman who had led that scorn. It cannot be mere coincidence that throughout his life Stephen continually forced himself to take on ventures far beyond his capabilities.

He began well enough. William Clito was soon killed fighting in Flanders, and although David of Scotland (who was Matilda's uncle) started hostilities in the north in her support, Stephen gained a valuable adherent in England. This was Robert of Gloucester who, as an illegitimate son of Henry I and a shrewd and experienced man, had been favored as king by some of the barons. His ambitions seem not to have gone beyond making himself valued, and he ignored the first summons to court; so that when he finally came he was received by Stephen with extraordinary favor, and his adherence was followed by the homage of most of the barons.

Some, however, were troubled by their broken oath of fealty to Matilda, and when the Archbishop of Canterbury died within the year, his death was said to be the vengeance of God on an oath-breaker. Stephen had taken the oath himself, and he defended it by asserting that it was void because it had been exacted under duress. The Pope had an ingenious justification for his accession: "The suffrages of so great a number of men could not have been obtained without an especial co-operation of the Divine Grace." Stephen had to pay for Canterbury's support, conceding the freedom of the Church in his coronation oath. But so anarchic was his reign to be, that the oath counted for little more than a precedent for more settled times.

The King's first task was to deal with the rebellious King David of Scotland. He raised an army and marched north to meet him. An uneasy compromise was reached, but within a few weeks he had to march again against a rebellious baron. When at last the rebel surrendered, Stephen let himself be persuaded by Robert of Gloucester to pardon him. It was a knightly action, but he should have suspected the advice of one as near his throne as Robert. "If he had then inflicted punishment," wrote Henry of Huntingdon, "so many castles would not thereafter have been held against him."

He then crossed to his other domain of Normandy. "He was welcomed there," says the Anglo-Saxon Chronicle (which was being kept up-to-date in fewer and fewer monasteries, and was soon to fall silent forever), "because they imagined he would be all that his maternal uncle was, and because he was still in possession of the royal treasury; but he gave away his wealth and squandered it foolishly." He did homage to Louis VI for Normandy, but failed to establish his own authority there, for Geoffrey of Anjou, now in pursuit of his wife's claim to England, had invaded the Duchy in force. Possibly Geoffrey pressed Robert of Gloucester to return to his allegiance to Matilda, for there were many rumors of Robert's treachery. With nothing achieved, Stephen returned aimlessly to England, and, having lost the loyalty of his barons, went on to quarrel with the Church, and in particular with his loyal brother Henry Bishop of Gloucester.

Bishop Henry has been described as "a man of extraordinary prudence and persuasive eloquence," and "a monstrous spectacle, compounded of purity and corruption, half monk and half knight." He seems, in fact, to have been anxious to stay loyal to his brother but to have found it progressively more difficult. Stephen now made quite certain of alienating him by giving the See of Canterbury to another. He did worse, by deciding to mount an attack on the whole power of the clergy. The Bishops of Ely, Exeter, and Salisbury were arrested on dubious charges and imprisoned until they surrendered their castles. By this foolish action Stephen raised up again the whole business of the respective authority of Church and Crown, on which William I and Henry I had so patiently compromised. Bishop Henry at once challenged him; but in 1138, before any conclusion could be reached, the country was plunged into civil war.

In Normandy, Robert of Gloucester had at last renounced his fealty to Stephen; the next month, David of Scotland invaded in the north, and many English castles challenged Stephen's authority. The Scottish invasion was particularly barbarous: "They ripped open pregnant women," wrote Henry of Huntingdon, "tossed children on to the points of their spears, butchered priests at their altars, and cutting off the heads from crucifixes placed them on the bodies of the slain, while in exchange they fixed on the crucifixes the heads of their victims." Stephen was busy in the south, and it was left to Thurstan Archbishop of York (another "half monk and half knight") to rally the north against David. In Yorkshire he set up a great standard, surrounded by banners from the bishoprics of Yorkshire, and at the Battle of the Standard totally defeated David's savage half-clothed warriors. The Scots fled the field, leaving eleven thousand dead. When Stephen had temporarily subdued the south, he led a punitive expedition into Scotland, returning with David's son Henry as hostage.

Meanwhile, Matilda and her new ally Robert of Gloucester had been gathering their forces, and in 1139 they landed in Sussex. Not even Gloucester's support could dispel the mistrust Matilda aroused in the barons, and when Stephen marched successfully on her he had every chance of ending her intervention altogether. Instead, with extraordinarily misplaced chivalry, he let her go under his safe-conduct to Robert's castle at Bristol; and the civil war continued. By this time Bishop Henry was "much perplexed; on the one hand there was the greatest difficulty in supporting the King's cause, on the other it was a serious affair, and indecent in the eyes of the world, to desert his brother in his adversity." He tried in vain to bring about a peace, while Stephen strengthened his own position by betrothing his son Eustace to the sister of Louis VII of France.

Stephen's downfall came suddenly, and at the hands of an aggrieved baron, Ranulf of Chester. Ranulf's wife and sister-in-law went on a social call to the Constable of Stephen's castle of Lincoln; Ranulf arrived later to escort the ladies home, had the gates hospitably opened to him, and promptly took possession of the castle. This was a serious loss, and Stephen hastily marched north and entered the town while Ranulf fled. But Robert of Gloucester was in the neighborhood, and the two of them returned in strength. Any sensible commander would have retreated; Stephen gave battle. Fighting on foot, deserted by his chief men, he was defeated and sent prisoner to a dungeon in Bristol Castle.

Matilda's triumph now seemed assured; but she was as incapable as Stephen of commanding the loyalty of barons or people. For some reason we do not know she was not crowned. Perhaps she thought English consecration unnecessary for the Empress of Germany (she certainly still used the empress's seal); or perhaps the barons had become cautious about swearing oaths. The citizens of London reluctantly admitted her to their city, but she seems to have been incapable of self-control, utterly unprepared for that compromise needed in dealing with the burghers of London. She alienated David of Scotland, Bishop Henry, and ultimately the general body of the clergy. When Stephen's wife (another Matilda) came to plead for her husband's release, the Empress repulsed her "with harsh and insulting language." Finally she demanded "an immense sum of money" from the Londoners, and when they attempted to persuade her to reduce her demands refused "in an insufferable rage and without any of the gentleness of her sex." London as a city already thought itself good enough to talk with empresses, and rose. To the sound of the bells of London pealing against her, she fled to Oxford. From there, typically, she vented her rage on the unfortunate prisoner Stephen, "with a woman's bitterness causing the Lord's Anointed to be bound with fetters."

Bishop Henry had reluctantly decided that Stephen was a poor better of the two claimants, and rallied his supporters. The Londoners, still smarting from their encounter with Matilda, joined him; so did Stephen's Queen, with powerful forces. Matilda met them at Winchester, where she was defeated and Robert of Gloucester captured. Since each side was in possession of the other's commander, they exchanged prisoners; and the civil war went on.

It went on year after year. Cities were besieged, minor skirmishes fought, alliances made and betrayed; neither side ever gathered strength or lost it to a degree necessary to bring about a solution. Stephen very nearly captured Matilda once again, at the siege of Oxford in 1141; but it was the height of winter, and she was able to escape from the city and cross the frozen river, wrapped in a white cloak to make her invisible against the snow. The real victims of these years were the common people, who had to endure the incessant fighting of the rival barons.

They spared not [says the Anglo-Saxon Chronicle, one of the last entries] —they spared not the lands of abbots nor of priests, but plundered the monks of the clergy, and every man who could robbed his neighbour. If two or three men came riding towards a village, all the villagers fled for fear of them, believing that they must be robbers. Even where the ground was tilled the earth bore no corn, for the land was ruined by such doings; and men said openly that Christ and His Saints slept.

It was only in Normandy that the war progressed at all. While Stephen was embroiled in England, Geoffrey of Anjou was steadily taking control of the duchy, and by 1146 was virtually its master. For some reason we do not know he never fought for his wife in England; perhaps because he took his marriage (which can hardly have brought him personal pleasure) as a weapon for increasing his own power; perhaps because in the end Matilda seems not to have taken her English heritage very seriously; or perhaps because he wisely decided not to risk offending Robert of Gloucester, who had been loyal and tireless as Matilda's commander in England. But in 1147 Robert died, and then Matilda gave up the struggle. To one who had been an all-powerful Empress, the possession of a ruined and ungrateful little island was perhaps of little interest. Early in 1148 she embarked for Normandy and never returned.

But England had gone past an automatic return to peace. David of Scotland remained Stephen's implacable enemy, and there was a formidable list of earls who would not submit to him. And to these was now added a new and greater opponent: Henry of Anjou, son of Matilda and Geoffrey of Anjou, who had been born the year before Henry I died. He was fourteen now, and had already on his own initiative mounted a slightly comic invasion of England. He had run out of money before long and been forced to return to Normandy, where his irritated parents had disowned him.

But Henry of Anjou, if precocious, was not comic. Even as a youth he was plainly what England so dearly wanted, an exceptionally capable leader. He could have been much less than this and still attracted the hopes of the despairing English swiftly by his descent. He was what Henry I had intended his successor to be, the undoubted heir of the two royal lines of England, the lines of Alfred the Great and William the Conqueror. In 1149, when he was fifteen, he returned to England, and made his unopposed way to Carlisle, where King David of Scotland knighted him. This was a challenge, for a King-to-be had to be knighted by a king. But Stephen, weary as he may have been of the struggle, had a son, Eustace, to fight for, and sent him north to capture Henry. Eustace instead justified the popular view of himself by first failing and then savagely wasting the countryside, and Henry went wisely home to Anjou, where his father rewarded him with the Duchy of Normandy.

The defense of this duchy occupied Henry for some time. In Paris on business he met a lady of European fame, who was then (but only reluctantly and because the Pope had personally put her to bed for a second time with her estranged husband) Queen of France; she was

Eleanor of Aquitaine, lady in her own right of half the breadth of France.

It was 1152 before Henry returned to England, and by then he was one of the greatest princes of Europe, by the side of whom the dubious King of England was a petty chieftain. Geoffrey of Anjou had died, and his great domains in France had passed to his son; the King and Queen of France had at last been divorced, and Henry had married Eleanor and become lord of all her vast lands. His possessions stretched from the Channel coast to the Pyrenees. He had only to set foot in England, and Stephen's barons began to leave him. His progress was all but royal, and baron after baron, town after town, came over to him. Only Stephen's son Eustace, in a raging impotence, devastated Cambridge and Bury St. Edmund's, and a few days later died (men said by God's vengeance for his desecration of the town where Saint Edmund was buried).

With his son dead, Stephen had nothing left to fight for. In his extremity his faithful brother Bishop Henry came to his help for the last time, and brought the tired old King and the vigorous young Prince together in the cathedral city of Winchester, Alfred the Great's capital. Stephen, still upholding his generous but irrelevant standards of knightly behavior, recognized Henry as his heir, and Henry, equally knightly, did homage to him.

For England it was peace at last, and under a strong King; for Stephen died within the year, and was buried in the Abbey of Faversham in Kent at the side of his wife and son. He was without doubt a good man, courageous, generous, and sincere, but his nineteen-year reign gave his country nineteen of the most wretched years of her history. His death at the age of fifty was unlamented, and even the chronicle written to celebrate his life breaks off before its conclusion.

House of

ANJOU

or

PLANTAGENET

HENRY II

✿

Born at Le Mans in 1133.

Son of the Empress Matilda, daughter of Henry I, and her
second husband Geoffrey of Anjou.

Married in 1151 Eleanor of Aquitaine, divorced wife of
Louis VII of France, from whom he took the title of
Duke of Aquitaine. Their children included:

> Henry, born in 1155, crowned as the Young King or
> *Filius Regis* in 1170, and died in France in 1173; Rich-
> ard, later Richard I; Geoffrey, born in 1158, married
> Constance of Brittany, by whom he had a son,
> > Arthur of Brittany, born in 1186 after his father's
> > death, and died probably in 1203;
> John, later King John;
> Joan, married William II King of Sicily.

Recognized in 1153 as heir to King Stephen.

Died at Chinon in 1189 and was buried in the Abbey of
Fontrevault.

Henry's father Geoffrey of Anjou was known as Geoffrey
Plantagenet from the sprig of broom *(planta genista)* he
used as his badge. Henry II and his immediate successors
are known as the Angevin Kings, but with the loss of
Anjou in the reign of King John, the House came to be
known by the family name of Plantagenet.

HENRY II

To those who try to understand history, Henry II is a rare figure: a man 800-years dead whose personality is still vital and present.

The Angevins were notorious for their energy, their turbulence, their terrible rages. They were said to be descended from the witch Melusine, and Saint Bernard of Clairvaulx said of them "From the Devil they came and to the Devil they will return." Henry II had all that temper: when a particular enemy of his was praised in his presence he fell into such a rage that he threw himself screaming out of bed and tore his mattress to pieces with his teeth. And he had all the energy, as a pathetically resigned description of his daily life by the chronicler Peter of Blois tells us:

If the King has promised to remain in one place for a day—and especially when he has announced his intention by public proclamation—he is sure to upset everyone's arrangements by leaving early in the morning. If on the other hand he orders an early start, you can take it for granted that he will sleep until midday. We have to go to the servants and whores to find out when the King is likely to make a start, for these are the people most likely to know the secrets of the palace. I have often known it happen, when the King seems safely asleep and peace and silence at last established, that word comes suddenly from the royal lodgings that he is starting for some other place. After all the day's delay and uncertainty it is naturally an enormous relief to have the prospect of staying overnight in a town, where there is a reasonable chance of getting a comfortable room and enough to eat. But, late in the afternoon, when the advance party have practically finished the day's ride, the King will change his mind and turn off to some quite different place, where there are quarters and food for him alone. We may wander for miles through some unknown forest, as often as not in pitch darkness, and think ourselves lucky if we come across some squalid little hut. I have seen men draw their swords over a broken-down shed that pigs would be ashamed to fight for.

It was said that the King never sat down except at table, and that when he had to be still (as in church) he would scribble or scratch or whittle. And yet this man had a passion for the smallest acts of justice, and would stay for hours in the courts, listening patiently to every man. Walter Map wrote, "Whoever has a good case is anxious to have it tried before the King, but whoever has a bad one will not come to him unless he is dragged." He was a compact, sturdy man, with gray eyes that blazed in his fits of temper; wherever he went crowds would press round him, begging him to hear their grievances, jostling to touch him or simply to look at him. He could afford to be easy, for his dignity was in himself, not in his position. The monks of Winchester once begged him to protect them from their tyrannical bishop, who had deprived them of three courses at dinner. Hearing that this atrocious act still left the holy men ten courses, Henry replied robustly, "In my court three courses is enough. Perish your Bishop if he doesn't cut you down to the same." And, riding one day with his magnificent Chancellor Beckett, Henry saw a half-naked beggar, and asked if it would not be Christian charity to cover the man's shoulders with a cloak. When Beckett piously agreed, Henry snatched Beckett's own furs from his shoulder and tossed them to the beggar. At the bottom of Henry's character there was always a stubborn human decency, as if he were not a remarkable man, but an ordinarily decent, generous, fair-minded man raised to a higher power. As a private citizen he would have been intolerable; as the King of a disorganized and demoralized country he was in his element.

In 1151 at the age of nineteen Henry had married Eleanor of Aquitaine, ten years his senior, a great heiress in her own right and one of the most beautiful and impossible women in Europe. She had first married Louis VII of France, a man of monkish disposition for whom she was altogether too much. She bore him one daughter, but there were many tales of her infidelity, and she became the inseparable companion of her uncle, Raymond of Antioch. Desperate, Louis tried to divorce her on the usual grounds that they were too closely related, although his advisers pointed out that her possessions in France were as great as his own. Louis appealed to the Pope, whose response was to confirm their marriage and personally bed them again. The result of this was a second daughter, but soon afterward Eleanor, too, was in favor of a divorce; it seems that she had now met Henry. In 1151 she got her divorce, and eight weeks later married Henry at Poitiers. Louis lost half his kingdom by the divorce, but said of Eleanor, "The poorest gentleman of my kingdom would not desire her for wife." Henry was made of stronger stuff than Louis; Eleanor's dowry helped to make him the most powerful European ruler since Charlemagne, and she was to bear him eight children; but still he was to have occasion to remember Louis's words.

His reign began peacefully enough. He had ruled as heir-apparent for the last months of the unhappy Stephen's life, and there was no one to dispute his succession. He was crowned at Westminster at Christmas, 1155, when he was twenty-one. Henry of Huntingdon tells us that the coronation was marked by universal rejoicing, and that was to prove prophetic. Henry was to bring to a stricken and exhausted country peace, security, law, and prosperity. He had to restore law and order, subjugate his unruly barons, resolve the quarrel with the Church, and maintain his other enormous domains, and he set about it all with only one aim. "Above everything in the world that is desirable," wrote Peter of Blois, "he labours for peace. All that he thinks, all that he says, all that he does, is directed to this one end: that his people may have peace."

Henry's misfortune is that he has been remembered by posterity chiefly for the murder of Beckett. Thomas à Beckett was typical of the "new men" Henry had introduced into his government, a Londoner of prosperous middle-class family, church-educated, who by the age of thirty-six had risen to be Archdeacon of Canterbury and an experienced lawyer and negotiator. His abilities were so plain that on Henry's accession the Archbishop of Canterbury recommended him as Chancellor.

Of all men in the kingdom, the Chancellor was the closest to the King; he was his confidential secretary and keeper of his Great Seal, and without his knowledge no matter of consequence could be transacted. Beckett gave Henry his total loyalty. He raised his taxes, fought in his wars, negotiated the marriage of his eldest son to the daughter of the King of France, and was the effective instrument of all his policies. He was also his closest friend, sharing his unresting life, his passionate energy, and his boyish humor; Fitz Stephen writes, "I do not think that two men have ever been more of one mind or closer in friendship than these two."

The one thing they did not share was Beckett's extravagance. Beckett lived in magnificent style, and loved to give sumptuous banquets; when he went to France on the marriage negotiations, he had an escort of 200 knights and squires, eight wagons of ermine, silks, furs, carpets and rich tapestries, two wagons of ale, 250 footmen and innumerable pack horses. Henry seems to have regarded this worldliness with an amused tolerance. Having himself no inner insecurities, he did not need outward magnificence, and he himself lived without display; but Beckett was a nobody who had risen to a dangerous height, and was soon to rise from a dangerous height to a fatal one. Henry was set on resolving the old conflict between church and crown by making himself master of the church in England, and Beckett had agreed that the policy was sound. In 1161 Theobald Archbishop of Canterbury died, and Henry nominated Beckett to the see.

Surprisingly, Beckett demurred; the archbishop, he warned the King, might be a very different man from the chancellor. Henry persisted, and Beckett accepted. He said later to the Prior of Leicester that now he was bound either to quarrel with the King or neglect the service of God.

To quarrel with the King was to do without his personal support, and from the hour of his appointment to Canterbury Beckett lived a life of extraordinary, sometimes grotesque, theatricality to mask his inner insecurity. He renounced his magnificent style, drank only water, wore a hair shirt infested with lice, and mortified the flesh by having his monks whip him. Gilbert Foliot said that the King had made an archbishop out of a man of the world; in fact, Henry had imposed on Beckett a role he was too weak to refuse and too weak to play out.

Beckett saw it as his duty as Canterbury to oppose the King on every important matter: on finance, on the appointment of the clergy, and above all on the jurisdiction of the ecclesiastical courts. The Church claimed the right to try all clerics on all charges, civil or not; and as the taking of minor orders involved no vows or duties incompatible with lay life any man with a smattering of literacy could escape trial by pleading "benefit of clergy." A cleric's duty to his church might properly sometimes supersede his duty to the state, but Beckett pushed matters so far that he protected acknowledged murderers if they claimed benefit, a course of action that he must have known was not only totally unacceptable to the King but totally incompatible with the rule of law. When Henry insisted that secular crimes must be tried in secular courts, Beckett replied that Canterbury was the representative of God on earth and as such was set above all Kings, at which Henry lost his temper and called him a low-born clerk.

In 1164 Henry attempted, in the Articles of Clarendon, to define the position of the Church in the feudal state. On the question of benefit of clergy, the articles stated that a cleric accused of a civil crime was to be brought first before a civil court, that any subsequent proceedings in a Church court were to be observed by an officer of the crown, and that if the cleric were found guilty he was to forfeit the protection of the Church. He summoned a council to ratify these articles, and Beckett, with blasphemous arrogance, said that the proceedings were like Christ's trial before Pilate. He came under heavy pressure to accept the articles, accepted, tried to withdraw, and, to the horror of his followers, attempted to flee the country and failed.

Henry now changed his tactics. It happened that one of his men already had a suit against Beckett on a charge of misappropriating money, and under Henry's new legal proceedings this was transferred to the royal court, and Beckett summoned to appear. It was a poor occasion for the representative of God upon earth, and Beckett neither defied nor complied, pleading illness, that the proceedings were incorrect because a witness had testified on a hymnal not a Bible, but eventually had to agree to a fine of £300 (a sizeable sum then). This was followed by a series of similar charges involving the great sum of £20,000, and Beckett was at last forced to agree to appear.

When he celebrated Mass that morning (October 13, 1164), Beckett used the Introit *Princes sate and spake against me.* When he came into court he carried even further his earlier comparison of himself with Christ by taking on his back his great pectoral Cross (except that Christ's Cross was not of silver). Whether from prudence, from regret, or from a disgust of histrionics, Henry refused to meet him. Whatever his emotion was, it was soon superseded by wrath, as he discovered that Beckett had already appealed his case to Rome, which was a violation of the Articles of Clarendon he had been thought to have accepted.

Accused of this faithlessness, Beckett first used a legal quibble, and then (the charge was still of misappropriating money) fell back on the thunders of the Church:

Have you come to judge me? You have no right. Such as I am, I am your father in God, and refuse to hear your judgements.

Henry behaved with such remarkable restraint that Beckett fell into panic; he fled the country, this time successfully, hidden under a bundle of old clothes on a pack horse. It seems that he never forgave Henry for inflicting this shame on him.

Louis of France helped him on his way to Rome, where the Pope advised him to wait in hope of a compromise. Beckett took refuge in the Abbey of Pontigny, where he began systematically excommunicating the clergy who supported the King, while Henry responded by expelling from the kingdom Beckett's numerous relations. Beckett stopped short of the ultimate sanction of excommunicating the King himself, writing to him that he would return to serve him in all matters "saving God's honour and that of the Roman Church," and at the same time threatening him with the vengeance of Almighty God.

This position endured until 1170. The King's eldest son, young Henry, was now fifteen, and to ensure the succession Henry proposed to have him crowned. In Beckett's absence the ceremony was carried out by the Archbishop of York, and for this uncanonical proceeding Beckett promptly got the Pope's permission to place all Henry's Continental possessions under the ban of the Church. A compromise was now essential, and in the presence of King Louis, Henry and Beckett met in France. Henry spoke kindly. "My lord Archbishop," he said, "let us return to our old friendship and each show the other what good he can; let us forget our hatred completely." He withdrew the offending articles, and gave Beckett permission to act against the bishops who had assisted at the coronation of the Young King (as the heir was now called).

Henry seems to have been sincere in his offers of friendship; but Beckett, who had spent four years in shameful impotence, was now actuated by a spirit of manic vindictiveness against the world. On his arrival in England he excommunicated the erring bishops and questioned the legality of the Young King's coronation. This amounted to treason, and was a total denial of the supposed reconciliation. When Henry heard the news he broke into an Angevin rage, shouting, "What idle and miserable and faithless men do I keep about me, who let me be mocked by a low-born clerk!" Henry's rages were well known, but four ambitious knights thought it politic to take this one seriously. Reginald FitzUrse, William de Tracy, Hugh de Morville, and Richard Brito arrived in Canterbury on Tuesday, the twenty-ninth of December. They saw Beckett in the cathedral, and demanded that he cease to question the validity of the Young King's crowning or leave the country. He refused, and they left him for a time to consider.

There was, in fact, no choice left to him. He could not accept yet another shameful flight, and he had finally put himself beyond the reach of the generosity of his old friend the King. In his last minutes his theatrical instinct served him well. He would not have the doors of the cathedral locked, nor conceal himself, and when the knights returned he went toward them to ask what they wanted. They cut him down at once, spilling his brains on the paved floor at the spot that is still called the Martyrdom. Later on, when he was known as Saint Thomas the "holy blissful martyr" (mostly to Englishmen who strongly disapproved of the ecclesiastical absolutism he had supported) an altar was set up to him called the Altar of the Sword's Point. It was an inspired choice of name, for the one thing in his life Beckett did not try to avoid was the sword's point.

And, after all, his vindictiveness caused his King less trouble than might have been expected. At the news of his death Henry wept for three days; then, with his characteristic good sense, he saw that he must make his peace with the Pope, and seized the chance of presenting him with a whole country. It happened that a Norman knight, Richard de Clare nicknamed Strongbow, had made himself King of Leinster. Henry took a force to Ireland, received Strongbow's homage, and imposed on the Irish clergy the authority of Rome. In return for the Irish Church, the Pope gave him a very light penance for the murder of an archbishop; he was to revoke the Articles of Clarendon, send 200 knights to the Holy Land, go himself to fight the Saracen in Spain if the Pope thought it necessary (he never did), and submit to a penitential scourging at Beckett's shrine. The ceremonial scourging, as it happened, fell on a day when Henry's armies captured his particular enemy William the Lion of Scotland, so even that sting could not have been too severe.

The fundamental disagreement with the Church, however—was the King or the Church sovereign?—was too great to be solved by the death of Beckett. It had to be left until later reigns, for virtually all the eighteen years left to Henry II were to be taken up by the rebellions of his sons.

There were four of them—Henry, Richard, Geoffrey, and John—and collectively they have been called the Devil's Brood. Behind them in most of their risings was their mother Eleanor, who now began to justify the opinion of her former husband. Nominally, Henry the Young King was lord of Anjou; Richard of Aquitaine; and Geoffrey (later) of Brittany. The youngest son, John, was given no lands, and nicknamed Lackland for it; was this Henry's unhappy attempt to stop his most dearly loved son showing his greed as nakedly as the rest? The problem of ambitious sons defeated Henry II as completely as it defeated the majority of his predecessors and successors; but, shameful as the sons were, the father was not wise. He consistently refused to allow them any real power (just as he consistently ignored the thwarted energies of his wife Eleanor).

The trouble began with John, who was on the point of betrothal and needed a proper establishment. Henry asked the Young King to give up some of his own fiefs. The Young King refused, and then, encouraged by Eleanor and by Louis VII of France, who was always ready to embarrass his great rival of England, rebelled and demanded either England or the French domains for himself. Richard and Geoffrey promptly joined him and Louis in an attack on Normandy, while William the Lion of Scotland, as well as some English barons, created trouble in England. Henry rode this trouble without any great exertion and characteristically forgave his sons (not for the only time). His general amnesty excepted only his wife Eleanor, who was held in prison. The princes were given extra lands to console them, and some minor revolts there kept them occupied for the next five years. Henry had peace enough even to think of organizing a Crusade.

It did not last; for in 1180 Louis VII of France died, and was succeeded by Philip Augustus, his son by his second wife. Philip Augustus reigned over only half of France, because his father had given away the other half rather than tolerate Eleanor of Aquitaine as his first wife, and it was reasonable that he should be determined to break the power of Eleanor's husband, Henry. But it was a struggle even more personal than that, because his weapon was the dissension within Henry's family. It was his cold intelligence that ruined the Devil's Brood; and yet he must have had charm, too, for much of his power over Henry lay in his personal attraction of the Young King and his brothers.

Perhaps Henry was too much used to grateful subjects to deal wisely with ungrateful sons. He tried to keep the Young King's loyalty by commanding Richard and Geoffrey to do him homage, which was in fact correct by feudal standards. Richard refused; the Young King attacked him, and while Henry was trying to quell the consequent war he was summoned to the Young King, who was said to be ill. He suspected treachery and refused to go, and his son died. Henry fell into agonies of remorse. He paid his dead son's considerable debts, saying, "He has cost me enough, but I wish he had lived to cost me more."

Yet he had learned nothing. Richard was now his heir, and he proposed a new division of his domains, which was fair enough except that it required Richard to give Aquitaine to John, and Richard had ruled and defended Aquitaine for years, and passionately loved it. Possibly Henry had no idea of this love; Aquitaine was the land of Richard's mother, and Richard was always a mother's boy. Richard refused to give up his lands; he also quarrelled bitterly with his father about his delayed marriage with Alice, half-sister of Philip Augustus. It was possible that Henry was keeping Richard, as his heir, free for a better match, but it was also rumored that Alice was Henry's mistress. Since Richard was a notorious homosexual, it was plain that his real purpose was a quarrel with his father.

John, meanwhile, still lacked land, and in 1185 the Christians of the Holy Land (still precariously in place, but not to last very much longer) were looking for an heir to their King Baldwin IV of Jerusalem, who was a leper. John begged on his knees for this heritage, but Henry wisely refused his permission. In compensation he made John Lord of Ireland; but in the hands of his sons even Henry's wisest dispositions went wrong; John sulked at what he had lost in the Holy Land and squandered what might have been a valuable opportunity in Ireland. Mostly he jeered at the wild Irish ways of his more powerful subjects.

Finally Henry had to release Eleanor, after eleven years of captivity, and beg her to influence the intractable Richard. If he again refused to give Richard power in his kingdom, at least by now he had evidence to spare of his disloyalty. Philip Augustus had been intriguing with Geoffrey, which was frustrated by Geoffrey's death in 1186, but he now came into real conflict with Henry over a border dispute: Henry called Richard and John to join him, and a truce was arranged. The truce was more fatal to Henry than any battle could have been, for it brought Richard within reach of Philip's seductions.

Soon they were (as the chronicle discreetly puts it) "eating from the same dish and sleeping in the same bed." This situation was only resolved by disastrous news from the East.

In 1187 the Christian princes of the Holy Land had been catastrophically defeated at the Horns of Hattin by the brilliant infidel soldier Saladin; the True Cross, the most holy relic of Christendom, had been taken, and the Holy City itself was threatened.

It was the ethos of those days that to all true Christians the fate of the Holy City was more important than life. Henry, Philip Augustus, and Richard agreed to a truce that would allow them to go to the defense of the Holy Land. The truce lasted for less than six months. It was Philip Augustus who broke it, and with it Henry's spirit.

Henry was an old man now, over fifty, worn out by his failure with the sons whom he still treated with a father's loyalty, and Philip's duplicity was beyond his powers to combat. Philip egged Richard into truce-breaking, complained of it to Henry, and when Henry refused the bait himself started the war again. Henry, naturally, fought capably; it was Richard who, with the Angevin perversity—or was it simply hatred of his father?—,forced him to a disadvantageous peace, and then refused to accept it. The poor little Princess Alice was involved in his demands again, and Henry refused to hand her over as Richard's wife. It is possible that she was Henry's mistress; but it is also possible that his generous spirit simply revolted at handing her over to his sodomite son, who slept in her half-brother's bed. By now Henry's fatherly feelings had reached their end. It is likely that he came finally to hate his heir when Richard committed the ultimate treachery of doing homage to Philip for his father's lands in France.

Henry's only counter was to have the Papal Legate threaten Philip with an interdict for his failure to go on Crusade. Undisturbed, Philip invaded Maine and beseiged Henry's birthplace of Le Mans, and neither Henry nor his commander, William the Marshal, could save it. Henry watched his city burning, and cried out against the God who had deserted him.

He met Philip and Richard at Colombières, so ill that he could hardly stay in the saddle. Even the cold Philip took pity on him, and offered a cloak for him to sit on. Henry refused; even when his mount reared at a sudden flash of lightning he kept his saddle. It was his only triumph. He had to agree to give Richard Alice and the homage of his barons, he had to do homage to Philip himself for his lands in France and agree to join him on Crusade. When he gave Richard the customary kiss of peace at the conclusion of the treaty, he whispered, "Let God only spare my life to be revenged on you!" He went, dying, back to Chinon, and there read over the list of those whose fealty he was to relinquish to Richard. Among them was the name of his best-loved son John. He turned his face to the wall, saying "Then let all things go as they must, for I care no longer for myself or my world."

He lingered for a few days longer, like a true Angevin raging to the last: "Cursed be the day I was born and cursed of God the sons I leave behind me." He was buried in the Abbey of Fontrevault, and it is said that as his body lay there in state Richard came and stood for a time in silence.

Yet England blessed the day Henry II was born. He found her wrecked by the worst and most sterile excesses of the feudal system, and he left her peaceful, prosperous, and law-abiding. It is not Beckett who has the last word on him, nor his capricious wife or treacherous sons, but Peter of Blois, the chronicler who speaks for the common people of his time.

I loved him [wrote Peter], I loved him, I shall always love him. Everybody loved him, because he exacted swift justice and made peace.

Something of the spirit of Arthur had come back with Henry II.

RICHARD I
Lion-Heart
1189–1199

✿

Born at Oxford in 1157.
Second son of Henry II and his wife Eleanor of Aquitaine.
Married in Cyprus, 1191, Berengaria of Navarre.
Died without children at Chalus, Limousin, 1199, and was
 buried near his father at Fontrevault.

RICHARD I
Lion-Heart

t is hardly worth our time to assess Richard I as an English King. He spoke no English, he spent only a few months in England, he gave no sign in the whole of his short life that the people of England had more claim on his attention than what sufficed to secure his own possessions. Indeed, he showed no sign that anything had a claim beyond his own desires, which were eternally bedevilled by the Angevin temper and the Angevin passion to thwart everyone he had to do with. Richard was vicious, homosexual, rash, indecisive, and avaricious. The comically sad fact that for many people he represents the ideal of Christian kingship is based on irrelevancies.

He was a perfect knight, in the most limited sense of that battered word: a splendid fighter and a good tactician. Physically he was strongly attractive, with red-gold hair, a noble face and long limbs, and he was a poet and troubadour. He had also, though it escapes us today, an inexplicable charm, commanding the devotion of his followers and the admiration of his enemies. Perhaps his homosexuality had a touch of the Greek ideal about it, the ideal of the man who cannot love women because they have no role in the life he has chosen.

His first exploit after Henry's death was to arrest Henry's seneschal, Stephen of Tours, and keep him in chains in a dungeon until the treasury had been handed over. He crossed to England then, and was duly crowned at Westminster on September 3, 1189, and did at least stop the Londoners from massacring the Jews that night (a habit of theirs when they were excited). His only interest was in the coming Crusade with Philip Augustus of France. He and Philip renewed the oath to take the Cross, swearing to fight together as brothers, to share the spoils of conquest, and to defend each other's territories while they were abroad. This oath was to prove as valuable as most oaths of the time.

Richard showed remarkable fervor—which may have been genuinely religious but did not benefit his kingdom—in raising money for the expedition. He sold towns, castles, domains, and offices of state to the highest bidder. "I would sell London," said Richard, "if I could find anyone rich enough to buy it." As a crowning act of folly, he sold the King of Scotland, England's oldest enemy, freedom from fealty to England.

Before he could leave, he had to find someone to look after his kingdom. He had no accepted heir. His brother John, now nearing thirty and Lord of Ireland and Count of Mortain, was the last of Henry II's sons; but the line senior to him, that of Geoffrey of Brittany, was since Geoffrey's death in 1186 represented only by his three-year-old son Arthur. John's main interest was in being assured of the succession if Richard should die in the East; and Richard neatly repeated his father's mistakes by denying him not only assurance but also power. He entrusted the kingdom to William Longchamps Bishop of Ely, and made the worst possible of his relationship with John by first exiling him for three years and then (at their mother Eleanor's request) revoking the exile. He may have been indecisive; more likely he was uninterested.

The beginning of the Crusade was unfortunate. The Emperor Frederick Barbarossa, who had gone in advance, was drowned, and when Richard received the staff and wallet, the traditional signs of the pilgrim, he leaned on the staff and it broke. Worse was to come. In Sicily, where they wintered, Richard heard the call of a falcon from inside a peasant's hut. In his lands only knights could own hunting birds, and he forced his way into the hut and seized the bird. The peasant and his neighbors resisted, the blade of Richard's sword broke, and he had to make an undignified escape under a shower of mud and stones.

His next trouble was of a more knightly kind. The island of Sicily (like the island of England) had been the prey of land-hungry Normans, and now King William III had died without heirs, and the Pope, anxious for Norman support against the Emperor, had chosen William's illegitimate cousin Tancred as King. Unwisely, Tancred took for himself ships and money William III had promised to the

Crusade, and imprisoned his widow. Since William's widow was Richard's sister Joan, Richard took and sacked Messina. This led to a quarrel with Philip Augustus, who had refused to join the fighting but claimed that their crusading oath gave him the right to share the spoils. This was the end of any trust between the former lovers, and to confirm the break Richard refused the marriage he had so wounded his father by seeking, with Philip's half-sister Alice. She had, he said (without any evidence that we know of), born his father a child.

The quarrel about poor Alice was brought to a close in March, 1191, when news reached Sicily that Richard's mother Eleanor was on her way with a new bride. Philip prudently sailed for the Holy Land before the ladies arrived. The new bride was Berengaria of Navarre, with whom later poets have taken surprising liberties, though not until after Richard's death. They sang of how he first saw her at the court of Navarre, and fell so deeply in love that he asked no dowry. Both ideas seem singularly uncharacteristic of the avaricious homosexual that Richard was in life, and in fact it is unlikely that he had ever seen Berengaria before her arrival with Eleanor. A contemporary writer calls her "sensible rather than attractive." Like his ancestor William Rufus, Richard did not feel obliged to provide his kingdom with an heir, however much he despised the one it had.

An oddly symbolic incident occurred before he left Sicily. He made a treaty (which Philip had tried secretly to thwart) with the new King Tancred, and it was solemnized by an exchange of gifts. Some years earlier a great tomb had been discovered in Glastonbury, where, it was claimed, Joseph of Arimathea had brought the Holy Grail, the cup used by Christ at the Last Supper; when the tomb was opened, the monks of Glastonbury claimed to have found there the bones of King Arthur and a sword that could only have been his renowned Excalibur. This event was so famous that the son of Geoffrey of Brittany (who as Richard's brother must have had a fair guess that he would have no children) was named Arthur, and a splendid future had been prophesied for this namesake of a great King. Richard gave Excalibur, the dearest relic of Britain, to Tancred.

On his way to the Holy Land Richard was forced almost by chance into the capture of the island of Cyprus. Its Byzantine ruler, Isaac, captured Berengaria and Richard's sister Joan when their ship was driven ashore in a storm, and in May, 1191, Richard assembled a fleet, sacked Limassol, and finally forced Isaac's submission. This incidental success was his most valuable contribution to the Crusaders' cause, for it gave them a convenient base and a safe port for the supply fleets. He married Berengaria in the Cathedral of Limassol, and then, with Philip Augustus, forced the surrender of the vital port of Acre in the Holy Land. This was the Crusaders' first victory since their disastrous defeat at Hattin, and it put new spirit into them. Characteristically it was marked by an incident that was to cost Richard dearly in a few years' time. Leopold of Austria, who now commanded the imperial army, flew his own banner beside those of Richard and Philip, and Richard (as he had done with Philip's at Messina) had it taken down and thrown into a ditch.

After the capture of Acre, Philip Augustus announced that he was ill, had accomplished his crusading vow, and was going home. In fact, he had inherited Artois, and wanted to return to France to secure it. Richard, who suspected that he also had designs on his own domains of Anjou and Normandy, raged in vain. Philip left, and that was the end of that comradeship-in-arms.

Richard now had the 2,700 citizens of Acre as a bargaining counter with Saladin, the famous Saracen commander. He offered them in exchange for the True Cross (captured at Hattin), 1,500 Christian prisoners of war, and a large sum of money. When Saladin was slow in raising the money, Richard had the prisoners herded outside the gates of Acre and massacred them. He stayed in the Holy Land for another year, and had some victories that were spectacular but indecisive. It was at this time that he won his reputation as the knightly warrior-King (the massacre at Acre being conveniently overlooked), but the evidence suggests that at least for some time he had in mind a solution of the problem of the Holy Land that was more diplomatic than military. The Saracen way of life was not unlike his own ideals, and he established a strong sympathy with Saladin. There was even talk of a marriage between Saladin and Richard's sister Joan, and perhaps the most solid result of his stay in the Holy Land was his agreement with Saladin that allowed Christian pilgrims to visit the Holy Places. But in the autumn of 1192, news from England forced him to sail for home, and that was the end of his Crusading.

If he had stayed another six months he might have achieved his ambition of freeing Jerusalem, for Saladin died the following March. There can be no doubt of the intensity of Richard's Crusading passion. It is said that when he was once riding in the hills near Emmaus, he came within sight of the faraway towers of the Holy City, and covered his face with his shield, not to look at them in their captivity.

In England, meanwhile, William of Longchamps, as might have been expected, was engaged in quarrels with his King's brothers. Geoffrey, who was Henry II's illegitimate son and had once been his Chancellor, arrived in England to take up his new see of York, and Longchamps (who was said to behave as if he were greater than the Pope) had him seized from the very altar. This sacrilege, so soon after Beckett's murder, so shocked the country that John had no difficulty in forcing Longchamps to flee. He disguised himself as a woman, but too successfully; on Dover Beach he was discovered by an amorous sailor, and exiled to Flanders. It did John no good, for Walter of Coutances took Longchamps's place, and only the intervention of the Dowager Queen Eleanor (now over seventy but as tireless for power as ever) kept the peace.

Richard, on his way home to deal with this situation, found his choice of route difficult, for in one way or another he had mortally offended every ruler through whose lands he might pass. When contrary winds prevented his making the Straits of Gibraltar and the long sea-passage round Spain and France, he decided for the German route. He disguised himself as a pilgrim, but characteristically refused to discard his jewelry or moderate his kingly style of traveling. He was arrested in Vienna by the men of Leopold of Austria, who was still smarting for the humiliation of Acre, and imprisoned. A captured King was then an object of immense value, since he could be used in negotiations or exchanged for ransom, and most of the Kings of Europe joined in the bidding for Richard. Leopold sold him to the Emperor Henry VI (he got nearly four times the sum Richard had got for remitting the homage of Scotland), and Henry VI, who hated Richard for his support of Tancred of Sicily, set to work to make an even better bargain. Two more of Richard's enemies, John Prince of England and Philip Augustus of France, were delighted by his capture; John could now secure England to himself and Philip set about the dismemberment of the Angevin lands in France. John did homage to Philip for the French lands, and even promised (he never kept the promise) to marry the pathetic Alice.

As the later song said:

> O Richard, ô mon roi,
> L' univers t'abandonne;

RICHARD I

Sur le monde il n'y a que moi
Qui s'intéresse à ta personne.

The only people who still interested themselves in Richard were his mother Eleanor and the faithful Walter of Coutances. It is said that his loyal minstrel Blondel de Nesle wandered the castles of the Empire, singing the songs Richard himself had composed, and found him when the voice of an unseen prisoner took up the song with him. Whether or not this story is true, it is a fact that two abbots from Walter's council reached Richard just as he was standing trial in Speyer. Richard defended himself with such nobility that the emperor broke into tears and gave him the kiss of peace; he did not, however, lower the price he asked for his release, and at the last moment Philip Augustus and brother John put in a counterbid. The price that England had in the end to pay for the King who took so little interest in her was appallingly high: England was to pay a sum down, yearly tribute, and become a fief of the Empire. It was a mark of the unreality of this game that Kings and emperors played that these conditions gradually lapsed once Richard was free.

At his release Philip Augustus sent a message to John: "Look to yourself; the devil is loosed." He was wrong. Perhaps Richard thought it unknightly to bear a grudge; perhaps he was too self-centered to understand others (certainly the light way he made enemies suggests this); or perhaps he retained his father's indulgent attitude to the youngest boy of the Devil's Brood. To the thirty-year-old man who knelt before him, he said, "You are a child; you have fallen into evil company. It is those who have given you bad counsel who will be punished." His fame as a Crusader made England forgive him much, and he had little trouble in bringing his kingdom under his control. Nottingham Castle held out briefly for John, but the rest of the people received him with joy.

He neither appreciated nor rewarded their joy. Instead, he left them Hubert Walter as his deputy and went back to Normandy and the war with Philip, which was to last for the rest of his short life. John, who had learned his lesson well, fought loyally for him, in spite of Philip's seductions.

It is a sad fact that although Richard I was a great tactical commander, not one of his victories achieved any lasting effect. Indeed, he hardly meant them to, for he was the product of a society that knew no other way of life but fighting and had no intention of ending that way of life. The art of warfare was now the art of living to fight another day, and the one thing that would infallibly bring about a truce was the prospect of a pitched battle. The one branch of warfare in which there were new developments was, typically, that of fortification; fortresses were being built so as to guarantee a defensive force the perfect answer to every possible move of an attacker. Richard planned a chain of such fortresses to hold his frontier in France, and put all his energy and knowledge into its vital point, the magnificent Château Gaillard. "If an angel had descended from heaven," wrote William of Newburgh, "and told him to abandon it, the angel would have had a volley of curses and the work gone on regardless."

In the winter of 1198 a ploughman near Chalus in the Limousin turned up in his furrow a Roman treasure-hoard. Dutifully, he handed it over to his lord, Archard de Chalus, and Richard, hearing of it, claimed it as his own. Archard tried to negotiate, and found his tiny castle under siege. One morning Richard went out unarmed, and a crossbowman in the castle saw him and sent a bolt into his shoulder. The bolt proved difficult to remove, the wound festered, and gangrene set in. Richard's captain of mercenaries, Mercadier, had meanwhile taken the castle, and massacred the garrison, except for the archer who had wounded Richard. The dying King asked the man why he had shot him. "You killed my father and my two brothers with your own hand," said the archer. "Do what you like with me; I can bear any torture to have seen you dying." Richard ordered him to be set free. Mercadier waited until the King was dead, and then had the archer flayed alive.

Richard was buried in the Abbey of Fontrevault, at the side of the father whose death he had done so much to bring about. He named John as heir to all his possessions both in England and in France. The shining reputation he left behind him was almost wholly spurious; the inhabitants of Acre could testify that he had not even the personal virtues of chivalry. As a King of England he can hardly be called a failure, for there is no evidence that he ever attempted to be such; England to Richard I was a purse of money. For ten years England had had no King, and only the excellence of Henry II's administrative machinery had saved her from chaos. Now Richard's brother had to take up Richard's legacy: an enormous debt, Continental frontiers in turmoil, and a general situation dangerously declining.

JOHN
LACKLAND
1199-1216

❁

Born at Oxford in 1160.

Fourth son of Henry II and his wife Eleanor of Aquitaine.
Married first, Hedwiga of Gloucester, by whom he had no
children, and whom he divorced in 1200 to marry Isabelle of Angoulême, by whom he had:

Henry, later Henry III;
Richard, born in 1209, elected in 1256 (during the
reign of his brother) King of the Romans (the title of
the heir of the Holy Roman Emperor; he was never
elected Emperor), and known in England as Richard
of Almayn; Joan, who in 1221 married Alexander II
King of Scots. They had one daughter,
Margaret, who married Eric King of Norway, and
had again one daughter,
Margaret, known as the Maid of Norway, heiress of Scotland, who died on the voyage from
Norway to Scotland in 1290.

Died in Newark Castle in 1216 and was buried in Worcester Cathedral.

JOHN
LACKLAND

To the schoolchild, John Lackland is the wicked prince whose efforts to usurp the throne were thwarted by Robin Hood (which is a completely false story). To the historian Matthew Paris, he was "a King whose fouler presence defiles the foulness of Hell." Even to the uninterested he is a joke, the King who lost his crown in the Wash. In fact, John was a conscientious and industrious ruler who had more than his share of bad luck (a great part of which was his spectacular and useless brother Richard I). He had the Angevin vices, but also the Angevin virtues, with the addition of a sense of humor that is probably funnier now than it could have been at the time. Forbidden the precarious throne of Jerusalem, and with three robust and ambitious brothers senior to him, he passed his youth, even as Lord of Ireland, without effort to learn the business of kingship; but when it came to the push he worked hard enough.

In spite of his brother's will, his succession was disputed. The heir of his dead elder brother Geoffrey, Arthur of Brittany, had at one time been named by Richard as his heir, and the right precedence in succession between a younger brother and the son of an elder brother had never been decided on in the feudal system. By one of history's ironies, John was the guest of Arthur (who was then only twelve) and his mother Constance of Brittany when he heard of Richard's death. He took horse at once and secured the royal treasury at Chinon; Constance moved with equal speed and placed Arthur under the protection of Philip Augustus King of France. In England, however, the wise and loyal old William the Marshal argued for John on a principle that had governed the Anglo-Saxon system of succession: that Arthur was too young to protect the kingdom. John had himself crowned in Rheims, and when William joined him later he brought the acclamation of England. John was crowned in Westminster Abbey on the twenty-seventh of May, 1199.

Philip had not the strength to enforce Arthur's claim, and John had not the strength to support his enormous French domains, so they agreed to the usual sort of compromise: Philip recognized John as King of England, John did homage to Philip for his French lands. Philip, however, did not play by the rules; he demanded not nominal homage but full feudal relief, which was a death-duty that amounted to an enormous sum. John could do nothing but pay, at which his subjects gave up calling him Lackland and instead called him Softsword.

John had earlier married Hedwiga of Gloucester, but she had given him no children, and when the chance arose to pacify the barons of Angoulême by marrying the young Isabelle, daughter of Count Audemar, it was easy enough to get the first marriage annulled. But Isabelle had been betrothed to Hugh of the powerful family of Lusignan, and soon John was guilty of an insult too to Hugh's brother Ralph of Eu. The Lusignans complained to John's overlord Philip Augustus, unhappily at a moment when John's confidence was high because of the death of Constance of Brittany. John was always at his worst when his confidence was high, and he first declared the Lusignans traitors and confiscated Eu and then flatly refused his plain duty of appearing to answer for this to Philip Augustus. Philip Augustus promptly took against him the steps he was entitled to take against any rebellious vassal, declaring his lands forfeit, knighting Arthur of Brittany, and giving him John's lands of Poitou, Maine, and Touraine (Normandy he kept for himself).

For once John had the good luck that Arthur's captain William des Roches deserted to the English side, and in July, 1202, they captured both Arthur and Hugh of Lusignan. As usual in success, John behaved foolishly, quarrelling with William, who deserted him, but was sobered by that into releasing Hugh and making peace with him. Arthur of Brittany simply disappeared from history. No one at the time was either surprised or concerned by this, for he was sixteen (a man by the standards of the time), and as a vassal who had rebelled against his liege lord his life was legally forfeit.

If it had not been for John's unfortunate reputation, Arthur would have been forgotten. The two accounts we have of his death bear all the marks of the manufactured horror story. The story that Shakespeare knew is certainly false; this says that John ordered Hubert de Burgh to castrate and blind Arthur, that Hubert, agonized by the boy's innocence, refused, and that Arthur died a mysterious death the next year. Hubert de Burgh was a great baron and not a hired bully; John was not cold-bloodedly cruel; castration and blinding were practiced on royal heirs not in England but in Byzantium; and Arthur was not a child, but a young man described by the sensible William the Marshal as "haughty and proud, and likely to do us harm if we put him over us, for he does not love the people of this land." A Cistercian abbey in Wales preserved the other story, that John himself murdered Arthur when he was "drunk and possessed of the Devil." This accords with the Angevin temper; but why should John resort to murder when Arthur's death was lawful?

The Bretons, however, cried for vengeance, and by the end of 1202 Normandy was hard beset by the Bretons in the west, Philip in the south, and the Poitevins in the east, with treachery rumored from every quarter. John hurried from corner to corner of his lands, giving battle to the Bretons, rescuing his Queen from siege in Chinon, desperately organizing relief for his brother Richard's prized Château Gaillard. It was in vain, but not from John's doing. Everywhere the barons, discontented by Richard's years of neglect, were going over to Philip; by the summer of 1204 Normandy was lost.

Hostile chroniclers assert that John greeted this with indifference and spent the next year feasting and making love to his young wife. Court records tell a different tale; he fell into an Angevin frenzy of activity, riding the country, inspecting towns and castles, personally dispensing justice. Within the year, his mother Eleanor of Aquitaine died, and Philip Augustus (who was her stepson) felt himself free to attack Aquitaine.

In the spring of 1205 John had a vast force ready to sail to the relief of Poitou. The barons refused to accompany him; Hubert Walter and William the Marshal claimed that England was in too much danger for John to leave, which may have been true, but the fact was that most of the barons had lands in France and had already done homage to Philip for them. John raged, and refused to give up; by the next year he had rallied enough of his barons to take a new fleet to save Aquitaine. But this lost him the loyalty of William the Marshal, and Hubert Walter, his other faithful counselor, was dead, and another crisis was in the making in which he was to feel their absence.

No more than the troubles in France was this one of John's own making. It was, in essence, the quarrel between Church and King that had been interrupted by the martyrdom of Thomas Beckett in the reign of John's father, Henry II. For a new Archbishop of Canterbury, John nominated the Bishop of Norwich, while the monks of Canterbury held out for their own Prior Reginald. As a compromise the Pope, Innocent III, proposed a third man; this was Stephen Langton, who was a distinguished scholar but not by upbringing an Englishman, and both John and his barons rejected him, united for once in a robust English dislike of foreigners. In reply, Innocent placed England under interdict, which meant that all church services were forbidden except for baptism and the last rites for the dying. With his sense of humor, John seized the property of the Church and arrested the concubines of the clergy (who had a robust English disdain of their vow of chastity), returning the concubines only on the payment of a fine. The people, finding the churches locked against them, with surprising calm held their services in the open air. In 1209 Innocent took the more serious step of declaring John excommunicate. This meant that his subjects were freed from their oaths of allegiance to him, and was an invitation to rebellion that many of them in Wales and Scotland promptly accepted. John's only comfort was that, at this, the faithful William the Marshal came back to his help.

But there was no solution now but complete submission; for to be excommunicate meant to be excluded from every normal way of life. The Pope ordered John's deposition, and Philip Augustus was happy to act as the Pope's executioner. He had his invasion fleet assembled when John accepted the Pope's terms. He had to welcome Langton to Canterbury, acknowledge the Pope as his overlord, and pay a heavy compensation to the clergy. It was a defeat, but not a disastrous one. It brought John a constant ally in the Pope (who later even suspended Langton for refusing to cooperate with him); moreover, during the years of the interdict he had reimposed on Scotland the homage Richard I had sold, subdued his rebellious Irish barons, and strengthened the Welsh borders. By 1213, though he still could not rely on the barons, he had England quiet and enough money to attempt the reconquest of Normandy.

It failed disastrously, and, again, it was not his fault. He had planned a double attack on Philip, from west and east, and his own part, from the west, he carried out in a way that was worthy of the son of Henry II. His allies in the east failed him, and he had to make peace with Philip. He complained bitterly: "Since I became reconciled to God and submitted myself and my kingdom to the Church nothing has gone right with me."

John returned to England to find a tangle of loyalties and alliances that would have been beyond any King. The barons blamed him for the loss of Normandy, yet were so jealous of their own Norman lands that they refused to fight against the King of France, who had captured Normandy. They disliked John's constant demands for money to pay mercenary troops, yet they refused to give the knight-service they had sworn, which would have made the hire of mercenaries unnecessary. They were, in fact, rebelling less against John than against his father, against the long years when Henry II's power had frustrated their lawlessness.

But, considering that they were the descendants of the Conqueror's men, there was a comic element in their demands; for what they wanted was a return to the charter of liberties of Henry I, which had been framed on the laws of the Anglo-Saxons and designed to appeal to the common people against the barons. What it amounted to was a limitation of the King's powers, and especially of his power to levy taxes. John inquired when he heard the demands, "Why not ask for my kingdom?" An appeal to his ally the Pope did not move the barons, and the King of Scots gladly seized the chance to renounce his alliance. Stephen Langton and the still faithful William the Marshal ended the indecisive fighting by arranging a meeting on an island in the Thames. Of this meeting the chronicler records: "A sort of peace was made." The date was the June 15, 1215, and the place Runnymede, and no one at the time thought it was more than a temporary truce which neither side had the least intention of respecting.

It was, in fact, an agreement on the side of anarchy, for by John's agreement to levy no taxes that were not approved by a council of twenty-five barons, who had the power to dethrone him, it strengthened the power of lawlessness and defiance of central rule. But, unobserved by any contemporary historian, the most significant words in the history of England had been slipped into the agreement: *To no one will we sell, and to no one will we deny or delay right or justice.* Was there, among the unknown clerks who drafted the agreement, one man who knew what gift he was bestowing upon England? This was the Great Charter, in which both barons and King agreed that no man was to be imprisoned without trial by his equals, and that all men were equal before the law; and no one noticed it, and when the signing was done the signatories went away to start preparations to fight again.

John now had only sixteen months of life left to him, and for him they were miserable months. The Pope excommunicated the barons, and the barons, true to form, invited Philip Augustus's son Louis to depose John and become King of England himself. (Louis had married Blanche, daughter of Alfonso of Castile and Henry II's daughter Eleanor, and thus had a faint claim to the throne.) Louis came in May, 1216. Hubert de Burgh in Dover defied him, but the barons acclaimed him in London. John, in an Angevin passion of activity, held off the Scots, held off the Welsh, and steadily brought the east of England under his control. He grew ill and exhausted. One night when he was crossing the Ouse in a heavy mist his baggage train was lost in the waters. Careless of anything but securing castle after castle to the defense of his kingdom, he pressed on to Newark. It is said that he was suffering from dysentery, and took peaches and new cider. This is not evidence of gluttony; there was little pure food or drink in those days except fresh fruit and brewed drinks. But he was plainly dying, and asked the Papal Legate and those barons who were still loyal to ensure his young son's succession to the throne. He was buried, according to his request, in the Cathedral Church of Worcester, the most misunderstood King in English history: his virtues seen as vices, his bad luck taken for malignancy, a mischance when he was dying turned into an overworked joke, and an unimportant incident in his struggle with treacherous barons making him appear to later history as the eternal enemy of the common man. His father had, after all, not been mistaken in his sons; of all the Devil's Brood, John was the best.

HENRY III
1216–1272

❂

Born at Winchester in 1206.

Son of King John and his second wife Isabelle of Angoulême.

Married in 1236 Eleanor of Provence, by whom he had:

> Edward, later Edward I;
> Margaret, who married in 1251 Alexander III of Scots.

Died at Bury St. Edmunds and buried in Westminster Abbey

HENRY III

enry III was crowned in the wrong place, by the wrong man, and with the wrong crown. The Papal Legate put a simple gold circlet on his head in the Abbey Church of Gloucester; Westminster Abbey was in the hands of the French, most of the rest of the kingdom was controlled by the enemy barons, and the crown jewels were at the bottom of the Wash. Worst of all, Henry III was the wrong man for King.

To begin with, he was only ten years old, and faced with a situation that would have taxed his grandfather the great Henry II. Then in him the Angevin blood had run thin; some of the perversity and rashness remained, but none of the military capability or the mental toughness. Personally he was undoubtedly the most agreeable of them all, sympathetic, kindly, courteous, pious, and devoted to his wife and children; he was also a friend of the arts and the rebuilder of Westminster Abbey. (Bad Kings in the Middle Ages were curiously apt to leave us good buildings.) Given peace, he might have been a competent and conscientious King, perhaps a little too piously ready to obey the Pope, but as it was he had long years of humiliation and struggle ahead of him.

The disastrous situation at the opening of the reign was saved by the two men who had done so much for his father, the statesman William the Marshal and the soldier Hubert de Burgh. Marshal at once reissued the Great Charter, though without the clause by which John had renounced the right to raise taxes without permission, and then wrote to each of the great barons asking them to return to their fealty. Perhaps the barons were a little aghast at the results of their treachery; they began to drift back, and the movement was completed by Hubert de Burgh's victory over a French invasion fleet in the Channel. The French withdrew from England and, to avoid the displeasure of the Pope, the French King Philip Augustus had to disown the expedition.

Wisely, Marshal declared a general amnesty. Since King John had submitted to the Pope the amnesty could not be extended to the clergy, and the Papal Legate saw no reason for mercy. He imposed enormous fines, by which the Papal treasury profited, but which perhaps made the clergy feel less kindly about Papal supremacy.

Marshal, who had served Henry's father, uncle, and grandfather, died not long after this, and Hubert de Burgh and Peter des Roches Bishop of Winchester took over the government. They could make little good of it, for nothing would quell the anarchic tendencies of the barons, who continued their futile squabbles, despising the King's pious gentleness. One spark of comfort must have been the death in 1223 of that bane of the Angevins, Philip Augustus; but his son Louis VIII was strong enough to seize and hold La Rochelle, one of the few remaining English possessions in France.

Disastrously, and for reasons unknown to us, Henry dismissed the wise and loyal Hubert de Burgh, and appointed in his place Peter des Roches. Peter came from Poitou, and was too fond of appointing his fellow-Poitevins to the chief offices of the kingdoms, which not only further angered the barons but also turned out to be expressly forbidden by the Great Charter. Henry, whose behavior often appears abstracted almost beyond sanity, took more interest in his own magnificent wedding, in 1236, to Eleanor, daughter of Raymond of Provence, and his pious obedience to the Papal Legate Pandulf, who was filling the great offices of the Church with Italians, further alienating the barons. They refused Henry money, and he had to take it from the Jews (whose interests, incidentally, he had sworn to protect). In 1242, in one of his spasmodic efforts for popularity, he led an army into France against another King, Louis IX, known to posterity as Saint Louis, and lost what had remained to him of Poitou. Like his father in 1215, he had to return to England to face the hostility of his scornful barons and a vast war debt. To pay the debt he had to sell his own jewels and plate. "If the treasury of the Emperor Augustus were brought to sale," he raged, "my people could buy it, while I am reduced to necessities."

He was soon reduced even further, and by his obedience to the

Pope, who was his only loyal ally. In its long battle for the hegemony of Europe, the Papacy was now in need of money and men, and offered Henry III the throne of Sicily for his second son Edmund Crouchback, the title of King of the Romans (by which name the heir to the emperor was known) for his brother Richard of Cornwall, both favors to be paid for by a crippling sum. The only way Henry could raise the money was from the clergy, but the Pope kindly helped by threatening excommunication to any who refused to contribute. Nothing came of the promised thrones, though Richard of Cornwall for some time contested the empire, and came to be known in England as Richard of Almayn (Germany). He was the only strong man at Henry's side, and his loss was soon to be felt.

By 1253 the barons had found a leader who was strong enough to make their unruly rabble into something like a united party. This man was Simon de Montfort Earl of Leicester, a name famous in the history of English freedom, though the fame can be justified only by a generous estimate of Simon's intentions. When the King summoned the barons to discuss raising money for the Sicilian venture, they arrived in full armor; he asked if he was their prisoner, and they said that he was their sovereign lord, but if he wanted money he must give them something in return. King and barons met at Oxford, in what has come to be known as the Mad Parliament. Mad its proceedings certainly were, and the name of Parliament then meant only *Parlement*—an assembly for talking. Like the Great Charter, this first Parliament contained its advance to freedom for the common people hidden in a minor clause.

The agreement that was forced upon Henry was that the country was now to be ruled not by the King but by a council of twenty-four barons, twelve from the King's side and twelve from the barons'; or, to put it more clearly, the anarchic side of the struggle for power was to be strengthened. The single new, and not much considered, idea in these Provisions of Oxford was a concession to the mounting discontent in the country at large: it was that each county should send four knights to a *Parlement* to discuss grievances and their redress.

This single step forward was promptly ignored. The barons in their new power humiliated the King, keeping him a virtual prisoner, exiling his family, forcing his heir Edward (a wary eighteen-year-old, at this time of his life more apt to observe than to act) to swear loyalty to the Provisions of Oxford, and dismissing the great officers of state in favor of their own inexperienced men. Worst of all, they wrecked the great achievement of the Angevins, the countrywide consistent enforcement of the King's law. The knights of the shire, summoned to this Mad Parliament, objected to this chaos, and, as they had been required to do, stated their local grievances; the barons ignored them.

To his credit, Simon de Montfort opposed the worst of the barons' excesses, but even as the head of the Council of Twenty-Four he could not control them; instead, he gave his support to the knights of the shires. They did not, of course, represent "the common people" as we understand that term now. What they represented was the class of smaller landowners, below the barons in rank, lords of countless manors whose chief interest was simply the peace and prosperity of those manors. The dissensions among the barons were now the King's only strength in England; but he received surprising help from abroad. It was to be expected that the Pope should free him from his oath at Oxford, on the grounds that it had been exacted under duress; it was not be expected that Louis IX of France, after his offer of mediation had been rejected by the barons, should generously and sensibly return to England the lost lands of Poitou and Guienne in return for the final cession of Normandy. Encouraged by this, Henry for once acted with Angevin speed and decision, dismissing the barons' officers of state and replacing them with his own men. Out-and-out civil war was joined.

It lasted in its muddled way until 1264. The Welsh Prince Llewellyn ap Gryfydd rose against Henry, but for his own purposes and not the barons'. London, traditionally anti-royalist, rose for Simon, pursuing Henry's Queen to sanctuary in Saint Paul's, pelting her with rotten eggs and screaming, "Burn the witch!" but taking the chance to massacre some five hundred Jews for its own purposes. Prince Edward was taken prisoner, which obliged the King to sue for peace, but also divided the barons even further, since some of them favored Edward for King. (Edward did not encourage them; he was too wary to be anything but royalist.) Finally, it came to a pitched battle, at Lewes in Sussex in 1264, when Simon decisively defeated Henry and took him prisoner. The defeat was chiefly due to Prince Edward; in front of the cavalry he commanded he found a band of Londoners, and remembered the insult to his mother so vividly that he pursued them until the rest of the battle was lost in his absence.

This famous battle of Lewes gave Simon de Montfort his brief term of authority. He had one constructive idea, which was tolerance; there were no executions and no reprisals. But that was all; having made himself virtual King, he found what an impossible situation it was. Not even his authority could hold men whose basic assumption was that a man's way of life was jealous defiance of authority.

Yet perhaps it was not all. Simon's period of authority was brief because he was opposed by a greater man than himself. Prince Edward set up alliances with various earls, captured Simon's son, and moved to meet Simon at Evesham (another famous battle). Simon, with the King a prisoner in his army, saw his son's standards appear and allowed them to approach; when he realized that they were captured standards it was too late. He was defeated and killed, and Prince Henry rescued his father, and the royal forces took no prisoners and gave no mercy; they cut Simon's body into pieces and sent the appropriate parts to his mistress. And yet! Prince Edward, this magnificent Plantagenet so unexpectedly emergent from what had seemed a dying family (no one could call them Angevins now that the French domains were all but lost)—this Prince, who was to succeed to the throne eight years later, proved to have a great many of the ideas of the enemy he had defeated and killed. Revolutions, after all, are successful only when they are educational. Simon de Montfort is remembered in England as a martyr to the cause of parliamentary government, when in fact it was the Prince who defeated him who really began parliamentary government as we understand it. Where else should Prince Edward have learned the ideas he applied successfully but from the man who applied them unsuccessfully? Perhaps the folk-memory that insists that Simon de Montfort is one of its heroes is a wise one.

But, more immediately, Henry III, with the Prince at his side, acknowledged the fact that his power depended on the barons who had stayed loyal to him. At a Parliament in Winchester, Henry and his son swore to abide by the conditions of the Great Charter and to rely on the counsel of the barons and of Parliament. For once, everyone respected the spirit rather than the letter of an oath. Perhaps the years of sterile warfare had merely exhausted them; perhaps it had given them a small measure of wisdom. At any rate, the years of dissension had somehow been resolved into a kind of national stability, and there was hope for the future in the splendid figure of Prince Edward. After the Devil's Brood, it is nice to record that the last years of Henry III were not darkened but glorified by his son. Prince Edward remained his ineffectual, pious old father's support until in 1271 he added to the Plantagenet glory by joining Louis IX of France on Crusade. Henry died the next year, while his son was away, in his sixty-seventh year, after a long, arduous and humiliating life, which it seems to us nowadays he was not mentally equipped to comprehend; but a life that was hopeful at its end, which was probably more than he deserved. He was buried in the Westminster Abbey that he had rebuilt from the humbler edifice of Edward the Confessor; it still stands as a record of one of his lesser, yet more enduring, virtues.

EDWARD I
1272–1307

☿

Born at Westminster in 1239.

Eldest surviving son of Henry III and his wife Eleanor of Provence.

Married in 1274 Eleanor of Castile, by whom he had:

Edward of Carnarvon, afterwards Edward II;

Married, secondly, in 1299, Margaret of France, by whom he had:

Edmund Earl of Kent, born 1301, who had a daughter Joan, known as the Fair Maid of Kent, who later married Edward Prince of Wales, son of Edward III.

Died at Burgh-by-Sands 1307 and buried in Westminster Abbey

EDWARD I

n 1264, when he was twenty-five, a terrible humiliation befell Edward Plantagenet, son and heir to King Henry III. He found himself and his father prisoner of their rebel barons led by Earl Simon de Montfort.

During the next year he had to watch the suspension of the monarchy. He had to swear obedience to Montfort's rule, surrender to him his own earldom of Chester, give up his other lands and castles as surety for good behavior, and observe the operation of the two Montfortian Parliaments.

Edward was not fitted by nature for submission. In May, 1265, he escaped from Simon's custody, defeated him at Evesham, and emerged triumphant as the heir to a newly pacified realm. In 1272, at the height of his popularity and considerable powers, he succeeded his father as King Edward I.

If Edward had been a lesser man, what he had learned from the Montfort rebellion would have been disastrous for himself and his country. What he did learn was that he must rule with the cooperation and consent of his people. Throughout his long reign he often had to force the cooperation, and did not always have the consent; but, in the main, he kept to his own high standards, and left England a better place.

Edward was a big man, with long legs "set far apart," probably slightly bandy from being much on horseback, and even in his old age "straight as a palm." As a child he was silver-fair, darkening gradually to brown, and finally impressively white; he had one drooping eyelid, said to have been inherited from his father, and a slight stammer, which he had conquered to make himself a good speaker. His temper was imperious, and he had a crisp and homely way of speech. He also had another attribute of the King: by his two wives he fathered fifteen children. His wives were Eleanor of Castile, whom he married in 1274, and Margaret of France, whom he married in 1299.

Edward was not the King to tolerate anarchy among his barons, and the outcome suggests that even the barons were thankful for this; no one had profited from Henry III's weakness. The truth was that in the face of an increasingly complex society, the feudal system was breaking down. The simple military relationship between lord and vassal, based on the ownership of land and the furnishing of knight-service, was no longer enough to direct a society that was growing more prosperous and mercantile and more influenced by the growing middle class of the burgesses or townsmen (who had as little use for the feudal system as the feudal system had for them). Even the very basis of feudalism was in confusion, for there were very few up-to-date records of the ownership of the land, and Edward began his reign, characteristically, with a countrywide inquiry to settle this. It was called the *Quo-Waranto* inquest, from the eternally repeated question, *"Quo waranto"*—"by what warrant is this land held?" It so irritated old John of Warenne that he drew his rusty sword, saying, "My ancestors came with Duke William Bastard, and this was their warrant." The words sound less noble when we remember that Duke William gave his ancestors Lewes, where he had last drawn his sword against his King, Henry III.

Edward's great achievement as a legislator, however, was in the beginning of statute law—that is, enacted law. Until then, laws had been of only two kinds: the fundamental and unalterable law of God, and the English traditional laws, which were the Anglo-Saxon un-written laws modified by Norman feudal law. The concept that laws could be made was wholly new. Edward changed all that, and with it the role of Parliament.

He has been called the Father of the English Parliament, but he was much more its schoolmaster. His only advisory body, as it had been with all the Kings since William I, was his King's Council, whose powers varied (like the King's) according to the situation. This Council the King efforced (to use the technical term) by sum-moning to it both knights bachelors and burgesses. The summoning of the burgesses was in particular a departure from feudal custom, for though they might be men of much wealth and influence they were not landowners and vassals. Edward did not give his Parliaments very much power; he did not always summon all the members to consultations, and he did not always take the advice they gave him; indeed, in his later and sadder years he often quarrelled with them. But, by summoning the Parliaments, he gave them the right to disagree with him, and he never tried to take away that right; he was willing to learn from them what his people wanted, and he went a long way toward taking them into his confidence. Nor did he summon them only when he wanted money (as many of his successors were to do). Parliament was also for the hearing of petitions and the redress of grievances, and Edward, who rightly mistrusted any court controlled by the barons, used it as a court of law.

But he saw attendance in Parliament not as a favor granted to members but as a duty laid upon them. The very coming and going of the local members tended to unite the country, and must have made even the little villages aware that government was a continuing civil process and not immutable but by the sword. Some say that England invented the rule of parliaments; it would be juster to say that the rule of Parliament invented England.

Another of Edward's nicknames was "the Hammer of the Scots." In fact, his hammering of the Scots was not effective beyond his lifetime, and he was much more successful with the Welsh. He regarded his battles with these two peoples as interruptions that kept him from his more vital effort to recover the Plantagenets' French possessions. In so far as the Welsh rebellions were rebellions of the Anglicized Welsh princes, who had long been in feudal relations with the English Kings, they were more wars between King and barons. Edward found the country, with its mountainous interior, difficult to subdue, but he had the advantage of controlling both the land-frontier, by means of the line of great Marcher castles and the sea-frontier by his navy, and by 1290 he had come to the bold conclusion that he must regard the whole of Wales as a hostile fortress and lay siege to it on all sides. In the end he was successful, and, on the whole, proved a merciful conqueror, wisely imposing on the people an amalgam of Welsh and English law. It is said that he made the conciliatory gesture of promising the Welsh a prince born in Wales and unable to speak a word of English, and at Carnarvon Castle presented to them his son Edward of Carnarvon, born there a month before. This is so old a tradition that even now the heir of the monarch is presented to the Welsh people at Carnarvon as Prince of Wales.

The problem of Scotland was more complicated, for the Scots had a ruling dynasty. But in 1286 Alexander III broke his neck over a cliff, and his only heir was a little girl of three, the Maid of Norway, daughter of his only daughter and Eric II of Norway, and she died in 1290. The Scots asked Edward to adjudicate the difficult question of the next heir.

It was one of those unresolved tangles feudalism had never developed to deal with, and came in the end to the choice between John Balliol, great-grandson of William the Lion by his elder daughter but through two females, and Robert Bruce the Elder, great-grandson by his younger daughter but through only one female. Edward decided for Balliol, who was crowned John of Scotland, but then quite legally claimed fealty from him. Balliol, whose nickname was the Toom Tabard, the empty coat, did his homage, which so infuriated his subjects that they elected a council to take his place and allied themselves for protection with Edward's enemy, France. Edward descended on them at Dunbar, defeated them, and regarded Scotland as conquered. The Scots lords did not; but they were so busy fighting among themselves about who was to be King now that it was only the French support that kept them going. The original Bruce claimant had died, and in 1296 Robert Bruce the Younger was foolish enough to put in a claim to the throne. Edward retorted, "Have I nothing else to do but win kingdoms for you?"

The only wholly admirable character to emerge from these wars was William Wallace, the Wallace of the patriotic songs. As the younger son of a small knight, he had no claim himself, and his patriotism seems to have been genuine. The purity of their motives did not soften the Scots' well-known savagery; after Wallace's victory of Stirling the English commander was flayed and his skin exhibited throughout the country.

What brought about Edward's final defeat of the Scots was a far-distant battle, when in 1303 he defeated Philip IV at Courtrai in France. Philip, who had earlier praised the Scots for their "constancy of perfect faithfulness and their vigour of proved courage," himself displayed neither; at the following Treaty of Paris he left the Scots to fend for themselves and Edward free to turn all his forces onto them. In 1303 he captured Stirling, hanged Wallace as a traitor, and drew up an ordinance that should have proved sensible and not unbearably oppressive.

The next year Robert Bruce the Younger, who had sworn fealty to Edward, killed with his own hand, and in sanctuary, a rival claimant to the leadership of the Scots, and had himself crowned at Scone. It was a small incident, for the so-called King then had to flee, and did not reappear until nine years had passed. We do not know what he did in those years, but the greedy and treacherous young man who vanished into the northern mists returned wise and patient and courageous.

It was, however, to the quarrel with France that Edward wanted to devote his energies. To do him justice, this quarrel, which in the end was to cause a hundred years of war, began on tolerably sensible issues. From his mother, Edward had inherited a neglected Gascony, which was a fief of France, and had turned it into a thriving province trading wine for English wool. The French tried to interrupt this trade, and the war started with a privateer's battle in 1293 between a French fleet and a combined English and Gascon one. Edward developed a strategy of encircling alliances against France, himself attacking from the west while his allies in Germany and Flanders attacked from the east. Unfortunately, as well as being distracted by the Welsh and Scots, he was constantly failed by his unreliable allies, whom, moreover, he had to subsidize until Parliament rebelled at the cost. In 1297 his hereditary marshal, Roger Bigod Earl of Norfolk, flatly refused to countenance a battle plan, on the purely technical grounds that it was the marshal's duty to fight only in the van of the King's own force, and Edward wanted him elsewhere. "By God, my lord Earl," said Edward, "you will either go or hang;" and Bigod made the famous reply "By that same oath, my lord King, I will neither go nor hang." He neither went nor was hanged, and the battle plan was reduced until it led to no more than a truce. Yet this kind of struggle between Edward and the marshal must not be seen as a continuation of the struggle between Edward's father and his barons. The tension between Edward I and his subjects was fruitful, each side urging its rightful needs, yet each responsible enough to know that survival depended finally on agreement.

The war with France came to a temporary end with the battle of Courtrai in 1303, and was not renewed for another twenty years. By the treaty that followed, Edward's heir, Edward of Carnarvon Prince of Wales, married Isabelle, daughter of Philip IV of France, a lady who was afterward to be known as the She-Wolf of France and to make a considerable mark on English history. From France, Edward went to the rebellion in Scotland, and if he had been a younger man perhaps Robert Bruce would never have become King of Scotland. But as Edward was gathering his forces against the conspirators of the coronation at Scone he was struck down by illness, and died at Burgh-by-Sands in July, 1307. He was sixty-four, a good age to be still commanding armies in those days when Kings mounted their horses and took their swords into the thick of battle. He had been a great soldier and a wonderfully cool head all his life, but it is as the great legislator that English still remembers him with gratitude.

In 1292 Edward had founded New Winchelsea on the South Coast, one of the Cinque Ports, laying it out regularly in squares on a plan he had invented for Gascony, and building a great gate that still stands on the coast road. In the east chapel of the Parish church there are two small heads at the springing of the canopy arch that are said to be portraits of Edward I and his second wife, Margaret of France. It is the only portrait of him that we possess; it shows a square, imperious face, with large straight-set eyes and a grimly closed mouth, surrounded by curling hair and beard. If it is not a true likeness, it shows very well what his subjects thought Edward Planta-genet was like.

EDWARD II
of Carnarvon
1307–1327

✿

Born at Carnarvon in 1284, created Prince of Wales in 1301.
Son of Edward I and his first wife Eleanor of Castile.
Married in 1308 Isabelle, daughter of Philip IV of France,
 by whom he had:

   Edward, later Edward III

Deposed by Parliament January 1327.
Murdered in Berkeley Castle September 1327 and buried
 in Gloucester.

EDWARD II
of Carnarvon

dward II was the son of Edward I and his first wife Eleanor of Castile. He was born in 1284 and was thus twenty-three when he succeeded his father. It should have been a happy succession: there were no possible rival claimants; his father had been a popular King; the war with France seemed to have been victoriously concluded; and the country was generally in good heart. This second Edward was a broad, fair, handsome Plantagenet, in looks very like his father. His looks belied him; he was lazy, incapable, and homosexual, and his reign was a disaster.

It has been argued that his ineffectual son was not the least of Edward I's gifts to his kingdom, and that another strong King would inevitably have drifted England into the path to absolute monarchy. Certainly, England emerged comparatively unharmed at the end of Edward II's reign because the administrative machine of his father was coherent enough to work in in spite of a weak hand at the center. In effect this was to be true of succeeding civil dissensions; for once such a machine is in working order it will not be mastered by a handful of discontented barons. Edward I had bequeathed to all his successors on the throne a built-in advantage.

The barons were not ignorant of the man who had come to rule them. In 1306 his father had sent into exile the Gascon Peter of Gabaston (whom Christopher Marlowe, in his great play *Edward II*, calls Piers Gaveston), for being an undesirable influence on his son, and one of Edward II's first royal acts was to recall this favorite. Unlike his predecessors William Rufus and Richard Lion-Heart, Edward did at least provide his kingdom with an heir, for his son

Edward was born in 1312; but, perhaps driven to resentment by a society which regarded homosexuality as a mortal sin, he not only insisted on having his "minions" about him, but loaded them with riches and took their advice before that of any others. The barons were outraged by the lands and titles granted to the inconsiderable Gaveston, and forced Edward to send him once again into exile. Edward complied, bided his time until the barons quarrelled among themselves, and then recalled him. It was a wretched business, partly because it was about an unworthy man, but chiefly because it engendered bitter hatreds, yet had nothing at all to do with the business of ruling that Edward and his barons should have been attending to.

One ought first to record, however, Edward's one moment of regal capability. Away in the north of Scotland was Robert Bruce, beginning to show that amazing change of character that was to make of the unscrupulous brawler of 1304 the wise and beloved King Robert I; he was quietly and patiently subduing his enemies in Scotland, and by the beginning of 1313 was able to move south. The famous Scottish legend is that one day, at the ebb of his fortunes, he was hiding alone in a cave and saw a spider starting to spin its web. Again and again it missed its first cast, and again and again it crawled back to its beginning and tried again. Bruce is supposed to have drawn a moral from this piece of natural history; but if he had really behaved like his spider he would have got nowhere. He behaved less with mindless patience than with a remarkable mixture of good timing and courage, and by 1314 had conquered all of Scotland but the great castle of Stirling in Perthshire. His brother Edward, impractically chivalrous, had granted the castle a year's truce, by which it had agreed to surrender if it were not relieved.

Some shred of his father's decisiveness entered into Edward II then; he gathered a great army and marched for Stirling. But the battle he was so uncharacteristically hurrying to was Bannockburn, the greatest battle of Scottish independence, and he was badly defeated. He fought bravely enough himself, and when the battle was lost saved himself by a courageous ride to Dunbar; but if the Scots had fought less well, would England have had a better King? It could not have been easy to follow the great Edward I; but Edward II had already been squabbling over his favorites for seven years, and it would have needed a very glorious victory indeed to make the barons trust him again.

As for Scotland, she was now independent under King Robert I,

Robert the Bruce. She was also isolated, all the civilizing work of the great and good Kings of Saint Margaret's line undone, cut off from European culture and given over for the next centuries to the sterile, and particularly brutal, warring of the great lords. Instead of civilization she had independence; but at least it was at her own choice.

Edward's inability to deal with the Scots made his barons even less inclined to acknowledge his authority, and they settled down to waging their private wars. As an example of them, Thomas of Lancaster had five earldoms, vast estates, and an immense private army, and made treaties with other barons as if he were himself King; he was stupid, selfish, brutal, and swollen with pride of birth, and no more fitted to control the destinies of the men he ruled than the King he despised, who at least had artistic taste and encouraged art and letters. In the intervals of their quarrelling the barons arrested Piers Gaveston, supposedly for fair trial; instead they allowed him to be carried off and hanged by his greatest personal enemy, Guy of Warwick. Edward countered with another minion, Hugh Despenser, who was worse than Gaveston; he became so arrogant that he acquired vast territories, and refused to let the King see anyone unless he himself were present. His greed was such that at last the Marcher Lords rose in protest, and in 1321 Parliament banished him.

But it was the Gaveston story once again. Edward waited a little and brought Despenser back, and then raised an army against his rebellious subjects. For as long as four years he was successful; but the victory was not his but Despenser's, and all Despenser's notion of ruling was to pile up land and power for himself. The besotted Edward gave him everything he asked for, and before long Despenser was the target of a bitter popular hatred perhaps unsurpassed in medieval England, and had brought on his King perhaps two of the savagest enemies an English King has ever had.

When he was seventeen, Edward had married Isabelle of France, the only daughter of that Philip IV, who had for children three Kings of France and one Queen of England. Isabelle came to be known as the She-Wolf of France, but there is no evidence that she was worse than a mistreated wife who, in despair, let another man rule her. Edward neglected her, confiscated her estates, and in 1325, in a fit of stupidity, sent her to her native France as an ambassadress to its King (now her third brother Charles IV). Not unnaturally, Isabelle did not return to England; instead, in Paris she met Roger Mortimer Earl of March, one of Edward's bitterest enemies. He had been defeated at Despenser's return to England in 1322, and been imprisoned in the Tower of London, but escaped the next year. Isabelle and Mortimer became lovers, and their enemy delivered them his most valuable weapon: Edward II sent his heir Prince Edward to France to do homage to Charles IV for Gascony.

In September, 1326, Isabelle and Mortimer, with the fourteen-year-old prince as their nominal leader, landed in Suffolk with an army. They were quickly joined by the greater part of the barons, and before the end of the year Despenser was executed and Edward deposed in favor of his son. It is worthy of remark that the deposition was nominally carried out by Parliament: so far had Edward I forced his subjects into sharing with him the burden of ruling that they could already put their names to the deposition of his son. The succession of Prince Edward, of course, was only nominal; the power was once again in the hands of the barons, the irresponsible, the anarchic, the essentially stupid. For them Edward's deposition was not enough; they wanted him dead.

There was a sensible, if brutal, statecraft in this, in that an imprisoned King would have been the center for every discontent; but the sequel showed that their intention was not embryonic statesmanship but plain hatred. They imprisoned him first in a small damp cell in Berkeley Castle, where it was thought he would not survive. He had his father's Plantagenet robustness, and refused to die. So, in September, 1327, they had him killed by the contemporary method of execution for a proved sodomite, a heated iron thrust up the anus. We do not know in what degree the guilt of this murder was distributed between Queen Isabelle, Mortimer, and the barons. It was not a pretty death, but it was actuated, not by matters political but by naked personal hatred, and that hatred Edward II had brought upon himself.

EDWARD III
1327–1377

✿

Born at Windsor in 1312.

Son of Edward II and his wife Isabelle of France, by
inheritance from whom in 1340 he claimed the title of
King of France.

Married in 1329 Philippa of Hainault, who died in 1369.
Their children included:

Edward of Woodstock,* known as the Black Prince,
born 1330, created Prince of Wales 1343, married in
1361 Joan, known as The Fair Maid of Kent, granddaughter of Edward I, and died in 1376. They had a
son,
Richard of Bordeaux, later Richard II;
Lionel of Antwerp Duke of Clarence, who married
Philippa de Burgh; their daughter,
Philippa, married Edmund Mortimer Earl of
March;
John of Gaunt (Ghent), by marriage Duke of Lancaster and King of Castile. He married, first, Blanche of
Lancaster, great-grand-daughter of Henry III, who
died in 1369; secondly, Costanza of Castile, who died
in 1394; and thirdly, in 1397, Catherine Swynford born
de Roet, who died in 1403. His children by these
marriages were:
by Blanche of Lancaster, Henry of Bolingbroke,
later Henry IV; by Costanza of Castile, Catalina,

*Kings' sons were often known by their places of birth.

who married Henry III of Castile and Leon, and
one of whose descendants, Catalina of Aragon, was
to marry Henry VIII of England; by Catherine
Swynford, before their marriage, John Beaufort
later Earl of Somerset, Henry later Cardinal Beaufort, and Joan Beaufort, who married as her second
husband Sir Ralph Neville of Raby and had a
daughter, Cicely, who was to marry Richard Plantagenet Duke of York, grandson of Edmund of
Langley Duke of York. The Beaufort children,
born illegitimate, were legitimated by Richard II
for all purposes but that of royal succession;

Edmund of Langley Duke of York, who married Isabel of Castile. Their son,

Richard Earl of Cambridge, who was beheaded in
1415, married Anne Mortimer, great-grand-daughter of Lionel Duke of Clarence, and had a son,
Richard Plantagenet Duke of York, who was to
marry Cicely Neville of Raby;

Thomas of Woodstock, murdered by Richard II in
1397.

Died at Shene (now Richmond, Surrey) in 1377 and was
buried in Westminster Abbey.

Edward III's mother, Isabelle of France, was the only
daughter of Philip IV of France. Philip IV was succeeded by his three sons, Louis X, Philip V, and Charles
IV, with whom the direct line ended; Charles IV was
succeeded in 1328 by Philip VI of Valois, nephew of
Philip IV. Edward III of England claimed that after the
sons of Philip IV his daughter should inherit, though
French law did not admit of succession through the
female line. He assumed the title of King of France,
which was borne by the Kings of England until George
III.

EDWARD III

Edward III was born, in 1312, of an inept homosexual father and a treacherous mother. He came to the throne in 1327 by means of the rebellion of his mother and her brutal lover, and before the year was out his father had been savagely murdered, probably with the consent of his mother and at the orders of her lover. It would appear to be the perfect way to produce a psychopathic King, and it failed miserably.

Edward III was the most humanly likable of the Plantagenets: strong, decent, intelligent, short-tempered, generous, a loving husband and father to a fine brood of sons; and his reign was, and still is, one of the most popular in the history of England. In his reign we see the first sure signs that the defeated Anglo-Saxons and the conquering Normans had at last come together to make the English people; in it the English language emerged with all the richness of the two languages that made it up, and with it a magnificent flowering of poetry; in it occurred the two famous victories that gave England European stature and confidence; and in it the King himself became not only a respected ruler but a loved and admired man with whom the people could identify themselves.

Edward gained his independence as a King by three qualities that were to last him his lifetime: courage, astuteness, and whatever it was that gave him his subjects' loyalty. For the first three years of his reign England was in chaos and his barons uncontrollable. He was already quietly corresponding to gain allies abroad, and by the time he was eighteen, in 1330, his plans were ready. His faithful friend Edward Montague arrested Mortimer; Mortimer was condemned by proper process of law in Parliament and executed; and Edward took over the government. Isabelle was quietly sent into retirement; her son continued to treat her with respect and affection, which leads us to suppose that she had been guilty of no more than obedience to Mortimer. Edward seems to have been accepted as King by the people with the simple cheerfulness that was so marked a trait of his own personality. Indeed, as much as any King of England, Edward III put on his reign the mark of his own personality. The people wanted no more Edward II's, but no more did they want strenuous Edward I's; Edward I had done his work, and they wanted to live their own lives in peace and enjoyment, with perhaps the added excitement of strenuous exertion well outside the kingdom; and this Edward III gave them.

Nowadays we pretend to find little moral worth in military victories, though we still hunger to prove ourselves better than our neighbors. In those days the values, which, as usual, were centuries behind the societies that professed them, were unashamedly military. As Froissart the chronicler wrote:

The English will never love or honour their King, unless he be victorious and a lover of arms and war against neighbours, and especially such neighbours as are greater and richer than themselves.

The Scots, having gained their independence, had found nothing better to do with it than go on harrying the English border, and in this annoyance they were openly supported by the French. Philip IV's three sons (Louis X, Philip V, and Charles IV) had all died without heirs within fourteen years, and the throne had gone to Philip IV's nephew, Philip VI of Valois. But Philip IV had had also a daughter, Isabelle wife of Edward II of England, and Edward III claimed that the rightful succession was his as Isabelle's son. It was a perfectly good claim according to some interpretations of the feudal laws of inheritance, but, unsurprisingly, these were not the interpretations the French preferred, and Philip VI announced that he was confiscating Edward's fief of Gascony. Edward, like his grandfather, set up his circle of alliances against France.

It was a popular war in England; perhaps Edward II's reign had taught the people that there are worse things than costly wars several hundred miles away. Edward III got his money from Parliament, his alliances, and into the bargain a bride he was to love all her life. This was Philippa, daughter of the Count of Hainault in the Low Countries, whom he married in 1329. She is said to have been a moderating influence when his short temper was irritated, and she bore him six sons and a daughter.

This grand alliance against France failed, as Edward I's had done, for lack of money. Even the English wool trade, which was prosperous and helpful, could not supply the subsidies needed by the Continental allies. Edward first borrowed from the great Italian banking houses, and then had to disclose to Parliament debts of over £300,000. This was an enormous sum in those days, several times his annual income. A shocked Parliament agreed to supply him with money only in exchange for many concessions; the greatest of these, fruitful of much to come, was that no lay taxation should be levied without the consent of Parliament.

Edward learned from his mistakes, and from the 1340s carried on the war with France by brief raids, *chevauchées* as they were called. The small, mobile, mounted armies lived by plunder, so the method was cheap, and it exactly suited the kind of army the English were developing.

Back in Edward I's reign the English had discovered a new weapon: the long-bow. The usual bow had been the short-bow, drawn facing the target and to the length of the extended left arm, a comparatively feeble weapon. The long-bow was larger and drawn with the archer standing at right angles to the line of fire (every woman knows how to measure a yard from her fingertips to her lips, and every child has heard of Robin Hood's "cloth-yard" arrow). An arrow from a long-bow could go through steel armor, but it was an immensely difficult weapon to use properly. Edward disposed of the difficulty of training a citizen army to a complicated weapon by the brilliantly simple idea of making it their holiday game. Under pain of imprisonment, he forbade the young men in the villages to waste their time on "hand-ball, foot-ball, hockey, coursing, cock-fighting, and other such idle games," and made them devote their leisure to the long-bow. The victories of Crécy and Poitiers were won on the village greens of England.

In 1346 Edward had an army in Normandy, and marching north to the Somme after sacking Caen encountered the French at Crécy on August 26, 1346. The English "chivalry," or mounted and armored knights, were far outnumbered by the French, so they dismounted and fought in line with the archers, who wore jackets of boiled leather, since they were not meant to come hand-to-hand with the enemy except in extremity. It was the "arrow-storm," the steady volleys of well-aimed arrows, that won the battle; when the remnants of the French had struggled through this, they came to the English line and the armed knights.

It was a great victory; and it seems past good luck that it could be followed by another equally great as little as ten years later. In the second battle, that of Poitiers in 1356, it was not the King who was in command, but his splendid soldier-son, Edward of Wood-stock Prince of Wales, known from the color of his armor as the Black Prince. The situation was much the same, a large French army opposed to a smaller English one, and this time the French tried the English tactics of dismounting their knights. But they had not the skill of the village greens in their archers, and were again defeated, and the French King Jean was taken prisoner.

The Scottish King David II was also a prisoner, and with two foreign monarchs at his court awaiting ransom Edward III was now at the height of his success. In 1360 France signed the Treaty of Brétigny, by which Edward renounced his claim to the throne of France in return for recognition of his French possessions (the Atlantic seaboard from Bayonne to south of the Loire, and east and south to beyond Toulouse) and a ransom for King Jean that must have comforted Parliament, for it was the equivalent of King Edward's income for five years. Edward's renunciation was not full, nor the full ransom ever paid, but peace was restored at least for a time.

But, while all this human turmoil was going on, disaster was preparing on an inhuman scale. From some unidentified spot in Asia or India an epidemic was creeping out along the trade routes. It came in the form of a "foul-smelling mist" in 1333 to China, and in 1347 twelve Genoese galleys put in at Messina in Sicily carrying an infection that was later calculated to have killed forty-three millions in Europe. It was the Black Death, which we now call the three forms of bubonic, septicaemic, and pneumonic plague; it was brought to England by ship in the summer of 1348, and by the next year was all over the country. When that attack had abated, it returned again in 1361, in what was sadly called the Plague of the Children, and there were recurrences in 1368 and 1375. Being carried on rats, it is a disease of bad hygiene, and in those days there was no protection but developed immunity or the gradual attenuation of the bacillus's virulence. It sank after 1375 to endemic form, but for the next three centuries broke out again and again in epidemic. In Shakespeare's time actors regarded the occasional closing of the theatres because of plague as a trade risk.

We cannot measure the effects of the Black Death in relation to Edward III's reign, for we lack short-term evidence. In local records we can find villages that died of the plague, but in general we must rely on such calculations as that by the last half of the next century the population of England had fallen from three and a half to two and a half million, or the remark of the overseas visitor nearly 150 years later that the land was devoid of people, considering how fertile it was. Modern historians have concluded that it was not until the latter third of the sixteenth century that the land was restored to the prosperity of the early days of Edward III. The consequences of depopulation are more easily observed, but belong to later reigns; yet even toward the end of Edward's reign we can see the social and economic situation changing under the pressure of the dearth of labor. In countrysides which had once been made up of thriving villages of mixed farming, landowners were being forced to take to sheep–rearing, while the common men, understanding nothing of economic forces but that one shepherd had been engaged to take the places of a dozen laborers, and their cottages torn down to make a sheep-run, harbored bitter grievances. Where sheep-runs were not practicable (and however much English wool was prized abroad, food still had to be grown) the common man was a little better off, for the scarcity-value of his labor was driving up wages. It is noteworthy that at this time there occurred the first effort by Parliament to impose a maximum wage. Since Parliament was controlled by landowners the wage was of course too low, yet the effort was not wholly despicable. It recognized the overriding power of law, for one thing; and, for another, the landowners were less greedy capitalists than men struggling with a system that was visibly going out of their control.

For Edward III and his people, however, these processes were slow to be seen, and the years following the peace with France were otherwise good years. Edward had arrived at a fruitful relationship with his barons. He was generous to his friends (in particular Salisbury, who had been Edward Montague and the hero of Roger Mortimer's downfall in 1330), but he also reconciled the great family of Mortimer by restoring Roger's grandson to the Earldom of March and marrying him into the family of his son Lionel of Antwerp, reversed the judgement against Despenser's friend Arundel, and in

1352 passed the just and sensible Statute of Treasons. This was a valuable attempt to define according to law the capital charge of treason, which in his father's time had come to mean any action temporarily irritating to those temporarily in power.

Of Edward's sons, Lionel of Antwerp Duke of Clarence, Edmund of Langley Duke of York, and Thomas of Woodstock Duke of Gloucester all married and had children who were to confuse the succession later; but the two most powerful were his heir, Edward the Black Prince, and John of Gaunt Duke of Lancaster. The Black Prince was the hope of England and his father's greatest supporter. He was married to Joan, the Maid of Kent, who was granddaughter to Edward I by his second wife, so that their son, Richard of Bordeaux, who was born in 1366, was doubly a Plantagenet. John of Gaunt was next in power and influence, and a great man by the standards of the time. He got the Duchy of Lancaster by marrying its heiress Blanche, a descendant of Henry III, and the year after the birth of Prince Richard they had a son, known as Henry Bolingbroke. When Blanche died he made an even greater match, getting himself a kingdom by marrying Costanza of Castile. But Costanza also died, and the succession in Castile went to their daughter; and back in England Gaunt was no more than a younger son of the King. He was too intelligent to resort to the methods of Henry II's sons, for by now it was the machinery of government and not a few castles that had to be seized by a successful rebel. So Gaunt took to playing politics, and often fell into company with some dubious allies.

But Gaunt would have been no more important to England than any other discontented baron if he had not, quite early in his life, fallen in love with a lady too socially inconsiderable for a bride, but to whom he was yet faithful in his fashion. She was Catherine Swynford born de Roet, daughter and widow of small knights, who bore him four remarkable children known by Gaunt's family name of Beaufort. In 1397 he married her, and in the next reign their children were legitimated, though specifically not for purposes of royal succession. Catherine's children were a stirring and ambitious lot, who perhaps made more mark on England than any other family excluded from the succession; but she has another claim on our attention. She had a sister, Philippa, two years older, who married (everyone must have said) much less well, a commoner, a civil servant who was capable in his degree but would never make a great man. He was Geoffrey Chaucer, the greatest poet of the spanking-new Middle English language.

The last years of Edward III were less happy. By a misfortunate chance the newly apparent consequences of the Black Death coincided with a renewal of the war with France, and a great French soldier, Bertrand du Guesclin, had learned how to beat the battle-line of Crécy and Poitiers by outflanking it. (The French, always haughty to new ideas, forgot this simple idea after Bertrand's death, to the profit of another generation of English archers.) Then two deaths brought about the personal wreck of the King. In 1369 Queen Philippa died; she must have been a good and kind woman, for without her Edward appeared an old, tired, lost man, with the weight of forty-two years of ruling behind him. He fell under the evil influence of his mistress, the greedy and unscrupulous Alice Perrers. Seven years later even worse befell. In 1376 his heir and support, the splendid Black Prince, died, leaving a boy of ten as heir to the throne, and the ambitious and slightly sinister Gaunt as the greatest prince of the blood. (In fact Gaunt was three years younger than Lionel of Antwerp, a fact that was to be of importance later.)

Possibly Gaunt was moved by a genuine concern for the kingdom so plainly soon to be ruled by a young boy; but if so, his methods amounted to a public scandal. They led to one of the great moments of the English Parliament, when the very properly named Good Parliament objected to Gaunt's doings, and the Speaker, Sir Peter de la Mare, a mere knight, rose to impeach some of the greatest men in the land. Gaunt had been too clever and escaped, but Alice Perrers and her allies were exiled. It did little good; they were back again within the year, and when Edward III died, a worn-out old man, after a reign of fifty years, in June, 1377, Alice Perrers was at his bedside to pick the rings from his stiffening fingers.

It was a sad death for a man who had deserved better of his people. The disturbances in his kingdom at the end were the outcome of forces no King could have either understood or controlled. Edward had been a warlike King, but in his own terms rightfully so, fighting only for what he thought his by right, and his people had loved him for it, for he had given them confidence and a sense of national pride. Under his rule, in spite of all her troubles, England had probably been a better place to live in than ever before. A contemporary of his, a scholar called Robert Burley, wrote a learned commentary on the *Politics* of Aristotle, and from his own experience added this note:

A profound love between subjects and King leads to a deep concord between the citizens and a very strong kingdom: as appears today in the case of the King of the English, on account of whose virtue there is the greatest harmony among the English people.

RICHARD II
of Bordeaux
1377–1399

✿

Born in Bordeaux in 1366.

Son of Edward of Woodstock, the Black Prince (who died
in 1369) and his wife Joan of Kent, grand-daughter of
Edward I by his second wife.

Married firstly, in 1382, Anne of Bohemia, who died 1394,
and secondly, in 1396, Isabelle of France.

Deposed September 1399, and died of unknown causes in
February 1400 in Pontefract Castle.

RICHARD II
of Bordeaux

ichard II was eleven years old when he came to the throne, and within three years he had to deal personally with something completely new in England: the Peasants' Revolt in 1381. The depopulation of the Black Death had brought about great social and economic dislocation, and ignorant efforts to right matters had increased the chaos. There had been a parallel movement in France in 1358, the murderous *Jacquerie;* that had been a gesture of despair and hatred against a society that treated its peasants as slaves. The Peasants' Revolt in England was, by comparison, law-abiding. The common man did not want to destroy the law because it denied him every human right; he wanted it altered because it was unjust to him. Once again we can see the operation of that continuing tradition of the Anglo-Saxon local law, the surprising confidence of the common man that he had rights before the law. The peasants rose all over the country, for the first time under their own leaders and for their own cause, and made their way to London, crying out for justice and for vengeance on those who had oppressed them. The young King was in the Tower of London (the Tower was a royal residence as well as a prison then) when the rebels were burning the city; he went himself

up to a high garret of the Tower to watch the fires. Then he came down again, and sent for the lords, to have their counsel. But they did not know how to advise him, and were suprisingly abashed. The next day the commons of the country and the commons of London were assembled in fearful strength. The King came to them at Mile End, with his mother and his lords and his sword carried before him; and when the people saw him they knelt down to him, saying, "Welcome, our lord King Richard, if it pleases you, and we will not have other king but you." Wat Tyler, their leader, prayed on behalf of the commons that the King would suffer them to take and deal with all the the traitors against him and the law. The King granted that they should freely seize all who were traitors and could be proved such by processes of law; that no man should be a serf nor make homage for any type of service to any lord, but should give four pence for an acre of land; that no one should serve any man except at his own will and by means of a regular covenant; and confirmed and granted that the commons should go free and have their will.

Richard's men, however, were less courteous than he, and called Tyler "Thou stinking knave" and killed him. The commons said, according to a contemporary account, "Our captain is slain, let us go and slay them all." The King said to his own knights, "Sirs, none of you follow me; let me alone," and rode out alone against the commons, saying to them, "Sirs, what aileth you? Ye shall have no captain but me; I am your King; be all in rest and peace."

And so the most part of the people that heard the King speak and saw him among them were shamefast, and began to wax peaceable.

It was a splendid scene, the lordly boy rightly trusting in his people's trust in him; but it was no more than a show on the King's side. All his promises to the commons were broken, and their leaders hunted down and killed. He was a minor in 1381, of course, and perhaps was not able to work his own will. But his later history makes this unlikely. For the rest of his reign he was to show himself as wholly occupied with his personal affairs, imperious, vindictive, and blindly set on the establishment of an absolute royal power. He also continued to show his mastery of the theatrical effect.

Richard II was doubly Plantagenet, descended from Edward I on both sides, and perhaps the double dose of royal blood was too much. Of all the physically splendid Plantagenets he was the most splendid, with an additional delicacy of feature that made his face hauntingly beautiful; his love of art made his court one of the finest in Europe, and his propensity for surrounding himself with favorites perhaps arose from the irritation of an artistic King surrounded by barbarous barons.

The unrest among the commons that marked the early part of Richard's reign was increased by popular discontent with the poor showing of the English in the continuing war against France. The pattern of this Hundred Years' War was basically simple: in both countries strong Kings alternated with weak, and the country of the strong King was for the moment in the ascendant. Richard refused to take any interest in the war. Perhaps he had perceived that good seldom came from it, but he never showed such a degree of political intelligence on any other subject, and it is more likely that his comtempt for war arose from the fact that he was the son of the greatest soldier of Europe, the Black Prince. All his life Richard had a childish tendency to refuse to do what was expected of him. The French war he left to Gaunt and the barons, and they contrived to make very little of it. Gaunt provided an original twist, by virtue of his marriage to Blanche of Castile, by proposing an attack from Spain, and in pursuance of the alliances necessary to this strategy Richard married Anne of Bohemia. He and his young Queen fell deeply in love during their short married life, and if she had lived longer she might have helped a personality so disastrously at odds with its circumstances.

By 1386, when Richard was twenty, Parliament had grown tired of his lack of interest in the damaging effect of the war on English trading interests, and demanded the removal of some of his favorites. By now Parliament had for convenience become divided into the two familiar Houses, Lords (which included the lords of the Church) and Commons, who were the representatives of the shires. The interests of the two Houses did not always coincide, and Richard tried to rule them by dividing them. He received the historic answer that the Commons stood with the Lords. He took this as rebellion, raised an army, and marched on London, but was defeated on the way. The assembly of barons who brought about this defeat included a young man he was to know better, that son of John of Gaunt who had been born the year after his own birth, Henry Earl of Derby, known as Bolingbroke. In the Parliament of 1388, known as the Merciless Parliament, there were menacing references to Edward II, and Richard had to submit to losing his friends; two were executed and the others exiled.

To do Richard justice, his friends were not to be compared with the minions of Edward II, any more than his rule was to be compared with the rule, or lack of it, of Edward II. Edward's minions were greedy men thinking of nothing but their own gain, but Richard's friends were his assistants in his kingdom. Richard's trouble was not that he governed badly, but that he attempted to govern in a way totally opposed by his subjects. Unbelievably, about this time of the

Merciless Parliament, he actually proposed to the Pope the canonization of Edward II.

Five years later, in 1394, Richard's dearly loved wife, Anne of Bohemia, died of the plague. Richard behaved like a man crazed. He had the palace where she died razed to the ground, and when one of the barons arrived late at her funeral he struck him down for the insult. Or was he, as ever, making a dramatic gesture? The man he struck was Arundel, one of his chief enemies, and Arundel never forgot it.

Still only in his twenties, Richard was now totally isolated, and in the next ten years he appeared a little mad. He did some very odd things, and did them with a superb disregard of their oddness. He suddenly had the idea of having himself elected King of the Romans, the title of the heir-apparent of the Emperor of Germany, and spent enormous sums in the necessary bribes. Then, when for a short time the war with France was in abeyance, Richard planned to help her King, Charles VI, in his invasion of Italy. Very luckily, nothing came of this, for the invasion was a piece of pure aggression that was to cause untold trouble and misery. Richard's only real military act was comical in its disdainful brevity. He accompanied John of Gaunt on an expedition to Scotland. The Scots wisely kept out of the way, and when they entered Edinburgh and found it deserted, Richard lost interest and insisted on going home.

But his chief interest in these years after the Merciless Parliament, as his people were to see from 1397, was in planning revenge for his defeat in 1388. There was nothing political in these plans; his revenge was purely personal. The only thing that can be said for this childish and suicidal plan is that it was executed with artistry; that was always Richard's gift. His chief enemies in his eyes were his uncle Thomas of Woodstock, Arundel, Warwick, Norfolk, the Archbishop of Canterbury, and his own cousin Henry Bolingbroke. In 1397 he had Thomas of Woodstock murdered, Arundel executed, Warwick and Canterbury banished. In its showy way it was a wonderful performance, for they were among the greatest men in the kingdom, and to banish the Primate of England was unheard-of. But this was not the end of the performance. He assured the two remaining enemies, Norfolk and Bolingbroke, that he was their friend, and even gave Bolingbroke a duchy. Next year he attacked Parliament, successfully reassuming control in some money matters, and significantly restoring the vague definition of treason which his grandfather had so wisely limited in the Statute of Treasons of 1352. In September, 1398, Bolingbroke and Norfolk quarrelled on some private matter, and Bolingbroke accused Norfolk of plotting against the King. Richard arranged one of his big scenes (familiar to us in Shakespeare). He let the two of them come to trial by battle, and had them armed in the lists, with himself presiding, and at the moment when they should have spurred their horses to the encounter stopped them, summoned them in front of him, and assumed judgment himself. He banished them both; his revenge was completed.

The triumph was too much for him. He seems to have imagined that he had established himself as an absolute monarch, and behaved like one. Next year old John of Gaunt died, and Richard confiscated the Lancaster estates that were the inheritance of Bolingbroke. To give Bolingbroke, of all men, a just cause for revolt was insane; Richard calmly compounded his insanity by leaving for Ireland.

With these heaven-sent gifts of a rightful complaint and an absent King, Bolingbroke landed on the Yorkshire coast. Many welcomed him, and as he marched south even Richard's deputy, who was his uncle Edmund of Langley Duke of York, came over to him. Richard hurried back from Ireland, but found that it was too late, and he had lost his kingdom without even a fight. There was only one thing he could do: on September 29, 1399, his abdication was presented to Parliament.

This raised the question of his heir, since he had no children. Richard himself named Edmund Mortimer Earl of March, grandson of the regicide Mortimer. If succession through the female were allowed, Mortimer was the legal heir, since he had married the daughter and heiress of Edward III's second son, Lionel of Antwerp. If Parliament decided that descent through the female were not allowable, the next heir would be Edward III's grandson by his third son, who was Henry Bolingbroke. It would have been a difficult problem if it had ever been debated, but it was not, for the simple reason that London was full of Henry Bolingbroke's army. Parliament chose Bolingbroke.

Probably no choice of king would have been altogether happy, given the absence of a strong son of Richard II's. Once the line had been broken, the Plantagenet fertility assured a mob of energetic ambitious children too conscious of the possibility of breaking it again. There were the Mortimers: Anne, sister of Richard's choice Edmund, married into another royal line, that of Edmund of Langley

Duke of York. There were the Beauforts, Gaunt's children by Catherine Swynford, whom Richard (in one of his pretenses of friendship for the House of Lancaster) had legitimated but for the purposes of succession; in the next generation they married purposefully into the lines of both Edmund of Langley and the murdered Thomas of Woodstock, and in the end John Beaufort was to father the line that ran from King Henry VII to Queen Anne, his daughter Joan to marry James I of Scots from whom was descended the line of Scottish Kings who inherited the throne of England from Elizabeth I Tudor, and his sister Joan was foremother of three kings in three generations. And there were others, swept aside in the end, but still making their small turmoil in the land.

As for Richard II, who had so abruptly quitted the turmoil, he died the next year, 1400, a prisoner in Pontefract Castle. We do not know the circumstances of his death. King Henry IV said he had committed suicide by starving himself to death; he was merciful enough then to add that he had repented his purpose and taken food again when it was too late, which saved Richard from the disgrace of a suicide's grave (that is, one not in sanctified ground). Later (the story Shakespeare knew) it was said that he was smothered, to show no marks of violence, by a man of Henry's. If there was a murder, modern historians tend to blame it on Sir Thomas Swynford, who is interesting in that he was the eldest son of Catherine Swynford by her first marriage, and thus could claim a kinship surely unequalled in English history, being related to all the royal lines fathered by the Beauforts, and nephew of Geoffrey Chaucer. It may well be that Bolingbroke was guilty of Richard's death, for it was of benefit to him, and in his strange character it is possible to detect later the shadow cast by guilt. But if we consider Richard's own character, his imperiousness, his vindictiveness, his obstinacy, and wonder what was the effect of total defeat on a mind with only a tenuous grasp on reality, we may even conclude that Bolingbroke's story was entirely true and that Richard starved himself to death. It would be like the young man who cherished his revenge through ten lonely years, and ruined himself in achieving it, to kill himself slowly because that was the one way left to him to embarrass his successor.

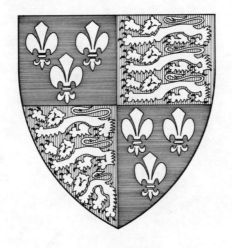

House of

LANCASTER

HENRY IV
of Bolingbroke
1399–1413

❁

Born in Bolingbroke in 1366.

Son of John of Gaunt, who was the third son of Edward III, and his first wife Blanche of Lancaster.

Recognized as king after the deposition of Richard II.

Married in 1380 Mary de Bohun, who died in 1394, by whom he had:

> Henry of Monmouth, later Henry V;
> John Duke of Bedford, born 1389, later Regent of France.

In 1403 he married secondly Joan of Navarre, but by her had no children.

Died in the Jerusalem Chamber of Westminster, March 1413 and was buried at Canterbury.

From the assumption of the Crown by Henry IV arose the dispute over the succession which was to lead to the Wars of the Roses between the contending parties of Lancaster and York.

HENRY IV
of Bolingbroke

When in 1399 Henry Bolingbroke Duke of Lancaster became King Henry IV he was a commanding figure. He was a distinguished knight, a proved soldier of European reputation, and well-skilled in the courtier's arts of music and literature. When he died in 1413, only forty-six years old, he had all the appearance of a broken invalid, old before his time and ruler only in name. Of all the Kings of England, he is to us the most withdrawn, the most difficult to see as a living man.

Politically speaking, he never overcame the situation he had created by his method of seizing the throne. When he landed in England in 1399, it is possible that he had no intention of making himself King; indeed, it seems that he took an oath before witnesses that his only object was to recover the inheritance that Richard II had confiscated. By the moral standards of the time, and probably by our standards, too, he was justified in this intention. He may honestly not have known the extent to which Richard II had alienated his subjects, and been himself surprised by the momentum that his rebellion gathered.

If he was so surprised, he was not happy with it. His expressed claim to the throne of England was curious in the extreme. The feeling against Richard being what it was, he could have asserted his right by conquest; or he could have asserted his right by descent from Edward III, since he descended from the eldest surviving male line, and Edmund Mortimer Earl of March, Richard's choice, descended only from the female line, which was sometimes considered junior to any male line. Instead he took the extraordinary path of asserting that his ancestor through the *female* line (by way of his father Gaunt's marriage with Blanche of Lancaster), Edmund Crouchback, was the eldest and not the second son of Henry III. Few claims can have been based on thinner material; if Crouchback had been Henry III's eldest son Edward I would have been a usurper. Perhaps this was a private fantasy of his own to hold off guilt, since when he finally laid his claim before Parliament it was couched in the vaguest terms possible:

I, Henry of Lancaster, challenge this realm of England and the Crown with all the members and appurtenances, as that I am descended by right line of the blood coming from the good Lord King Henry Third and through that right that God of His Grace hath sent me, with help of my king and my friends, to recover it; the which realm was in point to be undone for default of governance and undoing of the good laws.

He was to spend his unhappy reign in fighting the kin and friends who had helped him, and in persuading the Parliament who had sanctioned his succession to give him money to carry out his task.

Henry Bolingbroke had been born to authority. Although the throne of England could never have seemed within his reach, he was the son of John of Gaunt, sometime King of Castile, and with a place beyond question in the knightly aristocracy of Europe. He fought in ornate tournaments, went twice to the Baltic to fight with the Knights of the Sword against the Lithuanians, made the pilgrimage to Jerusalem, and in England took by right a leading place in the struggle between Richard II and his barons. He was a more honorable man than his father, never becoming enmeshed in dubious dealings; but he had inherited the imperious Plantagenet temper, and he never lost, however much it cost him, the impulse to assert his authority regardless of principle or practicality.

But the times were not propitious for the exercise of the Plantagenet temper, for Richard II had exhausted Parliament's tolerance of it. It was Parliament that had conferred the crown upon Henry IV, and Parliament now expected returns. Unhappily this was one of the times in English history when Parliament was less alive than the King to the necessities of the country. Henry spent the great fortunes of the House of Lancaster in rewarding his supporters and suppressing rebellions, and soon had to turn to Parliament for money.

Each of Henry IV's many Parliaments followed the same pattern.

He would summon them to ask for help in his wars against the Welsh, or the Scots, or the French, or his rebellious subjects; they were all necessary wars, for he was not an aggressive king (he never had the leisure to be so). The Speaker would first of all ask the King's forgiveness for anything he might say as the mouth of Parliament, and the King's assurance that no reprisals would be taken against him personally; then he would criticize the King's Council, try to reduce the King's household expenditure (which was not great), and insist that high office in the kingdom should be held only by those who were prepared to work for it—that if the King, for instance, chose to call his son Prince of Wales then the boy should go and fight the rebels in Wales. In fury at this presumption, Henry would dissolve Parliament, pause to reflect on his finances, and grant its demands. He did at least steadily progress toward political reality. It brought him little popular support, but in his reign this close struggle between monarch and Parliament came closer to the ideal of constitutional monarchy than was to be possible again for many centuries.

Henry was merciful by temperament, but it did him little good. There was an ill-supported rebellion in the early months of 1400, but when after this he announced the suicide of Richard II the legend started that Richard was still alive, and he was never able to free himself of it. That same summer he fought a costly and indecisive war with Robert III in Scotland, becoming the last English King to lead an army into that country, and while he was away the Welsh landowner Owen Glendower (popularly reputed a sorcerer) led the first of his many raids into England. The course of these raids was always the same. Glendower would sally from his mountains, devastate the countryside, and seize a castle or two; Henry would send an army, at first under his ally Henry Percy (the famous Hotspur), later under his own son Henry Prince of Wales; Glendower's men would fade away, the English would tramp for a few weeks in the rain looking for them, and then be forced to retire for lack of money; and after a decent interval Glendower would come back. Henry could never find the money to finance a decisive campaign, and by the summer of 1402 Glendower had allied himself with the great Marcher family of Mortimer, and Hotspur was advising peace.

Hotspur himself was busy defeating the Scots on the northern frontier. The Percys were the greatest family of the north, and, like most Kings, Henry IV was too much afraid of such powerful subjects to give them the rewards they deserved for their guarding of the north. He needlessly offended Hotspur by ordering them to hand over to him their Scots prisoners (he wanted, of course, their ransom value). He had to send an army to France, where the French King had given his eldest son the Prince of Wales's title of Duke of Aquitaine, and in the spring of 1403 yet another army was needed against Glendower. When the army in Wales as usual ran out of money, Hotspur and his father Northumberland, who were fighting the Scots, deemanded £20,000 they said was owing to them. Henry could not pay it, and was on his way to meet them when he found that they had joined Glendower and proclaimed Edmund Mortimer King.

The Percy claim was that Henry had tricked them in 1399 by swearing that he came to England with no designs on the throne; but they had fought for him too long and too faithfully for this to be credible. The truth seems to have been that Henry's demand for the wealthy prisoners taken on the Scottish border had at last broken a temper irritated by his suspicions of their power. It was, however, an ill-prepared rebellion, and Henry showed his old courage and energy in joining forces with his son at Shrewsbury before Hotspur could seize the town. Hotspur is said to have placed faith in a prophecy that he would die in Berwick, which he took to be the great border fortress of Berwick-on-Tweed, and was dismayed to find that he was to fight near a small village called Berwick. He was killed there by a stray arrow, the heart went out of his men, and Northumberland surrendered after a decisive victory for Henry. The only rebel who escaped was Glendower, for the usual reason that the King had not the money to hunt him out of his native mountains.

After all this expense, Henry had to summon two Parliaments next year, and not all the humiliating concessions he granted them brought him money. He could hold back Glendower but not defeat him, he could hold Guyenne in France but not stop the Bretons harrying the South Coast of England, and in 1405 came a revolt which in its consequences was to be the most serious of his reign. Glendower and Northunberland were involved again, but the central figure was Richard Scrope Archbishop of York. They appear to have had the extraordinarily naive idea of partitioning England between them, and were defeated even before Henry could reach York. The real problem lay in how to how to punish an Archbishop of York for the undoubted crime of treason. Arundel Archbishop of Canterbury hurried to York to advise sparing Scrope's life. Henry sent him to rest after his journey, and as soon as his back was turned summoned a court, sentenced Scrope to death, and had him at once beheaded.

It was a perfectly legal proceeding, and a sensible one, for Henry had pardoned many rebels (Northumberland the most recent) who had promptly rebelled again. But it was the most sensational act of sacrilege since the murder of Beckett, and while the world condemned Henry for it, Henry himself seems to have condemned himself even more strongly. He began to suffer from a mysterious "wasting sickness" that was written of with a peculiar note of horror. The only symptoms we know of are that he grew unable to ride and had to travel by barge or litter, that he withdrew into greater and greater isolation, and that his face showed signs of decay; it seems likely that he had contracted leprosy, and men said that it was the vengeance of God for the murder of Scrope.

Arundel of Canterbury became Chancellor and virtual ruler of the country, and Henry steadily yielded power to Parliament and to his council, whose membership was now out of his control. To add to his miseries, he came into growing conflict with his son Harry of Monmouth Prince of Wales.

The Prince of Wales had two heroes: Richard II and Hotspur. He had grown up in Richard's court, and when his father landed in England in 1399 Harry of Monmouth was actually serving under Richard in Ireland. His ideas of royalty he took from the absolutist Richard, and his ideals of knightly behavior from the courageous but hardly intelligent Hotspur; after Hotspur's death he took all his retainers into his own service. In 1409 he at last pacified Glendower by capturing his wife and daughters, and was able to return to London. It is from this time that Shakespeare took the stories of Prince Hal's riotous youth (the contemporary comment was that in his youth he served Venus as well as Mars); but in fact he seems from the evidence to have been in his twenties earnest, sober, and distressingly humorless. Falstaff is Shakespeare's invention; the Prince's chosen companions were such men as Richard de Beauchamp, flower of a chivalry still extant only in romance. He ousted Arundel from the council and brought in the intelligent and pushing Beauforts, and soon he was taking his father's place on the council with the Beauforts urging him to seize the royal power.

Around this time—it was largely a movement of the commons, and ill-recorded—there was developing a growing antipathy toward the Church. Dislike of a power extremely wealthy and chiefly Italian in its interests was far from new; but the Lollards, as they came to be called, were religious and not political reformers; in doctrine they were the forerunners of the Protestants. They influenced many of the knights of the Lower House to urge that the great and useless wealth of the Church should be taxed to raise money for the King's wars. Arundel of Canterbury was naturally opposed to these doctrines (even if Canterbury had not been the wealthiest see in England); he attempted to suppress the teaching of the Lollard doctrines in Oxford, and came into conflict with the Prince of Wales, who had that university under his protection. When the King, as he was bound to do, supported Arundel the breach between them was further widened. At this, Arundel used all his influence with the King, regained his position on the council, and ousted the headstrong Beauforts and the rest of the prince's supporters.

This was Henry IV's last rebellion, and he defeated it as he had defeated the rest. The prince came under suspicion of misappropriating moneys entrusted to him, and cannily dissociated himself from the Beauforts; but that mattered little, because by now the King was dying. He lay in his bed with the crown on the pillow beside him, and there is a story that the prince thought him dead and took it away. Waking, Henry had prince and crown brought before him, and asked his son: "By what right do you take the crown, seeing that I myself had none?" "As you have kept it by the sword," said the prince, not unjustly, "so will I while my life lasts." There had been a prophecy that Henry IV would die in Jerusalem, and he is said to have cherished it, thinking that his last years would be passed on the Holy Pilgrimage. Instead, the room in which he died was called the Jerusalem Chamber.

Henry IV had promised better than any King since Edward I, but because his usurpation had made him the servant rather than the master of Parliament he had never been able to show what kind of a ruler he could have made. Parliament does not emerge very well from his reign, demanding results it would not pay for. Personally, Henry seems to have been a kindly, patient, and reasonable man, faithful to his friends, devoted to his family, and not humorless. There is a nice letter extant written to Arundel about an otherwise unknown lady called only D:

We have, at the importunate suit of the aforesaid D, and in order to get rid of her out of our company, promised her our said letters; and we believe that you will be as weary of her company and persistence as we became before she would see reason.

But to his contemporaries Henry IV was the man who had killed an anointed King and executed a Prince of the Church. By his usurpation he had fatally weakened the principle—respected even by the murderers of Edward II, and none the less sacred for all the uncertainties of its application—of the royal succession. The crown was now open to legal seizure by anyone who could get it, and in the nature of things it could not be long before a weak King would tempt someone to try. The Wars of the Roses, in which nearly all of the great barons' families were to come to an end, was still two reigns off, but it had become inevitable.

HENRY V
of Monmouth
1413-1422

☼

Born in Monmouth in 1387.

Son of Henry IV and his first wife Mary de Bohun.

Married in 1420 Catherine de Valois, daughter of Charles VI of France, by whom he had one son:

> Henry, later Henry VI
> Catherine de Valois later married (at a date unknown) Owen Tudor, by whom she had several children, of whom the eldest, Edmund Tudor later Earl of Richmond, was to marry Margaret Beaufort, great-grand-daughter of John of Gaunt and Catherine Swynford.

Died at Bois de Vincennes August 1422 and buried in Westminster Abbey.

HENRY V
of Monmouth

hakespeare's Henry V is unforgettable and wholly false. The gay reveller, the devoted son, the merry lover, the flower of chivalry, never existed; instead there was a calculating fanatic obsessed by dreams of military glory and a cold merciless soldier with a liking for gratuitous cruelties. Even the hero-King who restored England to her greatness turns out to be the soldier of one victory who died on the verge of defeat.

Henry V's coronation took place in a blizzard, an omen whose interpretation baffled his contemporaries; his first acts as King were assertive and unfilial. He honored the memory of Richard II (in passing dishonoring that of his father) by re-interring his body with great ceremony in Westminster Abbey and restoring to favor many of Richard's supporters. He left Arundel on the council, but restored those who had been closest to him, particularly the Beauforts. Not entirely logically, he also set at liberty the rightful heir to England, the Earl of March. The only serious domestic problem at first was that of the Lollards, the forerunners of the religious reformers. As Prince of Wales he had appeared to favor them, in opposition to his father and Arundel; but his lack of sympathy had appeared during his father's final illness, when he had allowed Arundel to continue their suppression. He even personally supervised one peculiarly cruel execution; a tailor, John Badby, had been condemned to burning and in the middle of the burning Henry had the fire put out and offered Badby a pension if he would recant. Badby refused, and Henry had the fires relit. Badby's crime had been that he had asserted that the Sacrament was not the true

Body of Christ; on that argument the fires of England and all Europe were to be lit within the century.

Henry's reforming zeal did not return when he was King. He gave Arundel a free hand with his suppression, which led to a rebellion and plot against his life by a man who had been a friend of his, Sir John Oldcastle. It was Oldcastle who was Shakespeare's original of Falstaff, and at least the line he gave Henry to Falstaff on his accession was a true one:"Fall to thy prayers, old man." The rebellion was overcome and the rebels executed.

Meanwhile, the weak King of France, Charles VI, whose sanity was only intermittent, had so far lost control of his kingdom that the leaders of the two great fiefs, the Burgundians and the Armagnacs, were both angling for English support. England was still a power in France; Henry V held (from the days of Henry II) the great fief of Aquitaine, and although Edward III had agreed in 1360 to renounce his claim to the throne in return for King Jean's ransom, that ransom had not been paid in full. Richard II, from disinclination, and Henry IV, from lack of money, had let the claim stand, which had been another cause of disagreement between Henry IV and his son. Henry V was determined to revive it, and the internal dissensions in France played into his hands. He favored—perhaps because his father had not—the party of the Burgundians, whose leader, John the Fearless Duke of Burgundy, had in 1407 been murdered by the Armagnacs, led by Philip Duke of Orleans. Henry demanded the crown of France, the domains of Normandy and Anjou, the hand in marriage of Catherine de Valois daughter of Charles VI, and the ransom of King Jean, and to secure his help the Burgundians offered their neutrality toward these claims.

Where Henry IV had been unable to scrape together a force strong enough to oust Glendower from his Welsh mountains, Henry V could raise, within a few months, an army of 10,000 and and a navy to carry them to France. He had the gift of inspiring confidence; he could also tempt his barons with the spoils awaiting them in France. The Lord Mayor of London, Sir Richard Whittington (the classic example of the flexibility of English society, for he had come to London as a boy with nothing, probably not even the cat of the children's story) raised money for him in the city, and something like a war-fever swept the country.

Yet, the situation was not as secure as Henry had supposed. He was on the point of embarking for France when he had news of a major conspiracy against him. It was led (an omen for the future) by Richard Earl of Cambridge, who was son to that Edmund Langley Duke of York who had joined Bolingbroke on his march to London in 1399, and who had married Anne, sister of the true heir Edmund Mortimer Earl of March. Richard's supporters summed up the troubles of the previous reign; there were Hotspur's son, Scrope's nephew, rebellious Scots and Welsh, and some Lollards. They had adopted March as their figurehead, but had miscalculated his honorable gratitude to the King who had set him free; he betrayed them to Henry, and Cambridge and his companions were executed. The episode then must have seemed an epilogue to the reign of Henry IV; in fact it was a prologue to the Wars of the Roses. Richard of Cambridge had a son, Richard Plantagenet Duke of York, whose marriage to one of the Beaufort family Henry V so much favored was to bring Henry's only son to ruin.

Henry's campaign in France began well. He beseiged the port of Harfleur, in spite of the surrounding marshes which brought his army low with dysentery, and when the town yielded, he treated it with uncharacteristic clemency. He sent an extraordinary challenge to Charles VI's son the Dauphin, which reveals his curious clinging to chivalric ideas long outdated:

Considering that it hath pleased God to visit with infirmity our cousin your father, we offer you to decide this our quarrel, with God's grace, between our person and yours . . .

That is, he proposed to fight the Dauphin personally to settle the affairs of two kingdoms. The Dauphin had never been attached to the military virtues, and prudently refused. Less prudently, Henry set off for Calais, a march of more than 150 miles through enemy country with an exhausted and diseased army, and at the little village of Agincourt found a greatly superior French army barring his way. He did not, in fact, want to fight, and even offered to return Harfleur in exchange for a truce; but the French were set on wiping out the memory of Crécy and Poitiers, and thought they were in overwhelming force.

Unhappily for them, in remembering their defeats they had forgotten Bertrand du Guesclin, who had discovered how to deal with the type of army that had defeated them. The result of Agincourt is rather more due to French stupidity than to English valor. The French knights, unaccustomed to fighting as an army, rode toward the English battle-line as if at a tournament, and when the muddy ground and the English arrows hampered them, the sheer weight of knight and armor made them unable to maneuver; the English fell on them with swords and axes and anything that came to hand. Henry had ordered his men to give no quarter and take no prisoners but the valuable ones, and he himself fought with conspicuous valor. Ninety counts, 1500 knights, and 5,000 common soldiers were killed, and the Armagnac leaders taken prisoner.

Henry's cause in France seemed assured, and he returned to England in triumph to a new subsidy from Parliament. Yet, the results of Agincourt were more moral than material. The army of the King of England was now feared, but France was far from conquered, and the Burgundians very sensibly took to regarding him less as an ally than as a rival.

There was nothing for it but another campaign in France, this time a less impulsive one, with the object of securing Normandy by means of a series of carefully calculated sieges of the fortresses of northern France. The Conqueror's city of Caen was treated in the fashion of the Conqueror: the two great abbeys, in which the Conqueror and his wife were buried, were used as assault positions, and the city itself subjected to the worst excesses of pillage and massacre, so that after that no other town had to be taken by force. Rouen, which Henry regarded as his rightful capital, was literally starved into submission. Even in face of this, the French could not combine, and after some distasteful murders and intrigues a treaty was concluded at Troyes in May, 1420. The old French King was there, so witless that he had difficulty in making out who Henry was. His two elder sons were dead, and his present heir, the Dauphin Charles, was weak and epileptic. His daughter Catherine was a princess of more attraction, and at their first meeting Henry kissed her, causing something of a sensation. However, the treaty gave her to him in marriage. The old King could not in decency be deposed, and it was agreed that he should hold the throne during his lifetime and that Henry should succeed him. The Dauphin was entirely ignored.

There remained the Armagnacs, who had not been given a slice of the cake, and therefore continued to assert the rights of the Dauphin (whom they heartily despised). Two days after his wedding to the Dauphin's sister, accompanied by the Dauphin's father, Henry and Philip of Burgundy rode to war again. They made a festive campaign of it, watching the fall of city after city, and in December

Henry made a triumphal entry into Paris, with Charles VI at his side. Perhaps the Parisians thought even an English King better than the non-Kings they had had lately, and presumably on his next visit he would have been crowned and anointed King of France.

But the stubborn Armagnacs were still firmly entrenched along the Loire, and while Henry was enjoying his triumph in London they totally defeated an army of his. Henry hurried back to the Loire; and from now on he seems to have been fighting with a new brutality. It had never been a merciful war, but now pillage and hangings and torture became more common, and Henry and his men ever greedier for loot. Henry had every success, yet total victory seemed as far away as at the beginning; he fought in a kind of fury of frustration. Perhaps it was because his health was by now failing fast. By July, 1422, he could no longer ride. The dysentery to which he had so recklessly exposed his armies was now draining his own strength. He reached the castle of Vincennes and in August of 1422 realized that he was dying. At this last he tried to justify his actions:

It was not ambitious lust for dominion, nor for empty glory, nor any other course, that drew me to these wars, but only that by suing of my right I might at once gain peace and my own right.

But he had not gained peace, and his right was perilously insecure. He had brought England prestige; but to the son born to him only a few months before his death he left possessions in France that not even he had succeeded in controlling, and a situation in England moving inevitably toward anarchy. For all its glory, the reign of Henry V was merely an intermission in the real life of the country.

HENRY VI
1422-1471

❁

Born at Windsor, December 1421.
Only child of Henry V and his wife Catherine de Valois.
Crowned King of England at Westminster in 1429 and
    King of France in Notre Dame, Paris, in 1431.
Married in 1445 Margaret of Anjou, who died in 1482.
Margaret had one son:

> Edward Prince of Wales, born 1453, married in 1470
> Anne daughter of Richard Earl of Warwick (War-
> wick the King-Maker), killed at the Battle of Tewkes-
> bury 1471. Anne of Warwick later married Richard
> Duke of York, who was to become Richard III.

Henry was declared deposed by the Yorkist faction in 1461,
and his throne taken by Edward of York, but was restored
in 1470, sent to the Tower in May 1471 after the Yorkist
victory at Tewkesbury, and there died on a date unknown
and for reasons unknown, and was buried at Windsor.

In this reign began the Wars of the Roses between the
    Houses of Lancaster and York.

HENRY VI

I f Henry V had been less set on military glory, or even if he had lived longer and learned more, the Wars of the Roses might never have been fought. There is an air of nemesis about the reign of his son Henry VI, as if upon his head were laid all the crimes of the two royal houses from which he was sprung. From his French grandfather Charles VI he inherited a madness he accepted all too meekly; from his English grandfather Henry IV a usurped throne threatened by powerful rivals; and from his father a neglected kingdom, a long minority, and a disastrously mistaken education. When Charles VI died in 1422, the year-old child was proclaimed King of France and England, the most powerful monarch since Henry II of England. When he died fifty years later, a prisoner murdered in the Tower of London by an unknown hand, his life had horribly paralleled that of the poor mad old French King; he had come to the throne as a child, been forced to witness a struggle for power between enemies who called themselves his protectors, fallen mad while others disputed his throne, and been forced to disclaim his own heir in favor of a rival. The history of Henry VI's reign is not of what he did, but of what was done to him.

His father, never remarkable for a grasp of any reality that went beyond military tactics, entrusted his education to Richard de Beauchamp Earl of Warwick, the knight whose deeds of chivalry had made him renowned throughout Europe. Warwick was certainly a splendid figure, but had curious ideas of the qualities necessary to rule a kingdom in which even the military men were emerging from the feudal habit of thought. Nature must have assisted him, but he produced a man so concerned with the ideals of peace and justice that he was incapable of dealing with the realities of their opposites. Henry's only real achievements were the two colleges he founded, Eton and King's College Cambridge; when he met any of the Eton boys, he would give them money, advise them to follow the paths of virtue, and say, "Be you good boys, gentle and teachable, and servants of the Lord." His own simplicity of life verged on the eccentric. He wore a long, hooded, coarse gown and farmer's boots, and averted his eyes and left the room when ladies entered in low-cut dresses, saying, "Fie fie for shame!," which may have been moral but was not kingly. Throughout his life he exercised mercy, pardoning his enemies and working always for peace and reconciliation, and before the onset of his madness these undoubted virtues commanded some respect. But, since he still regarded himself as King, he stood by in his virtue while others fought for him. He had a lot in common with Edward the Confessor.

The early years of his reign were dominated at home by the rivalries of his protectors, while his uncle John of Bedford fought conscientiously to defend the French inheritance. Another uncle, Humphrey of Gloucester, locked in a stupid struggle with Henry Beaufort Cardinal-Archbishop of Winchester (Catherine Swynford's second son by John of Gaunt), contrived to offend Bedford's ally the Duke of Burgundy, whose commitment to the English cause slowly declined. Much more unlikely help to France came in 1429 in the person of a French country girl convinced that she bore a message from heaven to the French King. The message itself was unremarkable, being mostly an adjuration to have confidence and fight better; what was remarkable about Joan of Arc was that the French chivalry listened to her. The French King Charles VII (who was still known as the Dauphin because he had not been crowned) was persuaded to behave in something approaching a kingly fashion, the English were defeated, Orleans relieved, and Charles VII crowned. Within a few months of this triumph Joan had been captured and burned as a witch. The French were unperturbed by her death, even a little relieved, for she had given them back their confidence and had no more for them.

Their new belligerence brought them the alliance of Burgundy. When he heard that the Duke of Burgundy no longer considered him King of France, Henry VI burst into tears. By 1435 France and Burgundy were in alliance against England, and the French adventure was over. A few survivors of Agincourt fought manfully on, but it was now only a matter of time before England was driven entirely out of France. This loss naturally led to disaster in England, Henry VI finding, like Henry III and John before him, that powerful subjects deprived of loot elsewhere use their energies in rebellion and civil war. The struggle between Humphrey of Gloucester and Cardinal Beaufort ended scandalously with charges of witchcraft against Humphrey's wife and retainers, and Humphrey himself died a mysterious death in which Beaufort was suspected of having a hand. It did him no good, for he himself died six weeks later of natural causes, regretting to the last that money could not buy him a longer life and that he had to die before he had achieved the Papal crown.

By now Henry had long been of an age to govern for himself, but the system of protectors had become too entrenched in the struggles of the rival nobles for anyone to wish for change. Even Henry himself made no move to take over his own duties. In the year of his majority his mother Catherine de Valois died; she had not been given any part in his upbringing, and it seems to have been only at her death that Henry discovered that she had quietly married again and had four children.

In spite of all efforts to reinterpret the very few documents we have about this apparently unimportant marriage, which was to bring a new and brilliant dynasty to England, we know hardly anything about the man Catherine Princess of France and Queen of England married. His name was Owen Tudor, he was Welsh and undistinguished of birth and achievement, and in spite of later sneers there is no doubt that the marriage was lawful and the young Tudors legitimate. Henry took charge of their upbringing, but for all his virtue he seems to have found it difficult to show them any mark of favor for many years.

The new strong man in England's councils was now William de la Pole Duke of Suffolk, a supporter of the Beauforts, and he arranged the King's marriage with a brilliant and ambitious bride. This was Margaret of Anjou, daughter of René King of Sicily and Jerusalem, Duke of Anjou and Duke of Maine, a great title except that the kingdoms of Sicily and Jerusalem had long vanished and the duchies of Anjou and Maine were in the hands of the English. Margaret of Anjou was, in fact, a very poor match for a King, and Suffolk's persistence in bringing it about can only be explained by his infatuation with Margaret and his conviction that his own power lay in her.

Not only did Margaret bring no dower to the match, but Anjou and Maine were to be ceded to her father, the last defenses of England's fast-vanishing French kingdom, and Suffolk went to some lengths to conceal this part of the marriage contract. Henry was pleased with his young bride, but the deception could not long be concealed; the French demanded the immediate surrender of Anjou and Maine, and by 1453 there remained to England, of all Henry V's vast Continental empire, only the town of Calais and the marshes that surrounded it. The man who saved Calais was Richard Plantagenet Duke of York, son of that Richard Earl of Cambridge, who had been beheaded in 1415, and his wife Anne Mortimer. Richard of York was now heir to the line of Mortimer as well as that of York, and, being thus descended twice from Edward III, he married Cicely Neville, daughter of Joan Beaufort by her second marriage. When Henry VI did not prove to be a King who dealt capably with rivals, Richard of York was a tempting prospect as leader of a rebellion. It is just possible that he instigated the rising of the commons under Jack Cade, whose fate, like Wat Tyler's, was to be tricked into a truce and in the end killed. At any rate, he took the excuse of the rising to break into Henry's presence and quarrel with Suffolk. Henry moderated his wrath a little, but it was clear that civil war was now very near.

In 1453, as if in response to this situation, Henry's mind gave way. We do not know the exact nature of his madness, only that it involved depression, fits of terror, and a total incapacity to deal with persons or problems; it was certainly inherited from his grandfather of France, but we cannot doubt that Henry retreated into it without much resistance. He did however emerge from it into perfect lucidity when, in the same year, his wife Margaret had a son. He said the child must have been conceived by the Holy Ghost. Margaret ignored questions of the child's legitimacy; he was her son, and his defense her first object.

There is a legend that the Wars of the Roses formally began in the gardens of the Temple in London, when the two leaders picked roses for their badges, red for Lancaster and white for York. These wars were to divide, and ultimately destroy, the old aristocracy, and like most civil wars they were fought with ferocity and a total absence of mercy, chivalry, or moral principle. Nothing illustrates better the absence of the knightly principles on which Henry VI had been so disastrously brought up. Men changed sides with bewildering frequency and entire lack of faith, even in the midst of battle; personal advantage was the only principle followed, and battle followed battle with a terrible toll of slaughter, pillage, and wanton cruelty.

Richard of York was no general, but his wife's Neville kin supported him, and the greatest of these was Richard Neville Earl of Warwick. Warwick was the most formidable man in the kingdom and was to become known as the Kingmaker and to be responsible for the spectacular rise of the House of York. York began by forcing himself on the King as protector and sending to the Tower the Lancastrian leader Somerset. At this, Henry unexpectedly had a return of sanity, and he and York might have achieved a successful settlement, but Margaret would not have it. She freed Somerset and the two sides came to pitched battle at Saint Albans in 1455. York here won an easy victory, and, Somerset having been killed and Henry relapsed into madness, became protector again. But he could not maintain the position, and Henry had one of his oddly apposite fits of sanity and staged a ceremony of reconciliation of the kind so dear to him. Warwick, Exeter, York, and Margaret walked hand in hand in procession to Saint Paul's, and Henry (according to Hall's Chronicle)

promised so gently to entertain the Duke of York and his factors that all old grudges being not only inwardly forgotten but also outwardly forgiven should be the cause of perpetual love between them and their friends.

The fact that Henry was able to achieve even this impractical conciliation shows the reverence his piety commanded; but reverence was of little use against York's ambition or Margaret's determination to secure the throne for her son. At Ludlow on the Welsh border there was a Lancastrian victory, chiefly because of the treachery of men wearing the Warwick colors. Richard of York escaped to Ireland with his second son Edmund; his eldest son Edward went with Warwick to Calais; and his younger sons George and Richard were taken prisoner with their mother Cicely. Warwick raised an army in Calais, and in 1460 defeated the Lancastrians at Northampton; the King was taken prisoner and Margaret fled with her son to Harlech in Wales. As these two turns of fortune showed, neither side had either the military strength to defeat the other or the moral strength to retain its own supporters.

Warwick assured the King that he would not lose his throne, but York came back from Ireland and (says Hall) "with a bold countenance entered into the chamber of the Peers and sat down in the throne royal." Here Parliament had the final word, refusing to accept

York as King, and finally it was agreed that Henry should continue to reign for his lifetime and that on his death the succession should pass to York and his heirs.

Henry seems to have been willing to accept this solution in the interests of peace (perhaps also of justice, if we are to take seriously his remark on the conception of his son Edward), but Margaret was not. She assembled a formidable army and defeated York and executed him on the battlefield. His head was put over the gate of the city of York, crowned with a paper garland. But Margaret's triumph was as short-lived as all triumphs were in that sad time. In 1461 Richard's twenty-year-old eldest son, Edward Earl of March, defeated the Lancastrians at Mortimer's Cross. This army was led by the King's stepfather, Owen Tudor, and his son Jasper. Owen was captured and beheaded; "That head shall lie on the stock that was wont to lie in Queen Catherine's lap." Jasper lived to ensure the ultimate triumph of the Lancastrian cause by devoting himself to the safety of a young nephew of his, now only six years old, one Henry Tudor. Warwick, although he was defeated again at St. Albans—a battle remarkable for the behavior of the King, who sat under an oak tree singing to himself—still reached London before Margaret, and thus settled the loyalty of the Londoners. Against the poor mad King, dominated by his detested French wife, he could set himself, the mighty Kingmaker, and the splendid young Edward of March. Moreover, he could rely on the blessing of the Church, for the Bishop of Exeter was yet another Neville. As a popular orator put it, the people of England could "walk in a new vineyard, and make a gay garden with this fair white rose the Earl of March."

But Henry VI was still at large in the vineyard, and his forces met Warwick and Edward of March at Towton in 1461. His numerical advantage might have been of more use if he had not been piously reluctant to fight on Palm Sunday. He wandered about making aimless efforts to encourage his men, while Edward of March dismounted and killed his horse as a token that he would not flee the field. A defection from the Lancastrian ranks brought victory to the Yorkists, and so great was the slaughter that the snow was stained blood-red and the river ran with red waters. Margaret and the King escaped into Scotland, where Henry put his signature to an absurd alliance. And Hall wrote of his signature, "It was as long as the whole sheet of parchment, the worst-shaped letters and the worst put together that I ever saw."

This was, in effect, the end of Henry VI's reign, though his life was to go sadly on for another ten years. He was even to have another brief spell on the throne, as a helpless pawn. The truth was that he was now hated in his own kingdom, not for himself but for the ruthless ambition of his wife Margaret, and his people turned with relief from him to the glorious sun of York. For all his piety and humility, and for all his placid conviction of his right to the throne, he had never made any attempt at the real work of ruling, letting others act for him in time of peace, and in time of war all too obviously escaping into flights of madness. At the end of his life, when he was a helpless prisoner, he made a statement that in its saintly blindness almost excuses every rebel against his power:

My father had been King of England, possessing his crown in peace all through his realm [his education, we see, had not included history]; my grandfather had been King of the same realm. And I, when a boy in the cradle, had been without any interval crowned in peace and approved as King by the whole realm, and wore the crown for well-nigh forty years, every lord doing royal homage to me and swearing fealty as they had done to my forefathers; so I may say with the Psalmist, The lines are fallen to me in a pleasant place, yea, I have a goodly heritage.

House of

YORK

EDWARD IV
1471–1483

✿

Born at Rouen in 1441.

Son of Richard Duke of York and Cicely Neville of Raby, and thus thrice descended from Edward III: by his grandfather Richard Earl of Cambridge, who was son to Edmund Langley Duke of York; by his paternal grandmother Anne Mortimer, who was great-great-grand-daughter of Lionel Duke of Clarence; and by his mother Cicely Neville, who was grand-daughter of John of Gaunt and Catherine Swynford.

Proclaimed and crowned in 1461, but had to dispute his claim with the Lancastrians led by Margaret of Anjou, wife of his predecessor Henry VI, until the battle of Tewkesbury 1471.

Married in 1464 (though the marriage was probably bigamous) Elizabeth Grey née Woodville, by whom he had:

Edward Prince of Wales, later Edward V;

Richard Duke of York, born 1473, died probably with his elder brother in the Tower, on a date and for reasons unknown;

Elizabeth, known as Elizabeth of York, married in 1486 Henry VII, thus uniting the contending families of York and Lancaster;

Catherine, born 1479, married Sir William Courtney, from whom the Courtney family descended.

Died at Westminster in April 1483 and was buried at Windsor.

EDWARD IV

dward IV did not bely his promise; he proved to be one of the most popular of the English Kings. He was tall and handsome, a courageous soldier, courtly and yet easy of access; above all, after the meek abstinences of Henry VI, he had a tremendous zest for living. He enjoyed enormous meals, he drank his courtiers under the table, he seduced—with one notable exception—every woman who took his eye. His reign was greatly troubled by the continuation of the Wars of the Roses, but it still brought England stability and prosperity. He was one of the few English Kings to discover how to rule without dependence on Parliament, but this did no harm to the country because—perhaps because it did not suit his temperament —he never became tyrannical or detached from reality. His was not a great mind, but it nevertheless attained one idea wholly novel to his time: that the crown needed above all financial stability, and that stability now lay in the hands, not of the factious barons, but of the loyal and wealthy merchants, whose interests, like his own, were in peace. It was in Edward IV's reign that the middle classes began their rise to power. As one modern historian has pointed out, Edward did not frequent the houses of the great merchants simply for the sake of seducing their wives and daughters.

Can we put this down to the fact that it is extremely unlikely that Edward was a Plantagenet at all? Cicely Neville was said to have consoled herself during her husband's many absences with one Blackburn, the captain of her archers, and Edward bore no resemblance at all to his brothers, and both of them hinted at his illegitimacy. Since Cicely's own descent was splendidly middle-class (she was the great-niece of Geoffrey Chaucer), the situation gains interest when we consider that we have no idea who fathered Edward's rival, the son of Margaret of Anjou wife of Henry VI. Louis XI of France, a rarity in Kings of France by his wit, referred to his fellow-monarch as the *fils d'archier.*

Edward IV's coronation, on June 29, 1462, was spectacular, but one great figure was absent: Richard Neville of Warwick, the Kingmaker. His absence was significant, and not only because he was pursuing Margaret of Anjou. Margaret's supporters still held out, notably Jasper Tudor Earl of Pembroke, who was protecting a young nephew of his; but Edward's true danger was within his own party. He was only twenty-one, and like most men of his kind he was lazy until roused. While the Kingmaker fought and negotiated, Edward feasted, hunted, and pursued the prettiest girls. Louis XI said, "They tell me you have two rulers in England, Monsieur de Ouarouique and another whose name I have forgotten." Monsieur de Warwick wanted an alliance with France to deprive Margaret of Continental support, and after some demur, Edward sent him to France to negotiate for the hand of Bonne of Savoy: It was only in France that Warwick discovered that he was on a fool's errand; Edward was already married.

While he was hunting, the King had been approached by a certain Dame Elizabeth Grey (born Woodville); she was the widow of a Lancastrian knight killed at Saint Albans, and had a petition for the restoration of her property. She was (says Hall)

a woman more of formal countenance than of excelling beauty, yet of such beauty and favour that with her sober demeanour, lovely looking, and feminine smiling (neither too wanton nor too humble), beside her tongue so eloquent and her wit so pregnant, she was able to ravish the mind of a mean person, when she allured and made subject to her the heart of so great a King.

Edward no doubt expected an easy conquest, but Elizabeth (even on one occasion with his dagger at her throat) said calmly that "she knew herself unworthy to be a Queen, but valued her honour more than to be a concubine." Edward agreed to marry her.

His mother Cicely, horrified by the idea, urged that he be betrothed to a Lady Elizabeth Lucy, by whom he had two children (there is some evidence that he had in fact married her, and later another valid marriage was alleged to an Eleanor Butler; presumably these were passing mistresses with whom he had gone through some reassuring ceremony). Perhaps Edward intended this marriage to be of the same kind, for it was celebrated in secret and he visited Elizabeth only by stealth when he was hunting. But when the council pressed him for a decision on the marriage with Bonne of Savoy he revealed what he had done. The old nobility, including Edward's brothers George of Clarence and Richard of Gloucester, were deeply shocked; and not unreasonably, for Elizabeth turned out to be insufferable both as Queen and as woman. She was five years older than Edward, a Lancastrian, with no less than five brothers, seven sisters, and two children to be provided for, and her arrogance alienated even the most loyal of the nobles. She lived in magnificent state, allowing no one to sit or eat in her presence, keeping Edward's sister and her own mother for hours on their knees in her presence.

But the real disaster of the marriage was that Warwick took it as a mortal insult. He had, after all, put Edward on his throne, and was described by Philippe de Commynes as "almost the King's father." But he held his hand; indeed in the same year, 1464, he made a great contribution to the cause of York by capturing Henry VI. The poor mad old man had been wandering the roads of northern England disguised as a black monk, and did not seem greatly disturbed to find himself a prisoner in the Tower; he passed his time in prayer, not much troubling himself to wash or change his linen. Edward gave thanks for his capture at the shrine of that other lice-ridden saint, Thomas Beckett, and set himself to gently loosening Warwick's grip on the kingdom.

In spite of the Queen's pretensions, Edward's marriage to the daughter of a mere knight had endeared him to the rich middle class, and in essence the conflict between him and Warwick was that between a businessman and an old-fashioned statesman. Edward married the Woodvilles to nobles, but not of Warwick's kin; he made her father, now Earl Rivers, Lord Treasurer, and dismissed Warwick's uncle to make room for him; he proposed to marry his sister Margaret to Charles Duke of Burgundy where Warwick preferred a French alliance. Warwick responded by quietly circulating the old rumors of Edward's illegitimacy, and tempting the foolish George of Clarence with a marriage to his own daughter Isabel. Edward countered by having the Pope forbid the marriage, dismissing Warwick's brother George from his office as chancellor, and having the Pope deny him his Cardinal's hat.

At this Warwick lost his temper. "Did you see the traitors round the King?" he raged to the French ambassador, and retired to sulk in his castle of Middleham. Edward's success, however, was not entire, for the Burgundians were proving the better businessmen with the marriage contract between Margaret and their Duke. He could conclude the negotiations only by raising an enormous sum, which he got from Parliament by pretending it was destined for the invasion of France. Margaret and Charles of Burgundy were married in great splendor in 1469, and Margaret was to cause much mischief in England in years to come by her support of the cause of York long after it had gone down.

The intelligent Louis XI of France foresaw that, sooner or later, Edward would have to satisfy Parliament's expectations of a war against him, but his advances to Warwick were courteously rebuffed, and his support of an invasion by the loyal Lancastrian, Jasper Tudor of Pembroke, ended in disaster for Jasper. Edward's popularity was beginning to decline, for the astute Burgundians were attempting to ruin the English cloth trade, and he was also embroiled with the merchants of the Hanseatic League in the Baltic ports. But it was too late to consider reconciliation with Warwick. A revolt was raised in the north by a secret supporter of Warwick's, repeating the story of Edward's illegitimacy; Cicely Neville was said to be prepared to confirm it, and her second son, George of Clarence, so-called rightful King, went with Warwick to Calais, where at last he married Isabel Neville. Only Richard of Gloucester stayed faithful to his brother.

Warwick invaded England and at Olney in Buckinghamshire surrounded Edward's forces. With a neat sense of justice he left it to his brother George Neville to take Edward prisoner and escort him to Warwick Castle.

Warwick now had three possible Kings under his hand: Henry VI wasting away in the Tower, Edward IV in comfortable confinement in Warwick, and his son-in-law, the feckless Clarence, at large. He could trust none of them, and he had no claim himself to the throne, and when the Duke of Burgundy tried to foster rebellion in London he found himself in the foolish position of being able to crush it only by using Edward's name. Finally, he had to come to some sort of terms with him; the Croyland Chronicle describes them as "peace and entire oblivion of all grievances upon both sides," which was hardly likely. In fact, the quarrel had to be fought out to the end, and Edward, now at full liberty, still had his Woodville kin and

Richard of Gloucester to support him. Soon Warwick and Clarence were in flight yet again, and forced to seek refuge with Louis XI of France.

Louis was delighted to have the great rebel at his side. This little, bent, shabby figure, known to his friends as the "universal spider" (he wore a cap with the images of saints in the band, and in swearing a solemn oath took care to put his hand on the wrong saint), was hatching a plot that any reasonable man would have called impossible. He meant to ally Warwick with his sworn enemy Margaret of Anjou.

He brought them together, the dispossessed Queen and the man who had dispossessed her, and she left Warwick kneeling at her feet for a full quarter of an hour before she would even acknowledge his presence; but the agreement was made. Warwick was to return Henry VI to the throne of England and Margaret's son Edward was to marry his daughter Anne. They had Jasper Tudor and George of Clarence to support them, though as Clarence now saw himself no longer heir to the throne his loyalty was less reliable. The one thing that Margaret would not do was place her son Edward in Warwick's care. It was an understandable refusal, but it was to prove their undoing.

Meantime Edward, content to have Warwick out of the way, says Hall

left all purveyance for defence alone, and rode on hunting, hawking, and using all manner of pastimes with ladies and damsels for his disport and solace.

In 1470, when Warwick landed, he marched north, but delayed, while Warwick proclaimed him "usurper, oppressor, and destroyer." It took Warwick eleven days to conquer England. Edward could not at first believe it; but when he heard that George Neville was advancing to trap him at Donaster he quietly slipped out of the room "as if to make his water," and rode off to take ship on the Norfolk coast. He had a hard journey, "in the greatest jeopardy that it beseemed a prince to be in," and eventually arrived in Holland.

Philippe de Commynes, who as well as a historian was a member of Louis XI's council, said contemptuously of him: "What excuse could he find, after suffering this great loss through his own fault, but to say, I had not thought it could happen!" Warwick's recorded utterances were no more noble; his explanation of his rebellion was that Edward had "envied our house and tried every day to lessen our honour, as if he had given it to us and we had not raised him to royal power and authority."

Warwick, like Simon de Montfort before him, found it easier to conquer than to rule. He could wield the royal power only through Henry VI, whom George Neville, when he went to the Tower to fetch him, found "not worshipfully arrayed as a prince and not so cleanly kept as such a prince should be." They rode from the Tower to Saint Paul's; Henry was wearing a long blue gown that had once been Edward IV's, and the banners in the streets were not the Red Rose of Lancaster but the Bear and Ragged Staff of Warwick.

Henry VI was "the mere shadow and pretence of a King," "as mute as a crowned calf," and to arouse popular enthusiasm Warwick needed the young Prince Edward; but Prince Edward was with his mother in France. There is a tale (which does not seem altogether likely) that the young boy who did come to London, and of whom Henry VI said, "Lo, this is he to whom both we and our adversary shall give room and place," was not Prince Edward but the fifteen-year-old nephew of Jasper of Pembroke, Henry Tudor. Margaret would not trust Warwick so far as to bring Prince Edward to him, and the rich middle class refused to be placated. They liked the Burgundian alliance, which if it had not fulfilled all its promise had still brought prosperity; Parliament refused to sanction war against Burgundy, and without this commitment Louis XI would do no more for Warwick. Waiting at the court of the Duke of Burgundy was Edward IV. Duchess Margaret was always a firm supporter of her own family, and Duke Charles needed the support of England against France. In March, 1471, Edward landed in England.

He had, he declared, no designs on the throne and meant only to recover his own Duchy of York; but this was soon forgotten. The loyal Richard of Gloucester was with him, and on the Banbury road they came face to face with George of Clarence, with 4,000 men meant to reinforce Warwick. Richard of Gloucester rode forward alone and spoke to Clarence; Clarence embraced Edward, his men exchanged their red roses for white, and the three brothers set out at full speed for London.

George Neville was in London, parading poor mad Henry VI through the streets in an effort to gain public support. Finally, he opened the gates and begged Edward's pardon. Edward granted it readily; he was reunited with his wife, who had borne him a son and heir in his absence (safely in the Sanctuary at Westminster Abbey), and for once in his life did not linger, collecting an army and marching in search of Warwick. As so often, Henry VI went in the baggage train.

The battle of Barnet was one of the few battles of the time that were not decided by a commander's changing sides in the middle; it was decided by a Yorkist's only imagining that one had. Warwick was fighting on foot, and was killed trying to struggle back to his mount. It was perhaps an undistinguished end for a Kingmaker, but, with the exception of his first venture with Edward of York, Warwick's kingmaking had been actuated by nothing but personal pique; when he had power, he did not know what to do with it, and what finally defeated him was Edward IV's control of the middle classes, the one weapon he could never have wielded himself.

On April 19, 1471, Warwick's body was exposed to public view in Saint Paul's, and on that day Margaret of Anjou at last landed in England with Prince Edward. Against all reason she decided to join Jasper Tudor's still-intact army at Gloucester. But the city refused to open its gates to her, and King Edward was at her heels.

At the battle of Tewkesbury the Lancastrian turncoat was detected and killed before he could act, but the confusion led to a rout and massacre of the Lancastrians. Prince Edward was presumably killed on the field, though there is an unlikely story that he was "suddenly murdered and piteously manquelled" in the King's presence by Clarence and Gloucester. Margaret of Anjou was held prisoner for some years, but finally allowed to return to France, where she died in 1482. Jasper Tudor fled the country, taking with him young Henry Tudor. There remained now only Henry VI, whom the Yorkists could no longer afford to leave alive. One account says that he died "of pure displeasure and melancholy to hear of his son's death," but it is much more probable that he was murdered.

Characteristically, Edward returned to his old pursuits. The Queen was pregnant again, court life gay and slothful, and the administration of the kingdom left to the loyal and hard-working Richard Duke of Gloucester. In poverty and disgrace in London, Richard found the young widow of Margaret of Anjou's son Prince Edward, Anne Neville, daughter and co-heiress of the Kingmaker. They had been friends since childhood, and Richard asked the King for permission to marry her. It was granted, in spite of the opposition of the foolish Clarence (who hoped to inherit the Warwick property; Richard generously gave him the larger part of it).

There was still to be settled Edward's promise, both to Parliament and to Charles of Burgundy, that he would go to war against France; trade was doing well, but military prestige a little lacking. Edward sent Louis a princely letter of defiance, which that true Frenchman, Commynes, said was in such "fine language and elegant style I believe no Englishman could have had a hand in composing it." Edward landed with his army in Calais in July, 1475, only to find that Duke Charles expected him to march half across France instead of attacking on the spot in Normandy. The astute Louis XI, as soon as Duke Charles's back was turned, proposed to pay £15,000 down and £50,000 annually for Edward's withdrawal. Duke Charles rode hastily back to storm at his brother-in-law, but Edward had already calculated that Louis's money would more than compensate for the loss of the Burgundian trade. In an even more astute move, Louis sent 300 cartloads of wine as a gift to the English camp when he met Edward to discuss the Peace of Picquigny. Richard of Gloucester thought the treaty a shameful and mercenary betrayal of a true ally, but resigned himself to it, and the English left France.

The remainder of Edward's reign was passed in peace and prosperity. He was a lazy ruler, but a sensible and even wise one, and he had strong supporters in Richard of Gloucester, and an old drinking companion of his, Hastings. The only real trouble was the incorrigibly foolish Clarence, who was in fact lucky not to be in the Tower. When his wife Isabel died in childbirth, he attempted two matches with foreign princesses, and his household was involved in a plot by witchcraft against the King; finally, in 1478 he at last put an end to his brother's patience by being discovered behind an insurrection in Cambridgeshire, and was brought to trial on a charge of treason. His actual death is something of a mystery, for tradition has it that he was drowned in a butt of malmsey wine. Maybe he was given the privilege of drinking himself to death, but "whatever was the manner of it," wrote Hall, "justice was executed on him."

Throughout these last years, Edward encouraged Caxton's new printing press, began the collection of a rich library, and encouraged the building of the great chapels of Henry VI's college in Cambridge and of Windsor Castle. Elizabeth bore him yet another child, and he grew fat, but unimpaired in his appetite for living. More and more he relied on Richard of Gloucester for the business of government. In the spring of 1483 he was suddenly taken ill, with something we cannot identify, though a heart attack seems possible. Unable to sit up, he carried out a not unworthy last act, reconciling his old friend Hastings with an enemy, and thus died. He was only forty-one.

His reign had been marked by violent reversals of fortune, but, in sum, it had brought remarkable stability and prosperity to his country. For all his faults, he was a just and generous man, and perhaps his very laziness protected him from excesses of ambition like those of Margaret of Anjou. But his chief wisdom had been in the sensible conviction that the future lay not with the futile nobles who had no more in their heads than family pride and feudal honor, but with the merchants who could bring prosperity to a country.

It must be added that he could not have done all that he did to bring back to his people confidence in the monarchy if he had not had the loyal and capable Richard of Gloucester at his back; and that, in dying so young, he left a thirteen-year-old son surrounded by men who still thought in terms of the Wars of the Roses.

EDWARD V
1483

❁

Born in the Sanctuary, Westminster, 1470.
Eldest son of Edward IV and his wife Elizabeth Woodville.
Died probably in the Tower of London, on a date and for
  reasons unknown.

EDWARD V

dward V was the son of Edward IV of York and Elizabeth Woodville. He was born in sanctuary at Westminster Abbey in 1470, while his father was recovering his throne from the Lancastrians; his birth was very probably illegitimate, his father having married secretly at least once before the union with his mother. He reigned for two and a half months in the year 1483, and we do not know how he died.

In fact we know practically nothing at all about him, unless we like to believe such courtly eulogies as this one of Dominic Mancini, an Italian monk who witnessed the events of 1483:

In word and deed he gave so many proofs of his liberal education, of polite, nay rather scholarly attainments far beyond his age. He had a special knowledge of literature that enabled him to discourse elegantly, to understand fully, and to declaim most excellently from any work, verse or prose, that came into his hands.

Allowing for a courtier's flattery, and remembering that he was brought up in the last happy years of his father's reign, we may believe that he was a well-trained little Renaissance prince. But he ws a thirteen-year-old boy in a time when weak Kings meant anarchy, and a Woodville in an age that had learned to hate that family.

Edward IV had known this, and on his deathbed had given the boy, as his sole protector, the only man who had remained loyal against every stress: his brother Richard Duke of Gloucester. But Edward IV's death was sudden and unexpected, and Edward V was at Ludlow on the Welsh Marches, separated by the breadth of England from his protector, and in the company of his Woodville uncle Earl Rivers. In London the Woodville faction denied Richard of Gloucester his sole protectorship by packing the council with their men, though they had not the strength to exclude him altogether; then they had Rivers bring the boy south, hoping to have him crowned in Westminster before Richard arrived.

Richard, however, had been warned by Hastings, Edward IV's old friend, and moved so quickly that Rivers could only send him a courteous invitation to join the young King on his progress to London and then attempt to give him the slip. Trying to find his King, Richard found instead his friend and distant kinsman Henry Stafford Duke of Buckingham. The Staffords were of the royal blood, being descended from that Thomas of Woodstock, son of Edward III, who was murdered by Richard II, and Henry Stafford's mother was a Margaret Beaufort—not that Margaret of the elder Beaufort line who was the mother of young Henry Tudor sometimes Earl of Richmond, but a cousin of the younger line. Henry of Buckingham appears to have considered himself (with a fair justice) next in line to the throne after Edward IV's two sons and Richard of Gloucester, and was an inveterate enemy of the Woodvilles. He seems to have persuaded Richard that the Woodville power must be broken now, and in the morning Rivers and his men were arrested and Richard and Buckingham rode to find the King. It was a stormy meeting; young Edward defended his mother's family, but when Richard reminded him of his own loyalty to his father and promised equal loyalty to the son, the boy broke into tears. If he was as intelligent as the courtiers made out he may very well have wept at the rarity of the quality he so much needed.

The three of them, Edward V, Richard the Protector, and Buckingham rode toward London, and panic seized the Woodvilles. Elizabeth and her younger children (they included the next heir, Edward V's brother Richard of York, now ten) returned to the Sanctuary in Westminster. Richard entered peaceably, arranging with the Lord Mayor for an early coronation of the young King and settling him in the Tower (which was the royal residence as well as a state prison). These preparations were only interrupted by the discovery, at the beginning of June, of a plot to oust Richard from the protectorship.

It was naturally a Woodville plot, but Richard seems to have been shaken profoundly by the fact that the Woodvilles had been joined by his and his brother Edward IV's old friend Lord Hastings. Also implicated was Edward IV's middle-class mistress Jane Shore, whom Hastings had now taken to his bed and who had supposedly attempted to take Richard's life by witchcraft.

According to the colorful account of the chroniclers, Richard entered the council chamber and asked Hastings what punishment should be given to "those that compass and imagine the destruction of me." Taken by surprise, Hastings stammered the courtly opinion that they should be treated as traitors, and Richard had him taken from the room, given a few minutes for prayer and confession, and executed. This account is probably grossly exaggerated, but contains the truth that Hastings's defection had shocked Richard into the realization that his protectorship was not viable.

He had until now taken no part in court intrigues, insulated from them by his work as Edward IV's deputy and the wholly justified trust his brother had placed in him. Now he saw his years of work at peril from the irrepressible, and to him incomprehensible, ambition and selfishness of the Woodvilles; Richard had been born to his position and had not had to struggle for it. The only loyal friend appeared to be Buckingham, and the only sensible advice Buckingham's: to put aside the child-King and pass the succession to the next heir.

This was the easier to do in that it had always been an open secret that Edward IV's marriage with Elizabeth Woodville had been bigamous (even discounting that other equally open secret that Edward IV himself had not been fathered by his mother Cicely Neville's husband Richard Duke of York). In a sermon preached at Saint Paul's Cross on June 22, 1483, the text was "Bastard slips shall not take deep root," and two days later Buckingham enlarged on this theme at Guildhall, in a speech whose delivery was so impressive that, as Fabyan notes, he did not once pause to spit. "Woe is that realm that hath a child to their king," he declared, which to his hearers was a matter not of opinion but of fact and, to many, of experience. On June 28, Parliament was called to hear Richard of Gloucester's claim to the throne. It was asserted that the wicked Woodvilles had brought about Edward IV's marriage by sorcery (which Elizabeth had, by the oldest sorcery in the world); that at the time of his marriage to her "the said King Edward was and stood married and troth-plight to one Dame Eleanor Butler, daughter of the old Earl of Shrewsbury." Unanimously, Lords and Commons both assented to Richard's claim. There is no doubt but that that claim was correct and the vote legal. Richard was the heir in blood and Parliament was choosing what it wanted, strong government, the end of the hated Woodvilles, and a man proved loyal and capable.

The next day Buckingham led a delegation of lords and citizens to request Richard formally to assume the crown. He made the traditional show of reluctance, but assented, and was proclaimed King Richard III; and so ended the brief reign of Edward V.

The boy never reappeared. He and his brother and heir Richard Duke of York had been lodged with royal state in the Tower, and they never emerged from it. It is unlikely that we shall ever know what happened to them there. We do know what did not happen. They were not murdered by Richard's henchman Tyrell, for that story was invented much later by the Tudors. The most likely murderer was Buckingham, who was pursuing his own devious plots. From what we know of Richard III's character it is unlikely that he would have murdered his brother's children, and their lives did not in fact trouble him during his short reign; his enemies were different. It is possible that the boys lived on in obscure captivity and were put out of the way eventually by Henry VII; it is even possible that they died a natural death. Like their distant cousin, that other Edward once Prince of Wales, they were victims of their time, and the unhappy legend that still haunts the Tower stairways is condemnatory not of one man but of many.

RICHARD III
Crookback
1483-1485

❁

Born at Fotheringay, October 1450.

Third son of Richard Duke of York and Cicely Neville of
Raby, brother of Edward IV.

Married in 1472 Anne Neville of Warwick, daughter of
Warwick the King-Maker and widow of Henry VI's son
Edward Prince of Wales. Anne Neville died in March
1485, and had one son, Edward Prince of Wales, who
was born 1473 and died 1484.

Killed in battle on Bosworth Field, August 1485, by the
forces of the Lancastrian claimant, Henry Tudor of
Richmond, later Henry VII, and buried in the Abbey of
the Gray Friars, Leicester.

RICHARD III
Crookback

n the reign of Edward IV there is one figure that stands apart from the self-indulgent King and the blindly ambitious courtiers. Hard-working, honorable, generous, austere, above all selflessly loyal to his brother, Richard of Gloucester is one of the few attractive figures of the times.

It is therefore a shock to find him transformed into King Richard III, variously described by the chroniclers as "swollen with rage like a serpent that has fed on noxious herbs," "little of stature, ill-featured of limbs, crook-backed, hard-favoured of visage; close and secret, a deep dissimuler, lowly of countenance, arrogant of heart, outwardly companionable where he inwardly hated, not letting to kiss whom he sought to kill," and, most violently, "a scorpion mild in countenance, stinging in the tail, a monster and a tyrant, born under a hostile star and perishing like Anti-Christ." What is even odder is that this last quotation comes from John Rous, in the second edition of his history of the Earls of Warwick, and that the first edition read somewhat differently. He then described Richard as "a mighty prince and especial good lord, in his realm full commendably punishing offenders of the laws, especially oppressors of the commons, and cherishing those that were virtuous, by the which discreet guiding he got great thanks and love of all his subjects great and poor."

The explanation of all this is to be found in the next reign. Richard had an extremely good legal claim to the throne, his successor Henry VII an extremely poor one, and the House of York had to be blackened to justify the success of Lancaster. Edward IV must be left, for by then his daughter was Queen; so one of the few loyal and capable men of the time had to be turned into a monster.

It is difficult now to understand why anyone ever believed the Tudor historians so much did they overstate their case. At the end of the last century documents contemporary with his reign were found to contain another story, and after that there was a danger that the reaction would present us with something not much nearer the truth than the Tudor picture. Now at last, however, there emerges a Richard III both humanly credible and consistent with the available evidence: a ruler no more ruthless than Edward IV or Henry VII, and like them ruthless only with good reason and without enjoyment; a man probably more admirable personally than either of them, honorable, just, unselfishly devoted to his duty; but, after all, fatally flawed as a King by his blind conservatism. Richard was an aristocrat, both by birth and by temperament, and could not understand, as his brother had, that the prosperity of England lay in the hands of the middle classes.

Richard's coronation was the most lavish and spectacular seen in that century. Northumberland, come fresh from the executions at Pontefract, carried the Sword of Mercy; Lord Stanley, who was to betray Richard to his death at Bosworth, carried the Constable's mace; Buckingham, who was to attempt to dethrone him, carried his train, and Margaret Beaufort, mother of the man who was to succeed him, that of his wife. After his coronation, Richard went on a royal progress through his kingdom. He rewarded those who had helped him, but his first public acts showed generosity and a wish to help the new learning. The universities were especially favored, Henry VI reburied at Windsor, and Richard's ten-year-old son Edward invested as Prince of Wales.

Meantime, a most uneasy alliance was forming itself against him. Since York was victorious, the Woodvilles were prepared to change sides, and the most vigorous and resourceful of the remaining Lancastrians was to their hand. This was Margaret Beaufort, descended from John of Gaunt, who had married as her first husband that Edmund Tudor Earl of Richmond who was the eldest son of Queen Catherine de Valois and Owen Tudor, and had a son Henry Tudor, who was now the Lancastrian claimant. (It is quite possible that Henry Tudor knew nothing of his own claim, since his uncle Jasper had taken him abroad after the battle of Tewkesbury, and he was now half-prisoner, half-guest in the Duchy of Brittany.) This curious alliance needed a strong leader, and it found one in the man to whom a great part of the troubles of the times can be traced—Henry Stafford Duke of Buckingham.

Buckingham's behavior toward Richard III makes that of Warwick the Kingmaker toward Edward IV seem human and understandable. Edward had, after all, deeply offended the Kingmaker; Richard had done no more harm to Buckingham than to become his King. Even that Tudor historian Sir Thomas More (whose unfinished history of Richard III should seriously have affected his claim to sanctity) saw through Buckingham, and wrote of him:

I have heard some that say they saw it, that when the crown was first set upon King Richard's head, the Duke of Buckingham could not abide the sight, but wried his head the other way.

Having used Richard to destroy the Woodville succession, Buckingham presumably meant to use a Woodville-Tudor alliance to destroy Richard, and in the confusion to seize the crown himself.

The plan was that risings should break out in the south, converging on London, Buckingham advance from the west, and the Duke of Brittany land an army on the South Coast. Richard was in Lincoln, without an army, when he heard of Buckingham's treachery, and he wrote to his chancellor in London:

Here, loved be God, all is well and truly determined, and for to resist the malice of him that had best cause to be true, the Duke of Buckingham, the most untrue creature living; whom with God's Grace we shall not be long till that we subdue his malice.

Perhaps another flaw in Richard was his inclination to believe that others shared his own standards of honor. He marched south with his supporters, one of whom was Stanley, Margaret Beaufort's third husband, who was prudently cultivating both sides; and then found that the threat had disappeared. It had been a foolish conspiracy. The Duke of Brittany, whose support had been assumed because of his enmity to France, had merely lent young Henry Tudor a few ships in which he had prospected the South Coast and then wisely turned back. As for Buckingham's army, no one had joined it, and he himself was betrayed by a servant for money in Salisbury. He begged for a meeting with Richard, but Richard contemptuously refused his one-time friend, and Buckingham was beheaded in the marketplace of Salisbury.

The whole foolish affair had lasted barely two weeks, and Richard felt that he could afford to be merciful. Only ten men were executed, the common people spared, and Margaret Beaufort's only punishment was to have her lands handed over to her husband Stanley. Richard returned in triumph to London and his real concerns. He wrote about this time of his concern

that every person that find himself aggrieved, oppressed, or unlawfully wronged, do make a bill of his complaint and put it to His Highness, and he shall be heard and without delay have such convenient remedy as shall accord with his laws; for His Grace is utterly determined that all his true subjects shall live in rest and quiet, and peaceably enjoy their lands, livelodes, and good, according to the laws of this land, which they be naturally born to inherit.

Parliament assembled in January, 1484. Richard's son was named heir apparent, the judicial system overhauled, juries freed from intimidation, the system of bail enlarged, and a bill passed to prevent fraudulent property transfers—quiet stabilizing work of the kind Richard had been doing for his brother for years. With considerable tact he not only asked for no subsidy, but also abandoned Edward IV's habit of raising money by forced "voluntary loans."

In March he and his wife went north, leaving their son behind. He took the precaution first of having the lords swear an oath of allegience to "Edward, the King's only son, as their supreme lord, in case anything should happen to his father." The case was to be otherwise; in Nottingham they had news from which Richard was never to recover.

This only son of his, in whom all the hopes of the royal succession, fortified with so many oaths, were centred, was seized with an illness of but short duration and died at Middleham Castle. You might have seen his father and mother in a state almost bordering on madness by reason of their sudden grief.

This was the end of Richard's hopes. His dearly loved wife Anne had borne him no more children, and though he had two illegitimate children born in his youth his standards of honor would not allow him to pass the succession to them when he had denied it to his brother's bastard children. His brother Clarence had a son, Edward Earl of Warwick, but he was simple-minded. Finally, Richard chose the line of his sister Elizabeth, who had married John de la Pole Duke of Suffolk. It was a mere gesture; a childless King could not long survive.

All that he could do now was put his defenses in order against the expected invasion by Henry Tudor. Henry was now with Charles

VIII of France, who had not forgotten that Richard had favored the Burgundians during Edward IV's reign, and in the spring of 1485 Richard had firm news that the invasion was planned for that summer.

On March 16, 1485, there was an eclipse of the sun, and on that day Queen Anne died. Richard was struck down with grief, and then enraged to hear the Woodville's latest rumor, that he had poisoned Anne to secure his kingdom by marrying Elizabeth of York. (The Woodvilles were not the Tudors' equal in invention; marrying his bastard niece would hardly have helped him.) He wrote angrily:

It is so that divers seditious and evil-disposed persons enforce themselves daily to sow seed of noise and disclaundre against our person, to abuse the multitude of our subjects and avert their minds from us.

But he had to avert his subjects' minds from him himself to raise money for defense. He did his best to counter the Lancastrian propaganda, asserting that Henry Tudor was a pawn of France (which might have been true), that he was a bastard in the maternal line (which was true), and a bastard in the paternal line (which was not true). But his real danger, as he knew, was among his own nobles, and his suspicions centered on Thomas Lord Stanley, Margaret Beaufort's third husband. Stanley professed loyalty, but in July asked permission to visit his family in Lancashire. Richard had to let him go, but took the precaution of keeping his son Lord Strange as a hostage.

On the August 7, 1485, Henry Tudor landed at Milford Haven in Wales. Like the Conqueror, he knelt and kissed the sands as he came ashore, and as his banner he flew the Red Dragon of the old Kings of Wales.

He marched rapidly through Wales, gaining support as he went, while Richard, very doubtful about two of his absent commanders, Northumberland and Stanley, moved only slowly to meet him. He was, said Hall, "sore moved and broiled with melancholy and dolour, asking vengeance on them that contrary to their oath and promise had fraudulently deceived him." Northumberland joined him; but at the same time Stanley was secretly with Henry, where, wrote Polydore Vergil,

taking one another by the hand and yielding mutual salutation, they entered in counsel in what sort to arraign battle with King Richard if the matter should come to strokes.

Stanley could not openly declare for Henry, since Richard held his son Lord Strange, but when the enemies met, on Sunday, August 21, at a spot now known as Bosworth Field, he drew up his men at a distance from both armies. Since no one wanted to fight on a Sunday, they camped that night and waited for the dawn of August 22. A mysterious warning was put into the hand of Richard's supporter, the Duke of Norfolk:

Jockey of Norfolk, be not bold,
For Dickon thy master is bought and sold.

Richard himself took station in his center, while Henry, who had no experience of battle, stayed in his rear. When Henry sent to ask Stanley to join them, Stanley merely replied that he was still making his dispositions.

As for Richard:

Knowing certainly that the day would either yield him a peaceable and quiet realm from thenceforward or else perpetually bereave him of the same, he came to the field with the Crown upon his head, that thereby he might either make a beginning or an end of his reign.

At an early stage in the fighting, Norfolk was killed, and his men began to waver. Richard sent to Northumberland to reinforce him, but Northumberland did not move. Richard sent to Stanley; Stanley did not budge. Richard was now hopelessly outnumbered, and saw only one course open to him. It was a course worthy of his own austere standards, and it could be called out-of-date if it had not come so very close to success. Followed by the knights of his household, Richard set himself to cut his way across the field to where Henry's Red Dragon stood at the Lancastrian rear and to kill his rival with his own hands.

He got to within a few feet of the Red Dragon before he was dragged from his horse. His little band of knights was killed and he himself struck by dozens of blows. "If I may speak truth to his honour," wrote Rous, "although small of body and weak in strength, he most valiantly defended himself as a noble knight to his last breath, saying *Treason! Treason! Treason!*"

Richard's last words were entirely correct. It was Lord Stanley, who had brought his men into battle as soon as he was sure it was safe, who took the crown from the dead King's helmet and put it on the head of Henry Tudor.

House of

TUDOR

HENRY VII
1485-1509

❂

Born in Pembroke Castle, Wales, in July 1455.

Son of Edmund Tudor Earl of Richmond (who was the eldest son of Owen Tudor and Catherine of France widow of Henry V) and Margaret Beaufort, great-grand-daughter of John of Gaunt and Catherine Swynford.

Proclaimed king after the death at Bosworth Field of Richard III, August 1485.

Married in January 1486 Elizabeth of York, elder daughter of Edward IV and Elizabeth Woodville, who died in childbirth in February 1503. Their surviving children were:

> Arthur Prince of Wales, born in 1486. In 1502 he married Catalina, known in England as Catherine of Aragon, daughter of Ferdinand of Aragon and Isabel of Castile, but died in April 1503. Catherine later married: Henry, later Henry VIII; Margaret, born in 1489, married in 1503 James IV King of Scots, who was killed at Flodden in 1513, by whom she had a son,
>> James V of Scots, born 1512 and died 1542. James's only child was by his second wife, Mary of Guise, Mary Stuart Queen of Scots, born 1542;

In 1514 Margaret Tudor married as her second husband Archibald Douglas Earl of Angus, whom she
divorced in 1528 to marry Lord Methven. By Angus
she had one daughter,

    Margaret Douglas. She married in 1554 Matthew
    Stuart Earl of Lennox, and had a son,

        Henry Stuart Lord Darnley, born 1545, who was
        to marry his cousin Mary Stuart Queen of Scots;
Mary, born 1498, who married first, in 1514, Louis XII
of France, who died in 1515; and secondly, in 1515,
Charles Brandon Duke of Suffolk, by whom she had
a daughter,

    Frances, who married in 1535 Henry Grey Mar-
    quess of Dorset and had a daughter,

        Jane Grey, who married in 1553 Guilford Dud-
        ley son of John Dudley Duke of Northumber-
        land and was proclaimed Queen by her father-
        in-law 7th July 1553 and executed 12th February
        1555.

Died at Richmond in April 1509 and was buried in his own
chapel in Westminster Abbey.

Henry VII had no legal claim to the throne, since his
descent from Edward III was illegitimate for purposes of
the royal succession.

Although Henry VII was the Lancastrian claimant, his
own family name was Tudor. After his marriage to Elizabeth of York he signalized the union of the two opposing
Houses by adopting as his badge the double Tudor Rose,
formed by joining the (single) Red Rose of Lancaster with
the (single) White Rose of York. Later heirs to the claim
of the House of York were often known as the White
Roses of England.

HENRY VII

I t is not likely that Thomas Lord Stanley, when on Bosworth Field in 1485 he took the crown of England from the head of Richard Plantagenet and put it on the head of Henry Tudor, understood that he was thus closing the Wars of the Roses; indeed, his record suggests that he was willing to uncrown any Kings available. It is not possible that anyone for many years yet could have foreseen that he had thus brought to a close the age of the great feudal nobles.

They had lingered long after society elsewhere was ready to do without them, long after the changes in their world had robbed their values of any good they might once have had. They went out in a blaze of incomprehension, reducing their own system to such a pitch of absurdity that they destroyed themselves in the process.

The destruction was literal. Very few of the old Anglo-Norman nobility were left alive in 1485, and those who did survive did not last long, especially if they had the least touch of royal blood. The problem of unwanted claimants to the throne had so far proved intractable, so the Tudors solved it by a method that was at least efficient: extermination. One by one the successive and hapless White Roses of England were hunted down and killed. It at least cost fewer lives than a rebellion, and many of them invited sacrifice by their inability to stop conspiring. Some of them were pitiable, but collectively they were better gone. Between that and the casualties of war there are very few families in England now who can trace their descent from before Bosworth, and these are of the lesser nobility. In 1625 Sir Ranulphe Crewe could write of the great medieval families:

Where is Bohun? Where is Mowbray? Where is Mortimer? Nay, which is more and most of all, where is Plantagenet? They are intombed in the urns and sepulchres of mortality.

—of Tudor mortality, which was high but salutary.

The Wars of the Roses had had their effect on the English commons, too. Once, they had had a stubborn reverence for their King, a reverence that was partly Christian, mostly Anglo-Saxon Christian, and hardly at all Norman. To the commons of England their King was different not in degree but in kind from all other men. As they put it, he had been hallowed by God; and they were capable of a remarkable degree of charity in recognizing that God's instruments are necessarily imperfect. As we would put it, meaning much the same thing, good government is only possible by consent, and in this the governed bear as much responsibility as the governors. It is unlikely that the commons would have consented to quite so much responsibility if they had not been upheld by that gift from the distant past, the old Anglo-Saxon laws that gave them confidence in the rights of every one of them.

But this view could not survive the unhallowed crownings and hallowed uncrownings of the Wars of the Roses. The process was slow, and interrupted by many other processes, but in the long run it was irreversible: the English of the future were going to require a King to be worthy of reverence before they gave it to him.

It is possible that Henry VII understood something of this; there are very few recorded instances when he did not thoroughly understand what was going on. But this did not appear on the morrow of Bosworth Field, when the inexperienced young man who received Richard Plantagenet's crown received it only as the nominal leader of his party. Henry Tudor attaindered Earl of Richmond did not appear promising material for kingship then. He was not quite twenty-nine, a tall man, not big but surprisingly strong, with a sallow skin, small blue eyes, and a big mouth tightly shut. It was often recorded that the "cheerfulness" of his expression, and the liveliness of his eyes, "especially when speaking," made him attractive. He had shown, in the years before Bosworth, some tenacity and discretion and courage, but nothing very remarkable; he was the Lancastrian claimant only because there was no one better, and it is likely that he knew nothing of his own claim when his mother Margaret Beaufort put it forward during Buckingham's stupid little revolt of 1484.

Indeed it is a sign of the coming end of the great houses that Lancaster had no better claimant. Henry's only English royal blood came from his mother, and hers was bastard as far as the succession was concerned. He knew nothing of war (he was kept quietly in the rear at Bosworth), nothing of the business of ruling, and nothing except by hearsay of England, for most of his life had been spent as a near-prisoner in Brittany.

He had been born in 1455, of a father two months dead and a mother not quite fourteen. Margaret Beaufort had remarried twice before her son was six and virtually disappeared from his life, and we may take it that to her he was little more than a political counter. He owed his survival almost entirely to his father's brother Jasper Tudor (whom, like many of this time, it is only possible to describe as sometimes Earl of Pembroke, since he was deprived of the title when the opposing faction was in power). Jasper was a valiant supporter of the Lancastrian cause who, after the battle of Tewkesbury in 1471, when Edward IV was finally victorious, wisely fled abroad with the young Henry. He had meant to seek refuge in France, whose King Louis XI was then at odds with England for its alliance with Burgundy. Luckily for Henry, they were driven off course to Brittany, which was then a duchy whose independence was threatened by France. By all the rules of international alliances, Duke François should have embarrassed his enemy France by handing over to France's enemy England, England's enemy Henry Tudor; but Duke François was that odd thing, a man of strict honor. To this stray young man he promised his protection, and he kept his promise. He kept it far better than Louis XI would have done, since in 1475 Louis made peace with Edward IV of England at Picquigny (with the help of some cartloads of wine), and would undoubtedly have handed over to him as well any young rival he had under his protection. Edward protested to Duke François that he only wanted his young kinsman in England because of the great love he bore for him, and once fooled him; Duke François insisted on sending Henry off with a returning English embassy. At the port of Saint Mâlo, Henry pretended to be too ill to travel, while his friends behind in Rennes argued his case with Duke François. This was not to be the only time the duke woke just in time to what was going on under his very nose. His treasurer, Peter Landois, was sent galloping after the English ambassadors, and reached Saint Mâlo in time to distract them while Henry escaped by hiding in the town. But Duke François remained true to his old-fashioned honor; Henry was under his protection, but was still kept in light confinement so that he could not conspire against Edward IV.

He did not need to conspire; his mother did all that. When Edward IV died, the duke considered himself free of his obligation, and without much enthusiasm gave Henry his freedom and some ships in 1484 to go to the help of his mother in their rebellion. Henry seems to have shared his lack of enthusiasm; he dutifully sailed, took a distant look at Plymouth, and then tranquilly returned to Brittany. But the situation in Brittany was now becoming complex, for Duke François's only heir was a little girl, the Duchess Anne, for whose hand—and land—both France and the Empire were quarrelling. The duke had fallen ill, and Henry's old savior, Peter Landois, proposed to hand over Henry to Richard III in exchange for men and money. The proposal somehow reached the ears of John Morton Bishop of Ely, then in exile for his part in Buckingham's rising, and he sent at once to warn Henry of his peril; Morton thereby made his own fortune, for Henry never forgot his gratitude for the warning. Henry went off one morning for a little exercise, slipped into a wood to change into servant's clothes, and with one man of his own as guide escaped into France. The thwarted Landois at once took as hostages the friends he had left behind; but at this point Duke François recovered a little, once more realized what was going on, and honorably sent Henry's friends to him, with apologies and compensation. Henry never forgot this debt either, and after the old Duke's death tried, though in vain, to help the little Duchess Anne.

These mild adventures, and this wholly un-English life, were the experience with which Henry Tudor faced his task of ruling England. Perhaps his very ignorance helped him to see things as they were and not as tradition taught him they should be. But, if he followed any tradition, it was that of the Yorkist Edward IV, the businessman who understood money, ignored aristocratic pretensions, and liked life to be peaceful and pleasant.

Henry had temperamental advantages over Edward IV. He was not lazy, and he was not tempted to entangle himself with the wrong women. He had no natural love of magnificence, though he understood the use of it. He had no false pride (it had probably been beaten out of him by his years as a pensioner). But chiefly he seems to have been by nature a worker: a man who sees his position not as a glory but as a job to be done.

Personally, he was ruthless when he thought it necessary, almost humorously mild when he did not. Like Edward IV he was easy and accessible to everyone, and liked and encouraged a rich and gay court, though unlike Edward his sexual life was irreproachable. The one vice that all contemporaries attribute to him was avarice, and he was certainly greedy for money. Together with John Morton Bishop of Ely, whom he made his chancellor, he explored every possible means of raising taxes, and made both of them disliked for it. But Henry's avarice was not personal but professional. Wealth had been terribly squandered in England during the Wars of the Roses, and wealth, above all, was what was needed to restore her.

Henry VII was crowned in Westminster on Sunday, October 30, 1485, and summoned his first Parliament for November 7. A feature of his grants in reward of his supporters is the number of unknown common people who received material benefits "in consideration of true and faithful service." Margaret Beaufort was royally endowed, and Jasper Tudor had unusually affectionate terms in his letters patent. The current White Rose, Clarence's son Warwick, who was mentally subnormal, was merely lodged in the Tower. To reconcile the two Roses, and to strengthen the Tudor's almost nonexistent claim to the throne, Henry had agreed to marry Elizabeth, daughter of Edward IV and Elizabeth Woodville. This was a problem legally, as Elizabeth had been pronounced illegitimate by Parliament, and she was also related to Henry (technically in the fourth degree, which the Church considered a bar to marriage). It must have been also a problem personally, since the couple could not have met at all until after Bosworth. We should not, in the case of a marriage so desirable dynastically, consider this a problem if it were not for the undoubted fact that the marriage was an entirely happy one. It is typical of Henry VII, though the mechanics of it escape us now, that what was necessary to his kingdom he somehow made happen; so we may assume modern ideas in this first of the modern English Kings, and believe that he was glad of four months' delay to do his courting.

In only one point was this most significant marriage unhappy. Of the seven children Elizabeth bore to Henry, only three, the second son Henry and the two girls Margaret and Mary, were to live to maturity. For some reason we do not know, the Tudor stock, so strong in other ways, was genetically weak, surviving in the direct male line for only two generations.

The battle of Bosworth had by no means finished the Yorkists, and to them Henry's accession seemed only another swing of the seesaw. The immediate heirs, Edward V and his brother Richard Duke of York, were in the Tower, and their sister Elizabeth had deserted the cause by marrying Henry VII; but Edward IV had no fewer than seven nephews by the marriage of his sister Elizabeth to John de la Pole Duke of Suffolk, and to her line Richard III had transferred the succession after the death of his own only son in 1484. In 1487 two of these nephews, John of Lincoln and Edmund of Suffolk, were involved in an absurd imposture that goes a long way toward reconciling us to the extermination of their foolish and irresponsible class. A boy of fourteen claimed to be that young Earl of Warwick, Clarence's son, who was a prisoner in the Tower and feeble-minded at that. The Irish, who knew no better, believed him, and crowned him in Dublin as Edward VI, but Lincoln and Suffolk were well aware that the boy was Lambert Simnel, the son of a joiner, and had been trained in his imposture by a priest called Simons. Henry took the sensible course of parading the real Warwick through the streets of London to prove the imposture, but he had reckoned without another Yorkist—perhaps one of the worst, because she was far from the mischief she caused. This was Edward IV's sister, Margaret Duchess of Burgundy, who could always be relied on for money to support her House. Henry had to meet the rebels in arms at Stoke. He defeated them, but he now had a son, Arthur, born in September, 1486, and the risk that his death or capture in battle might leave this child in peril determined him thereafter always to seek solutions by negotiation. John of Lincoln was killed at Stoke, Edmund of Suffolk fled, and Henry correctly judged poor Lambert Simnel by giving him work in the royal kitchens. It was not a malicious judgment, for Simnel prospered and was later promoted to King's Falconer.

A second imposter was more serious, for he was supported by the King of France, Charles VIII. Charles had succeeded in getting little Duchess Anne and her land of Brittany, and was to cause untold misery by leading France into naked aggression in Italy; he has been described as a licentious hunchback of doubtful sanity. He claimed to believe that one Perkin Warbeck was Richard Duke of York, the survivor (he said) of the princes in the Tower. Warbeck made a career out of his shrewd judgement that any power interested in harassing England would support him. When Charles VIII tired of him he went to Burgundy, where the ruler was now the powerful Archduke Maximilian, heir to the emperor but still nephew to Duchess Margaret. His supporters in England did less well, since Henry was informed of the plot and in early 1495 seized and executed its leaders. The chief of these was his own stepfather, Lord Stanley, who by his calculated desertion of Richard III at Bosworth had secured Henry's accession. He is an illustration of the state the old nobles had sunk to. Rebellion for its own sake had become their way of life, and with no sign of regret Henry made it also their way of death.

Warbeck, however, continued to threaten from his usual safe distance, circumnavigating England in his travels from court to profitable court. He fetched up finally in Scotland, where his undoubted talents even fooled James IV into giving him a kinswoman of his in marriage. Henry was not to be hurried; with infinite patience he had followed Warbeck around, negotiating and renegotiating, and he had something of value to offer James—his daughter Margaret. In the end James took Margaret and peace with England, and Warbeck was gently eased out. He had now exhausted everyone's generosity, and in the end surrendered to Henry and confessed his imposture.

At first, Henry—as he'd been with Simnel—was lenient, and even spared him the Tower; but evidently plotting was going on of which records have not survived. Perhaps Simnel could not abandon the habit of a lifetime and got in touch with a possible ally, poor young Warwick in the Tower; perhaps others did the plotting for them, or perhaps it was all a subtle plot of Henry's, using Warbeck to bring down Warwick. The latter supposition seems over-elaborate for Henry, who could easily have executed Warbeck on his surrender, but there may have been plots unknown to us centering on Warwick. Whatever the truth, Warbeck and Warwick were both executed for treason in 1499.

The marriage of Margaret to the King of Scots was by no means Henry's sole triumph in this field. Europe was now entering on the great age of the dynastic marriage, where the fate of countries might hang on the availability of a marriageable princess, and the success of a King be gauged by the number of his children married into powerful foreign dynasties. The acceptance or bestowal of a bride by a foreign ruler was a mark of confidence, and by the time Henry had been ten years on the throne it was beginning to penetrate even the thickest royal brains of Europe that this King of England was not only permanent but confident and powerful. Henry's chief concern, of course, was for the marriage of his heir, Prince Arthur. Having in his lineage the undistinguished Tudors, the illegitimate Beauforts, and the very dubious Plantagenets, Arthur needed impeccable royal birth in his bride, and there was only one family with a suitable princess.

This was the family of the Catholic Kings in Spain, Ferdinand of Aragon and Isabel of Castile, two independent monarchs who had united in marriage to drive the Moors out of Spain. More exactly it was Isabel, a fiercely religious woman, who wanted to drive out the Moors; Ferdinand, known as the Spanish Fox, simply wanted power. The Catholic Kings were implacably opposed to France, and, moreover, had Lancastrian blood in them by way of that Infanta Catalina of Castile who was the daughter of John of Gaunt by his second wife. It took Henry VII many patient years of diplomacy, starting from a dubious succession, an empty exchequer, and a people who had been a byword in Europe as ungovernable, to establish England as worthy of a daughter of Spain; but in 1502 Prince Arthur, not quite fifteen, was married in England to the Infanta Catalina, not quite sixteen.

There is a nice story of how Henry arranged a slow stately progress through England for the Infanta, and then impulsively interrupted it one night by taking the boy Arthur with him on a ride through the darkness and insisting on defying the Spanish custom that a bride must not be seen unveiled. Catalina in those days was a lively pretty young woman, glowingly fair, brought up to be obedient to her duty as a daughter of Spain but eager for dancing and hunting and jousting. She was plainly happy to find a handsome young husband (a little quiet and modest), a charmer of a father-in-law, and a splendidly gay court. There was a magnificent wedding, the customary ritual of putting the young couple to bed together, and it seems that in the morning Prince Arthur boasted a little to his friends, which was equally a ritual, and the Infanta, now Catherine Princess of Wales, went off with her husband to his own castle of Ludlow in the Welsh Marches. Five months later Prince Arthur was dead.

There is a touching contemporary account of how this news reached the court: how the Queen at first thought only of her husband, and ran to his room to comfort him, and when she had done what she could and gone back to her own room was so much overcome with her own grief that they had to call the King to comfort her. It was a severe blow both personally and politically, and by the next month the Queen was pregnant again. In February, 1503, she died in childbirth, and the child "tarried but a short time after."

With these three deaths the gaiety of the English court died. More than gaiety died in Henry. The charm of this gaunt unhandsome man was gone, his lively eyes and cheerful ways; his reserve, his caution, his evasiveness grew all the stronger.

With the death of her husband the charm of the little Spanish Princess of Wales died too. She could not be treated as a sad little widow, for she was a political counter again, and the reminder of a lost hope, and in that atmosphere she grew peevish and arrogant, let her Spanish pride and her Spanish suite lead her into foolish mistakes. No thought of comforting her entered into the calculations of the Catholic Kings; on the very day they heard of Prince Arthur's death they instructed their ambassadors in England not only to demand the return of Catherine's dowry (a demand they knew would be embarrassing) but also to open negotiations for her betrothal to the King's new heir, Prince Henry.

Prince Henry was only nine, so the negotiations could comfortably be prolonged for many years: comfortably, that is, for Henry VII, for whom the policy of the Spanish Fox, Ferdinand, was soon to grow too blatantly aggressive to make Spain a safe ally for England, but not in the least so for Catherine, doomed to live out a miserable life of waiting, and in the end to be denied even money for food because neither father nor father-in-law would yield legal ground in a foolish quarrel about the dowry. What seemed of little importance at the time, but was later to be the proximate cause of one of the greatest upheavals in English history, was the question of whether Catherine's marriage to Arthur had been consummated as well as celebrated. In those days it was quite usual for consummation to be delayed for young couples; neither Catherine nor Arthur were considered too young, but Arthur was not strong and there may have been private arrangements we do not know about. If the marriage was consummated, then she was within the forbidden degrees of marriage to Prince Henry. The necessary Papal dispensation for the marriage with Prince Henry was easily obtainable, and Henry VII obtained it, and Catherine herself gave no indication that has come down to us that it was not necessary. We can only note that her first child was born within the year of her second marriage, and that in five months of marriage to Prince Arthur she had no recorded signs of pregnancy. But that the King got his dispensation did not mean that he meant to use it, and that the Princess allowed him to get it did not mean that she knew it to be necessary. All we know for sure is that the King was less happy than he had been about the Spanish alliance, but not yet ready to give it up entirely, and that the cunning that had served him so well all his life did not desert him now. Catherine was betrothed to Prince Henry, but not married, and England with its full exchequer and its complete freedom from foreign entanglements was a worthy heritage for its waiting heir.

At the death of his wife Henry VII was still in his forties, and could have married again and had other children. This most curious of Kings, who could make a dynastic marriage with a woman he had never seen and in life and in death behave as if she had been the love of his life, never did marry again. A few enquiries were made, but in only one case was Henry's own interest aroused, and the way he behaved in this case makes him even more worthy of respect.

In 1506, because of a Channel storm that drove their ships off course, he had one short meeting with his daughter-in-law Catherine's elder sister Juana, heiress to Castile. Juana had been married to the Imperial Archduke Philip, heir to half of Central Europe and Italy, a brainless athlete who neglected her and with whom she had fallen deeply in love. Almost at once after that (in circumstances deeply suspicious to Juana's father Ferdinand), Philip had mysteriously died in Spain. Juana was naturally deeply affected by his death, but soon Ferdinand began to hint at worse. He was too wary ever to commit himself to more than the statement that Juana had to be confined for her own safety, but terrible stories of her madness soon began to circulate in Europe (*Juana la Loca* is the *King of Spain's daughter* of the nursery rhyme). The stories were false; Juana was sane, but the heiress through her mother to the throne of Castile, which her atrocious father coveted. The heiress of Castile would not, in fact, have been at all a suitable wife for the King of an England set upon avoiding European entanglements; yet Henry VII persisted in trying to rescue this sad lady he had seen only once. Long after Ferdinand had made it clear that he had Juana in prison and was not releasing her for any offer, Henry went on pestering the Spanish ambassadors for news of her, pushing his interest with Ferdinand as far as it would go, breaking the habit of a lifetime and trying to push it a little further. There seems to us, at this distance of time, some kind of unassimilated moral about the career of Henry VII, some sort of conclusion to be drawn that it is possible to be politically successful and yet humanly decent.

But this story has no happy ending. In April, 1509, Henry VII died, aged only fifty-two. He left his eighteen-year-old son Prince Henry, as he had wished, a secure succession, a full exchequer, and no foreign embarrassments. Of his two surviving children, his elder daughter Margaret was Queen of Scotland, and the younger, Mary, who was then only eleven, was to become (if briefly) Queen of France. England, at his accession despised in Europe as bankrupt and ungovernable, was now respected as a stable and responsible power. Somewhere around his court, in a darned dress and eating stale fish because she could not afford fresh, was a not-now-young Spanish Princess his son could do as he liked with. The only curious thing about Henry VII's dispositions for the future of his kingdom, otherwise so shrewd, was the state of the Prince to whom he had left it. Prince Henry was a splendid young man to look at, but he was very ignorant.

As for Queen Juana, she stayed in her father's prison. He died seven years after her would-be rescuer, in 1515, and his successor was her own eldest son Charles. From his mother's parents Charles inherited Spain, from his father's parents (the Emperor Maximilian I and Mary of Burgundy) the whole of what is now Germany, Holland, Belgium, Bohemia, Hungary, Switzerland, Sardinia, Sicily, Milan, and the kingdom of Naples. He never mastered the whole of it, Europe rebelled at his swollen power, and he abdicated in exhaustion before his death, taking great care to divide his heritage into reasonable slices of the cake. But in 1515 all he did for his mother was to leave her in prison as mad. She stayed there until her death in 1555 (the year when Charles gave up his monstrous power), and by that time, unsurprisingly, she was mad. There can be few other ladies whose lives so condemn the values of their times as the wretchedly sane Mad Juana of Castile.

And while all this was going on, in fact when the little Catalina was still a child in Spain, a Genoese Jew mostly thought to be mad got a little money from the Catholic Kings and sailed west into the blue to deliver a letter to the Great Khan who lived in the east. He fetched up on a whole new continent no one had suspected was in his way; but no one thought the discovery of any great importance.

HENRY VIII
1509–1547

❁

Born in Greenwich Palace, June 1491.

Second son of Henry VII and his wife Elizabeth of York.

Married: 1. in 1509, Catherine of Aragon Dowager Princess of Wales, widow of his elder brother Arthur (who had died in 1503), and daughter of Ferdinand of Aragon and Isabel of Castile Kings of Spain; divorced May 1533; by whom he had:

>Mary, born 1516, later Mary I;

>2. on a date unknown, Anne Boleyn, daughter of Sir Thomas Boleyn later Earl of Wiltshire, divorced and executed May 1536, by whom he had:

>>Elizabeth, born September 1533, later Elizabeth I;

>3. in May 1536, Jane Seymour, daughter of Sir John Seymour, died October 1537, by whom he had:

>>Edward, born October 1547, later Edward VI;

>4. in January 1540, Anne, daughter of John Duke of Cleves, divorced July 1540;

>5. in August 1540, Catherine Howard, daughter of Lord Edmund Howard, executed in February 1542;

>6. in July 1543, Catherine Lady Latimer, formerly Burgh, and born Parr, daughter of Sir Thomas Parr, who survived him, later marrying as her fourth husband, in 1547, Thomas Lord Seymour of Sudeley, brother of Jane Seymour and the Lord Protector Somerset of the following reign, and dying in 1548.

Died at Whitehall, January 1547 and buried at Windsor.

In 1519 the Pope granted Henry VIII the title of *Fidei Defensor* or Defender of the Faith, which the Kings of England have used to the present day.

HENRY VIII

And now, as if all the patient years of Henry VII, the caution, the diplomacy, the economy, had been meant to lead only to this joyous occasion, there succeeds to the English throne the perfect English King. Henry VIII, a magnificent youth of eighteen, handsome, athletic, gay, artistic, steps into the enjoyment of his father's industry. It was like the opening of spring; no more pennypinching, no more ailing King and peevish princess; England was to be merry and peaceful and prosperous, and her King the greatest and most beloved of history.

The effect of this adulation on a youth so inexperienced that he had never gone outside of the palace grounds alone was disastrous. If Henry VIII had had a little hardship in his youth he might have made a good King, for he had inherited to the full his father's intense silent shrewdness. But he was given no chance. He even found at once, waiting in his very court, a betrothed wife to whom he could appear magnificent simply by announcing that he would marry her; and when he had married her he found that she was more than he could have expected.

Catherine of Aragon was twenty-four now, and since her first husband's death had been living a wretched life on the fringes of the court. Buffeted between Spain and England, belonging to neither, refused money by both, she and her dwindling band of Spanish attendants had been reduced to mended clothes and stale food, with no hope of amendment in the future. Catherine was a daughter of Spain and deeply religious, determined to suffer anything in the course of her duty, but she was also a highly intelligent woman. In those painful years she taught herself the art of diplomacy, forcing on to herself discretion, judgment, political wisdom, and a great self-control. Her father came to value her so much that he used her as his virtual ambassador.

But she was still a forlorn young woman, and when, against all expectation, the young King rescued her by the marriage she had long despaired of, she responded with all her natural warmth. The love between the King and the Queen lightened court and country, and everything was dancing and hawking and jousting. Henry called himself Sir Loyal Heart, and boasted tirelessly of the lady he loved. And well he might, for he discovered that she had the wisdom and political experience that he lacked. A great King could not admit to ignorance and uncertainty, but without any loss of dignity he could learn from his loving and obedient wife. Catherine was to be the first of the advisers this incapable shrewd King took to support him. He was to ruin them all one by one, but none so cruelly as he ruined Catherine.

As for Catherine herself, she was all her life a good and dutiful wife, and even at her death not one word critical of her husband escaped her. Was she, in the early years, a little contemptuous of the games, of the masked outlaws who broke into her rooms and played at abduction, until they unmasked and she had to be vastly astonished that the tallest of them was her King? A daughter of Spain could hardly have thought this part of the business of ruling. But then in these years Henry did very little ruling, being content to hunt while his clerks did the daily business, and confining himself mostly to a glorious dream that was a hundred years out of date. His mind dwelt on the field of Agincourt, and he fancied it his duty to reconquer France. France (its population perhaps twenty million to England's four) was now so powerful that not the combined powers of Europe could stop her piracy in Italy; but then France was the object of Ferdinand of Spain's ambitions, and for years after his accession Henry VIII was through his wife the tool of the Spanish Fox. An invasion of France that was to have been triumphal turned out an absurd fiasco that somehow benefited Spain and left England humiliated and suffering in the exchequer. (Later on Henry complained to all Europe that Ferdinand had deceived him twice. "He lies," cackled the Fox; "it was five times.")

In the end, like the good and honest woman she was, Catherine sickened of her father's plots and abandoned him, thereafter considering her country to be England. But by that time Henry had found a rival councillor, another who understood how to support while appearing to be subordinate, and English politics became a battle between the Queen and Cardinal Wolsey. But even before this there were flaws appearing in the picture.

One was the state of the army. Oddly, Henry was entirely in touch with reality about the naval situation, and one of his few ventures of real wisdom was the establishment of a regular navy with its dockyards at Woolwich and Deptford. But then he was no seaman, and in military matters he prided himself on his prowess, which meant that he was an athletic jouster, a form of sport that consisted of setting two mounted knights at either end of an enclosed course and letting them run at each other. This was the outlook that had lost the French the battle of Agincourt a century before, but Henry never grasped that the tactics and weapons of his army were long outmoded, and made no attempt to improve them.

Another, and as it was to prove more serious, flaw showed itself first in 1510, with the birth of Catherine's first child. It was stillborn. Nine months later she had a boy who survived for fifty-two days. After a series of miscarriages (to our modern eyes far too close together) she had a second living boy, "who lived not long after." It was not until February, 1516, that a child was born who survived, a girl who was christened Mary. Henry refused to be worried, saying, "The Queen and I are still young." He was twenty-five and in the best of health, but Catherine was thirty-one and suffering from these repeated pregnancies.

She was no longer the lively, glowingly fair princess Henry had fallen in love with. She had grown broader, and a little hunched; her hair had darkened and her skin become sallow; she had given up dancing and spent long hours on her knees in her own chapel. Presently, Henry began to wonder why God refused him the children his splendid manhood so plainly deserved.

Why the Tudors so signally failed in this respect we do not know. Henry VIII was half Plantagenet, and that House, heaven knew, was prolific enough. Catherine's own family seemed sound enough (her sister Juana had six children), only petering out in the idiocy of Carlos II nearly two centuries later after horrific incestuous inbreeding. From six wives Henry VIII had three children, of whom one died in adolescence and two were barren women; even allowing for bad luck, late marriage, and medical ignorance, that seems to argue some congenital infirmity. A clue may possibly be found in the years 1513 and 1514, though the evidence is not convincing.

In 1513 Henry set off on his one campaign, a magnificent venture to the Continent that was of course engineered by the Spanish Fox, who liked to use English men and money for his own ends. In his absence the Scots, in their normal way, invaded the north, and to Catherine, left behind pregnant as regent, fell the ordering of the defense of the realm. It is a mark of her capability that she also looked after the supplies sent to the King. She was ably supported by the house of Howard, and the man who was later to be the Duke of Norfolk (he was then only the elder son and known as the Earl of Surrey) utterly defeated the Scots at Flodden. The Scottish King James IV was killed there, and his widow was Margaret Tudor, Henry VIII's elder sister, and Catherine, with that blend of the human with the political that was her great gift, sent an envoy to "comfort her," and thus paved the way to peace between the countries. This effort cost her the child she was carrying, which perhaps was natural; but when Henry came home from his campaign (which had been a party of chivalry with no action and no political advantages) she had to nurse him through a serious illness. It was variously said to be measles, smallpox, or the greater pox, syphilis. If it was syphilis, it could explain the gross ill-health he suffered from later, and the miscarriages and stillbirths of his second wife and the ill-health of the two children yet to be born.

We do not know when it was that Henry finally grew tired of his marriage to Catherine. Possibly, in the way of such things, he did not know himself. It seems clear that he never understood the one serious crime he could undoubtedly have charged her with, that of forwarding the interests of Spain rather than those of England. But he no longer needed Catherine's support now, for he had his great minister, Cardinal Wolsey, and while Catherine still represented the pro-Spanish and Imperial party, Wolsey urged a French alliance; and where Wolsey was a magnificent Prince of the Church, whose very magnificence enhanced the King he served, Catherine was an aging woman, fonder of the chapel than of the court, and incapable of giving the King children.

It is impossible now to disentangle the complexities of "the King's Great Matter," as Henry's divorce from Catherine was to be called. On the one side, it involved itself with the greatest religious and political upheavals of the time, on the other, it concerned the intimate emotions of people who were very careful indeed never to let them be known. (Henry himself once said, "If I thought my cap knew my counsel, I would destroy it.") We may grow suspicious over points that are not wholly explained by the accepted story—why, for example, was Henry so inexplicably infatuated for so very many years with a young woman who represented the party opposed to Catherine, and then make it quite clear that he disliked her intensely? And how was it arranged, after six years of impasse, that the way was cleared for Catherine's divorce only four months before the birth of her rival's child? The more "the Great Matter" is studied the less explicable it appears, and we can only be sure of its results.

There was of course no bar in Church law to an annulment of Henry's marriage. Monarchs had always wanted to be rid of inconvenient marriages, and with the good will of the Pope canonical ways could always be found. The most usual was the discovery of consanguinity (that is, that husband and wife were too closely related to marry), and since Catherine had first married Henry's elder brother Prince Arthur it would seem that he had good grounds for an annulment. Their father, Henry VII, of course, had not neglected this and a dispensation for the marriage had been obtained, but flaws can always be found in such things. Unfortunately Henry had chosen the worst of times to ask for a divorce from a daughter of the Catholic Kings, since in 1527 the grandson of the Catholic Kings, the Emperor Charles V, had sacked Rome and put the terrified Pope in daily fear of his life. Charles V was the son of Catherine's elder sister Juana, and not remarkable for his family sympathies (he was keeping his mother imprisoned that he might enjoy her kingdom), and it is possible that if he had been approached diplomatically, and if Catherine herself had been appealed to, and generous provision made for her daughter Mary, the matter might have been settled sensibly. Henry VII at any rate would surely have attempted it. Henry VIII did not. Instead, he announced that (after eighteen years of marriage) he had found a text in Leviticus that revealed the cause of his troubles. It stated that a man who took his brother's widow was committing incest, and that his progeny was accursed. (He did not explain how he missed the other text in Deuteronomy that urged a man to take his brother's wife for the sake of progeny.) And since the law against incest was a law not of man but of God, could even the Pope dispense from it?

It seems that Catherine knew that Henry was infatutated by Anne

Boleyn, an inconsiderable young woman of the pro-French party, and had taken as little notice of it as she took of other mistresses. She did not know that Anne had refused to become Henry's mistress until he consented to a divorce, and—a little aging lady, worn out with the vain effort to bear a son, happy in the daughter whose education she lovingly oversaw and the charities that made her people love her—she appears to have missed entirely the hatred of the pupil for the teacher he had discarded. One day in early 1527 Henry made Catherine one of the rare domestic visits of which their life together now consisted. He sat talking for some hours, while Mary studied and Catherine sewed. Then he sent Mary away and told Catherine that they must part. It was her single moment of weakness; she did nothing but break into a terrible weeping. Henry fled; and that was the end of their married life. From then onwards he treated her with a brutal cruelty.

An inconclusive process took place in June, 1527, that has come to be called the Queen's Trial, though there was nothing with which Catherine was legally charged. Its purpose was to set out Henry's case, and he had seen to it that Catherine was deprived of friends and legal counsel. She had to speak for herself, and when she did she was clear, concise, and legally devastating; in one breath she swept away Henry's case for annulment.

Her marriage to him, she said, could not be incestuous because it had been her first marriage. The union with Prince Arthur had never been consummated, and she had come to Henry "as virgin as I came from my mother's womb." Kneeling submissively in front of the King, she challenged him to deny her virginity on their wedding night. Henry said nothing; and she rose and left the court. One of her own men said timidly that she should stay, in case she were called again. She said, "It matters not. This is no indifferent court for me, and I will not tarry."

Her political judgment, as always, was sound. Any court in England that sat on her case was bound to be "not indifferent," and Henry was bound to get his divorce in one way or another. We cannot say that Catherine would not have lied, for the future, even the life, of her daughter Mary was at stake. Catherine was a deeply religious woman, but for all we know she would have lied to any extent, and taken the sin upon her own soul, to save her daughter. But she was also an experienced and sensible woman, and it is inconceivable that she would have lied in public on a matter on which the King could at once have corrected her. Perhaps in her youth, as a wretched young widow, she had at least prevaricated in allowing it to be assumed that her marriage to Arthur was complete; it had mattered very little then. Now, with her daughter at risk, we can only believe that she spoke the exact truth.

It made, of course, no difference, except that if Catherine had complied with his wishes Henry might have been less cruel to her and to her daughter. But his marital problems had not occurred in isolation. Ten years before, Martin Luther had nailed to the church door of Wittenburg, in Germany, the Ninety-five Theses that contested the power of the Pope, and the European Reformation was in full swing. For a man who wanted to contest the powers of the Pope in the small matter of one divorce the possibilities were enormous.

It is a paradox of English history that the English Reformation was made possible by a King who to the end of his life considered himself a faithful son of the Roman Church. When Luther had started his career of challenging Rome, Henry had written a pamphlet confuting him, and for that the Pope had bestowed on him the title of *Fidei Defensor,* Defender of the Faith. Henry treasured it, and four and a half centuries later his distant descendant Queen Elizabeth II still has the two letters *F.D.* on her coins (to the mystification of most of her subjects). Henry was completely satisfied by his relationship with God, regarding it in virtue of his royalty as a special one, and seems to have thought that God would not object if for his own purposes he made some adjustments in the upper echelons of the Church. For the purpose of marrying the woman he thought could give him a son, he repudiated the authority of the Pope and proclaimed himself Head of the English Church.

The greatest paradox of them all was that while his divorce was hated by the people as a whole (Catherine was much loved, and Anne Boleyn commonly known as the Concubine), the break with Rome was welcomed. As history shows, England had resented the Papal rule for centuries, hating Italian priests, Italian taxes, and Italian policies; and in recent decades there had grown up the popular (and therefore ill-documented) movement of the Lollards, common people with genuine religious feeling who objected to the Roman dogma as inconsistent with the teachings of Christ. It is difficult now to understand the feelings of those years. Did men sincerely find other men worthy of a terrible death by burning because they believed that a piece of bread either did or did not turn into the flesh and blood of their Savior? (for it was on the question of the celebration of the Mass that the doctrinal arguments were to center). We can only be sure that, however the great men judged their political advantage, the common people were honestly moved by religious feelings.

But of the great men, some saw their own advantage in an anti-Roman and pro-French policy, and among these the most powerful were those who supported Cardinal Wolsey and thus disliked Queen Catherine.

It was weary years before this divorce from Catherine was accomplished, chiefly because the legal machinery for it had to be established. Henry found a useful tool in the obscure Cambridge scholar Thomas Cranmer, and it was because the Pope was foolish enough to accept Cranmer as Archbishop of Canterbury that Henry had an archbishop who would cut the ties with Rome. On May 23, 1533, Cranmer pronounced Henry's marriage annulled and the King free to marry again. Rather less than four months later his second child to survive, Elizabeth Tudor, was born at Hampton Court. It is not surprising that the date of the King's marriage to her mother Anne Boleyn was kept secret.

More than the date of her marriage was kept secret about Anne Boleyn. Her daughter was to become Queen Elizabeth I, who would see to it that all records were destroyed. The story we know is that with her wit and charm Anne had kept the King unsatisfied until she was sure of marriage. We have some of his letters to her, and they are touchingly honest; what does not quite fit is that this pursuit went on for at least six years, and that six months after the birth of the Princess Elizabeth Henry was tired of Anne, and telling her so. Anne was not beautiful, except for her expressive eyes and splendid dark hair (she went to her coronation "sitting in it"), but she was spirited and sophisticated; she was not a solitary girl using her wits to rise in the world, but the willing weapon of a powerful and unscrupulous political party. We may guess that she was also the unwilling weapon of the King, who, having set out on his way in 1527, found it longer and less rewarding than he had thought it, and when he reached its end in 1533 destroyed his weapons in hatred.

Henry always came to hate his weapons. Having used Wolsey to destroy Catherine, he used Catherine to destroy Wolsey, dismissing him in 1531 in such disgrace that Wolsey died of it (luckily for him), because he had failed to secure the divorce.

As for Anne, it seems from the records that she knew she was doomed, and her courage gradually failed her. Less than a year after her marriage Henry had a new mistress, and when she broke out at him in a fury he told her brutally that as he had raised her up so he could cast her down. Her sole chance of life after that was to bear him a son, and that she could not do. It is said that she had her final miscarriage when she found a lady-in-waiting of her own sitting on the King's knee. The lady's name was Jane Seymour; the Seymours were not of Anne's party.

Catherine meanwhile was living out her life in a series of dank manors to which she was banished. It is said that after her divorce the Imperial Ambassador, Eustache de Chapuys, who so loved her that he was was more her advocate than his master's, had plans ready for the escape of the Queen and her daughter to the Low Countries and an invasion of England by the Emperor. Catherine refused to have any part in any such plan. She was, and in her own estimation she remained for the rest of her life, Queen of England and the obedient and faithful wife of its King, and nothing made her move one inch in any way incompatible with those roles. She was denied friends, attendants, the comforts of life, above all the sight of her beloved daughter; she was threatened with death for her contumacy, her daughter and her servants were threatened with death, she was confined in places blatantly chosen to ruin her health, and was in such fear of poison that her few faithful ladies allowed her to eat nothing that they had not cooked and tasted themselves; and in all that time she is not recorded as having said or written anything remotely critical of the man she still regarded as her husband. At the very end, the dearest friend of her sad youth, Maria de Salinas, now the Dowager Lady Willoughby, came by night to Kimbolton where she was imprisoned, and by sheer force of personality overrode the King's orders and was with her mistress when she died. Two days before her death, on January 7, 1536, Catherine dictated a last letter to Henry.

It began, "My most dear lord, king and husband." It pardoned him the wrongs he had done her, prayed God also to pardon him, begged him to be a good father to their daughter Mary (who at the time was proclaimed a bastard and forced to act as lady to her half-sister Elizabeth), asked him to give her maids marriage portions ("which is not much, they being but three") and her other servants their due wages and a year's more "lest they be unprovided for." It ends "Lastly, I make this vow, that mine eyes desire you above all things."

Henry ignored her requests. At the news of her death he dressed himself from top to toe in yellow, the color of gaiety, and gave a party, telling everyone, "The old harridan is dead." Queen Anne Boleyn, in one of the few utterances to remind us that she was the mother of the greatest of English Queens, said, "I am her death, as she is mine." In May of that same year, 1536, she was divorced and executed. The charge was adultery with five men, one of whom was her brother, George Lord Rochford, and another of whom had accused her only under torture. Rochford's wife was to live on as a noted royal procuress; the rest of Anne's family obediently gave their votes for her death.

In the last days Anne's courage, which at best had seemed hysterical, deserted her at times, and she clung to some hope of banishment to a convent. But at the very end she sent a message to Henry (or so it is said) that tells us whence came her daughter's gift of phrase:

Commend me to His Grace, and tell him he hath been ever constant in his career of advancing me; from a private gentlewoman he made me a marchioness, from a marchioness a queen, and now he hath left me a higher honour, he gives my innocency the crown of martyrdom.

Chapuys, who loathed her on Catherine's account, records private information that "the Concubine" had sworn on the Sacrament, "qu'elle n'avais jamais méfaicte de son corps envers ce roy."

Anne Boleyn was beheaded on the May 20, and Henry married Jane Seymour on the twenty-first—again dressed all in yellow.

Once more we can only guess at the truth of the stories we have. Jane Seymour was the weapon of another powerful party; her part in the death of her predecessor can hardly have been pleasant. She was Queen from May, 1536, to October, 1537, when she died in childbirth, and little is known of her. Considering the manner of Anne's death, not to have been pregnant at marriage seems a small moral advantage, but some kindly thoughts are recorded of her. She persuaded the King to invite the wretched and maltreated Princess Mary back to court, and there took pains to see that she was treated with respect; it was noted that if they came to a door, where Mary would have had to give way to her, Queen Jane took her hand and went through at her side. Perhaps she can best be regarded as a tepidly nice woman who did what her menfolk told her. It is worth notice for the complications that were to follow that no one of any party or religion could assail the legitimacy of her son Prince Edward. Henry now had two disputed marriages and two illegitimated daughters, but neither Catherine of Aragon nor Anne Boleyn was alive at the time of his marriage to Jane Seymour, and as a son, Prince Edward took acknowledged precedence of both girls in the succession. He was a handsome, healthy boy and the succession seemed secured and indisputable. It was to be two years before Henry married again.

The fall of Anne Boleyn had not meant the fall of the reforming party. Henry's new supporter, Thomas Cromwell, successor to Cardinal Wolsey, was a reformer; so were the Seymours. They had to be; the work of tearing the Roman church from its English roots could not be accomplished in a year or two. In its greed and its foolish policies the Church was much disliked in England, and by some more religiously inclined its dogma was hated, but its social presence had been in the land since Saint Augustine landed at Dover in the eighth century. The great religious houses were centers of literacy, art, and banking; the smaller houses were familiar neighbors, refuge of the unwanted, both rich and poor. That they were disposed of with relatively little difficulty is because the weapon used against them was that most powerful of all: their own wealth. Henry took the treasure and the lands of the Church and distributed both to his men. No one whose wealth was even in part the looted wealth of the Church would be easily reconciled with the Papacy. It was a cruel business, but nothing at all in comparison with the process of Reformation as it was practiced in other countries (or as Henry's daughter was to attempt to practice Counter Reformation), and there can be no doubt that it took England in the way she wanted to go. Tudor security and Tudor prosperity after the long years of the Wars of the Roses had brought confidence back to England, and the progress of the Reformation on the Continent had made it imperative that she choose one side or the other. The choice was a historical imperative; with her rising nationalism, her long history of unrest toward Rome, and her geographical position, she could only choose the side of reform. We do know that many of the common people would have made this same choice from purely religious conviction, but we also know that it was many decades before the majority of them willingly considered themselves members of an established reformed church.

We must remember, however, that in Henry VIII's reign the Church of England remained Catholic. The pressures for religious reform came chiefly from below, and were severely repressed—one of the more useful results of the political reform being that now heresy had become also treason. To Henry, the Church of England was precisely what it had always been, the only true church of Christ, improved under new management.

He had, of course, needed legal instruments to bring about this change, and, to add to the paradoxes of this most paradoxical of all reigns, he chose to operate through Parliament. The only other possible instrument would have been Convocation (the Church assembly), but Convocation was not over-ready to give away its own rights, and Parliament was lamentably anxious to be subservient. Morally speaking, it was a sad spectacle, for there is little doubt that individual members were actuated mostly by fear of the King and lust for loot; but as Parliament had evolved, it kept what powers it gained, and from its subservience to the royal will it emerged with greatly enhanced powers.

This eager subservience was a feature of the later years of Henry VIII's reign. After a reign of thirty years Henry had at last come of age; Thomas Cromwell was his last great minister, and though he always had his party of supporting nobles, these years were those of his personal rule. No immediate danger threatened from overseas; the succession was secure; and the dangers at home, the state of the army and the exchequer, were not appreciated (indeed the financial trouble was dealt with by the dangerous expedient of debasing the coinage). Henry was sole master of his kingdom, and his kingdom responded by a religious regard for his every wish.

This feeling was the dying kick of the old English reverence for the office of the King, for it vanished with the death of Elizabeth I, and only reappeared as a political tenet of those whose safety lay with the safety of the King. Partly it must have come from the devout thankfulness of the common people for a strong King and a stable kingdom after the uncertainties and dangers of the Wars of the Roses; but it was also a widespread politico-religious theory in Europe, where the common people were perhaps blindly looking for a safe authority to replace the lost authority of the Pope. "The will of the King is the law of the people": in a country with England's history, the idea should have been laughable. That it was taken for a short time with the utmost seriousness—one of its greatest upholders was that most humanly failing of great and good men, Thomas Cranmer Archbishop of Canterbury—is a measure of how incapable not only the common men found themselves in face of the political and religious problems of the day. (It is likely that such great problems had never before been presented with such immediacy to the whole people in their everyday life.) Since God had given them their King, ran the theory, it was the King's duty to take the people's decisions, and the people's duty to abide by them religiously.

In the years around 1540 a new distribution of power was emerging in Europe, making a new foreign policy necessary. For many years now the two great states of Europe, France and Spain, had been opposed, and this opposition only grew when the heir of Spain became also the Holy Roman Emperor Charles V. England had preserved herself by playing off the one against the other and refusing entangling alliances with either (except for Henry VIII's youthful enthusiasm for the Spanish Fox). This began to change with the Reformation, for many of the states adopting the reformed religion belonged to the vast and unwieldy tangle of more or less autonomous states that made up the empire. Charles V's control of his empire was always tenuous, and, unluckily for him, many of the rebels, though small, occupied strategic positions. The chief of them, and also the most stubborn in their heresy, were the Low Countries (roughly, modern Holland and Belgium), and they could control the mouths of the Rhine and the northeast frontiers of France. Being great seamen, they also controlled their own seas, which meant Charles could not send men or supplies from Spain to the empire except by the southerly route through Italy, which was long and vulnerable.

The command of the Channel passage was to dominate European politics for decades, and in the face of it Charles V for a short time allied himself with France. In England the reform party, led by Cromwell, persuaded the King to abandon his father's old policy and make a firm European alliance with the reforming countries, and in pursuance of this policy picked out a fourth wife for him from these countries.

She was Anna of Clev-Jülich, whom the English called Anne of Cleves, sister of the duke of a small duchy in the very storm-center of the European battle. Once again a marriage of Henry VIII hides its secrets from us; something went wrong, but we shall never know exactly what it was. The lady arrived by night, her eager bridegroom rode to meet her alone, and in that time alone they quarrelled fatally. The marriage ceremony was gone through, the King never went near the Queen, and within six months they were divorced. At the same time, Cromwell was executed, France and Spain were quarrelling again, and England had returned to her old policy of refusing all permanent European alliances. Once again in Henry's life, private and political were inexplicably mixed.

It was said publicly that Henry found Anne so ugly that he was reluctant to marry her and incapable of sleeping with her. Against this we have only the portraits of Anne painted by a man of genius, Hans Holbein the Younger, who was Henry's court painter. Anne's face is far from ugly, and very far from unintelligent, and at that time in his life Henry was too bulky to move freely, with an ulcer on his thigh that periodically discharged and crippled him with pain, and his face is the familiar broad ham with small eyes and a tiny compressed mouth. We can only make our own guesses, knowing too that at court was the powerful family of Howard (now headed by that Duke of Norfolk who, as Surrey, had won Flodden Field for Catherine of Aragon), a conservative Catholic family, hating the Protestant alliance and the men who supported it, and having on their fringes a so-far-neglected little beauty of eighteen who was appointed one of Anne's ladies-in-waiting.

At the end of the six months Anne quietly consented to divorce on the grounds of non-consummation, and thus gained Henry's good will so that he gave her a pension and a house in Richmond, where he visited her and is said to have enjoyed her conversation. She is recorded as being always very merry, and became great friends with his children, who, heaven knew, needed such friends.

So the Howards were now in the ascendant; but no one can say why they chose, of all people, Catherine Howard as their tool. She seems to have been born doomed; she was a cousin of Anne Boleyn, and had been left to grow up unwanted and unwatched; she had had at least two lovers before her marriage, one of them apparently for the reward of a silk cap embroidered with true-lover's-knots. It seems that Norfolk put her into Henry's path, and that Henry, with his amazing capacity for suiting his emotions to his politics, or vice versa, fell in love with her and married her. If we are to consider Catherine's actions as dictated by reason, or even by Norfolk, we may assume that if Henry was still capable of normal sexual relations (rumor said that he was not) she continued her own relations with her lovers in the hope of fathering a child on Henry. Nothing so considered appears from the depositions at her examination on a charge of treason (as cuckolding the King's Grace was now called); there she seems only a pathetic corrupted child too frightened and bedazzled to be more than greedy.

Henry was undoubtedly stricken when he heard of her adultery; but by now power and flattery had made him incapable of normal personal relations. The best he could do for his young wife was to order that her execution should be hurried on without further saddening him with the details. At the end Catherine showed courage, dying more bravely than any of the wretched men condemned with (and by) her. Henry was at a party when he heard the cannon that signalled her death; his eyes filled with tears.

That was the end of the Howard ascendancy, and now it was again the day of the Seymours, the family of the heir Prince Edward. They even contrived to marry Henry again to one of them, the childless widow of two elderly husbands who had sadly fallen in love with Thomas Seymour, who was to be a stirring man in the next reign. This union with Catherine Parr was Henry's only honorable marriage since his first. This Catherine had neither the intelligence nor the courage of the first, for she could be terrorized as no one had ever terrorized the daughter of the Catholic Kings; but she was a kind and dutiful woman, and gave Henry in his old age the care he had deserved from no one.

When in 1547 Henry's constant ill-health was plainly bringing him near death, his heir, Prince Edward, was only nine. Henry left the Seymours to look after him, but appointed a Regency Council for the country. His two wretched daughters were put into the succession after the prince—Mary, now a brooding bitter woman of thirty-one, and Elizabeth, a tense young girl of fourteen, already marked down as worthy of notice. As a final act to mark his dying powers, Henry ordered the execution on a charge of treason of two of the greatest men in the kingdom, the old Duke of Norfolk and his son, the poet Surrey. Surrey was executed; but when it came to the old duke's turn Henry was in the state of all Kings at the point of death: no one would obey him for fear of what was to come, and Norfolk stayed in the Tower.

King Henry VIII died with his hand in the grasp of Thomas Cranmer, a man who had condoned many royal crimes in the honest belief that in this way he was doing God's will. In this belief he was joined by most of Henry's subjects. Henry's children were to change their ideas.

EDWARD VI
1547–1553

❁

Born at Hampton Court, October 1537.

Son of Henry VIII and his third wife Jane Seymour.

Died unmarried at Greenwich Palace, July 1553, and was
buried at Westminster.

Upon his death the Crown was assumed for the nine days
7 July–16 July by Lady Jane Dudley, known as Lady
Jane Grey, daughter of Frances Grey of Suffolk, who
was grand-daughter of Henry VII by his younger
daughter Mary, who had married in May 1553 Guilford
Dudley, son of John Dudley Duke of Northumberland,
and who with her husband was executed by the orders
of Queen Mary I in February 1555.

EDWARD VI

The death of Henry VIII left England with a depleted exchequer, a debased coinage, a neglected army, and a religious life in profound confusion. The chief interest of his successor should have been in putting some of this to rights. But Edward VI was a child of nine, and the history of his reign is that of the battle of the nobles to rule the King.

At the time of Henry VIII's death, the Seymours (Edward's maternal family) were the uppermost faction, and he was hardly dead before Edward Seymour Lord Hertford, the boy-King's uncle, had upset the dispositions of his will. Instead of a council to hold the Regency, Hertford established himself as Lord Protector and filled the great offices of state with his family and friends. For all practical purposes Hertford was dictator of England.

King Edward, contrary to later legend, was not a sickly child, but normally healthy and a little more than normally intelligent. Perhaps he had been too young to have been affected by the horrors of his family life, and he had had the good luck of having two affectionate sisters in the Princesses Mary and Elizabeth, two kind stepmothers in Anne of Cleves and Catherine Parr, and a tutor to whom both King and Reformation probably owed more than they knew or suspected. This was John Cheke, a scholar, a reformer, and a teacher of great kindliness and wisdom. Because of his teaching, the reign of Edward VI was a reforming reign, and it was to Cheke, too, that Edward owed his greatest (though pathetic) kingly virtue, his deep awareness of his responsibilities to his people.

Edward seems to have been a nice-natured child, perhaps taking after his mother Jane Seymour in this. He was readily influenced by those he trusted, but capable of a quiet and decisive withdrawal when his trust was abused. He did not much like the Lord Protector, but, perhaps with comprehension that Edward Seymour was an honest man in his own way, concealed the fact. Seymour was undoubtedly loyal to his King, but only in pursuit of his own ideas, which were reformist and tolerably liberal and humane. He had a younger brother, Thomas (Lord High Admiral, Lord Seymour of Sudeley— all the great men of this reign are difficult to keep track of because of the self-promotion they indulged in; Edward Seymour is first the Earl of Hertford and then the Duke of Somerset), who thought he had not been rewarded according to his merits. He was brave and charming, but also vain, stupid, and irresponsible. Henry VIII's last wife, Catherine Parr, had long been in love with him, but he proposed marriage to both Princess Mary and Princess Elizabeth before contenting himself with a mere King's widow. Edward VI, who loved Catherine, approved of the marriage, but Somerset did not, knowing the dangers of marrying into the royal family. Catherine quickly ended her frustrated life by dying in childbirth, and Thomas turned to realizing his ambitions by charming the young King.

One of Edward's boyish worries was that the protector allowed him no pocket money. Thomas lent him small sums; Thomas was so fatuous, when the small sums had mounted to above a hundred pounds, as to think he could embarrass Edward into asking the council to transfer the protectorate from his brother to him. Cheke extracted the little King without too much loss of dignity, and Thomas turned instead to bribing members of the council. He financed this scheme by getting the Master of the Mint to debase the coinage still further and share the proceeds with him, and when this proved insufficient came to an arrangement, in his capacity as Lord High Admiral, with some Channel pirates to ignore their depredations in return for a share of the loot. About the same time he also engaged in a dangerous attempt to seduce the Princess Elizabeth.

It seems to have surprised him then that Edward would no longer see him alone. One night in January, 1549, armed with a pistol and a set of keys, he tried to break into his bedchamber. He may only have wanted a private word, but when Edward's pet dog barked he shot it, and within minutes was under arrest.

He was executed for treason, after a long and savage investigation of his accomplices which very nearly dragged Princess Elizabeth into the Tower with him. After this betrayal of his trust, the King might have arrived at a sympathy with Somerset, but Somerset was too deep in troubles. He had failed to bring about the King's marriage, planned by Henry VIII, to the Queen of Scots, little Mary Stuart; he was making himself unpopular with the people by his efforts to impose an extreme Protestant ritual on the Church; and at the same time he was alienating a powerful body of the landowners by his attempts to stop them from illegally enclosing common land for their own use. He was popular with the commons, who called him their Good Duke, but his religion was too extreme for them. They rose in revolt as the nobles threatened to do the same, and the situation was saved only by the prompt military action of John Dudley Earl of Warwick. Warwick was a coming man, quietly building up his position with an eye to the future.

By 1549 Somerset's only advantage against his enemies was his possession of Edward's person. Telling the boy that the revolt was against the throne itself, he hurried him away on a dramatic night ride to refuge in Windsor Castle. It did him no good; he had to make peace as best he could (Archbishop Cranmer was one of the mediators), and Edward discovered that yet another man had been unworthy of his trust. Somerset had to agree to a formal arrest and banishment to the Tower, but he was still too powerful for that to last, and before long he was back on the council and on such good terms with the subtle Warwick that he was marrying his daughter to Warwick's eldest son. But he had forfeited the chief weapon of his power, the confidence of the King, which Warwick now held, and soon all that stood between Somerset and the Tower was his popularity with the people.

To counteract this, Warwick started negotiating a French marriage for the King, and professed himself an extreme reformer, which brought him a party of strong supporters and the enthusiasm of the King. Edward's Protestantism was already growing a little extreme for his age; he rebuked his mature sister Mary for playing cards, and his adolescent sister Elizabeth took good care to please him by the modesty of her dress.

Warwick's religious policy naturally brought him into conflict with Mary, who clung stubbornly and dangerously to her Catholic practices. In early May of 1550 she was ordered to give up her household celebration of Mass (it was supposed to be a private celebration, but she interpreted this very liberally); she refused, and the next day the Spanish Ambassador warned the council that if her

Mass were denied her her cousin the emperor would at once declare war on England. This was not to be risked, and she was grudgingly allowed Mass "for the time being," while Warwick hurried on the negotiations for the French alliance. Edward's precocious bigotry was growing, and he had to be persuaded to spare Mary, making it clear that it would not be for long. The emperor continually urged her to escape to his protection, but she persisted in living her quiet and perilous life in England.

It was Mary's position that led finally to Somerset's fall. Protestant though he was, in September, 1551, he kindly suggested better treatment for her, and was at once sent to the Tower and convicted on a charge of high treason. Edward appealed to Warwick to spare his life, but was told that it would be dangerous, and given a series of Christmas festivities to distract him. Somerset was executed in January, 1552; and when Edward had at last been betrothed to the French princess, thus securing a friend against the emperor, it seemed that the ascendancy of Warwick—now Duke of Northumberland—was complete.

Northumberland's time has been described as a high-water of greed and corruption, for, shrewd as he was, he had no principles beyond personal ambition. He would surely have come to grief in time, for the King was now fifteen, intelligent, sadly experienced, and above all ambitious for the good of the people he believed God to have given, body and soul, into his care. Northumberland had to take good care to stay close to him, visiting him in secret each night to coach him in the next day's council business, and Edward was already showing signs of struggling free from this tutelage. In January, 1552, he proposed twelve Bills to Parliament for the righting of various economic and religious abuses, and it seems that they were his own ideas rather than Northumberland's. They were rejected; but in February of that year Nicholas Ridley, unable to contain his anger at the state of the country, preached at Westminster, in Edward's own presence, a sermon passionately attacking the greedy men in office and describing the miserable state of the poor of the kingdom. It was a brave thing to do, and he could have been in the Tower by the evening; instead he was closeted with the King, devising a scheme of hospitals, orphanages, and schools.

In April, 1552, Edward suffered a feverish illness that was most likely measles. He seemed to recover well, and in the summer made a royal progress through the southwest that was a personal triumph.

Northumberland was hated, but the King was still what he had been called as a baby, England's Treasure. In September he was back in London, eager to deal with a controversy that Northumberland had been fomenting over Cranmer's Prayer-Book of 1552. Cranmer, a reformer while denying the Real Presence of Christ in the Host, still had the communicant kneel to receive it, and was accused of idolatry. Edward had himself had a hand in the preparation of this Prayer-Book, and keenly felt the attack on it.

This attack by Northumberland on Cranmer's power and influence with the King suggests that he was becoming increasingly aware of danger. He had no great party of his own either among the nobles or in the country, but relied only on the King, who was fast developing independent ideas. Worse than that, his health was giving cause for alarm. He had not recovered as completely as he insisted from his 1552 illness, and less than a year later, in February, 1553, caught a chill that turned to congestion of the lungs. Again he declared himself ready for work, and this time it was very clear that he was wrong. In April he left London for the purer air of Greenwich, and here Northumberland came to him with the plan he had conceived that would lead to the continuance of his own power.

In 1515 Henry VII's younger daughter Mary, widowed after a brief marriage to the elderly Louis XII of France, had made a scandalous runaway match with the handsome Charles Brandon Duke of Suffolk, and their granddaughter was a young, scholarly, dogmatically Protestant and pathetically prim girl called Lady Jane Grey. Northumberland married her to his fourth son, Lord Guilford Dudley, and proposed to the King that he should make a will passing over the Princesses Mary and Elizabeth and leaving the throne to Jane Grey. This was plainly illegal, since, even if the illegitimacy of both Mary and Elizabeth were upheld, the next legal heir was Mary Stuart Queen of Scots, granddaughter of Henry VII's elder daughter Margaret. But Mary Stuart was a Catholic, and betrothed to the heir to France, and Edward believed that it was his duty to secure a Protestant succession in England. He was reluctant to upset his father's will, but in the end he signed.

To give legal effect to this will, the Bill of Settlement had to be drawn up and signed. This proved so difficult that Northumberland began to fear that Edward would die first, and when the orthodox doctors failed to rally his strength brought in a terrible old woman who claimed an infallible nostrum, which seems to have contained arsenic. The Lord Chief Justice refused to draw up the bill, saying it could not be done legally; and when he had done so only on the King's express command, many of the council refused to sign it, having no wish to prolong Northumberland's power. Finally, only Archbishop Cranmer held out, a good, utterly confused man refusing to do what he thought wrong even when it meant delivering his people (and also himself) into the hands of a Catholic Queen. After two long interviews, he seems to have given in and signed out of love for the dying boy.

The forces were arrayed for the battle of the new reign; news was secretly sent to Mary, Northumberland was collecting his supporters; no one now regarded the last male Tudor. Edward VI died at Greenwich Palace in July, 1553, and was buried in Westminster Abbey.

MARY I
1553-1558

❀

Born at Greenwich, February 1516.

Daughter of Henry VIII and his first wife Catherine of
Aragon; after Catherine's divorce pronounced illegitimate, but restored to the succession by Henry VIII's
will.

Succeeded after the unsuccessful assumption of the Crown
by Lady Jane Grey.

Married in 1554 Philip, son of the Holy Roman Emperor
and King of Spain Charles V, later Philip II of Spain.
Charles V was the son of Philip Archduke of Austria
and Catherine's sister Juana Queen of Castile.

Died childless, November 1558 and was buried at Westminster.

By Mary's marriage Philip of Spain was styled King of
England and Mary Queen of Spain; these titles lapsed
with her death and were not inherited.

MARY I

ary Tudor is the most pitiable of the English monarchs. She was in every sense a good woman and a courageous one; she perseveringly did all her life what she devoutly believed was her duty; and she died forlorn and hated, leaving a name that is still synonomous with cruelty.

As a child she was the darling of everyone, charming, pretty, a prodigy of learning, her father's pride, the betrothed of the great Emperor Charles V. Her father showed her off to foreign ambassadors, her mother supervised an education that was in the best traditions of an age that admired the intelligent woman. Even when her proposed husband (in spite of being the greatest prince of Europe) proved too poor to wait for her and married a rich Portuguese princess Mary was still the heiress of England. She was twelve years old when the Portuguese princess who had superseded her gave birth to an heir to Spain, who was christened Philip, and it was about this time (we do not know the exact date) that her father started the long process of ridding himself of her mother.

To Henry VIII it seems to have been a matter of indifference to bastardize his daughter; no one existed for Henry but in relation to his own wishes. But Mary was a true daughter of Catherine of Aragon; to her, her mother was Queen of England and she herself the King's legitimate daughter—after the birth of Elizabeth the King's only legitimate daughter. Henry was no less monstrously unkind to her than he was to her mother. He kept her in confinment, deprived her of her friends and her household, refused to let her see her mother, even when either of them was ill, and forced her to become lady-in-waiting to her half-sister. It is greatly to Mary's credit that brutal humiliations like this never succeeded in making her hate her sister. Perhaps she was helped at first by her love of children; it was clear now that there would be no marriage arranged for her.

Under the strain of this life her health broke down. She lived in constant fear of being poisoned, and in obedience to her mother's urging ate nothing that had not been prepared and tasted by her own maids; Henry stopped this by taking her maids from her. But there is one small incident recorded that is interesting. Mary had a chance meeting with her father in the country; he spoke to her kindly, but left at once when two of Anne Boleyn's people came up as if to listen.

Mary's pride, and her simple passion for truth and duty, remained unshaken. When Anne Boleyn sent her a message "from the Queen," she replied calmly, "It is not possible my mother can send me a message, being so far from here." She was forbidden to enter the King's presence, and then forbidden to go out, because the people cheered her. To threatening messages from her father she replied inflexibly that she was the obedient servant of the King's Grace, saving her honor and her conscience.

She had some savage consolation when Anne was executed and the second daughter declared bastard. ("Why, governor," the child said, "how haps it, yesterday Lady Princess and today but Lady Elizabeth?": the first step in a long and hard education.) With the King's marriage to Jane Seymour, Mary's life should have been easier, for there could be no doubt about the legitimacy of any children born of this marriage; but before she could be left in peace she had to sign the Oath of Succession. This acknowledged her father as head of the English church, repudiated the "pretended authority of the Bishop of Rome," and acknowledged that the marriage of her father and mother was by God's law and man's incestuous and unlawful.

It was of course a political necessity, for a rebellious legitimate princess of the Catholic faith could have been a terrible weapon in the hands of the King's enemies. But Henry pursued his daughter with a vindictiveness that must have been personal. She wrote him a dutiful letter, but put in it the damning words "After God." Cromwell (perhaps kindly) refused to show it to the King, and sent back a draft of what was required. Mary copied the draft, but again put in "Next to Almighty God." Cromwell sent that back too, and she deleted God, but that did not satisfy her earthly father. He sent a commission to examine her, and to them she would not, or could not, repeat the Oath of Succession. They abused her as a bastard and worse than a bastard, threatened her with violence, and gave her four days to submit.

She submitted. She did so under duress and with the mental reservations permitted by her church, and at once wrote privately to the Pope for absolution; but to her devout Catholic faith, her pride, her stern conscience, and her love for her dead mother, the submission must have been a terrible blow.

Henry received her again as his daughter, and in Queen Jane she found a kind friend; but there was again no peace for her. In 1535 the men of the north rose in what they insisted was not a rebellion but a pilgrimage—the Pilgrimage of Grace. They were protesting against the severance from Rome, but inevitably one of their demands was the repealing of Mary's bastardization. She was forced to publish her submission, addressing herself to the rebels, to the country at large, to the Pope, and to the emperor (who was her cousin and ready to take advantage of any troubles that befell in England). When Henry cynically withdrew the pardon he had promised the pilgrims and took a terrible revenge on them (their leader hung in chains at York until he died), Mary fell ill from the strain. She returned to court only when Queen Jane, nearing her confinement, asked to have Mary with her. Prince Edward was born in October, 1537, and as he was a boy, Mary could with good conscience acknowledge him heir to England.

For the rest of her father's life she had a little peace, for the three children were sometimes together, and both Anne of Cleves and Catherine Parr were kind stepmothers. Mary was now a woman in her thirties, small, proud-mannered, the fairness of her complexion giving her a deceptive air of youth, but always ailing, and, with her stubborn adherence to her faith, still too dangerous to be allowed to marry.

In her brother Edward's reign her sad state appeared permanent. There was (until the last year of his life) no apparent reason why he should not marry and have heirs, and his extreme Protestantism made it plain that he would have no return to Rome. Even his youthful fondness for his sister began to give way to his dogmatism, and from lecturing her on her frivolous ways (by which he meant dressing richly and playing cards) he advanced to a determnation that she must give up her faith. But Mary was no longer the terrorized girl of her father's reign. When the council wrote to her reminding her that the celebration of Mass was forbidden, she wrote calmly back that she had offended against no law except one of their own making that her conscience told her was an offense to God, and instructed her chaplain to say three daily Masses instead of two. After the fall of Somerset she was called to account before the council, and there reminded her brother that he was still a boy and the lords that she was the daughter of the King who had raised them from nothing. She rode to London with a great retinue of her supporters, all wearing the Catholic badge of the black rosary. It was dangerous, but where her religion was concerned Mary was fearless; and she had the support of her cousin the emperor, who threatened reprisals if she were forbidden her Mass.

In February, 1553, when she was thirty-seven, she rode to Westminster again to visit her brother. He was ill, clearly dying; and she was not only his heir by Henry VIII's will, but the hope of many of the people besides. Edward's Protestantism had hardly yet penetrated the conservative mass of the people, and Northumberland was widely hated; and, religion and politics apart, Catherine of Aragon was still remembered with love and pity, and her brave daughter had the loyalty of many who might still incline toward reform.

Five months later Mary was summoned to the King's death-bed, and set out at once. On the way news was brought to her that he was already dead, that he had disinherited her and that Northumberland had had his daughter-in-law Lady Jane Grey proclaimed Queen and was waiting to capture Mary. She turned north at once and rode to the strong castle of Framlingham in Suffolk; and while she waited there England rose in her support. That must have been one of the few happy times of Mary's life, for it was a triumph for her own courage and steadfastness.

She came to her coronation in London in triumph, even though there were threatening murmurs from the Protestants. Jane, the little Nine-Days-Queen (whose reign was ended when her father-in-law Northumberland broke in on her at dinner and pulled down the royal canopy over her head), and her husband Guilford Dudley were only put into comfortable confinement in the Tower, though Northumberland was executed, cravenly protesting his loyalty to Rome. In the Tower Mary found the old Duke of Norfolk, the victor under her mother of Flodden Field, who had escaped death in Henry VIII's last hours; Stephen Gardiner, the Catholic Bishop of Winchester; and a pathetic young man of twenty-seven who had been there since he was twelve, Edward Courtenay, descended from Catherine of York, sister to Henry VII's Queen, the last White Rose to fall to Henry VIII's vengeance. She released them all, and thankfully took Gardiner as her chief counsellor, and received with genuine kindness her half-sister Elizabeth, whom she kept with her during these first happy weeks. Elizabeth was far too wary to have become even tacitly allied with any party in the land, and the astute Imperial Ambassador wrote of her, "She is greatly to be feared; she hath a spirit full of incantation."

Mary took it as her duty to re-establish the Catholic faith; no thought of compromise could have entered into the head of one who claimed it as a virtue that she had never opened a heretical book. It is not likely that she would have succeeded in the long run, even if she had had a Catholic heir, because of the growing English hatred of interference from overseas; but she made sure of failing almost at once by her decision to marry. A Queen Regnant had to provide an heir, but it was also thought then that a woman, being unable to provide military leadership, could not rule alone. We may suspect that Mary also quite simply wanted the support of a husband and the joy of children. Gardiner, to whom she turned for both political and spiritual advice until the arrival of the Papal Legate, Cardinal Pole, told her outright that England would never consent to be ruled by a foreigner, and advised her to marry Edward Courtenay. Mary showed him her coronation ring, the symbol of her marriage to England, and told him that she would never be false to her coronation oath, but that nevertheless she had decided to marry Philip heir to Spain, son of that Emperor Charles V to whom she had once been betrothed.

She could not have made a more disastrous choice. Not only did it indicate beyond doubt that England was to be taken forcibly back into the Roman allegiance, but it tied her to the Spanish-Imperial party in Europe and made her a mere province of Spain. England rose in revolt at the prospect. The Midlands and the West Country rose, nominally in favor of Lady Jane Grey, living harmlessly in the Tower, and in the southeast Thomas Wyatt led Kent in a march on London. But it was not the name of Jane Grey that brought Kent to arms; it was the names of Elizabeth Tudor and Henry Courtney.

The issues were too many, the active leaders irresolute, the figure-heads inactive. In extremity, in refuge in the Tower of London, with

Wyatt nearing the city, Mary showed her Tudor courage and her own humanity; she refused to turn the guns of the Tower on Southwark over the river for fear of killing the innocent, and when the news came that Wyatt was at Hyde Park she said, "Fall to prayer then, and I warrant we shall hear better news soon." They did: the news of Wyatt's capture.

After that, of course, Jane Grey was too dangerous to be left alive, little though she had ever done to harm anyone. Mary delayed her execution in the hope of converting her to Catholicism, but in vain, for Jane's faith was as strong and narrow as her own, and even Mary's chaplain pitied her. The day before her own execution she watched through the window her young husband Guilford Dudley going to his death, and herself died with courage and dignity, the sixteen-year-old victim of a greedy man's ambition.

There remained Courtney and Princess Elizabeth. Courtney was of no account, and died in exile on the Continent. Elizabeth, with precocious wisdom, had stayed quietly at her home while Wyatt's men were cheering and dying for her. Mary sent for her, and she came obediently (though as slowly as possible) to London, and found herself dispatched by water to the Tower. She was landed at Traitors' Gate, through which her mother had gone in and never come out alive. She sat down on the landing stage outside the gate, with the river water washing over her shoes, and refused to move. This so affected one of her attendants that he burst into tears. Elizabeth's response was worthy of the old cunning magnificent Queen of thirty years ahead: captious, splendid, and a stately withdrawal from an untenable position. She turned on the unfortunate man, tongue-lashed him for not giving her proper support, declared, that, thank God, her truth was such that her friends did not need to weep for her, and marched into the Tower.

She was right, too; nothing could be proved against her of complicity with Wyatt, and she was grudgingly released. For the rest of her life Mary mistrusted her and hoped to prevent her succession; yet she loved her dearly and never forgot that she too was Henry VIII's daughter.

This sisterly feeling was soon to be tested to the utmost, for the ambassador of the emperor stipulated that the Princess must be executed before Philip of Spain could arrive to claim his bride. Mary refused and the stipulation was dropped, but Philip came only very slowly. He took the opportunity before he came of holding a ceremony before witnesses in which he swore that he consented to his marriage contract, which had been carefully drawn up to prevent his having any power in England, only to secure the marriage and did not consider himself bound by it. He was twelve years Mary's junior, having already being married and widowered, and had been accustomed to refer to her as his aunt. He was extremely polite when he did come, making himself agreeable to everyone and taking care to adopt the English manners. He and Mary were married in great state in Winchester, and Mary at once fell deeply in love with him. His attendants were sorry for him; they found Mary older than her years, badly dressed, and embarrassingly affectionate to him.

Philip was was completely indifferent to Mary; but then Philip was all his life completely indifferent to anything human; he seems hardly to have been human himself. In a long friendless and arduous life he did his duty to his God and his position, becoming guilty of monstrous cruelties in the process, and it is no more possible to hate him for his cruelties than to pity him for his friendless labors.

Or perhaps he had one spark of life, though we have only hints of it. His position in England suited him excellently, giving him control of the short sea-route from Spain to the Low Countries, and various other advantages his loving wife willingly gave him, and soon Mary discovered signs of pregnancy, and was so happy that she restored her sister Elizabeth to court. Elizabeth had been the center of an embarrassing display of public loyalty before the wedding, but had behaved herself impeccably; and Mary sent her, in her best dress, to see Philip. At this time of her life there seems to have been a kind of magic about Elizabeth, a glitter drawn from her fleeting beauty, her pride, her intelligence, and the tautness of her peril and her relish in meeting it. Many years later she said that Philip had been in love with her, and Philip confirmed it.

Mary's pregnancy was to come to term in April, 1555, but it did not; her doctors said May, then June. By this time she was so ill that even a difficult pregnancy (she was thirty-nine) could not account for it; she sat all day on cushions on the floor, her women said, weeping with the pain. In August, Philip left her to visit his father, saying that he would be away for a fortnight, and did not return. By the autumn Mary had accepted that there would be no child, and took up her burden of ruling alone.

By now she had forced through Parliament the revival of Henry VIII's laws against heresy. Parliament had reluctantly consented in the expectation of the moderate persecution that the old King had sanctioned (Edward VI had not punished by death). To their horror they found that Mary was resolved to apply the laws in all their rigor. The fires of Smithfield were lit, and burned fiercely for the rest of her reign; three hundred men and women were burned in less than four years. What makes this particularly odious is that chiefly it was the common people who suffered; those nobles who had enriched themselves in Henry VIII's reign with church lands and church wealth not only avoided the fires but contrived to keep their loot in all legality.

What was it that moved the kind and generous Mary to such atrocious cruelty? She believed (difficult though this is to understand) that it was her duty to God to stamp out heresy; and by the standards of the day the cruelty was not so very atrocious: far too moderate, indeed, by the standards of her husband. Probably some of the responsibility was Philip's, for Mary submitted herself entirely to his needs, and he needed a secure England. But it may be that Mary's own unhappiness had become so intense that she was grown incapable of compassion for others. Philip did not return, though he continued to make demands on her that neither Parliament nor the people would accept. He wanted the Crown Matrimonial—that is, he wanted to be King, which would have brought about rebellion in England. He wanted Elizabeth married off, to remove her from England, and Elizabeth contrived to refuse all offers without putting herself in the wrong. He wanted England to join his war against France, and in this at least Mary gave him what he wanted. The sole result was the loss of Calais, England's last remaining possession in France. After that the English called the Queen *Maria Ruina Anglica* instead of *Regina,* and it hurt her to the heart; "When I am dead and opened," she said, "you will find Calais engraved upon my heart."

Inevitably the burnings threw up their martyrs, whose memories remained to condemn her. They did not go unrecorded, for they went into *Foxe's Book of Martyrs,* which for the next 200 years was said to have been more widely read in England than any book but the Bible, and which kept alive the conviction, started by Mary, that Catholicism meant fire and torture. Of the greater victims, one was Nicholas Ridley, who had spoken out for the poor to Edward VI; and another that most unlikely of martyrs, Thomas Cranmer, very long Archbishop of Canterbury. Cranmer had honestly believed in royal absolutism, and this belief had clashed inexorably with his equally strong Protestant faith. In face of the fire the Protestant faith lost, and Cranmer recanted; then, with who knows what strength, he withdrew his recantation and went to the stake, and put first into the fire the hand that had signed the recantation. That hand had also written the Prayer-Book, in the purest and most beautiful English of any age yet.

Philip did come back to Mary once, for a few weeks in the summer of 1557. When he had gone she wrote to him that she was pregnant. She was forty-two; no one believed her, least of all Philip, whom she never saw again. Again it came to nothing, and by October, 1558, she knew that she was dying of a tumor of the womb. She dutifully made her will. There was a possible Catholic heir in Mary Queen of Scots, but in obedience to her father's will and the laws of England she left her crown to the next legal heir, Elizabeth (though she could not bring herself to mention her by name). In obedience to her coronation oath she added, "My most dear Lord and Husband shall have no government within the realm." It is possible that she hoped that Philip would secure England for Rome by marrying Elizabeth.

In her last days she was faithful to her old affections; she sent a kind message to her sister to tell her that she was glad she was to succeed to her father's throne. Toward the end she fell into a coma, waking only now and again and speaking kindly to her people. Once she told them not to weep for her, because she was having a good dream of children singing. She died on November 17, 1558, a good, kind, and courageous woman, pitiably mauled by life.

She left her country at its lowest ebb for centuries: ill-armed, ill-governed, disunited, disgraced in war, and devoid of all spirit and purpose. Yet it was not a poor country, materially or morally. Its riches wanted only a ruler who could release their potential; and living quietly at Hatfield, sewing, studying, playing skillfully on the virginal, was a young woman of twenty-five wanting only a kingdom that could release her own hidden riches.

ELIZABETH I
Gloriana
1558-1603

✿

Born in Greenwich Palace in September 1533.
Daughter of Henry VIII and his second wife Anne Boleyn; declared illegitimate at her mother's divorce and
   execution in 1536; restored to the succession by her
   father's will.
Died unmarried at Richmond, March 1603.

Elizabeth's legitimacy was never accepted by the Roman
   Church or the Catholic Powers, who claimed that on
   the death of her sister Mary I the succession devolved
   upon Mary Stuart Queen of Scots, who was great-
   grand-daughter of Henry VII by his elder surviving
   daughter Margaret Tudor, wife of James IV King of
   Scots. By her marriage with her cousin Henry Stuart
   Lord Darnley Mary Queen of Scots had one son,
      James VI of Scotland, later also James I of En-
      gland.
      She was deposed in her son's favor in 1567 and ex-
      ecuted at Fotheringay in 1587.

With the death of Elizabeth I the House of Tudor became
extinct in the male line. James Stuart's claim to the throne
of England was thus undisputed.

ELIZABETH I
Gloriana

lizabeth Tudor, who knew the value of the gesture, liked to boast that she was Henry VIII's daughter. She was much more Henry VII's granddaughter.

The three Tudors before Elizabeth had all promised more than they had performed. The founder of the dynasty, Henry VII, had set the stage for them, but Henry VIII had been frustrated by his deficient personality, Edward VI by his youth, Mary I by her age. Only now, in this long reign covering nearly half a century, full of fundamental political, religious, and cultural upheavals, did England find precisely the monarch she needed. Evasive, pragmatic, pennypinching, blandly dishonest under an honest face, patient, indomitable, tireless, a sick woman all her life, shameless, shaming all others by her single-minded devotion, Elizabeth was Henry VII over again but for one thing, she had in a high degree what Henry VII had only had quietly and by the way: magnetism. As a young woman she outshone crowned Queens and great beauties; as an old raddled woman, all red wig and blackened teeth and shriveled body held up by corsets, she was the center of every occasion by her mere force of personality.

She once said to Parliament, "I thank God I am endued with such qualities that if I were turned out of the realm in my petticoat, I were able to live in any place in Christendom." She was undoubtedly right, this formidable woman; but if this had happened (it was unlikely: she would more likely have been at the meeting of axe and block on Tower Hill) she would not have been the same woman. As Elizabeth ruled England, so England ruled Elizabeth. It was a perfect marriage, a symbiosis. England made Elizabeth; Elizabeth made Renaissance England.

Elizabeth's early years had been less harassed than her sister Mary's, but by her fifteenth year she was deep into the dangers that surrounded princes. When Henry VIII's widow Catherine Parr at last married her first love Thomas Seymour, out of her kindness she gave her younger stepdaughter a happy home. A little too happy: Elizabeth's high spirits and Seymour's charm led to such rompings in the princess's bedroom that she had to leave, and Seymour's idiotic behavior toward King Edward led to suspicions that Elizabeth had been part of a plot to dethrone her brother. Only her own wits stood between her and the Tower; she used them, but then had to hear the news of Thomas Seymour's execution as a traitor. One wrong word might have taken her to the block after him, for though Elizabeth could lie and evade and equivocate there was a steely vein of integrity in her that forbade her to cower. She said, "Then today died a man of much wit and little judgement." Pure Elizabeth Tudor: the undoubted truth beautifully phrased, the best defense possible, and her own feelings hidden from present and future.

Under Edward the Protestant she was quiet, modest, demure of dress, so that he called her his sweet sister Temperance. Under Mary the Catholic she did nothing so vulgar as recant, but begged her kind sister to give her instruction in the Catholic faith, and ended by going to Mass. Undoubtedly she knew precisely what she was doing, as she did when she refused all offers of marriage that would have removed her from England (she said, and even seems to have convinced her sister, that this was due to "none other than maidenly shamefastness"), and when she remained silent during Wyatt's rising. This, with Wyatt's men fighting their way down Ludgate shouting her name, could not have been easy; she had to be a calculating woman, but all her life she loved the grand gesture. Even while Mary was celebrating her wedding to the King of Spain, the people of England were cheering Elizabeth. She could afford to wave them down and beg their cheers for her sister; she was Elizabeth Tudor. When Mary was dying the courtiers left her bedside and rode to Elizabeth's house at Hatfield; and Mary's dying words went to Hatfield too, with all Mary's warmth and generosity. But Elizabeth's first great triumph, and it was splendid and unexpected and stunning in its effect even on her, came from the common people. When she entered London as Queen the people flaunted their love for her in a wild carnival, and she, as wild as they, accepted it. That was to be the keynote of her reign. She was "mere English," she told her English people. The Spanish ambassador said, "This woman is possessed by a hundred thousand devils." He meant the same thing.

As a child Elizabeth had been pretty, with the red-gold hair and fair skin of her father. Her looks soon faded, though she was never, even in her extreme of skinny and raddled old age, less than stately and magnificent; but for these few years around her accession she was something more than beautiful. There is a miniature of her at this time: a small triangular face with narrow eyes and level lips, a little face almost plain but for the effect it conveys of tenseness, of promise, of a brilliant intelligence held in taut control.

She had need of all her qualities, for she succeeded to little enough. No one could even be found to crown her but the obscure Bishop of Carlisle. Only with her sister Mary's death had her kingdom ceased to be an appanage of Spain, and all the powers of Europe were on the prowl to see who could snatch it—and its marriageable Queen —first. The country was rent by religious strife; the coinage was debased; the exchequer was empty. It was a dismal beginning.

It was meat and drink to Elizabeth. She found good men to help her, and hosts of willing servants, but from the start it was she herself who felt the infinitely delicate way through the complexities of home and European politics, and brought her country out rich, powerful, independent, and, above all, confident in itself.

She had to evolve her own style, for she was only the second Queen Regnant in English history. She was a woman unsupported in a man's world—a world that was man's to an extent difficult to imagine now—and she used with genius all the vices that men attributed to all women. She flirted, she coquetted, she was capricious, she was unreasonable; she would agree to a course one day after a flood of tears, and repudiate it the next, probably boxing her ministers' ears into the bargain; she would hang endlessly on a decision until her counsellors would despair of her; she would say one thing to one man and another to another, and taxed with it would blandly prove that she had not been in the least inconsistent; she would lie, prevaricate, and play the innocent with no conscience at all. And somehow, at the end of all the comedy, she would have arrived at what she judged the right thing to do, and her judgment was seldom wrong.

These feminine wiles were of course entirely in their place in the matter that engaged the attention of all Europe for nearly fifteen years after her accession: the question of her marriage. They were also, we may guess, something of a necessity to her because of her health. It is on record that all her life nervous stress induced illness in her, and the self-subjugation necessary to surmount this weakness produced a hysteria which was very likely valuably relieved by her tantrums. There is no record that any hysteria of hers ever affected her judgment. Nor, though it exasperated them almost past bearing, did it repel her servants; they came back, despairingly and devotedly, for more.

The personal ascendancy she exercised over her people—in which term is included not only her immediate servants but a large part of her subjects—tends to obscure the basic nature of her rule. Elizabeth I was the end of that process which had started just short of 500 years before, when Henry I had issued his first charter to those subjects whose good will he thought it would be useful to have. Elizabeth appears, because of the uniquely personal nature of her government, to have been an absolute monarch; in fact, her rule was based wholly on the principle that the King rules only with the consent of the people. It is as certain as any guess can be that anyone who voiced this principle to Elizabeth Tudor would have been soundly rated, and probably smartly slapped, for insolence verging on treason. She voiced the principle often, but only rhetorically (and generally with stunning effect), and would instantly have resisted any effort to have it put into practice by anyone but herself. Elizabeth was a pragmatist, but a long-sighted one; if she could only rule with the consent of her people, she made sure that the consent was deep and whole-hearted; she made it her business to keep so much in touch with her people that she seldom made a mistake about their feelings. But here comes the marriage, the symbiosis; who knows now—indeed, who could know at the time?—how much was Elizabeth's wisdom leading England's opinion, and how much England's wisdom trusting Elizabeth? This trust developed very fast, and in the nature of things declined into weariness a little at the very end of a forty-five-year reign, but while it lasted it merited the words Walter Burley had written two hundred years before: "A profound love between subjects and kings leads to a deep concord between the citizens and to a very strong kingdom."

A lifelong quality that Elizabeth inherited from her grandfather —it had entirely skipped her father—was economy. All her life she was poor—in wartime her revenue did not amount to half a million pounds—and all her life she was deeply conscious of the country's need for money. Early in her reign she told her council, "No war, my lords!"; wars settled too little for what they cost. She might equally well have said, "No religion, my lords!"; for all her efforts in that direction were set on peace.

In religious matters Elizabeth had a curiously modern outlook; she was, after all, a child of the Renaissance, which reached England late and with a cast that today we should call humanism. She said, "There is one Jesus Christ and one faith, and the rest is trifles," and on that principle she acted all her life. If later on she mildly persecuted both Catholics and Puritans (using this term in its broadest sense to indicate the extreme of Protestantism), it was not for religious reasons but for purely political ones. The Catholics stood for foreign domination of England, and the Puritans for domination of the crown by the clergy. She persecuted as little as possible, and only when she was politically driven to it, framing her laws for religious rites to be observable by all but fanatics. She also—and this is very rare indeed in history—persecuted successfully, neither so little that it had no effect, nor so much that it was counterproductive (as poor Mary's persecution had been). Her method was to establish the order she wanted, which was a moderate and respected Protestantism, and to support it until it became part of the peaceful prosperous life that was her gift to England; while in her councils she saw to it that in matters religious the English church was independent of anyone, and in matters secular the English crown was independent of the Church. In other Protestant countries the reformed religion had established theocracies that were quite as repulsive as anything dictated by the Vatican and enforced by the Inquisition; there was no chance of that in the England of Elizabeth.

It is a curious coincidence that in a brief time the British Isles had three Queens Regnant, and that two of them came to grief because of their marriages, and that the one who was a success never married. We can surely be certain of one thing about Elizabeth Tudor: that if she could have left her country a secure succession she would have done so. And as for the problem that a Queen married was a Queen who had to bow to the wishes of her husband, someone remarked of the brief suggestion that she should marry Ivan the Terrible of Russia that if the marriage had come off that Tsar would now be known as Ivan the Terrified. In those days when the internal disorders of a princess might make the difference between a kingdom and a dependent province, it was well-known throughout Europe that even in her youth Elizabeth suffered (like her sister) from amenorrhea (the interruption of the monthly periods); this can come about through nervous stress, or it may be a symptom of a more serious gynecological malfunction. It is possible that Elizabeth knew that she was incapable of childbearing; if she did, it was entirely characteristic of her to have turned this disability into a political weapon by concealing it from everyone. From herself we have only one recorded word, and it sounds uncommonly like a cry of anguish. It was when the boy who was eventually to succeed her was born in 1566; on hearing the news Elizabeth said, "The Queen of Scots is the lighter of a fair son, and we are but barren stock."

But, whatever her true intentions, she kept her mouth shut and her suitors dancing, and wrung every ounce of possible political advantage from them. Philip of Spain was at first her friend, to begin with hoping for marriage and later, when it had become plain that Elizabeth was reversing Mary's religious policy, hoping to prevent an alliance with his enemy France. The possibility of a French marriage went on even into Elizabeth's middle age, and she flirted outrageously with her "Frog," as she called her stout goggle-eyed French Prince. She insisted, incidentally, on having her marriage negotiations accompanied by a proper courtship, where possible in person. But there was one man she genuinely loved, with whom for all his life she had a deep and faithful relationship. This was Robin Dudley Earl of Leicester, who was a son of Northumberland's and brother-in-law of Lady Jane Grey. He had something of his father's short-sightedness, and though Elizabeth wholly trusted his loyalty his bull-headedness sometimes led her into trouble. An English marriage would have been popular, but most likely she felt that she could not survive the difficult early years of her reign without the advantage of the foreign-marriage bait. Whatever the truth of this, it is pleasant to record that their relationship endured and deepened, thwarted lovers, lifelong friends, great Queen and loyal servant.

European politics then were a bewildering set of cross-currents between dynastic ambition and religious struggle. The old enmity between France and Spain still held, but was complicated by the fact that both powers were fighting battles with the Protestants, and that neither side scrupled to ally itself with the anti-Catholic enemies of the other. Spain's trouble was in the Low Countries, roughly comprising modern Holland and Belgium, a Hapsburg inheritance which Charles V on his abdication had attached to Spain and the kingdom of Philip II. The Low Countries were passionately Protestant, and passionately independent; Philip's religion could not permit the one, and his Hapsburg passion for territory could not permit the other. He tried to "pacify," as the phrase was, the rebellious provinces by the sword and the stake, and they did not respond obediently. The French, rejoicing at his embarrassment, gave help to the rebels. Philip's only direct supply route to his armies was the sea-passage through the Channel, which was controlled by the increasingly powerful English seamen. English seamen in any case hated the Spanish. They were beginning to venture out to the Americas; Elizabeth could not afford great imperialist ventures, so they went as private traders (she was often canny enough to secure the crown a financial interest); and the Spanish, whose financial mismanagement was remarkable even in an age notoriously at sea on economics, had closed their overseas possessions to foreign traders. While England and Spain might be technically at peace, English and Spanish ships exchanged broadsides in American waters. Philip addressed protests to Elizabeth; she blandly replied that she had given no such orders, and in return demanded the release of British seamen taken in those waters, who often enough came to a miserable end in the dungeons of the Spanish Inquisition.

The French had the disadvantage that their Protestants, called Huguenots, were at home. They were a very sizable minority who came to acknowledge the leadership of an inconsiderable little ruler from the south. This was Henri of Navarre, later the great Protestant hero, and later still the Catholic King of France, who when he found himself heir to the throne on condition that he abandon his own religion decided that "Paris is worth a Mass." But before this his situation was as difficult as that of the Low Country rebels; and all of them applied to the Protestant Queen of England for help.

Elizabeth could not afford to help others; nor could she afford to let these co-religious suffer for lack of help. She gave it when she could, always niggardly as she always had to be, always firm in repudiating more involvement than she judged strictly necessary. Henri of Navarre took her help and cheated her over it (possibly the only man ever to get the better of her, and a man after her own heart, provided a couple of kingdoms' space separated the two hearts). Elizabeth let her young men go and fight, and she sent an expeditionary force, with strict instructions not to become deeply involved. Leicester was in command, and he committed her further than she wanted. They had their most serious quarrel about this, and she wrote to him:

Jesus, what availeth wit when it faileth the owner at greatest need? Do that you are bidden and leave your considerations for your own affairs. I am assured of your dutiful thoughts, but I am utterly at squares with this childish dealing.

In reply Leicester ruefully begged to be allowed to come home and be a groom in her stables.

Today, comfortably three centuries distanced, we can give all our sympathy to the brave Netherlanders, who suffered horribly and fought with immense courage. Elizabeth could afford no such luxury. She did not like their religion, which tended to produce a moral tyranny matching that of the Inquisition; she quite rightly mistrusted their good faith (they took her money and then undercut her ships in the cloth and carrying trades); and she feared that they would drag her deeper than was wise into European entanglements. Once she was offered a partial sovereignty and turned it down flat. Her father would have swelled to accept.

But the chief trouble during the earlier years of Elizabeth's reign was that other Queen Regnant, that exact contrary of her, that sad and silly woman, Mary Queen of Scots.

Mary Stuart was the granddaughter of Henry VIII's sister Margaret, and thus in Catholic eyes Mary Tudor's heir. She had been destined from birth to marry Edward VI and thus unite the two kingdoms. A Scots noble had remarked sourly to Edward that the marriage might be well enough but he did not hold with the wooing of it; Henry VIII tried to kidnap the infant Queen, and Edward's uncle killed 11,000 Scots at Pinkie Cleugh. Mary's mother was Marie of Guise, a member of the most powerful and most unscrupulous family in France, and they brought the little girl up as a princess of France and in due course married her to the boy who was to be until his death in 1560 François II. This might mean the eventual union of France, Scotland and England under one ruler, a possibility that explains Philip of Spain's favoring of Elizabeth as England's heir. But, while the little Queen of Scots was enjoying an idyllic upbringing as the darling of the French court, Scotland was suffering the Reformation in a peculiarly passionate form, thus becoming the natural ally of England and the Low Countries—except that the Scots loathed the English, whom they suspected of designs on their independence, and Elizabeth loathed the Scottish form of Protestantism, where the *Kirk* claimed complete ascendancy over crown and people.

Mary professed herself willing to reign as a Catholic over a Protestant country; but, brought up wholly in a court whose political principles might be described as monarchic absolutism well-tempered with treason, it is doubtful whether she fully appreciated what this meant. Indeed, for a woman bejewelled with so many kingdoms, it is doubtful whether she ever fully understood what to do with them; certainly her actual experience of ruling was brief. Mary is a pathetic figure, less because of her troubles, most of which she brought on herself, than because of her inadequacy to deal with them. Even her later reputation as a great lover is wholly false. Her first husband was known to be impotent; her undoubted passion for her second, Henry Lord Darnley, turned to disgust in a matter of months; and her third husband, Bothwell (who probably murdered Darnley), she married, she said, only because he raped her first. Her complete sexual discretion during the long years of her last virtual widowhood suggests that she was frigid.

Mary's Scots nobles were a brutal and selfish lot, but in tiring of a Catholic Queen incapable of controlling either her kingdom or her private life they showed a little good sense. Revolting against her and her murderous Bothwell, they imprisoned her on an island in Loch Leven. She escaped from there, and after some confused fighting in 1568 rode south with a few supporters and took refuge in, of all places, England.

Why she did this we shall never know. We know of no reason why she should not have gone back to France, and all these years, though she had been on graciously sisterly terms with Elizabeth, she had regarded herself, as the Catholic powers of Europe regarded her, as the rightful Queen of England. Did she trust her wits to fool Elizabeth, who had been living on her own wits for as long as Mary had lived her sheltered life? Or did she, fooled herself by that sheltered life, expect romantic generosity?

In fact, she did get something like that, for there is no doubt that Elizabeth had a strong feeling of, as it were, trade solidarity; and perhaps even sisterly solidarity to another woman in trouble in a world of greedy men (she had complained years ago of their "insatiable cupidity"). But Elizabeth, as always, could not afford luxuries of feeling; she firmly sent Mary (whom she was never to see) to comfortable but secure imprisonment in the north, and settled down to make what she could of this political counter so unexpectedly put into her hands.

It was far from being a useful counter. About the only people who were happy to see Mary where she was were the Scots, who had put her infant son James on the throne, and were bringing him up as a Protestant while the nobles fought out their own ambitions. The French were wholly on Mary's side, both as French and as Catholics. Perhaps the unhappiest of them all was Philip of Spain; as a Catholic he had to pretend to vast indignation at Elizabeth's action, while knowing that any decisive effort to free Mary could lead to her accession to England and a vast anti-Spanish *bloc* from Scotland to the Mediterranean.

Elizabeth knew this; she also knew that the time was near when England and Spain would inevitably clash. England was by no means settled in the Protestant faith; there were English Catholics in Rome actively plotting treason, as well as a great body of peaceful Catholics at home whose faith would be sorely tried in the case of a Catholic invasion. All that had saved England from this had been the fear of the French Mary.

Elizabeth did not want the faith of her Catholic subjects tested; she wanted them converted to her way of life (it is putting it too high to write *her religion,* because she thought a man's private religion none of her business) in the only fashion she thought possible and safe, that of liking the life they lived. She put her position quite clearly in a verse she wrote herself; the *Daughter of Debate* was Mary Queen of Scots:

The Daughter of Debate, who discord eke doth sow,
Shall reap no gain where former rule hath taught still peace to grow.

Yet, since Elizabeth had at some time to come to grips with the Catholic question, it could hardly have been posed to her kingdom in a more fortunate way than this. Mary was to be a prisoner for twenty years, during which Elizabeth's hold on her subjects' love and gratitude grew enormously. To all but the most fanatically Catholic, Mary was to come to represent everything that was undesirable: civil strife, foreign domination, loss of independence abroad and peace and prosperity at home.

That it was only Mary's life that stood between England and an attack from Spain was not apparent to the people. Whether purposely or not, Spain's intriguing in France had brought the French to the brink of civil war; the emperor was a dallier and anyway eternally bankrupt; so Spain was left the greatest power in Europe and the only upholder of the Catholic faith. She was in direct conflict with England in other ways, too; there was the war in the Low Countries; there was the command of the sea-passage through the Channel; and there was the question of what the English called honest trade and the Spanish piracy on the high seas.

A great part of English life had always centered on the sea, and these were the great days of the English seamen. In the early days of discovery of the New World, the Pope, with a blandness perhaps proper to the voice of God upon earth, had drawn a line through the Americas and bestowed upon Portugal all that was on the east side of it, on Spain all that was on the west; this alone was enough to convince the English of their right to take what they could get in both quarters. The real value of the Americas seems not yet to have dawned upon the world; most of it was hypnotized by the single fact that gold could be found there. But the Spanish and the Portuguese were already settling there, and it was in the reign of Elizabeth that the first English settlers went out, seeking the parts further north that the Spanish had not yet taken.

This battle in the western seas naturally spread east over the Atlantic, and was exacerbated when the Spanish took to treating captured English seamen not as pirates but as heretics, and handing them over to the Inquisition. Stories of honest English sailors chained in the dungeons of the Inquisition and burned at last for refusing to abjure their honest English faith, combined with Foxe's *Booke of Martyrs* to confirm the English conviction that Catholicism was mainly the Inquisition (which it was not, but there is little doubt that given the chance in England it would have been for some time).

The most famous of the English seamen of the time—though there were many like him—was Francis Drake, whom the Spanish so feared and hated that they called him *El Draque,* the Dragon. Drake was the man who had the courage to sail off into the blue and not turn back until he had circumnavigated the world; he was also the energetic bellicose seaman who was forever pestering the Queen to let him go and attack the Spanish in home waters. Elizabeth was the despair of both orthodox soldiers and individualists like Drake; she was immensely cautious, eternally niggardly of money, and, for all her bland disclaimers, kept a very firm hand on her men. Drake's time was not yet, while Mary Stuart was still alive.

Queens Regnant cannot abide twenty years in captivity entirely inactive, even if only in courtesy. No one knows now how much

Mary was personally involved in the plots that raged around her during those twenty years, when outwardly she lived the quiet life of a retired widow; but there is a certain tinge of her style in the last fatal plot. The only personal relationships she ever seems to have conducted successfuly were those of chivalry, of the beautiful unattainable Queen and the adoring young courtier (in her early days in Scotland she had conducted one of these so successfully that the adoring young courtier had to be executed). In 1552 the Pope excommunicated Elizabeth and freed her subjects from their allegiance. This was an open invitation to anyone who fancied the job to assassinate the Queen. Personally, Elizabeth took the danger with composure; politically, it must have delighted her, for it was the kind of foreign arrogance that could be counted on to infuriate even a moderately Catholic Englishman. It proved to be the death of Mary Stuart; a young man who adored her (we do not even know if he ever met her, and she was into her forties by now) set up a crazy plot, unsupported but by a few friends, to assassinate Elizabeth and rescue Mary. The plot became public, and England howled for Mary's blood.

It was the perfect political opportunity; and yet Elizabeth was reluctant. Certainly she was casting about, even at this last moment, for some method of avoiding personal responsibility; but it is one of the more heroic qualities of this heroic woman that, evasive, cunning, unscrupulous as she was, her emotions were always honest. She liked not, she said, this killing of Kings (it was an uncomfortable precedent), and she knew she was delivering her kingdom to the chances of war with Spain. Her tantrums when she did let herself be persuaded into signing the death warrant were thunderous.

Mary Stuart, on the other hand—she cannot any longer be called Queen of Scots, because her son James, now twenty-one and deeply involved in the battle between crown and Kirk was reigning in Scotland and coldly signifying to England that he would not make an issue of it if his mother were put to death—Mary Stuart rose to the occasion with all the splendor of a Queen who thought she had a right to three kingdoms. It was a brave and beautiful performance. She was beheaded on a dais set up in the great Hall of Fotheringhay, where she had lately been imprisoned; when she stepped out of her black gown for the execution, her petticoat was all of crimson, the color of martyrdom. But when her head was severed, and the executioner, as the custom was, took it by the hair and held it up, the glorious red-gold hair that had been celebrated throughout Europe came off in his hand, and a skull with a thin wisp of gray hair rolled at his feet.

England was now at great risk. Elizabeth's next heir was the Protestant James VI of Scotland, so that the way was clear for Philip II to launch his great stroke for the punishment of heretics and the return to Rome of the kingdom of England. The Queen collected her forces.

It looked like the battle between David and Goliath: poverty-stricken England, whose only allies were some rags of Protestants depending on her for help, against the mighty Spanish Empire with the gold of the Indies to draw on. In fact it was a far more equal fight than it appeared. Tactically, Elizabeth's pennypinching foresight had provided England with a fast, weatherly navy and a whole generation of experienced seamen, while the gold of the Indies had only served to bankrupt Spain to the point where Philip found it difficult to raise the money to equip his ships. (One modern historian attributes a great deal of the Armada's tactical failure to Drake's attack on Cadiz in 1587. In the course of it Drake burned a great consignment of seasoned barrel-staves, and seasoned barrel-staves were the stuff of life to any fleet, since water had to be carried in barrels, and if the wood were unseasoned the water went bad.) Strategically the Spanish advantage was even less, for the whole concept of the Enterprise of England (as the Spanish called the Great Armada) was astoundingly mistaken.

Philip's basic strategy was to coordinate the sailing of the Armada up-Channel with the movements of his army in the Low Countries. They were to rendezvous at the east end of the Channel, and from there launch their invasion of England. It is just understandable that Philip should not have known that in 1588 his commander in the Low Countries, the very capable Alexander of Parma, had not an army fit for this; Parma was, after all, fighting his own battles, and the military situation changed very suddenly. What is hardly believable is that Philip did not realize that the rendezvous could never have been made, since the Armada was made up of deep-draught vessels, and Parma would have had to put out from the shoaly Netherland coasts in shallow-draught vessels.

He could not, in fact, even do this, as during this summer the Protestant Justin of Nassau was in command of those coasts; but Justin, with the lack of brotherly feeling the English complained of in the Dutch, neglected to tell them this.

None of this, however, made the Armada less tactically dangerous, since a naval defeat would have stripped England of any defense. She had no standing army, only what were called the train-bands, who, however willing, were very little trained. Her navy was a bold step, being largely experimental. The Spanish ships were built as small battlefields, decked amidships and with immensely high turrets fore and aft; the soldiers were the important folk aboard, the sailors being there to get the ships into position beside the enemy. The agreed method of battle was to run aside your opponent and strike your topsails as an invitation to board and fight it out hand-to-hand. The English battleship, on the other hand, was built as a mobile battery, and the most important folk on board were the seamen to maneuver it and the gunners to lay and fire. (There is a social moral to all this; the Spanish used galley-slaves, and Drake said of his crews: "I must have the gentleman to hale and draw with the mariner.") To go with this new tactic the English had been building a new type of warship: low and narrow, very weatherly, lacking unwieldy top-hamper of turrets and decking.

The English ships had another advantage over the Spanish: their crews had not been long at sea, and so were healthy. In fact, the anguished feeling throughout the seamen in the weeks while they waited for the Armada to haul in sight was that the crews had not been long enough at sea; even at that crisis the Queen persisted in saving money by keeping her men ashore.

Contemporary accounts make it clear that (perhaps for the first time since Harold Godwinson marched the South Coast and the York Road in 1066) the whole of the country was waiting for the news of battle. The beacons were ready, piled for lighting all along the South Coast and northwards across country, so that they would know in Northumberland and Durham when the Spanish sails were sighted off the Lizard; the Lord High Admiral, Howard of Effingham, and the Vice-Admiral (who but Francis Drake?) were waiting in Plymouth; every port and little harbor along the coast was in readiness. After dinner on Friday, July 29, 1588 the little *Golden Hind,* Captain Thomas Fleming, sailed in to report the sighting of a Spanish flotilla off the Scillies. This is the time when Drake is reported to have said, "We have time to finish our game [of bowls] and beat the Spaniards too."

They showed at once that their little craft could outsail the cumbrous Spaniards, for after the difficult warping-out from Plymouth Lord Howard gained the weather gauge and thereafter held it. But the Armada sailed in its magnificently disciplined crescent of ships along the vulnerable South Coast, and nothing the English could do could break that formidable formation. Where individual ships broke away, they pounced, and in their presence the Spaniards could not attempt a landing on the undefended shores; but otherwise they never truly discovered the power of their deadly new fleet during the whole ten days of the up-Channel chase. (What they did discover was the enormity of their under-estimate of the powder and shot necessary for these tactics; all those days little boats were putting off from the warships with urgent pleas for more of both and scuttling back with what could be raked up from the South Coast arsenals.) But, worried as they were by their failure to force a battle, they were doing the right thing, shepherding the Spanish commander, the luckless Duke of Medina Sidonia, toward utter disaster.

On August 6, the Armada came to anchor in Calais Roads. The neutral French offered no shelter, and of the rendezvous with Parma there was no news. (Parma was having his own troubles in the Low Countries.) There was a northeasterly blowing, and at anchor the fleet was the perfect target for fireboats. The patient and courageous Medina-Sidonia took the correct precautions, putting out a screen of small boats equipped with grapnels and ordering his ships, if the screen were to be broken, to slip and buoy their cables and stand out to sea, letting the unmanned fireships drift by inshore.

Effingham loosed the fireships just after midnight, eight of them, crammed with combustible material, their guns doubleshotted and waiting for the heat to set them off, driving down with wind and tide behind them. The Spanish screen took off the first two and towed them away (a fair test of seamanship); but as they closed on the next pair the white-hot guns began to go off at random. Under that fusillade the screen broke, and the six remaining ships bore on toward the Armada.

Medina Sidonia slipped his moorings and got out of the way; but the necessity of scattering was too much for the discipline of the rest of the fleet. They broke up and, broken-up, became an easy target. At Gravelines the remnants recovered the old formidable crescent, and withstood Effingham's attack. But they were terribly battered, and by now the wind had strengthened and gone round into the northwest, and the great ships were being driven into the shallows round the Zeeland Sands, and the murderous little flyboats of Justin of Nassau were out picking up stragglers; the Great Armada was defeated.

They escaped running aground by a change of wind, and then ran north, and kept running, northabouts round Scotland, down the west coast of Ireland, and so home; very few of them got there. Medina Sidonia did his duty in seeing them home and then died of the defeat. King Philip is reported to have said, "I sent my ships to fight against men, not against the winds and waves of God"; which was a correctly Christian response to the chastening of God, but a terrible admission from a sovereign who claimed to be the sword of God upon earth.

And Elizabeth of England? She had defied the convention that because she could not lead her people into battle she could not rule them alone; she had given them everything it was in her power to give them for this battle, from time and confidence to the last penny her niggardly ways could scratch up; she was not going to sit quietly at home while the fighting went on. She rode out in state to Tilbury on August 18. She wore a gown of white velvet with a silver cuirass with diamonds in her red-gold hair, and, in state, she reviewed her train-bands. She was fifty-five then, and gaunt, and the red-gold hair was a wig and the train-bands would not much have worried Parma; but she was excommunicate and a target for assassination, and she walked among her people with an escort of four men and two boys. And she said to them:

My loving people, I do not desire to live to distrust my faithful and loving people. I have always so behaved myself that under God I have placed my chiefest strength and safeguard in the loyal hearts and good will of my subjects. And therefore I am come amongst you at this time, being resolved to live and die amongst you all, and to lay down for God and my kingdom and my people my honour and my blood even in the dust. I know I have the body of a weak and feeble woman, but I have the heart and stomach of a king, and of a king of England too, and I think foul scorn that Parma or Spain or any prince of Europe should dare to invade the borders of my realm; to which, rather than any dishonours shall grow by me, I myself will take up arms, I myself will be your general, judge, and rewarder of every one of your virtues in the field.

It was probably the most accomplished piece of showmanship in English history, and the most honest. England has been in love with Elizabeth for 400 years after that, and the love shows no sign of subsiding.

But that time had a sadness for this aging woman. Leicester had been in command at Tilbury, and a few days later he left her to ride to his castle at Kenilworth. He was stout by then, florid and graying, and was taken ill of a "continual fever." On August 29, he wrote to ask after her health, "the chiefest thing in this world" that he wanted. He died on September 4, and she put away the letter, writing across it, "His Last Letter."

She had another fifteen years to rule after the Armada, and none of them was easy; but by then she had laid down her pattern and had only to follow it. She wanted "still peace" to grow; she wanted a peaceful prosperous kingdom where the quality of daily life persuaded men that loving their neighbors was more important than the exact way in which they did it. She was rewarded by an upsurge of confident excitement such as England had never known before (or since). Everyone knows that the golden age of English art was the Elizabethan Age: so much so that we tend to go on calling writers Elizabethans when (as might be said of Shakespeare) the greater part of their work was accomplished under her successor. It doesn't matter; it was the Elizabethan world they wrote from. The English of the Elizabethan Age were not poverty-stricken and despised, but on the other hand they were not fat with good living; everything might be within their reach, but they would have to work for it. It was a state of tension between a hostile world and a confident people, and while the tautness endured, it produced a wonderful blossoming of all the arts. It did something, too, to the English language, as we can see from Elizabeth's own utterances. We can expect her public speeches to be splendid, but her most hastily written letters have a marvellous conjunction of the homely and the stately that can be found in the whole of the preserved papers of the kingdom. It is as if suddenly the commonest Englishman was presented with all of life from its highest spiritual visions to its lowest domestic details, and discovered that he could take part in as much of it as he pleased.

As for Elizabeth herself, in her later years she grew, inevitably, a little odd; she was the repository of more knowledge and wisdom than any other woman in English history, but she was also Gloriana, and one human spirit might have contained them all but one human frame could not. England was as kind to her as possible; she went on being Gloriana long after she had lost her hair and her teeth and everything but her magnificent spirit. It is said that in her old age she fell in love with a boy thirty years her junior, but this is mere ill-natured gossip. The boy was the young Earl of Essex, son of Lettice Knollys, an aristocratic whore who later married Elizabeth's Robin, the Earl of Leicester, and the probabilities are that Essex was Leicester's son. He seems to have been at first glance Robin Dudley over again, with a certain fineness that Robin never had; but experience proved that the fineness encompassed a streak of pure silliness. Elizabeth always had an eye for the promising young man who might be useful to her when he had been taught, and advanced and even indulged him. Essex was too silly to be taught, and when he had finally disappointed Elizabeth, she waited grimly for him to ruin himself. He obligingly did so, thinking he could raise a revolt in the fashion of barons centuries dead, marching through London calling for supporters, knowing nothing at all of the intricate machinery of government that those centuries had brought into being. He went to the meeting of the axe with the block, and Elizabeth reigned on. What it cost her to kill Robin Dudley's son is sad to imagine.

When she was seventy, and visibly dying, and refusing to take to her bed in the decent fashion of the normally dying, her loved godson said to her, "Madam, you must go to bed." "Little man, little man," she said wickedly, "*must* is not said to princes." It was the truth of her life. *Must* had been said to Elizabeth Tudor first when she was four years old ("How haps it, governor, Lady Princess yesterday and today but Lady Elizabeth?"), and *must* she had fought and mastered all her days. Illegitimate in the eyes of half her people, too weak to rule without a husband, too poor to challenge the powers of Europe, a barren woman, a deprived personality, a diseased body and a neurotic mind, she did what no one but herself had ever expected her to do, and she did it with splendor and relished it in the doing. As an English Queen, we respect her for her sensible, healthful, and forward-looking mind. As a woman, we are eternally grateful to her and eternally regretful that we never saw her in her glory.

At the beginning of 1603, her coronation ring, which she had never taken from her finger since it was put there on January 15, 1559, had so grown into her flesh that it had to be sawed off. She nominated as her successor James VI of Scotland, and then asked for her spiritual adviser, Archbishop Whitgift. When he had done, she turned her face to the wall, fell into a sleep, and in that sleep died.

> As the most resplendent sun setteth at
> last in a western cloud.

Her heir was the great-grandson of Henry VII, but there was nothing of the Tudor left in him; the dynasty had died with Elizabeth. He was a very odd fish for Elizabeth Tudor to leave her people to the mercies of. Or did Elizabeth Tudor leave James Stuart to the mercies of the people she had taught to be independent?

House of

STUART

JAMES I *of England*
and VI *of Scotland*

reigned in England

1603–1625

✿

Born in Edinburgh in June 1566.

Son of Mary Stuart Queen of Scots and her cousin and second husband Henry Stuart Lord Darnley, and thus twice descended from Henry VII of England by his daughter Margaret.

Succeeded to the Scottish throne in 1567 on the deposition of his mother.

Succeeded undisputed to the throne of England on the death of the last Tudor monarch, Elizabeth I.

Married in 1589 Anne, daughter of Frederick II of Denmark, who died in 1619, and by whom he had:

> Henry Prince of Wales, born in 1594 and died in 1612; Charles, later Charles I; Elizabeth, born in 1596, who in 1613 married Frederick V* Elector Palatine, briefly elected King of Bohemia, who died in 1632. Elizabeth died in 1662, and among her children were:
>> Rupert, known as Prince Rupert of the Rhine; Sophia, born in 1630, who in 1658 married Ernst August Elector of Hanover and had a son,
>>> George Elector of Hanover, later George I.

Died at Theobalds in March 1625 and was buried in Westminster Abbey.

*The Electors of the Holy Roman Empire (seven in number) were those reigning Princes of the Empire by whose votes the the Holy Roman Emperor was elected.

JAMES I *of England* and VI *of Scotland*

ngland now had need of everything Elizabeth had given her, for down from Scotland were coming the Stuarts, that dynasty of destruction for absolute monarchy. As Mary Stuart had forced England to Protestantism in sheer self-defense, so her descendants forced England to parliamentary government.

By presenting the issues so clearly, perhaps the Stuarts had their uses; but while they were busily destroying themselves they made terrible havoc in their kingdoms. Perhaps even in this they were valuable; they seem to have implanted in the long, stubborn memory of the English people the determination that civil violence must never again be allowed.

The Stuarts as a family showed a remarkable consistency. Clever, tricksy, devious, stubborn, immovably uninstructible, they were anachronisms in England, and they never admitted it. James I wrote a little book, *Basilicon Doron,* on the duties of a King, and both he and his son made it clear that they believed every word of it.

A good King [announced James] acknowledgeth himself ordained for his people, having received from God a burden of government, whereof he must be countable.

An unimpeachable sentiment, but for its gloss (from another of James's literary works, for he published voluminously):

A good King will frame his actions to be according to the law, yet he is not bound thereto but of his goodwill.

He could not have put more clearly the single reason for all the troubles of the Stuart reigns. He showed it even before he had completed his first triumphal journey to his new capital. A thief was taken at Newark, and James ordered him to be hanged: without trial, on the King's word alone. The ineptitude astonishes us even now, and must have struck cold then; the new King had not acquainted himself with his new country's laws even so far as to discover that not the King but the law ruled English lives.

James I was the lucky one—the only lucky one—among the reigning male Stuarts, for much of his reign was passed in the afterglow of the Elizabethan reign, and that sheltered him; though he did little to deserve it. We think, for example, of Sir Walter Raleigh as an Elizabethan: almost as the archetypal Elizabethan, throwing his rich cloak in the mud for his Queen to walk dryshod on, combining immortal poetry, broad learning, and daring action in a way that no one has done since. But it was by James's order that Raleigh was executed, a servile surrender to that Spain whom Elizabeth and her seamen had despised and beaten.

James I of England and VI of Scotland was the son of Mary Queen of Scots and her second husband Darnley. Mary had been six months pregnant when Darnley and his friends had forced their way into her private rooms and murdered her secretary David Rizzio in front of her. Darnley, a pathetically worthless young man, had professed to believe that Mary's child was not his but Rizzio's; Darnley's word was worth nothing and Mary's later behavior makes it clear that she was a chaste woman; but the slander endured. James prided himself in later life on his wisdom, and it was said that naturally he was the latter-day Solomon, since he was the son of David. (Even if Mary had been guilty of adultery, her behavior after Rizzio's murder saved the life of her son, and is one of the few times when we must admire her.) Ever afterwards (or so he said) James could not recover from his pre-natal shock, and naked blades were not permitted in his presence (a very useful pre-natal trauma to suffer from in James's place).He had been taken from his mother almost at birth and soon put on her throne, brought up as King in a savagely Protestant country. He had, in fact, done not so badly in Scotland, for he had discovered how to balance the power of the Kirk against the power of the nobles (the Scottish Parliament had little power). Unhappily, it never seems to have occurred to him that England was not Scotland, so that the fine balance of Elizabeth's religious policy was lost in the hands of a man who thought that the small and moderate party of English Puritans had to be dealt with like the arrogant extremists of the Scottish Kirk.

The English Puritans petitioned for certain relaxations that would allow them to conduct their services in a way that was both legal and satisfying to their consciences—a course that Elizabeth would thoroughly have approved of. James fell into a rage; "I shall make them conform themselves," he said, "or I shall harry them out of the land. No Bishop, no King!" He had needed his Scots bishops to rule Scotland; it was past the comprehension of this modern Solomon that England was different.

However, he was irreproachably Protestant, and thus gave the country time to become settled in that religion, or in their own curious blend of it. Moreover, his characteristic ineptitude led to that curiously formative episode, the Gunpowder Plot of 1605.

In the modestly literate England of the time, the most popular book, after the Bible, was Foxe's *Book of Martyrs*—of, naturally, Protestant martyrs; it formed, and was to form for many generations, part of the Englishman's mental furniture, and accounted for much of his firm belief that Popery was not only theologically wrong but damnably cruel, cunning, and untrustworthy. James underestimated the anti-Catholic feeling in England, and found himself forced to offend the Catholics by not fulfilling a promise of toleration; and a few noblemen and gentlemen started a plot to take over the government by assassinating its officers. The conspirators were wiser than their King, because they planted their barrels of gunpowder in the cellars of the House of Commons and sent a minor plotter, Guy Fawkes, to light the fuses. They were betrayed; and to this day, at the beginning of November, small boys in England make Guys out of straw and masks and old clothes, and on the night of November 5, burn Guy Fawkes in effigy, and derisively set off fireworks all around him. It is not by chance that we still celebrate what was not really much of a plot, for its effect was great. It had been a treacherous plot, a violent plot, a plot to force the English against their will, and a tremendous moral blow to the forces of Catholicism in England. For centuries after that the English Catholics had to live under unjust legal discrimination, when most of them were honest people clinging to their own faith without a wish in the world to bring back the rack and stake of Mary Tudor.

James I was called "the wisest fool in Christendom," and personally must have had a good deal of *outré* charm. All the Stuarts had charm, but the others had style, and James never had that. He was a slovenly, shambling, dribbling little man, living always in a cheerful mess, ready to dispute anything with anybody in the conviction that he would never lose dignity thereby because his intellect was bound to be the superior. "Have I three kingdoms," he said to a fly, when out hunting, "and you have to stick in my eye?" He married Anne of Denmark, and they had three children. There was Prince Henry, who seems to have been a promising boy; he refused to marry a Catholic princess, saying, "Two religions shall never lie in my bed." There was Baby Charles, that stately, dutiful, disastrous young man, who was privately shocked at his father's undignified ways, though he never permitted himself to say so. And there was the beautiful, brilliant, energetic Elizabeth, who married the most charming, handsome, disastrous young man in Europe. It was not James's fault that his daughter's marriage was the immediate cause of the most appalling and cruel and unreasonable war that has ever occurred in Europe. It was his fault that after it England could exert no influence in Europe because he had deliberately run down her pride and her safety, the navy. He had consistently refused money for its upkeep, and thereby made himself hated and laid up a great store of trouble for his son. When the Thirty Years' War broke out in Europe, the foolish little man saw himself as a wise arbitrator to whom the belligerent powers would turn for mediation. The belligerent powers saw him as King of an unarmed country anxiously appeasing the Spanish in all that they asked.

If Elizabeth Stuart had not married Frederick the Elector Palatine and the two of them set up as King and Queen of Protestant Bohemia in the lands of the Catholic emperor, something else would have started the Thirty Years' War, for this war was the result of two irresistible historical forces. One was the old satanic one of dynastic ambition, and the other that of the Counter-Reformation, the ambition of the Catholic powers to win back the countries gone over to the Protestant side. The Elector Frederick was an inconsiderable German prince whose Protestantism led him to compete for the elective throne of Bohemia. Bohemia was one of the oldest and proudest Protestant monarchies, but it was technically part of the empire, and the emperor naturally wanted a Catholic on the throne. Disastrously for Bohemia, Frederick was elected in 1615, and he and Elizabeth came to be known as the Winter King and Queen; for after a season of brilliant celebrations in Prague the incapable young man was decisively defeated in 1616 at the Battle of the White Hill, a defeat which lost to Bohemia forever its ancient religion and freedom. But this was only part of the war, for by now all the powers of Europe —except England—were moving into the battle. We cannot even thank the Stuarts that England escaped this terrible war; England had her own to come.

The old question of the Channel sea-passage from Spain to the rebellious Protestant Netherlands now came up again; and, shorn of his navy, James had no choice but to make Spain free of it. Attempting to disguise this as an alliance with Spain, he proposed that his heir should marry the Spanish Infanta.

Prince Henry, the sensible young man who had refused a Catholic marriage, died in 1612, and the heir was now Baby Charles. By now, too, another of James's weaknesses had gained the upper hand of him, and he was hopelessly infatuated with the handsome young "dear Steenie," George Villiers Duke of Buckingham. (It is more than curious to note how some names in English history seem fatal to their owners. Arthur for a prince is one; Buckingham for a noble another.) James was certainly homosexual, but what is odd about this infatuation is that it was shared with his son Charles. As with so many others, Buckingham's fascination escapes us, and to us he seems an arrogant, foolish bore; but he ruled the policy of England for many years. With father and son he hatched an incredibly absurd plot for the two young men alone to visit Spain and make the triumphant match between English prince and Spanish Infanta that was to bring peace to Europe, fame to Buckingham, and a great marriage to Charles.

It was, of course, a humiliating failure. The Spanish had not the least idea of giving a princess in marriage to a powerless kingdom that already did everything that they asked, and, to put it as moderately as possible, Buckingham's views of the way to woo an Infanta did not correspond with the stately ways of the Spanish court. The two young men had to come shamefully home alone, and the chief result of the escapade was the more-than-Spanish stateliness of the court etiquette introduced by Baby Charles after his accession.

Not even this humiliation taught these Stuarts anything. Buckingham remained in favor for the rest of James's life, and was to go on leading the submissive Charles into trouble until his death in 1628. Charles married another Catholic, Henrietta Maria daughter of Henri IV of France; it is doubtful if even the Spanish match could have been a worse one.

James I died in 1625 at the age of fifty-nine. It is an unremarkable and mostly unremarked date in English history, because his reign had been passed largely in the afterglow of the previous reign, and because his heir had all his own more unfortunate qualities to a much higher degree. If we remember James I these days it is as the author of the first pamphlet in history against tobacco.

CHARLES I
1625–1649

✿

Born at Dunfermline, Scotland, in November 1600.
Second son of James VI King of Scots (later James I of
   England) and his wife Anne of Denmark.
Married in 1625 Henrietta Maria, daughter of Henri IV of
   France (Henry of Navarra) and his second wife Marie
   de Medici, who died in 1669 and by whom he had:

Charles Prince of Wales, later Charles II; James Duke of
York, later James II; Mary, born in 1631, who in 1648
married William II Prince of Orange, and had a son,
         William III of Orange, born in 1650, who later
         married his cousin Mary, elder daughter of James
         II, and became William III of England.

Executed in Whitehall, 30th January 1649, and was buried
   at Windsor.

With the death of Charles I England ceased to be a Kingdom until the Restoration in 1660.

CHARLES I

ngland had now arrived at a point in her history when three vital matters had to be settled. The first was whether the English church should retain any secular power; the second, whether the law of the land should remain the old English common law; and the third, whether the final power in the realm was to be with the King or with Parliament.

With all these three questions Charles I had to deal; and with all three of them he turned out to be wholly, unintelligently, and immovably on the wrong side.

Personally, Charles was entirely unlike his shambling unkempt little father. He was a small man with a stammer, who kept his dignity by decreeing a royal distance between King and subject; the dignity, however, was genuine, and never failed him in even his worst days. He was chilly, humorless, and reserved, and seems to have had little talent for making himself loved; his most faithful subjects felt loyalty for him, but not affection. He seems to have had only two deep relationships in his life, those with Buckingham and his Queen. So impeccably virtuous was his later life that it is difficult to remember his infatuation with Buckingham; but at first he disliked his frivolous little French bride, and she did not become pregnant until after Buckingham's death at the hands of a Puritan fanatic in 1628 (their son Charles was born in 1630). After that their devotion was deep and exclusive. Charles I was so much the most purposefully disastrous of the English Kings that it is only fair to record that in one way he was the best of them: his artistic taste was infallible, and but for him England would have been poorer in art, in letters, in music, and in architecture. However, even this had its unfortunate side, for he spent on his arts money and time that should have gone to more important causes. As a modern historian has pointed out, the solemn nature of Charles's private enjoyments has led people to regard him as a dutiful King; in fact, he was a lazy one, and would not be drawn from his cultured life by the mere necessity of dealing with matters of state. Indeed, perhaps his real trouble was connected with this life, with his hunting, his tennis, his pictures, his wonderful theatrical entertainments; for, like his grandmother, Mary Queen of Scots, and for much the same reasons, he was ignorant of life. There are recorded instances where he dealt with difficult decisions of state by going hunting; there is even one slightly shocking one (the Scottish revolt) where he refused to tell his ministers what had happened.

The first twelve years of his reign appeared peaceful. To be just to him, he attempted to put right much of the muddle left by his father; but he would not ask Parliament for money when Parliament would only give it in return for concessions to its own power. Moreover, until 1628 he was at the mercy of Buckingham's fantasies, of which Parliament emphatically did not approve. In 1629 he dissolved Parliament, and did not recall it.

He then had to find other means of raising money. He succeeded to a certain degree, but only in ways that today would horrify a small shopkeeper—for example, impoverishing the crown by disposing of estates for a lump sum instead of continuing to draw rents from them. He explored the financially ticklish business of monopolies, and found various other useful taxes, but it was always at the expense of his subjects' good will. Because of the centuries-old insistence of Parliament that money had to be paid for in power, there had grown up in England the firm conviction that taxes could only be raised with the consent of the people. Respect was lost to the crown as well as good will, for there was much that was inept and some that was irresistibly comic in Charles's wrestlings with finance. The history of his attempt to give a London firm the monopoly of the soap trade is uproarious, with the laundresses of Bristol anticipating Brand X by several hundred years in conducting public washing tests to prove that London soap was worse than Bristol soap.

Charles had troubles, too, with his family, many of them with his wife. Henrietta Maria was a Catholic, and not a discreet or sensible one; she had her own elegant chapel, she made a noble convert or two, and she welcomed various distinguished foreign Catholic visitors, with whom her husband found it courteous and pleasant to talk. To the people, foreign Catholic visitors meant war, rebellion, foreign domination, the rack and the stake. There were also the disturbing Protestant Palatinates, Charles's beautiful widowed sister Elizabeth and her children, now in exile from lost Bohemia and roaming the courts of Europe looking for homes and livelihoods— that is, for power. Charles was honestly unable to help his sister; his father's foolish policies had left England too weak to exert influence, and in any case the band of brilliant energetic children with their determined beautiful mother were a downright danger to peace. But it did not endear him to his people when the Queen's Catholic visitors were welcomed by the King, or when arrogant Spanish captains lorded it in London (since Charles tried to raise money by ferrying Spanish troops to the Protestant Netherlands), and nothing was done for the Winter Queen.

There was, however, much more serious trouble within the English church. Charles's own religion was deep and sincere; he was, after all, the first English monarch to have been brought up within this new church. Nowdays we would call it High-Church Anglicanism—that is, not far from Rome in ritual, but denying the authority of the Pope; certainly the popular suspicion that he wanted to submit England again to the authority of Rome seems to have been unjustified. But—except for James I, who, poor child, had been exposed to the Scottish Kirk from birth—there seems to have been something about the Stuarts that responded instinctively to the Roman church. Charles regarded the English church as The Church, the only true Church of God, and looked forward to the time when all other churches would be reconciled to it. Now the English church had two qualities, remarkable for the time, which made it popular and often deeply loved: it was under the control of the common law, and it allowed a high degree of freedom of conscience and worship. Charles, with his willing abettor Archbishop Laud, would not allow this freedom to continue. Their way was a middle way between extremes, but in this middle way they were as intolerant as any extremist. They were also astonishingly foolish; for they tried to treat Scotland as they treated England, and they went about it in exactly the way that would most successfully unite the Scots and the English.

James I had made mistakes in his religious policy because he thought the English were like the Scots. Charles I made worse mistakes because he thought the Scots were like the English. They were wholly unalike. For one thing, the Scots were not Anglicans but Calvinists, a narrow and harshly intolerant sect, and they had learned by experience that bishops were an invention of James I to keep them down. The Scots had no tradition of Parliamentary government, and looked to the Kirk and the great nobles. In 1638, with a purely Stuart simplicity, Charles contrived to offend Kirk, nobles, and people alike with his order that the Laudian prayer book should be used throughout Scotland. The faith of the Scots was harsh and intolerant, but in this crisis its grand certainties of moral right gathered in all that was good in the people. It also gathered in a great deal that was prideful and sadistic and downright insane; but it was a genuine upsurge of religious feeling that resulted in the signing of the nation's "Covenant with God." It was very well directed, and, as one modern historian has pointed out, it was the Scots' single outlet of political protest in the absence of a Parliamentary tradition; and no doubt that what many a Scot thought was a truly religious feeling was simply one of sheer outrage at being dictated to. But in essence this was one of the few genuinely religious outbreaks.

The Scots, at any rate, queued up to sign the covenant, and then put an army in the field as an earnest of the determination to resist the Laudian reforms. Charles, who had imagined himself reigning over a peaceful pair of kingdoms, had to give himself time to collect his forces against Scotland. He summoned a Parliament, known as the Short Parliament; deceived by the quiet on the Scots borders, he dissolved it, and then had to recall it, and this was the Long Parliament. He had no idea what he was doing in summoning the Long Parliament, which was to outlast him.

The Long Parliament was to sit for seven years. Among its members were to be the greatest names in the history of English constitutional liberty—Pym, Hampden, Hyde, Falkland, Oliver Cromwell. It was to conduct great and successful military campaigns (which was not in the nature of Parliament at all), make England once more respected and feared abroad, change entirely the nature of monarchy in England, bring about the execution of the King, and, its inspiration exhausted, go out in a blaze of idiocy.

However, the English had not yet been driven so far as to attack their King personally, and, as always in times of trouble, the first target was "the King's evil counsellors." There were two of these: Archbishop Laud, the author of the church reforms, and Thomas Wentworth Lord Strafford, Charles's greatest and most faithful servant and a name of ill-omen to him.

Few men have ever been hated as Strafford was. He seems to have been a man naturally tactless to a curious degree in one so intelligent; he suffered from painful ill-health exacerbated by constant overwork, and he had to struggle always against the frustrations of a fine administrator faced by obstruction and stupidity. Yet, his private letters show a man most endearingly loyal, sensible, patient, and cheerful in adversity. With the Stuart (not to say royal) suspicion of great servants, Charles had sent Strafford out of the way to Ireland, but with the gathering of troubles was forced to summon him home. Strafford went, as he always went when his King called him, but he was not happy about it. In the winter of 1640 Charles gave him a written promise that he would not allow him to suffer in life or in fortune, whatever else happened.

There had been a lull in the Scottish trouble since the signing of the covenant; Charles had marched north with an untrained army, met the Scots, and, after some wholly inconclusive conferring, withdrew, leaving the Scots to continue their efficient preparations for rebellion on a large scale. It is typical of the style of Charles's rule that this absurd sally was presented by the court as a great victory.

The Long Parliament was determined less to make the King pay in power for what he got in money than to mount an attack on his whole method of government. They began by arresting Laud and Strafford, and Strafford's trial opened on March 22, 1641, in Westminster Hall, a place Charles was to know himself before long.

The charges against Strafford were many and detailed, but what they chiefly amounted to was increasing the direct power of the King by various means, chiefly those of the tyrannical courts Charles had come to use for his own purposes during his time of rule without Parliament; according to the indictment, he had said he would make "the little finger of the King heavier than the loins of the law." He was in such visibly poor health as to win pity from some of the spectators, but he defended himself magnificently. The heart of his defense, in which he himself wholly believed, was quite simply that there were circumstances in which the King's prerogative (power overriding the law) was necessary to good government.

The prerogative must be used as God doth his omnipotency, at extraordinary occasions; the laws must have place at all other times, and yet there must be a prerogative if there must be extraordinary occasions.

The most liberal of nations in times of crisis find it necessary to limit some freedoms; but Strafford, whether consciously or not, had completely missed the point: The English no longer trusted their King, and were set on denying him his prerogative.

Charles all this time was blindly confident that, even if the impeachment succeeded, he personally could save Strafford's life. During the seven weeks of the trial another important business for him was going forward: the marriage of his daughter Mary, still a child, to the young Prince William of Orange, who was only twelve. It was designed to persuade the people that the King's foreign policy was turning toward the Protestant powers; in fact, it was mostly for money, and the supporters of the Queen thought the match beneath her daughter. *"Jésu-Marie,"* they said, "the daughter of a daughter of France!" (Henrietta Maria herself was the daughter of Marie de Médici, whom her father had dubbed "my plump bankroll.") But Pym, who was the chief actor in the attack on Strafford, brought into the House also a Bill of Attainder, which was, in effect, the assertion of the prerogative of Parliament; it was a legacy of the Wars of the Roses, and permitted Parliament to condemn a man to death on the grounds that his life was a danger to the realm. The King, meanwhile, with his curious talent for fighting simultaneously on two levels, one of unimpeachable faith and virtue and the other of extraordinary slyness, was attempting an armed rising in London to rescue Strafford from the Tower. Naturally enough, hints of this leaked out, and ruined Strafford's chances of having the Bill of Attainder rejected by the Lords. Strafford himself, in the Tower, with the promise of the King in his pocket that he would come to no harm in life or fortune, saw that his own fate had put the crown itself into great danger. He knew that Charles had not the strength to save him in the face of Parliament, and he feared dreadful results if he tried and failed. He sacrificed himself for the Crown in his famous letter to the King:

May it please your Sacred Majesty: I understand the minds of men are more and more incensed against me, notwithstanding your Majesty hath declared that I am not guilty of treason and that you are not satisfied in your conscience to pass the bill. This bringeth me in a very great strait; there is before me the ruin of my children and family; there are before me the many ills which may befall your Sacred Person and the whole Kingdom should yourself and Parliament part less satisfied one with the other than is necessary for the preservation both of King and people; there are before me the things most valued, most feared by mortal men, Life and Death. To set Your Majesty's conscience at liberty, I do most humbly beseech Your

Majesty (for preventing of evils which may happen by our refusal) to pass this bill.

This noble letter was written on the evening of May 4. On May 9, the Bill of Attainder, duly passed by both Houses, came before the King for signature. The King saw it as his duty to chasten his man's conscience by consenting to Strafford's death. He signed, weeping and saying, "My Lord of Strafford's condition is happier than mine."

Later in his life, when Strafford's fate threatened him, Charles often said that all his sufferings were a result of his betrayal of Strafford. It was a characteristic reaction, to put down the sufferings of two kingdoms to the personal sin of one man. Strafford's policy had been precisely the policy that England would not abide, and Charles's betrayal of Strafford was precisely the symbol of that in Charles that made his kingdom distrust him. He never saw it in this larger light; all he saw was the narrow limit of his own salvation.

Charles's other servant, Archbishop Laud, was also in the Tower, and wrote in his diary that the King whom he and Strafford had served (Strafford had been his close friend) had not been worth their devotion; "He knew not how to be or to be made great." From his window Laud saw Strafford go out to the scaffold, and lifted his hands to give him his blessing. Strafford died as bravely and as simply as he had lived, saying:

In all the honour I had to serve His Majesty, I had not any intention in my heart but what did aim at the joint and individual prosperity of the King and his people.

The control of Parliament was now with the Presbyterians, and they had made common cause with the Scots. With his fatal lack of realism, Charles now decided that he could persuade the Scots to desert their English allies. He went north to Scotland, held court in style, enjoyed himself very much, and by graciously giving them all they demanded seems to have thought he was winning them to his cause. He was not; the Scots frankly did not trust him any more than the English did—probably rather less, for to them he was, in spite of his Stuart blood, an English King. And, once again, his fatal habit of laying off his bets betrayed him. He undoubtedly gave license to his courtiers to set up some kind of plot that was to involve the assassination of his enemies Argyll and Hamilton (though Hamilton had once been a friend). It was a duplication of the Army Plot during Strafford's trial, and only emphasized what the leaders in both countries knew already: that the King was not to be trusted in negotiation. Back in England, where he had left her, his Queen's attempts to whip up support for him made her even more hated. Charles's confidence in this faithful and wholly unintelligent little woman, who was liable to fall into hysterics in times of trouble, and apparently never understood what was going on, went a long way toward causing his final disaster.

However, before the Scots could be called on to declare for either Parliament or the King, an overriding emergency arose in Ireland. Strafford had had a powerful army in reserve there, but had warned the King that it must not be allowed to get out of control. Charles ignored the warning, and the army melted into the native Irish, and the native Irish rose in rebellion against years of neglect and exploitation.

In his leisured way Charles came back to England, and in an extraordinary fashion appointed to the government of Scotland exclusively his enemies. He had, in spite of his troubles, enjoyed himself in Scotland; it may have been that in that country without an active Parliament, where the relationship between lord and vassal was in the Lowlands still feudal and in the Highlands paternal, he had felt himself spiritually at home. But in London Pym had seen the chance that presented itself to him. Whatever the concessions the King had made in the last years, and however clearly both sides realized that he would repudiate them at the first opportunity, the King still held unimpugned the final power: the command of the armed forces. To defeat the Irish rising he would need an army; and Pym was determined that the control of this army must be with Parliament.

As always with Charles, negotiations proceeded in an atmosphere of calm and good faith. The more one studies Charles, the more impossible it is to reconcile his open, honest, if not very intelligent public negotiations with the rather pathetically muddled underhanded private ones. What is one to make of a man openly willing to become a martyr to the cause of his royal conscience, who at the same time is planning flights down backstairs and assassinations by hot-headed young courtiers?

But he had already long overplayed his hand on that game. He could force his enemies into a show of ruthlessness, but he could not for a moment make them trust his word. The struggle over the command of the armed forces led in the end, past many intricacies, to the most famous scene in the history of the English Parliament.

In January, 1632, Charles decided that he must arrest the Five Members—Pym, Hampden, Holles, Hazelrigg and Strode—who chiefly stood in his way, and took his armed men into the House to arrest them. The Five Members, in fact, had been forewarned and had cannily taken refuge in the safety of the city, but the act was fatal to Charles, for the inviolability of the House, and the privilege of the members who spoke there, was a sacred tradition.

Charles led in his men, and went straight to the Speaker, William Lenthall, demanding that he produce the Five Members. Lenthall, on his knees, responded that he had no tongue to speak but as the House commanded him: responded, in fact, that the command of the House was above that of the King. The Civil Wars had begun.

What made the English Civil Wars so peculiarly distressing was the cross-cutting of its issues. A man might serve the King on religious grounds while agonizing to join Parliament on political grounds; and vice versa, with all possible permutations. Falkland, for example, had supported Pym and Hampden in the House on constitutional grounds, but could not follow them the whole way; noble and wretched, he fought for the King and hoped to die in battle, so that he should not have to see his side either victorious or defeated. Very roughly speaking, the feudal gentry, the smaller-scale landowners, declared for the King. These in the first stages of the war gave the Cavaliers—as the King's men came to be called—their advantage, for at first the war was a matter of dashing affairs of cavalry on unenclosed ground. Moreover, the King had one great commander in his nephew Prince Rupert—"Rupert of the Rhine," son to the Winter Queen. Rupert was a dashing cavalry commander who soon gave the Cavaliers so great an advantage that Pym, dying before he could see the victory he had done so much to achieve, gave his cause a last gift by negotiating an agreement with the Scots.

But dashing cavalrymen, faithful squires, enthusiastically ignorant peasants might win skirmishes; they could seldom win battles, and they could never win countries to a cause that was mistrusted—worse, to a cause that was short of money. Henrietta Maria might sell her jewels, Charles his plate, loyal baronets (who, after all, had only had to pay £450 for their titles) might melt down their dishes for silver. But Parliament held London, and most of the ports and all of the shipping of the country. Parliament held many of the best businessmen of the realm, and put them to work; its fiscal system was admirable. It had control of trade, and it could negotiate with foreign governments; and the foreign governments, who were not made up of fools, had already judged Charles very much as his subjects had judged him, and were not disposed to allow him credit or send to his aid. The organization of all these advantages took time, but the Long Parliament achieved it. Moreover, they achieved the organization of what was probably the most efficient army that had yet been seen in Europe: the New Model Army.

Coming to prominence in the later stages of Pym's battle with the King was a stout, ugly, undistinguished squire from the Fenlands, one Oliver Cromwell. His looks were uninspiring, but when he spoke he had a gift of turning a magnificent phrase in homely language, and of seeming so passionate in what he said that lesser men, studying his words later and not able to find much sense in them, came to the conclusion that the fault was in themselves. Later on they were confirmed in this view when the cloudy words of General Cromwell turned out to have been based on extreme common sense. Cromwell, in fact, seems to have been one of those characters (Joan of Arc is the archetype) who can only function in an age intensely religious. He was intensely religious himself, and when he was perplexed about his course would seek guidance in prayer. How he thought God gave him that guidance we do not know; we only know that the guidance was normally what we should expect to have come from the unaided mind of a man intensely clear-headed, courageous, and suited for power. A small squire from the Fens would probably have thought it improper to assume that he knew better than anyone else, if it had not been that he was assured of the guidance of God; but no one who studies Cromwell can assert that he did not believe wholly and piously that he had such guidance. His family background is interesting; the family were Welsh by descent and had been called Williams, but in the reign of Henry VIII, Morgan Williams, a brewer and innkeeper in Putney, had married the sister of the minister Thomas Cromwell, and taken his name out of gratitude. It must have been a gesture requiring courage in Morgan Williams; Thomas Cromwell had seldom been a popular man.

In the Civil Wars, his descendant Oliver suddenly discovered a talent for warfare. It was more than the merely capable man's notion that armies had to be run with efficiency. Oliver had that, but also he had that extra apprehension of strategy and tactics and country that belongs only to the great general. And to Oliver his men were not cannon fodder, but immortal souls fighting evil, and (it seems)

he did not think they could withstand evil unless they lived godly
lives; and his raw young Puritans were taught to regard themselves
as elect of God; to take care of their consciences as much as of their
weapons; to use their native wit in securing salvation as well as
victory. Cromwell's army defeated Charles in the end, at Marston
Moor in July, 1644; but after that it very nearly defeated Cromwell.
When he wanted to consider what to do with the realm, he had to
spend his time on his mutinous soldiers, who had been taught that
they were valuable, every man. They even demanded universal fran-
chise, as well as the pay Parliament was refusing them. Cromwell did
as best he could for them about the pay; the men who wanted votes
he abandoned as mutineers.

The final victory, however, had only been won with the aid of the
Scots, and thanks to Pym's dying efforts, and it was obvious to
everyone that the alliance was too uneasy to last. (Except possibly
to the Scots, who in the flush of their own religious fervor were
inclined to think that the rest of the world would very soon fall into
step with them.) In payment for their help, the Scots demanded the
complete reformation of the English church on the Scots model. It
was not likely that England would want anyone else's model, but
Parliament dealt tactfully with the Scots, assuring them that the
Church would be reformed on the example of the best Reformed
churches and in accordance with the word of God, which to any Scot
meant exactly the same thing as on the Scots model. The King,
however, once again certain that he could assert his own ascendancy,
tried to split the allies by surrendering in the spring of 1646 to the
Scots. It was a reversal of his grandmother's move in 1568, when she
fled from the Scots to the English, and equally fatal. The Scots,
turning practical, sold him to Parliament for the price of money to
pay their troops. The First Civil War was over.

From now onward, Parliament—still officially the Long Parliament of glorious memory, though soon to be so depleted by deaths
and expulsions and abstentions that it is derisively called the Rump
Parliament—loses a great part of its glory. The truth was that it had
played its part and was exhausted. In the times for which it had been
elected, when an uneasy country, bedeviled by religious worries, had
had to withstand the attack of a determined absolutism, it had bat-
tled its way through perplexities to an admirable clarity of view on
what was needed, and it had held to that view and supported it with
efficiency and inspiration.

The Rump of the Long Parliament had no such wisdom. With the King its prisoner, it had the utter unwisdom to quarrel with the army, refuse its pay, and attempt to disband it. The result of this was the Second Civil War, in which Cromwell was the hero, defeating the remnants of the royalists, who had tried to take advantage of the falling-out of the victors, defeating the disappointed Scots, who had invaded the country yet again, and defeating, morally speaking, Parliament, whose trump card he took over when a certain Cornet Joyce, probably inspired by Cromwell's orders, seized the King and brought him a prisoner to army headquarters. There were thus in 1648 three parties in England: the King, Parliament, and the army —which for most purposes was Oliver Cromwell.

For most people in England the struggle with the King now must have seemed over; possibly he would abdicate in favor of his son, the Prince of Wales (now in exile, along with his mother and second brother); possibly he would continue on the throne, ruling as a strictly constitutional King under the peaceful orders of an elected Parliament. Most certainly few of the participants in the wars had entered into them with the formed idea of ousting not only the King but the monarchy from England; even Cromwell at one time began negotiations with the King. The King, still Charles Stuart, benignly negotiated in the light, and in the darkness fled. He was recaptured in the Isle of Wight and imprisoned at Newport. He had shown once again that he was not to be trusted; and Cromwell never again did trust him; and the logical outcome of that was to put the King on trial.

He was tried in Westminster Hall, where Strafford had suffered not so very long before, and like his grandmother he made a brave showing. He had his advantages; public opinion was not ready for such a drastic step, and English law, which specifies trial by peers (that is, by equals), had no provision for the trial of Kings. The whole process is a fascinating study of the English passion for law, and the English respect for law. Everyone knew that what they were doing had never been done before; except for the impervious royalists, for whom the will of the King was above the laws, everyone knew that trial was justified after the immense suffering brought on the land by the King's actions; yet all through the trial the prosecution was searching blindly for a properly legal procedure. If they were clumsy, they should not be despised for it. Their position was that the law is above the will of the King, and they tried to base their case on nothing but the law.

The charge against Charles was that, being as King "trusted with a limited power to govern according to the laws of the land and not otherwise," he had conceived a "wicked design to erect and uphold in himself an unlimited and tyrannical power to rule according to his will, and to overthrow the rights and liberties of his people," and had "traitorously and maliciously levied war against the present Parliament and the people herein represented," and further attempted to procure "invasions from foreign parts"; he was thus held responsible for all the "treasons, murders, rapines, burnings, spoils, desolations, damages and mischiefs to this nation committed in the said wars," and was a "Tyrant, Traitor, and Murderer, and a public and implacable Enemy to the Commonwealth of England."

To this, Charles, with a bearing described by a royalist as "undaunted" and by a Parliament man as "impudent," replied sharply:

I would know by what authority I am called hither; there are many unlawful authorities in the world, thieves and robbers by the highway. Remember I am your lawful King, and what sins you bring upon your heads, and the judgment of God upon this land. I have a trust committed to me by God, by old and lawful descent; I will not betray it to answer a new unlawful authority; therefore resolve me that and you shall hear no more of me.

This in fact was the sole defense Charles ever made: that the court was unlawful and he did not recognize its competence. He was justified, in his own terms; the court was equally justified, in its own terms—it was constituted "by the Commons of England assembled in Parliament." They were, in fact, fighting not only the Civil Wars but a fair number of the other wars of the past centuries over again in words. On the final day John Bradshaw, the president of the court, made the crucial point to Charles:

There is a contract and a bargain made between the King and his people, and your oath is taken; and certainly, Sir, the bond is reciprocal: for as you are the liege lord, so are they liege subjects. The one tie, the one bond, is the bond of protection that is due from the sovereign; the other is the bond of subjection that is due from the subject. Sir, if this bond be once broken, farewell sovereignty! Whether you have been, as by your office you ought to be, a protector of England or the destroyer of England, let all England judge, or all the world that hath look'd upon it.

Visibly, these words—with the reiteration of the words of the charge, "Sir, the charge hath called you a Tyrant, a Traitor, a Murderer and a public enemy to the Commonwealth of England"—wounded the King. It is difficult to see why; but he was so moved that a little later he interrupted Bradshaw, saying, "I would desire only one word before you give sentence, and that is that you would hear me concerning those great imputations you have laid to my charge."

It was a complete reversal of his defense; and Bradshaw, though courteous, was firm in rejecting it at this late stage: "Truly, Sir, I would not willingly, at this time especially, interrupt you in anything you have to say that is proper for us to admit of. But, Sir, you have not owned us as a Court; and therefore for you to address yourself to us, not acknowledging us as a Court to judge of what you say, it is not to be permitted." He declared the King guilty and had the Clerk read the sentence:

that the said Charles Stuart, as a Tyrant, Traitor, Murderer and public enemy, shall be put to death by the severing of his head from his body.

Charles asked to address the court again, not knowing, apparently, that a prisoner condemned to death was regarded as dead in law from the moment of sentence. When he was denied, for the first time he lost his composure; it seems from the broken phrases recorded that the stammer that had been absent all the time of the trial afflicted him. It lasted only a short space; from then until his death three days later, on January 30, 1649, he behaved with admirable calm and nobility. The executioner (in spite of later tales that the public executioner refused to kill his King and it was Cromwell who used the axe) was the man, Richard Brandon, who had beheaded Laud and Strafford. In his last speech from the scaffold Charles did not mention Strafford's name, but he said, "An unjust sentence I suffered to take effect is punished by an unjust sentence on me." With him he had Bishop Juxon, who had once advised him not to betray Strafford; to him he said at the very last, "I go from a corruptible to an incorruptible Crown, where no disturbance can be, no disturbance in the world."

A young boy too far back in the crowd to see the King when he knelt at the block saw the axe rise and then fall; and he heard from the crowd then "such a groan as I never heard before, and desire I may never hear again."

A few hours earlier, suddenly recalling that in law the throne cannot be vacant and the moment of death of a King is the moment of succession for his heir, the House of Commons had forbidden the proclamation of a new King. The order was disobeyed here and there, but to no lasting effect; foreign governments professed themselves shocked, but proved themselves largely indifferent. The poor stupid little Queen exiled in Paris wept, and then transferred to her eldest son the title of *le Roi;* the exiled son in The Hague was told the news in two words: "Your Majesty . . ."

England was now a Republic.

THE INTERREGNUM

I n a history of the Kings and Queens of England Oliver Cromwell has no place. Though he became as powerful as any King, and (with his magnificent army) more powerful than many, he refused to take the royal power.

There has to be more to kingship than a man's capability. Even today, when universal suffrage is practicable and well understood, we elect our rulers for a limited term only, and keep a very sharp eye on them for that term; we acknowledge that no one man can be infallible as a ruler. How then is a King for life to be chosen?

Certainly not, as in the Wars of the Roses, by armed power. Anyone can win a battle; no one can convince everyone else that he will win the next one. As the Commonwealth itself proved, not even a powerful standing army could make the English accept a rule they disliked. Certainly not by any method of human choice practicable then. The choice had to be non-human, yet of such authority that it was wholly acceptable to the great majority of the people; in fact, it had to be divine; it had to be of the eldest son of the royal dynasty.

A King is more than a ruler; he can be no ruler at all, and not for that cease to be King. His secret is that he is hallowed as King: we would say by the faith of his people, the seventeenth century said by the will of God; it comes to the same thing. What else is required of him—to be the best soldier, the smiling figurehead, the conscientious civil servant—varies from time to time; the necessity for hallowing does not.

In effect, both Charles I and his people believed in the divine right of Kings; but his people also believed in the human rights of subjects.

The seventeenth century was, so far, the most tumultuous in the history of England: not so much in that it suffered from great civil disorders as in that for the first time every man in the land felt himself entitled to take a rightful part in them. This was admirable; but it was also damnably awkward, for so many and so intricate were the issues of the day, religious tangled with political and economic intertwined with both, that no one would live at peace with his neighbor.

Not only had the King, with whose office law, custom, Parliament, the Church, the very background of men's lives had been intimately connected, been deposed; he had also been executed as a traitor. The land had not begun to recover from its "treasons, murders, rapines, burnings, spoils, desolations, damages and mischiefs," nor the people from the inevitable human miseries. Religious differences had been hardened by persecution and deformed by being forced into political moulds, and had grown bitter beyond any hope of toleration on the wise Elizabethan model. And, worst perhaps than all, the Parliament that had been the hope of the common people had in the end failed them.

The Long Parliament had had to endure, because it was the leader of the people in their war with the King; but seven years of constant upheaval was too long for a body of men, all with differing purposes at the outset, to remain firm to the inspiration of the first emergency. If Pym had lived, matters might have been different. As it was, Cromwell in the end grew contemptuous of that Parliament as whose loyal servant he had begun his life. "Take away that bauble," he said of the Mace, the symbol of Parliamentary sovereignty, and quite justly; he had no time to spare for pettiness. Yet, as his many hesitations show, he was aware all the time that he was being pushed in a wrong direction: the road to military domination. In the end, he ruled by the authority of his army, and was hated for it. Military rule is always hated; and Cromwell's army, being deeply conscious of itself as called to purge the country of sinfulness, could be peculiarly unpleasant to the English, who are not as a race inclined to dwell much on anyone's sins. Moreover, in England almost alone among nations at that time, there was not only no tradition of a standing army but also a very strong feeling against one. (In islands, standing armies are for repression, standing navies for defense; the English have always had a very warm feeling toward seamen in general.)

Oliver died in 1659, and by then it was plain to everyone that the Commonwealth had failed. His ineffectual son Richard for a few months occupied his place, to disastrous effect; there was no authority but that of the sword, and generals with regiments began to behave like fifteenth-century barons with armies. Everyone knew where it had to end, for the heir of the Stuarts, Charles sometime Prince of Wales, was living in Holland (and finding it very cold without money to buy firing). All that was needed was a man of enough authority to call him home.

And once he was called home? It seems that few people worried. Peace, freedom from army rule, above all something to restore the country's good humor, were more important now. England had gone sour; her lazy individualist people were being hounded into fanaticisms they hated and adopted only because the neighbors had adopted worse. They did not like it, and they wanted to stop it at any price.

They were fortunate in having a man who understood all this. General Monk was a distinguished soldier, and at the end of 1659 he and his army in Edinburgh were in a position to settle the matter. On January 1, 1660, Monk left Scotland for London; at the end of March he was in communication with the second Charles Stuart. Charles responded with the Declaration of Breda, in which he affirmed himself willing to abide by "the will of a free Parliament," and the second Charles Stuart, elected by nothing but the will of God that had decided he should be born the eldest son of Charles I, was invited back to his kingdom. The diarist John Evelyn wrote of his return in May 1660:

I stood in the Strand and beheld it, and blessed God. And all this was done without one drop of blood shed, and by that very army which rebelled against him.

It was the end of the Commonwealth, and its failure. The men who had voted for Charles I's death were executed, and the very decaying bones of the great Oliver dug up for public scorn. Yet, in their outcome the next two reigns were tacitly acknowledged to have been disastrous, and the resolution of the disasters was to lie always in the directions Oliver had wanted to take. Moreover, in that history of England which a great (if not very flexible) historian has characterized as what "every schoolboy knows," Oliver is done justice to. Every Englishman now knows that the Commonwealth was that time in English history when England did not stoop to serving the ambitions of dynasties but tried to live by a rule of conscience. He is ignorant of the many failures but clear on the principle, and he can always name Oliver Cromwell as the man who presided over the attempt. He can further remember him, endearingly, as the man who, when he came to have his portrait painted, asked for it to be done "warts and all." It is a better monument than the one his contemporaries gave him, which was his body on the gibbet at Tyburn and his skull over Westminster Hall.

THE
RESTORATION

CHARLES II
1660–1685

❁

Born at St. James's Palace, London, in 1630.

Elder surviving son of Charles I and his wife Henrietta Maria of France.

Lived in exile on the Continent during the period of the Commonwealth, 1649–1660.

Married in 1662 Catherine of Bragança, daughter of João IV of Portugal, but had no children by her.

Died at Whitehall in February 1685 and was buried at Windsor.

The Restoration in 1660 is generally regarded as the beginning of Charles II's reign, but he himself dated it from the death of his father in 1649.

He had no legitimate children, but among his children by mistresses was James Duke of Monmouth, son of Lucy Walter, born 1647, who was executed by James II after the Battle of Sedgemoor in 1685.

CHARLES II

harles II was possibly the cleverest of the English Kings, certainly the most agreeable personally, and arguably the most dangerous. So profoundly human were his loyalties and so stubborn and humorous the ways in which he pursued them, that it is easy to be caught into sympathy with his wry honesty. But it is no good trying to make an honest King out of him, for he had his father's fatal flaw, though he did not compound it with his father's complacent stupidity: his own principles were clear to him, but when he became King he swore vows he did not believe in and never intended to keep.

At fifteen he had been sent to fight for his father; at eighteen he was a King in name, disowned by his country and dependent on reluctant charity. In 1649 he made the disastrous, but instructive, mistake of accepting the throne of Scotland; the offer was made partly in a fit of pique at Cromwell's defeat of the Scots forces at Preston, and on condition that he accept the covenant. This got him a bellyful of bigotry and a decisive defeat by Cromwell at Worcester in 1651. For the next six weeks he lived the life of a hunted fugitive, cold and hungry and with blistered feet; significantly, those who sheltered him and took him to ship in safety were either Catholic gentry or plain common people. He never forgot any of them: any of those, that is, who survived.

The life he escaped to was neither comfortable nor hopeful. He had a small band of faithful friends around him, of whom the greatest was Edward Hyde (later to be Lord Clarendon and grandfather to two Queens Regnant), but Cromwell's army was so much respected that no one thought Charles useful even as a political pawn. He lived in the common man's poverty of one meal a day, no money for fires in the winter, and a landlady threatening eviction. But, perhaps from his frivolous mother, Charles had a natural proclivity for enjoying life, and being personable he found his comfort in mistresses. Lucy Walter comforted him in those days, and gave him the son, later the Duke of Monmouth, he was mostly dearly and painfully to love. Charles's mistresses were to cause him and his kingdom a deal of trouble, and to all of them he was unvaryingly kind.

The change in his fortunes came when he was thirty. The death of Oliver Cromwell had appeared to make no difference in England; but at the beginning of 1660 General Monk declared himself for both King and Parliament. Charles promptly affirmed himself in favor of the will of a free Parliament, and was invited home.

Charles II had been no Baby Charles, cherished and sheltered. He had lived by his wits, and he intended to go on living by them. He seems to have had no political principles at all, only some intensely human ones. He clung to his throne because it was his living, and he pursued the interests of his unattractive brother James from family loyalty. He hated cruelty and inhumanity in any form; he was lazy and cynical, but never intolerant and never unintelligent. His interests were admirably wide, including science as well as the arts; he had a gift of making life pleasant and stimulating; he could be easy with cockney whores and serious with the Royal Society, and entirely himself with all of them.

The beginning was happy. Charles returned to England in May, 1660, and the people cheered for him as they had cheered for Elizabeth Tudor in 1558. He was kingly, courteous, and modest; he greeted General Monk with a marvelous combination of the youthful host and the respectful pupil. He charmed everyone, and even his irony was completely void of malice; he was made so welcome, he observed, that he wondered why he had stayed away so long.

One of his first measures was the Bill of Indemnity and Oblivion, decreeing pardon for all but the regicides; and later he even contrived to save some of them, on the grounds that he was sickened by the hangings. When this bill was before the House, Edward Hyde made a remarkable speech which we cannot doubt sets out Charles's personal position:

The King is a suitor to you that you will join with him in restoring the whole nation to its primitive temper and integrity, its old good manners, and its old good humour, and that you will by your examples teach your neighbours how to learn this excellent art of forgetfulness.

Unhappily, though the King had come into his own again, countless Englishmen had not, and there was no religion that had not learned to fear the persecution of some other. Moreover, because the Civil Wars had been fought not King against Parliament, nor Anglican against Puritan, nor persecution against tolerance, but in a hugger-mugger of them all, no clear resolution had been arrived at on anything. Charles's Parliament had learned too well the lesson that its power lay in its control of taxation; it kept him always short of money, and this was the cause of the third of the three great disasters that befell England early in his reign. These are three dates that every schoolboy knows: 1665, the Great Plague of London; 1666, the Great Fire of London; 1667, the Dutch in the Medway. And though none of them could be blamed on the King—indeed during the Great Fire he showed conspicuous courage in the fire-fighting, and lent his good taste to the replanning afterwards—they did much to dissipate the good humor of his early years on the throne. The episode of the Dutch was particularly unfortunate, in that, in the series of wars which their rivalry in the sea trades had brought about between England and Holland, England in 1667 had the upper hand, and by the Treaty of Breda signed in that year had been ceded New York. But what money there was had not stretched to the coast defenses, and a few weeks before the treaty was signed the Dutch Admiral de Ruyter sailed unopposed up the Medway and burned the English warships as they lay off Chatham. However unjustly, a people already deeply shocked by the Plague and the Fire blamed the King for this; he took, they said, more trouble to reconcile his whores when they quarrelled than ever he did about his kingdom. This was not only unjust but ungrateful, for the best of Charles's human qualities was symbolized in the way he reconciled his whores. When in 1662 he married his plain little wife, Catherine of Bragança, he stubbornly refused to be unkind either to her or to his flaunting mistress, Barbara Palmer; heaven knows how he did it, but he contrived to make both ladies happy.

In Europe, where Spain had collapsed from her earlier position as the dominating Catholic power, France was now the rising threat. These were the early years of the reign of Louis XIV, that paranoiac Sun King whose magnificence was to drive his hapless successors into the French Revolution; and Edward Hyde Lord Clarendon clearly saw the threat. In 1668 the great Protestant powers of the North, England, Holland, and Sweden, took the first step in a war that was to last for generations by forming the Triple Alliance against the advance of France in the northeast of Europe. If Charles II had honored this agreement, he would have saved Europe many years of war. But he did not; and unhappily one of the powers left to the King was the conduct of foreign policy, and in the shameful Treaty of Dover of 1670 Charles showed all the ineradicable Stuart traits. It was a treaty between two sovereign Kings (though Louis of France had taken care to add to his own negotiating strength Louise de Quérouaille, who became one of Charles's most intelligent and most dangerous mistresses), arranging for France and England together to attack and partition Holland. (One of the clauses was that a small part of the defeated Holland—when it was defeated—was to be given, under the sovereignty of France, to one of Charles's family, William Prince of Orange, the son of that sister Mary who married at the time of Strafford's trial. It seems that this twenty-year-old prince, whose position was dubious and whose health so frail that he had only recently been judged strong enough to ride a war horse, was not consulted about the arrangement. He was to have his say in later years.) It was a devious treaty, for one half of it was kept secret, and that half of it bound Louis to provide Charles with money and troops to enable him to declare himself a Catholic and bring England back to the Church of Rome.

This, only four years after the Restoration, was a shocking betrayal of the King's own country. But though Charles was a Stuart he was a very intelligent one, and while he never did declare himself a Catholic (though he died one), and never was within hailing distance of bringing England back to Rome, for the rest of his life, he still drew a sizable subsidy from Louis. To secure this treaty he had to dismiss his old and loyal counsellor, Clarendon, and surround himself with men much less honest. (The initials of five of the chief of them, Clifford, Arlington, Buckingham, Ashley Cooper, and Lauderdale, have given us a useful word: *cabal*—a private intrigue of sinister character by a small number of persons.)

What saved Europe from French domination in that generation was the magnificent Dutch. Holland, or the United Provinces as they were then called, was the Protestant part of what had been the Spanish Netherlands (the Catholic part is present-day Belgium). Its provinces and cities were so passionately independent that often they preferred to die rather than take orders from their own side; how they ever survived their own liberty is one of the miracles of history.

They were a maritime nation, like the English, and these were the great days of the maritime nations with their overseas riches. The Dutch battle for survival, in their small country without natural defenses, was bitterer than that of the English on their island, and it is one of posterity's reproaches against that supporter of the arts and sciences, Charles II, that he should have attacked the land of Rembrandt and Vermeer, of Descartes and Spinoza.

In 1670 the French invaded Holland, and the Dutch, morally and materially unprepared, yet did the one heroic thing that saved their land at the price of ruining much of it; they opened the dykes, and drowned their fields along with the invaders. They also did what probably appealed to their independence as much more heroic, and installed a chief officer of state, a *Stadhouder,* choosing that inconsiderable young William of Orange, Charles II's nephew, to whom Louis XIV had been willing to allow the governorship of the Provinces when he had conquered them. William was then just twenty, and from that moment was to dedicate his life to the fight against French domination.

In accordance with the Treaty of Dover, Charles also declared war on Holland. Parliament, who at first saw nothing in the war but the chance to put a trade competitor out of business, was willing enough, but the King had miscalculated the costs, and soon Parliament saw also that a Dutch defeat would put the vital mouths of the Rhine into the hands of France, and in 1674 insisted on withdrawing England from the war. Their fears of Rome now revived, they also forced Charles to consent to the Test Act, a piece of intolerance against the Catholics which served one useful purpose in revealing that the heir presumptive, Charles's brother James Duke of York, was a Catholic himself.

Louis XIV was checked but not defeated, and many years of misery were before the Dutch. Neither was Charles II defeated, but he was the intelligent Stuart; seeing that his country would never accept a return to Rome, he abandoned his crypto-Catholic policies entirely, and for the rest of his reign devoted himself to the implementation of one policy alone: his resolve never to go on his travels again. With tact and intelligence he became a devout Anglican and a loyal Parliamentarian. This was the more difficult in that he was determined also to secure the accession to his neither tactful nor intelligent brother James, and to retain the subsidy Louis XIV paid him.

Nor did he intend to give up Louise de Quérouaille, or Madam Carwell as the English called her. She stayed in England and became Duchess of Portsmouth, as Barbara Palmer became Duchess of Cleveland; Charles was generous to his mistresses (whom Parliament called sourly "the chargeable ladies about court"), and even more generous to the many children he had by them. When he fell in love with the beautiful Frances Stuart, and she refused him, he was her friend for life, and perpetuated her beauty by putting her on his coins as Britannia. The country was enjoying its liberation from the stifling morality of the Commonwealth, and the court led the way. It was a gay court, dedicated to enjoyment; and if the King set the pattern here, he set it also, for those who were able to follow him, in the gaiety and culture of his other enjoyments. The love affair that most endeared him to later times was that with "pretty witty Nelly," the unaffected little plebeian actress from Drury Lane, Nell Gwyn. The best of the many stories about Nelly is of the time when her coach was mistaken for that of Louise de Quérouaille, whom a crowd in the London streets (who never, quite rightly, trusted Louise) were abusing as the "Catholic whore"; Nelly put her head out of the window and called, "Be quiet, good people, I'm the Protestant whore." It may be that it was England's tragedy as well as Charles's that his wife, whom he appears to have loved tenderly, was barren. If he had had a legitimate son to succeed him he might have acted differently. What calls for our pity for the King here is his dearest child, the eldest boy born in his father's exile to Lucy Walter, now James Duke of Monmouth. Monmouth was handsome, arrogant, stupid, and ungrateful. He allowed himself to be adopted as the Protestant rival to the Catholic Duke of York, and became implicated in a plot to assassinate his father. Charles professed not to believe this, but Charles was seldom deceived. Much of his attention in his later years was taken up with his efforts to save this worthless boy from his own foolishness and bad faith; he exiled him to keep him out of trouble, and when he went straight to the King's enemies in Holland he called him home again and sent the Duke of York to Scotland to keep them away from one another.

For, as well as the illegitimate Monmouth, there was another possible Protestant heir to the throne of England. After the Duke of

York and his family, the next heir was William III of Orange, *Stadhouder* of the United Provinces. He had been born in 1650, a week after his father's death from smallpox, and was fast making a name for himself as a defender of Protestant liberty against France. Just before the Restoration, a scandal had occurred in the English royal family: the Duke of York, having made Clarendon's daughter, Anne Hyde, pregnant, insisted on marrying her. The Duchess of York was a sickly girl and lived only ten years, and her two surviving children were not expected to live to maturity; but they did, and the elder of them, Mary, was remarkably pretty. In 1677 she married William III.

Charles II's loyalty to his brother James is one of the more inexplicable facets of his character. It was not that he was blind to James's qualities; he spoke tolerantly of the *"sottises de mon frère."* Did the royal Stuart in him cling to the principle of right descent by God's will? Or was he, after all, so deeply Catholic that he could give over his kingdom to a brother he knew was incapable of keeping it simply because his faith forbade him to give it over to a heretic?

Into this problem fits one of the most disgraceful episodes of English history: the so-called Popish Plot. This was alleged to be a plot by the Catholics against the kingdom, the discovery of which was engineered by a man for whom it is impossible to find the least extenuating word. Titus Oates was not only utterly unscrupulous, arbitrarily destroying men on nothing but his lying words, but he was loathesomely hypocritical with it, claiming to do so in the interests of true religion. In fact, there was no plot at all; the whole thing was a fabrication of Oates and his unsavory associates; it was disgraceful because from the beginning it could offer little in the way of credibility, let alone proof, yet the anti-Catholic party in Parliament, the Whigs as they were called (in opposition to the Tories, who were royalist), continued to exploit it long after it was plain that the whole thing was a fabrication and thus foolishly discredited themselves. The passion of support that Oates aroused in England was a plain sign of the ineradicable mistrust and indeed terror felt by the English for the Church of Rome. They had got tired of the Commonwealth, but many Englishmen still lived by the personal Puritan faith; Puritans were Englishman and neighbors, while Catholics were, in effect, foreigners, subject to the dictates of France or Rome. In fact, time had justified Elizabeth Tudor's strategy; the English now knew which religion gave them the best life.

This, however, did not mend Parliament, in which the religious and political issues had become so inextricably entangled that any kind of moderation seemed impossible. Louis XIV, who was zealously persecuting his own Protestants, the Huguenots, was also giving help to Monmouth, and his wealth had contrived to corrupt the Whig party. Their extremist attitudes had a miserable effect on the Tories, who were driven into an abject royalism, which the King punctually noted and made the best of. In 1683 the Whigs destroyed themselves—some of them on a traitors' scaffold—but the consequent Tory reaction was almost as bad. For the last four years of Charles II's reign the country was governed not by Parliament but by court intrigues. One party was for the French, the other against. The Duke of York, as a Catholic, was of course for them, and the King was dependent on Louis's money. It was a shameful time, for while these two royal Stuarts were comfortably pensioners of France, Louis XIV continued his aggression in Europe. Louis wanted territory, and to him his want was moral ground enough. Every inch that Charles II allowed him to take had to be won back later by the loss of Dutch and English blood.

And yet, while he was acting thus indefensibly, Charles II was also approaching his death with a courage, a serenity, and a kindness that should serve as an example. His hitherto admirable health began to decline, and he took it quietly and without complaint. One night in February, 1685, he slept badly, appeared ill at ease, and while he was being shaved suffered what seems to have been a stroke. He was in no doubt that he was dying, but in great pain and discomfort he retained all his courtesy and kindness. The Queen could not bear to see his suffering and was taken away fainting, for which she sent to beg his pardon; he said, "Take her back this answer, I beg hers with all my heart." He saw his brother James, whose grief was genuine; he recommended to him the Queen and all his children, and asked him to take care of Louise, and "not to let poor Nelly starve" (alone among the chargeable ladies Nelly had refused to take much). In between spasms of pain he prayed for God's blessing on his country, and asked for pardon if he had not been a good King. But also, when James whispered something in his ear, he said, "Yes, with all my heart." James went out, and came back with a Catholic priest. It happened to be a man Charles had known for more years than he had been King: the aged Father Huddleston, who had helped him escape from England after the defeat of Worcester thirty-four years ago. Father Huddleston received him into the Catholic Church and gave him Extreme Unction, the sacrament for the dying.

His two most famous dying words were to apologize for being such an unconscionable time a-dying (brave words when dying was extreme pain), and the request: "Open the curtains that I may once more see the day." He died as he had lived, a kind and cheerful and courageous human being and a faithless and disastrous King.

JAMES II
1685–1689

❀

Born at St. James's Palace, London, in October 1633.
Second surviving son of Charles I and his wife Henrietta
  Maria of France.
Married, first, in 1659, Anne Hyde, daughter of Edward
  Hyde later Lord Clarendon, who died in 1671, of whose
  many children only two daughters survived:

  Mary, later Queen Mary II, and
  Anne, later Queen Anne;

secondly James married, in 1673, Mary Beatrice of
Modena, by whom he had a son,

  James, born in June 1688, later known in England as
  the Old Pretender; he married Clementina Sobieska
  and died in 1766; their son was:
    Charles, born in Rome in 1720, later known in
    England as the Young Pretender, died 1788.

James II was deposed by Parliament in February 1689. He
lived in exile on the Continent until his death in 1701. His
son James was then recognized as James III by some
Continental powers, but this recognition gradually lapsed.

JAMES II

ames II was the last Stuart King of England, and he deserved to be. He united all his father's blindly stubborn belief in the divine right of Kings with a blinder fanatical Catholicism. It is recorded that when someone pointed out to him that his determination to make England into a Catholic country was endangering his throne, he replied simply that for his memorial he wanted a red-letter day. (In the Catholic calendar martyrs are commemorated with a red letter.) It did not prove to be a good way of achieving his ambition; he ran away long before he was martyred.

Yet, thanks to the loyalty of his brother, he succeeded to a reasonably secure position. Since the collapse of the Whigs after the Popish Plot the Tory party had carefully rigged the elective system. The Tories were chiefly the great nobles, the High Anglican churchmen, and the wealthier country gentlemen; the Whigs were the rich merchants, the Dissenters (the term that was coming to cover most shades of dissent on the Puritan or Low Church side of the Anglicans), and the opponents of the monarchy. But the lines of natural loyalties were by now so tangled that the Whigs, who should by rights have supported the Dutch alliance, were as often as not prevented by suspicions (quite justified) of the Dutch as overseas trade rivals; while the Tories, upholders though they were of the fatuous policy of non-resistance to the Crown, balked like good patriots at the whiff of Catholicism in a French alliance.

With a little of his brother's tact and patience James could have survived. No one, for example, took the chance to weaken his rule during the rising of the West Country Puritans under Monmouth in

June, 1685. These rebels were mostly honest country people driven to extremity by persecution, and they deserved a better leader than the worthless Monmouth. Their final defeat at Sedgemoor came in a matter of weeks; yet James allowed them to be punished with such merciless barbarity—this was the time of the sadistic Judge Jeffreys —that for the first time for decades the English began to find their own bigotry sticking in their own throats.

They soon had much more than cruelty to worry about; for James was in a short time not even attempting to cover up his moves in the direction of the Roman Church. The most dangerous of these were his attempts to terrorize the country, and in particular the sturdily independent City of London, by keeping a large army on foot. Monmouth's rebellion provided him with an excuse for this, and when once he had his army he tried to fill it and officer it with loyal Catholics. This attempt was a dismal failure, though it ruined the army that had once been the best in Europe. What James seems not to have realized was that there were very few (in his terms) loyal Catholics left in England. There were plenty of Catholics; but on the whole they were quiet Englishmen who wanted only to be allowed to live their private lives in private peace. In default of them, James imported droves of Catholic Irishmen; the difference in religion, loyalties, and culture between English and Irish wrecked the regiments.

In the same way, James attempted, first by legal means and then by increasingly and brazenly illegal ones, to fill his magistracies— both the local ones and the state ones—with Catholics. Again he failed; even though in the four years of his reign he progressed as far in that direction as to propose quite seriously religious toleration for Catholics. His appeal was largely to the smaller Catholic gentry to come forward to fill local magistracies, and that they on the whole resisted it seems to show that if they were Catholic in faith they were English in understanding. In an extraordinary gesture—he appears to have thought it was politic, which is the last thing it could have been—James extended the offer of religious toleration to the Dissenters. That he could have imagined that any Dissenter would have been foolish enough to believe in his honesty makes James the crowning example of the impossibility of the Stuarts.

During this time, of course, the question of the succession had been simmering. The obvious Protestant candidate—and thus quite clearly the one James would oppose—was the Dutch *Stadhouder*

William Prince of Orange, who by his double claim as the son of the King's sister Mary and the husband of his elder daughter would plainly be a formidable contender. James took the view that he himself had the only right to dispose of this throne. His younger daughter Anne had been married also to a Protestant, an inconspicuous prince of Denmark, and the couple lived in England. James tried to convert her to Rome, but Anne, whose part in politics had so far been to show jealousy of her sister Mary, evinced a surprising firmness and announced publicly that nothing would make her change her religion. After the death of Anne Hyde in 1671 James himself had married Mary Beatrice of Modena, and she had suffered so characteristic a series of miscarriages that it was believed throughout Europe that James was syphilitic and unable to father a living child, and while he had two firmly Protestant daughters, one of them married to a bulwark of the Protestant cause, England could afford to wear out his reign in the sure hope of better things to come.

This comfortable state was abruptly stayed at the end of 1687. Mary Beatrice was pregnant, and contrary to all precedent and expectation she did not miscarry. Her pregnancy was due to come to term in June 1688.

England, shaken to the core at the prospect of a legitimate heir who would be brought up a confirmed Catholic, took refuge in the wildest calumnies. It was all a plot, the people swore; and when, in June, 1688, in all the usual publicity of a royal birth, with the curtains of the bed providing the only privacy, Mary Beatrice gave birth to a healthy boy, he was christened the Warming-Pan Heir, the story went that the midwives had smuggled him into the birth-chamber in a warming-pan.

James was wild with joy at this birth; it did not occur to him that in having a Catholic heir he had gone too far. But quite possibly he had already gone too far, for by now his kingdom was almost wholly united against him (he did at least this good to his country, in uniting it for the first time for decades). He had issued a Declaration of Indulgence (that is, of religious indulgence, which would have allowed him to appoint Catholics to any office of state), which he had no legal right to do, and he had commanded the preachers to read it from the pulpit to their congregations. Seven bishops petitioned him against it; he put them on trial for seditious libel. On June 30, 1688, three weeks after the birth of the young prince, the jury acquitted the bishops. That night the chiefs of both parties signed an invitation to Prince William of Orange to come to England.

William was an experienced soldier and statesman and was hard-pressed in his own country; he did not move until he was sure of himself on both sides of the sea. His very sizable, but extremely peaceable and unaggressive, army did not land in England until November 5, the anniversary of the Gunpowder Plot, and then he was met by the country people calling to him "God bless you!"

At the very least, James could have made a fight for it. William had left Catholic enemies in his rear, and James had a vast army camp set up on Hounslow Heath which he had established for the sole purpose of terrorizing London. But at this crisis James seems to have gone slightly crazy. He was tormented by sleeplessness; his most decisive actions, even so late as a month before William's landing, were to tell his courtiers vengefully that they would find William a worse man than Cromwell; and at the moment when he brought himself to make the decision to join his army he was incapacitated by a violent nosebleed. And meanwhile, William was slowly marching through the south of England, and common people and leaders alike were flocking to join him. Distraught, James sent his wife and son to France; and on the December 10, 1688 fled himself. He wrote first a fretful letter to Dartmouth, who was in command of the fleet, complaining of having been basely deserted by his soldiers: "I could no longer resolve to expose myself for no purpose to what I might expect from the ambitious Prince of Orange and the associated rebellious lords, and therefore have resolved to withdraw till this violent storm is over." He advised Dartmouth, if he had any men left who were still "free to continue serving me," to go to Ireland (where the Catholic forces were concentrating against William); concluding, however, "If they will not, there is no remedy, and this I say, never any Prince took more care of his sea and land men as I have done, and been so very ill repaid by them."

Even this dispirited apology for an order arrived too late. Dartmouth had had to join William two days earlier to prevent a mutiny among his seamen.

James was not even capable of escaping efficiently, for he was recognized and taken in Kent, and treated without too much respect. He took refuge in Scripture, comparing himself to Abel and then to Joseph on the flight to Egypt, and addressing a man who cursed him as Shimei—"for Shimei cursed the Lord's Anointed."

He was a pathetic encumbrance in England now, for William's bloodless triumph was so entire that there was even a moment of sympathy for James as a suffering father. An escape route was quietly left open for him, and much to everyone's relief he took it. He went to France, keeping up his state in a court-in-exile, and his cause, at least, remained a nuisance to England for years. It is difficult to believe that even the most fanatical Catholic ever wanted James himself back again, but as the years went on there was always his son, and then his grandson, for the English malcontents to hope for. James himself made one more effort at action, when in 1689 Louis XIV gave him some French troops to take to the wars in Ireland. The result was a defeat for the Irish but a fiasco for James personally. He found himself helpless between Louis's commanders and the Irish Viceroy Tyrconnel (who had notions of securing an Irish kingdom for himself). It was a brutal war; the French were trained to brutality and ordered to use it as a weapon, and the unhappy Irish were driven by the despair of their long years of alternate neglect and exploitation. To his credit, James used what little influence he had to prevent the brutality. He was present at the decisive Battle of the Boyne, where he had to face William himself; and when he saw that the day was going against him, or rather against the troops who were nominally fighting for him, he retired as fast as he had gone in 1688 and took refuge in the French fleet. Again it must be said for him that he refused the French advice to burn Dublin behind him.

But it was the end of his active political career. He kept himself occupied; for instance, he kept in touch with that formidable lady, Sophia Electress of Hanover, who was a daughter of the Winter Queen; and apparently he was concerned in some attempts at assassinating William of Orange; and, in the nature of such things, when matters looked less than well for William there were always courtiers who thought it a good idea to be on speaking terms with the Jacobite court, as it soon became known. But after a time James became an embarrassment even to Louis XIV. Louis always referred to James as the King of England and to William as *"M. le Prince d'Orange,"* but as *M. le Prince d'Orange* won more battles, Louis had to negotiate with him. In 1694 William's wife, and James's daughter, Mary died, and James refused to go into mourning for her. James himself died in September, 1701, at the age of sixty-eight, and William, always cool and correct, went into mourning for his father-in-law. Louis at once recognized the Warming-Pan Heir as King James III of England; the impertinence of the foreigner outraged the English, which just at that time was very convenient for William.

Louis's James III, known in England as the Old Pretender, is a shadowy figure to us. His title is an example of a very rare type of English joke, a bilingual pun that really understands a foreign word. In French, *Prétendant* means claimant, and the English joyfully seized on the word as their view of the claims of the Stuarts. The later lives of the descendants of James II belong to later reigns in England; but long after their political importance had vanished, the Jacobite cause remained a romantic fashion in England. It was a useful safety-valve for a people irritated by the entire lack of charm in the English Kings of those days. The Scots proprietorially kept the legend alive long after the English had given it over to the novelists, cryptically honoring the Loyal Toast of *The King, God Bless Him,* by passing their glasses over a decanter of water before they drank, signifying *The King over the Water.* It is reported that in the the First World War some Scots officers of this mind were disconcerted to discover that the German commander in the trenches facing them was Prince Rupprecht of Bavaria, whom they had been accustomed to toast as the rightful King of England.

House of

ORANGE

WILLIAM III
AND MARY II
1689-1694

WILLIAM III
1694-1702

❂

William III Prince of Orange, born in 1650, son of William
of Orange and his wife Mary daughter of Charles I and
Henrietta Maria: married in 1677:

Mary, elder surviving daughter of James II and his first
    wife Anne Hyde, born 1662.

Recognized as joint sovereigns after the abdication of
    Mary's father James II; reigned jointly, with the execu-
    tive power vested in William, until Mary died in
    December 1694, and was buried at Westminster;
    thereafter William reigned alone until his death at Ken-
    sington Palace in March 1702; he was buried at West-
    minster.

William and Mary had no children, and by the Act of
    Settlement of 1701 the Crown devolved upon only the
    Protestant heirs, of whom the first was Mary's sister
    Anne; thereafter, as Anne's only surviving child had
    recently died, upon the Protestant line of the Electors
    of Hanover, descended from James I by his daughter
    Elizabeth, wife of the Elector Palatine.

Orange was a sovereign Principality in the south of
    France. William III held also, both before and after his
    accession, various offices in the United Provinces (mod-
    ern Holland and Belgium) which were not hereditary.

WILLIAM III
AND MARY II

William III was something new to England since the days of William the Conqueror; he was a foreigner and an experienced ruler.

He was from birth a sovereign prince, hereditary ruler of the tiny state of Orange in the south of France. In the United Provinces he had no authority but what was bestowed on him, and so fanatically independent were the Dutch that although they owed a great part of their liberty to the House of Orange it was only the French invasion of 1679 that persuaded them to name William III of Orange their *Stadhouder,* or chief officer of state. Even this authority was always hedged about by the suspicions and jealousies of the individual provinces and cities. Indeed, William fought for them for thirty-two years until his death in 1702, and in only two campaigns did he have enough trained troops, enough money, and an unquestioned command.

The Dutch were an unfortunate people in the sixteenth and seventeenth centuries; after having with great labor struggled free of the Spanish threat they found themselves the first target of an aggressive France at the height of her power. The struggle was a political one, religious only to the extent to which the Protestant powers found themselves with similar interests. Spain, who a hundred years before had been burning and torturing in the Low Countries to bring them back to Rome, was to be found allied with the Dutch; the Pope, to whose church Louis XIV, Charles II, and James II were attempting to return forcibly millions of souls, distrusted them all and favored the Protestant cause; and the two chief Protestant powers, England and the United Provinces, were sporadically at war with one another because of their trade rivalry. In such an atmosphere alliances sprang up and were disavowed within months, so that the disavowal coincided with the implementation; peace negotiations began with the opening of hostilities, and the military position was even further confused by the number of small states who lived by hiring out mercenaries and instructed their troops to change sides for purely mercenary reasons. Nevertheless, for those who could see it there was one purpose behind it all, and that was the determination of the French King Louis XIV—the Sun King—to dominate Europe.

After years of anarchy France had emerged as probably the most absolute of all absolute monarchies, and the richest nation in Europe. The character of Louis XIV, who exhibited his bowel movements as matter for public congratulation, is a caricature of an absolute monarch. He was undoubtedly a little less than sane at times, driven to it by power and adulation; but there were many in the position of William of Orange, who fought the power of France all his life and all his life admired and loved things French.

No one admired Louis's methods. He considered himself bound by nothing, not even his own word, for it is hardly possible to find a treaty he did not break. He would invade a peaceable country for no more reason than that he wanted a man of his own on some petty throne. His arrogance was so absurd that he made it a habit when dictating terms of peace to include the demand that the defeated should send him a yearly deputation to thank him for the favor of having defeated them, with a gold medal specially struck for the occasion. But undoubtedly his worst crimes, and his most foolish, were committed in his own country, where he cruelly persecuted the Huguenots, who were mostly a peaceable people. It was this, with the stories carried abroad by the escaping Huguenots to the Protestant countries, that provoked a public anger that made the war against France a popular one that the common people were willing to make sacrifices for.

In 1670, however, the war was between France and the United Provinces, and William of Orange, not quite twenty-one, was called to lead against the strongest nation in Europe an army that hardly existed, because the Provinces would not pay their taxes and were not convinced that France was their enemy. He was not even equipped to command, for so suspicious were the Dutch that they had refused to allow him to receive any training in the military art. Moreover his physique was so frail that for a long time he was thought not strong enough to manage the great warhorses of the time. The Dutch, it was plain, could not alone withstand France, and hurriedly, showing a flair for the diplomacy he had not been allowed to learn, William patched up an alliance. It was neither stable nor lengthy, but it did for the time.

William was something entirely unknown in England, an aristocrat. The Continental aristocracy was a closed class (they despised the English peers for having common blood), with their own inflexible standards and their own way of life; their chosen profession was the military profession. Although in fact William's best work was as a diplomat, personally he had all the virtues of the soldier in the days when that was an honorable profession. His morals were simple, straightforward, and a little austere, his talents those of clear thinking and of decisive and patient action. He had a certain inability (which he struggled against) to be gracious to those he despised, but he seems never to have been affected by the power he attained in later life. His courage in battle was a necessary disregard of danger, and to the end of his life he fought personally; when he was fifty-one and very near death he mounted and led an attack that held a vital counterscarp at Namur. He was small, with one shoulder higher than the other, was chronically asthmatic, and suffered from ill health all his life; but he was never so well as when on campaign, riding all day and writing all night.

He succeeded to great estates burdened by debt, which he paid off by living simply and reading his personal accounts once a week (an incredible proceeding for a nobleman); a great deal of his wealth later went into the struggle with France. He was a quiet, reserved man, easy with only a few friends and of them demanding a high standard of probity and an even higher one of hard work. His religious faith was strong, but private to himself, and not puritanical; he drank, sometimes too much but not often because of his health; he gambled on cards and liked the theatre, on all which amusements the Dutch frowned. His taste in art and architecture was remarkably good. Most of all he loved making palaces with gardens, and England would have been the poorer without him. There was a famous palace at Enghien in Holland with splendid fountains, and whenever he was near he would ride out alone to look at the gardens.

In 1677 he brought about a precarious alliance with England and married his cousin Mary, elder daughter of James Duke of York. Since his mother had been another Princess Mary, daughter of Charles I of England, he had always regarded himself as legitimately within the line of succession to the English throne, and the marriage strengthened this claim. Even if he were not to succeed, the safety of the United Provinces, and thus of the base for the struggle with France, depended on a firm alliance with England. The irrepressibly suspicious Dutch, however, took the chance to accuse him of preferring England's interests to theirs. Nor was his bride happy about it. Mary was then fifteen, twelve years younger than William, tall and stately and beautiful, and she wept for a day and a half after her first meeting with her quiet hunch-backed suitor. The marriage did not promise happiness; Mary had considerable charm but no education, knowing nothing but cards and the theatre, and could not even speak Dutch. Yet, she was a woman of intelligence and strong character as well as of charm and honesty, and somehow this disparate couple came to fall deeply in love. Mary took immense pains, even to almost losing her sight, to educate herself to William's standard, and he came to value her for her judgment as much as for her loyalty. He is only once recorded as having been unfaithful to her. Lady Betty Villiers had missed the famous Villiers beauty, but she was lively and witty and intelligent. In 1683 Mary discovered that she was William's mistress, and there were tears and scandal. Yet, in the end Lady Betty stayed at court and remained excellent friends with both William and Mary, which seems to have been an example of Mary's genuine sweetness of temper.

About the time of his marriage William's fortunes fell to their lowest. There was no campaigning in the winter, and every spring he was at a disadvantage because Louis could establish magazines for foddering his horses, while William never had the money, and had to wait to open his campaign until the fresh fodder was ready in May. The Dutch were disheartened, his allies deserted him; his wife's country went on its crypto-Catholic way; and he was forced to make peace. It seemed that the whole of Europe united to shower humiliations on him; it seemed that William of Orange was finished. He was not, of course; he went quietly on, dealing with petty details of troops and taxes and titles, winning this small man by giving him a good dinner, that larger one by convincing him of his interest, dealing as patiently as he could with the antics of his two impossible uncles of England (with whom he lost his temper very often). His forms of expression are a study in themselves; if he said something was outrageous and intolerable, he was irritated; if he said he was "not a little surprised," he was dangerously angry.

The one trouble that he did not surmount was his wife's barrenness. He must have been prepared for this when he married her, for their father James Duke of York was currently supposed to be syphilitic (though in fact the weakness must have been on the side of her mother, Anne Hyde, and Mary's sister Anne had the same trouble). Later on he did consider Mary's position if she were to survive him and have children by a second marriage, but this may have been mere precaution, for very early he seem to have been convinced that he would have no children of his own. Characteristically, he made an advantage of the lack, using the bait of his wealth to bring to his side his uniformly nasty Nassau relations. He used to say that he cared nothing for how the world went on after his death, which is a curious remark from a man who spent himself fighting for the future of Europe. The resolution of the curiosity seems to lie in a word he used with surprising frequency for a man not addicted to the gesture: honor. There were things he would not do because they were "against my honor." What set him fighting a lifelong battle that profited him nothing? The word *honor* is as good as any other.

There is ample evidence that various English parties urged William to intervene in England for the Protestant cause very early in James II's reign. William was courteous, but always made it clear that James was his wife's father, and that he could interfere only if the people of England as a whole asked for his help and if Mary's inheritance was endangered.

In June, 1688, this moment appeared to have come. King James had had a Catholic heir, and it was clear that nothing now would stop him in his determination to return England to the Roman allegiance in spite of the protests of most of the English. The dangers to William's cause were enormous; he could not go without an army (no one appears to have foreseen James's collapse), and that army had to be taken from his Continental defenses against France. Once he was decided, he had the advantage of living always on a war footing; he mounted his invasion with remarkable speed, and on November 5, 1688, disembarked on the English soil at Torbay in Devon. It is worthy of remark that the Dutch found the English disgustingly dirty, but liked the way they offered cider and called "God bless you!" to William. William was determined not to antagonize the English. Slowly and patiently, giving them plenty of time, he moved north and east. No great army marched out to confront him. Instead, countless individual Englishmen rode in to join him.

James II put himself out of the running; he was gently nudged out of the country, while slowly and patiently William negotiated with what he regarded as the authority in the land: what the Stuarts had left of Parliament.

What he wanted was quite simple: authority that he could commit to the war against France. In effect this meant the throne, and he persisted quietly until he got it: joint monarchy for himself and his wife, with the executive power vested in himself. It took a long time, and was an earnest of what the future in England was to be for him. Few people have William's single-mindedness, and he was a Continental with a view far broader than any Englishman's. He was using England in a Continental quarrel, and the result could have been disastrous for England; that it was not was because William's clarity of mind had correctly seen that the French threat was a threat to England, too. He was many times to despair of the English (as he had many times despaired of the Dutch), and once he wrote, "I see I am not for these people, nor they for me." But he was wrong; for the day of his landing at Torbay is one of the greatest days of English history.

We in England call this revolution of 1688 the Glorious Revolution. This is partly because it was a very successful revolution, getting rid of an impossibly incapable King and replacing him by a remarkably capable one, and destroying in one stroke the two dangers of the preceding reigns, the secret encroachment of the Roman Church and the claim of the throne to override the will of Parliament.

But chiefly we call the year 1688 Glorious because it did not demand bloodshed. Not one life was lost in the change of dynasty, law, and religion. After decades of intolerance and cruelty, the people themselves made it clear that what they wanted was civil peace and kindness—"the nation's primitive temper and integrity, its old good manners and its old good honor." Because of this glorious year, the English still (so far) believe that governments can be moved by peaceful means to what the governed want.

This is a dangerous state of mind, as was noticeable in the reigns following William's. The very virtues of moderation and good-neighborliness needed to make it work easily degenerate into the vice of slavish complacency, so that reformers find it very hard going. But, governments being what they are, reformers very seldom find their paths easy; and at least in England after 1688 those who did not need changes were able to go on with their private lives in peace.

Scotland was still a separate kingdom, and had a sentimental attachment to the Stuarts; but it was still a Protestant country, and after a brief flurry accepted William and Mary. William was not, of course, of the Scottish communion; but nor had he been of the English communion, and it is a sign of the growing religious sanity of the times that no one wanted to be too precise about the details. Ireland, however, was a different matter. To England, Ireland was always a possible base for enemy invasion; to Ireland, England was an occupying power dragging a weaker country in her wake. The English thought the Irish savage and uncivilizeable, the Irish thought the English brutal and aggressive. The problem had come to a head in the time of Cromwell's ascendancy, and indefensibly (it is still difficult to understand why so practical a man could have been so foolish) Cromwell had settled for the short answer of terror. He had brought in Protestant settlers to the northern province and supported them by fire and sword, beginning centuries of irreconcilable strife. James II had had a vague idea of making it into a Catholic fortress, and Louis XIV intended using it as a military base. It was more ill luck for the Irish; Louis cared nothing for them, the French regarded them as savages, and James II was no inspiring leader. But the Irish, faithful to their passionate Catholicism, rose for James, and, after some inconclusive fighting, William himself had to come over. The Battle of the Boyne, at which the matter was settled, was in fact a small skirmish, where William's trained and disciplined men defeated the Irish who were not trained and the French who were not disciplined. William was able to return to England and set his new kingdom to rights.

He was not now the half-distrusted general of a half-defeated state. He was the ruler of two countries and the greatest statesman of Europe, and he had realized now that the way to defeat France was by the war of attrition. Let him but bring an army into the field every spring, keep his alliances on foot in however divided a way, and sooner or later even the immense natural resources of France would give way under the strain. The business of running two countries almost single-handedly nearly killed him; the business of fighting invariably restored him for the next stint.

His industry in administration is awe-inspiring. As he found it necessary to enquire into the running of one department of state after another he found such a dearth of any tradition of responsible public service, so complete a lack of skilled men, that all he could do was take it over himself. The harm done to the country by the Stuarts is nowhere clearer than in this: that a King who cared nothing for a man's politics, only for his honesty and his capability, could nowhere find men to run his government offices for him. Almost alone, William created the departmental framework of government that endures until today: the difference is that in those days William ran the lot of them. The men about court might have had a hand in turning out the Stuarts, but they were still Stuart creatures, and had been Stuart creatures for nearly three generations. In their way they differed little from the medieval barons who had been their precursors. They were settling roughly into two parties by now, but as political, financial, and religious factors often contradicted one another, the division was by no means definite in Parliament or outside it. One might find a convinced royalist whose trade interests favored France and who was yet a Puritan; or a Puritan Parliamentarian whose fortune had been ruined by the Dutch. For the first time, the names Whig and Tory were applied to these two parties; oddly enough, both names seem originally to have been given to obscure parties of Celtic outlaws, Scots for the Whigs and Irish for the Tories. The original English Tories were those who had opposed the exclusion of James Duke of York from the succession; now they still kept up their communication with the Jacobite court in France. The Whigs tended to support William because they had most to lose from a Stuart restoration; very roughly speaking, the Whigs were the bourgeois, the businessmen, the Dissenters, and the Tories the peers, the landowners, the Catholics, and the fanatical royalists. They were mostly a poor lot, as Stuart courtiers had learned to be, fickle, treacherous, and unaware of the necessity of hard work.

The one place where William had no trouble was that place where the English were accustomed to look after themselves: among the local magistrates. Very likely, the local justices of the peace had their politics, but their business was the conduct of day-to-day justice, and for them the advent of William and Mary was heaven-sent. The country was positively governed again; there was no sly pressure from above to favor one side or another, there was no religious persecution; trade was beginning to flourish. As they had always done, the local magistrates remained loyal to a King who permitted life to be what they knew it should be, peaceful enough for the people to live their lives as they liked.

For the rest of his life William divided his year between winters in England and summers—the campaigning season—on the Continent. Being King of England had not solved his chief military problem, that of finding fodder for his horses to start the campaign early. He had once had to wait for the hay in May; now he had to wait for the Parliamentary terms to get his money for the year. He had no great victories, no great defeats; indeed, for a great soldier William probably had defeats above the average. But he kept on forcing France to fight, and with each year the French potential was declining and William's rising. In 1690 Savoy joined the Grand Alliance against France, and a new southern front was opened; that year was marked by anxiety about Princess Anne's loyalty and the next year there was more serious trouble, led by a man of the princess's—or, more correctly, by a man who had found it convenient to attach himself to the princess.

This was John Churchill, later Duke of Marlborough, whom William frankly detested; understandably so, for Churchill was not in his sense an honorable man, being moved by nothing but personal ambition. Churchill was later to be one of the great men of Europe, though he was never to approach William's stature as a human being; he was always remote, lofty, emotionally null in success, peevish in defeat, totally unreliable as an ally. He was said to have begun his public life as a spare lover of one of Charles II's mistresses, and had once had to tumble out of her window in a hurry at the King's unexpected arrival. She paid him, and he, refreshingly enough, carefully invested the money to make it the basis of the enormous Churchill fortune. In 1688 he as carefully went over to William when it was clear that William would be the next King; but after that his fortunes lagged. William, who had been fighting the French when Churchill had been profiting from the royal bed, desperately wanted soldiers who had military experience, and saw no reason to give Churchill, who had none, the dukedom and the Garter he thought he was worthy of.

William was carrying out a lengthy retraining of the English army, which had been wrecked by James II's foolish policies, and trusted only the men he knew; Churchill attacked him for preferring Dutch officers to English, and demanded equal preference for the English. Considering what the Dutch had done in the last twenty years, it was an insolent attack; and it was an unscrupulous one, dictated by Churchill's naked ambition; and it was the more dangerous in that he had married the scarifyingly ambitious Sarah Jennings, who had established a complete ascendancy over the foolish Princess Anne. William dismissed Churchill, and Mary demanded that Anne should dismiss Sarah. Anne contrived to keep Sarah, and later on William came to appreciate Churchill, though never to like him. The Churchills were not at this time an attractive couple, but they had their way to make in an unattractive society. It was to be England's luck that her advantage was later to coincide with the course of the Churchill aggrandizement.

In 1692 there was a Jacobite plot to assassinate William. Both Louis XIV and James II were implicated in this, and as usual the threat of foreign interference brought about a useful surge of anti-Stuart feeling in England. In May Louis took the vital fortress of Namur, but in August William inflicted heavy losses on him at Steenkirk. In 1693, by accepting odds of 50,000 to 80,000, William saved both Liège and Brussels at the battle of Landen. Like so many of William's battles, Landen was not a victory, but it achieved his object. A week after the battle his own army was larger than on the day before, while the French casualties were so great that the French surgeons had to abandon their habit of estimating amputations by the number of patients and reckon instead by the wagonloads of severed limbs. The Grand Alliance still stood firm; and meantime the embargo that William had put upon trade with France, enforcing it by the two greatest navies of Europe, Dutch and English, was slowly eating into France's strength.

At the close of the campaigning season of 1694, William for the first time had the military initiative for the next year. He came back to England in poor health; during these years he was always emaciated, coughing, and liable to fevers. He had improved a little when, toward Christmas, his wife Mary was taken ill. Soon the fatal rash of smallpox showed—the disease from which William had lost both father and mother. In spite of the danger of infection he would not leave her room, even when his tears disturbed her rest. He was in more anguish than she; she suffered so little pain that she said, a few hours before her death, that it was amazing that one could die without feeling ill. She took her last Communion, said goodbye to him, and quietly grew weaker until she died at eleven at night on the December 27, 1694. She was only thirty-two, and they had been married seventeen years.

William collapsed at her bedside, and as she died his faithful friend Portland had to carry him away. It was a month before he even began to recover. He told Portland, "I keep thinking it's time to go and have supper with my wife." Very slowly he adjusted himself to his loss, and took up again the purpose of his life, but he was a changed man. He never afterward lost a sadness in his look; he went to prayers twice a day, and dismissed Betty Villiers from court. It is pleasant to record that his sense of having sinned with her did not stop his generously giving her husband an earldom when she married later that year. He began, for the first time, to voice doubts whether he would be strong enough to fight for another season.

In fact, the very summer after Mary's death he had his greatest military triumph in the capture of Namur; after that he carried through the negotiations in which an exhausted France agreed to a European peace; and then lived another hard-working five years, and at the end of it found the strength to set up another Grand Alliance against the next European crisis. For a man who had been too weak to handle a warhorse at seventeen, and had professed himself indifferent to how the world went after his death, it was a remarkable performance. We can only assume that he thought it necessary to his honor.

European peace, as Europe understood it, was attained at the Treaty of Ryswick in 1697. In all the intricacies of alliances, betrayals, threats, promises, ambitions, a sort of stability had been arrived at, and it satisfied William because it was a stability that kept France within her own bounds, and that had been the purpose of his life. It is not likely that he had ever expected thanks for what he had done, and he never got any in his lifetime, though posterity has been more generous. In England the great men loved him only when they contemplated how difficult life would be without him; but the commons of England loved him without qualification because he had given them peace. Mary's death had left him open to assassination, since his death would not now leave her in possession of the throne. Another plot in 1696 brought the country as a whole to his side; yet, as he seems to have known, few of the men in high places were entirely guiltless of correspondence with James II.

It must have been a lonely life, and in England he never found a man he wholly trusted; he had to rely on his few personal friends. The chief were Hans Willem Bentinck, who had been his page as a boy and stayed with him as his lifelong friend and ended as Earl of Portland; and Arnout Joost van Keppel, later Earl of Albemarle, who as a young man had taken his attention by a display of courage under pain. Both acted at different times as his secretary, a post of awesomely hard work. But for his wife and Betty Villiers they seem to have been his only confidants. Louis XIV's propagandists started a homosexual scandal about the handsome Albemarle that was particularly inept. Like many men of industry and poor health, William slept badly and worked far into the night, and required his poor secretary to be within call if he wanted him. Albemarle was notorious as a womanizer, and must have been considerably thwarted by his King.

After Mary's death, of course, the most important question in England was that of the succession. At her death William was forty-four, and in frail health, and that he should marry again in hope of an heir was out of the question, for a child-King would have been worse than none. The next heir, if the Catholic line of James II was disregarded, was his wife's sister the Princess Anne. Perhaps—because for all her faults Anne was a good and honest, if not very clever, woman—she was sobered by her sister's death; she was reconciled with her brother-in-law, and the succession was understood to go to her one surviving son, Henry Duke of Gloucester. But in 1700 this little boy died with great suddenness. As had happened before, the danger of a Catholic succession—or could it have been simply the succession of the ineffably foolish James II?—brought out the good sense of all English parties. By the Act of Settlement of 1701 the succession, after a nominal bow to William's and Anne's descendants, was limited to the Protestant heirs of the line of Stuart. This in effect meant a return to that line that had so troubled Europe, the family of James I's beautiful daughter Elizabeth of Bohemia, the Winter Queen. Elizabeth had had a daughter, Sophia, who had married the Protestant Elector of Hanover. Sophia was still very much alive, and had a son, Georg, who though far from being an attractive character (indeed Sophia herself was a formidable woman), was impeccably Protestant and one of the most reliable generals against France. This famous Act of Settlement made explicit once and for all the new English view of kingship. It was, the preamble stated, "an Act for the better securing of the rights and liberties of the subject." It spoke the last warning word from the people of England to the Kings of England, and since that word was spoken it has always been heeded.

It also marked the ending of the Arthurian dream in England. After so many centuries of hope that each new King would prove to be the awakened Arthur, the English people had sensibly given up. They had decided to do Arthur's work for themselves. It is odd that this should have come about in the reign of one of England's most Arthurian Kings.

The Treaty of Ryswick and the Act of Settlement did not, alas, conclude William III's labors. Some devil of ill luck placed in the hands of Europe's rulers the chance to upset once more the peace of the Continent. It was France who took that chance, but if she had not, the empire would have done so.

The trouble arose from the insane Hapsburg policy of inbreeding. Possessing in their two great branches (the Imperial and the Spanish) a large part of Europe, the Hapsburgs would not part with an acre of it and consequently, after decades of incestuous marriages, found themselves with a congenital idiot as the King of Spain. This was Carlos II, who had inherited the famous Hapsburg undershot jaw so many times that he could not eat, and was plainly incapable of giving his wife Marie Louise of France a child as his heir. The best candidate for his throne was Joseph Ferdinand of Bohemia, who was grandson to Charles's sister Margaret, who had married her first cousin the Emperor Leopold; Margaret was the younger sister, but had been recognized by her father as Charles's heir, since the elder half-sister, Maria Teresa, had renounced her claim when she married Louis XIV of France. Unfortunately, Joseph Ferdinand died in 1699, leaving two other candidates whose claims were of a surely unexampled complexity. Maria Teresa's claim had passed to her grandson, Philip of Anjou, and was strengthened by the fact that another Infanta of Spain, Anne, had been Louis XIV's mother, and Louis characteristically asserted that both she and his wife had renounced their claims to Spain only under conditions that had never been fulfilled. Her sister Margaret's claim had passed, on Joseph Ferdinand's death, to her husband, the Emperor Leopold, and he passed it to a son by a later marriage, the Archduke Charles. The opposing parties were thus, in effect, France and the Empire.

Spain owned the rich Spanish Netherlands (roughly present-day Belgium), a vast amount of Italy, and great possessions in the New World, and if this were to pass to one single power the balance of Europe would be upset. William of England had to start his diplomatic labors again. He tried to arrive at a compromise with Louis XIV; Louis had become much more polite to him since Ryswick, and when in 1701 James II died, the Jacobite danger lessened in England. But the loot from Spain was too great for even an aging Louis XIV to exercise moderation. William stitched together another Grand Alliance, and again it had to be against France, and again Europe moved into years of warfare.

William was just over fifty, and frailer than ever, but as always his frailty responded to emergency. He prepared for the summer campaign on the Continent, sending Albemarle ahead of him to The Hague to hurry things on for his own coming. Then in February, 1702, he went for a gallop in Richmond Park and fell and broke his collarbone. It was said that his mount put its foot into a molehill, so that for years to come Jacobites would toast the Little Gentleman in Black Velvet. He took little notice of the injury, and when he could wear a coat again appeared "very merrily" in public. But that night, in his favorite Kensington Palace, he woke feverish. Even then he rallied for two days, but the fever returned. Albemarle, back from Holland, tried to cheer him, but William knew the truth; *"Je tire vers ma fin,"* he said. He was in such pain that he asked one of his doctors if it could go on, and the man said, not for long. He was quite calm; he received Communion, and gave his keys to Albemarle. At the last moment, Portland, his friend of forty years' standing, got in to see him; William was so near death that he could only take Portland's hand and hold it over his heart. He died on March 8, 1702, the French Prince, the Dutch *Stadhouder,* who was one of the greatest Kings of England. Bishop Burnet called him from the Psalms "The man of God's right hand, whom He made strong for Himself." A less famous Englishman noted two years later, on the anniversary of Queen Anne's accession:

Yesterday was generally observed here as a day of mourning, not of thanksgiving. Several sermons were preach'd in most churches, and in our market the butchers shopps were generally shut up, they postponing their gain tho it was market day.

House of

STUART

ANNE
1702–1714

✿

Born at St. James's, February 1665.

Younger daughter (to survive) of James II and his first
   wife Anne Hyde.

Married in 1683 George Prince of Denmark. Of her numerous pregnancies the only child to survive infancy
   was William Duke of Gloucester, born 1689 and died
   1700.

Recognized by the Act of Settlement, 1701, as the heir of
   William III, her sister's widower.

Died at Kensington Palace, August 1714, and was buried
   at Westminster.

In 1707 England and Scotland, which had until then been
   separate Kingdoms, were united by the Act of Union as
   Great Britain. Ireland was regarded as a separate Kingdom, and the claim to the throne of France (which had
   been put forward by Edward III by virtue of his mother
   Isabelle daughter of Philip IV of France) was still maintained. Anne's title after 1707 was therefore Queen of
   Great Britain, France, and Ireland.

Queen Anne was regarded as of the House of Stuart because she succeeded to the throne in her own right.

ANNE

Anne was a lucky Queen. Probably she would have denied this, for she was not a happy woman. Troubled in her childhood by the early loss of her mother (who was in any case regarded as a disastrous misalliance for her royal father) and the religious divisions in the family, her own position insecure, eternally jealous of her more favored sister Mary, she was married in 1683 to the Protestant nonentity George Prince of Denmark and saddened by a long series of miscarriages and stillbirths that culminated in 1700 in the death of Henry Duke of Gloucester, her only child to survive infancy. She had not, or perhaps she had never exercised (for it seems that it was only Mary's deep love for her husband that made her do so), her sister's intelligence and strength of personality; she most certainly had not her beauty and charm (which may have accounted more than anything for William III's recurring worries about her loyalty). Her health, as might have been expected of any woman who had had an almost yearly miscarriage or stillbirth, was poor, though she never let it interfere with her conduct of business. But she took refuge in favorites, with whom she could drink tea and gossip and complain of her headache and play absurd pretense-games that she was just an ordinary married woman. (She liked to call herself, symbolically she thought, Mrs. Freeman.) The poet Pope wrote:

> Here thou, great Anna! whom three realms obey,
> Dost sometimes counsel take—and sometimes tea.

For a great part of her life her chief favorite was the beautiful and bossy Sarah Jennings; and Sarah, who was ambitious and not over-scrupulous or over-, or even at all, principled, had married the equally ambitious and unprincipled John Churchill, later Duke of Marlborough, who, with neither birth nor wealth to help him, found his wife's domination over the Queen his most valuable asset (indeed, his devotion to his impossible Sarah is the most, perhaps the only, endearing thing about him). A weak monarch dominated by a personally ambitious favorite: it was the classic position for disaster. Queen Anne's good luck lay in the fact that her favorite was married to the most brilliant soldier of his time in an age when what England and Europe needed was such a soldier. England's good luck lay in the fact that after William of Orange she should have also John Churchill. Perhaps it was tipping of the balance after so many Stuarts. But as William was to Churchill, so was William's war to Churchill's. William's war was a desperate and comparatively honest affair of self-defense; Churchill's degenerated into mean calculations as often as not directed against allies rather than enemies.

The war began officially in the spring of 1702, though there had been fighting in Italy before that, and it was not until the end of 1703 that the full Grand Alliance was deployed against Louis XIV and his grandson, now crowned Philip V of Spain. This Alliance included the English; the Dutch, who as usual were fighting for their very existence against France on their frontiers; Austria, whose Emperor was the grandfather of the opposing claimant to Spain and who was hoping for pickings in Italy; Savoy, whose Duke also (and more justifiably) wanted territory in Italy; and Portugal, who had an interest in who was to rule in the Spanish Peninsula. The two latter were especially useful to the Alliance, since they provided much-needed bases in the Mediterranean. Marlborough and the Dutch started well in the Netherlands, but the Emperor was much hampered by a rising of the Hungarians, which was backed by France. In the winter of 1703–04 it became plain that the Grand Alliance would not endure unless the difficult situation in the south of Germany were relieved, and the English and the Dutch collaborated in a daring plan that sent Marlborough and his combined army in a great march from the North Sea to the Danube. At the end of it, on August 13, 1704, he fought and won the battle of Blenheim. It was a pitched battle in the grand style, with nearly equal forces (Marlborough had 52,000 to the French Tallard's 54,000); five hours were first spent in deployment, and, once joined, battle lasted the rest of the day. It was Louis XIV's first resounding defeat, and was the battle that saved central Europe from French domination; but by now much more than central Europe was engaged in the struggle.

Peripherally, the war involved the Americas; and here the Allies had the advantage in that among them were the two great seafaring nations, the Dutch and the English; but the significant victories were gained in and around the shore of Europe. In the spring of the year that saw Blenheim, 1704, the Hapsburg claimant, Charles III (as he is known, though he was not crowned and cannot be said to have reigned in Spain), landed in Spain. In this year, England happened to capture Gibraltar, though for fifty years or so the significance of this valuable naval base seems to have escaped her. The next year, Marlborough had a plan, which he was to maintain for the rest of the war, to ensure the utter defeat of France by a march on Paris; he had to give it up now because the promised Imperial forces never arrived to his aid. Savoy was in danger, and Marlborough's comrade-in-arms, and probably his equal as a general, Prince Eugène, could not break through to relieve her. The Dutch also began to be uneasy at seeing England winning the advantage of her for future trade. The last decades of struggle were to exhaust the magnificent Dutch people; they had had to fight longer and more desperately, and not for their advantage but for their existence, than any other country. They never stopped fighting, but their contribution in men and money was beginning to fall; and England, it is sad to record, was not to be generous about it. But in May of the next year, 1706, Marlborough fought the second of his great victories at Ramillies, and in Italy in September Prince Eugéne had a success at Turin, and won Italy for the Allies. In May, 1706, all of Aragon rose against Philip V, and he had to escape to France, and it seemed that the war in this third theatre was won by the Allies too.

But their success was fleeting; Charles III was not a resolute man, his armies were ill-equipped and ill-disciplined, and in Spain the friendship of Aragon meant the enmity of Castile. Moreover, whatever his background or loyalties, Philip V was an anointed King, and that weighed with the Spanish much as it did with the English. By August, Philip V was back and Berwick had occupied Madrid.

Still, the chief danger seemed to be past, and the Allies began to quarrel over the spoils. The emperor offended everyone by his high-handedness in Italy, and then again by offering to Marlborough the great office of Governor of the Netherlands. Marlborough, who had everything that England could give him—a dukedom, the Garter, immense wealth—coveted this almost royal power, but the Dutch made it quite clear to him that they would accept no Imperial nominee.

In 1708 Marlborough dealt Louis XIV the most crushing blow yet, at Oudenarde; and by the end of that year France had not only lost all of the Netherlands but had suffered the breaking of the first barrier on that road which Marlborough had for years been straining for—the road to Paris. This year of 1708, when France was further weakened by a disastrous famine, and Austria at last got the better of the Hungarian rebels, it seemed that the next year might see the Allies in Paris.

So thought the French, for they opened peace negotiations; or possibly only appeared to do so, for their first action was to encourage the perfectly just suspicions of the Dutch about the English. The Allies, in any case, had demands which they knew France would not grant while she could still fight. The emperor was greedy for territory, the Dutch wanted a strongly fortified frontier. The English, entirely unreasonably, wanted victory in Spain. It grew to be a byword with the people and a policy with some politicians: *No Peace without Spain.* All of them knew they would never get their demands without the total conquest of France. So the war went on; and, if we like to apply the principle of poetic justice while neglecting the tens of thousands of common people of all nations who died during its application, the Allies got very much what they deserved. The French still had more fight left in them than the Allies had reckoned on, and by the end of 1710 it was plain that there was at least another year's fighting to be done. The inevitable in such an alliance happened. The Portuguese started peace negotiations on their own account; Savoy began to drag her feet; Prussia quarreled with the Dutch, and also started negotiations. They came to nothing; the Allies wanted too much, and with every month the French agreed to concede even less; but meanwhile in England things had been quietly changing to an extent that now revolutionized the whole of the peace negotiations.

William III had been totally indifferent to the party system that was beginning to evolve in English politics; he would make use of any man so long as he was efficient. Inevitably, however, his religion, his toleration, his steadfast opposition to France and thus to the French-supported Jacobite cause, had made him appear a Whig. Anne had disapproved of his religion, which, though Protestant, was not her

High Church Anglicanism, and illogically she also disapproved of his (as she saw it) usurpation, though she also believed that as a Catholic her father should not have been permitted to reign and was markedly jealous to preserve her own right to the throne. Her religion and her temperament thus inclined her to the Tories, who were glad to support her. When she came to the throne, she did not persecute the nonconformists, but saw no reason not to thwart them by every legal means, and she never had any doubts about using her own influence vigorously in support of the Tories. But she was a dutiful, sensible, practical woman, and perhaps had learned something from observing her father's methods; she might hate a man for his opinions, but if he was useful to the state then she would employ him.

Her chief man, naturally, was Marlborough. Marlborough had political acumen but no political principles; he had been a Whig in 1688, but as a supporter of Anne had to be moderate Tory. But as his chief principle was to continue with the war against France, he found himself working with the moderate Whigs. No changes of government occurred, for the party system was not entirely established (there was, for example, no such thing as prime minister, though the dominant man in a government is often so named); but the ministry grew more pronouncedly Whig until by 1708 it was almost entirely so.

But by that time it was felt in the country, and with justice, that the war was dragging on too long, and Marlborough and the Whig ministers were under criticism. The Queen, too, was coming to dislike the men she had been forced to work with; and, more importantly to her, she was beginning to quarrel with the Duchess of Marlborough. Sarah had admirable energy, shrewdness, and devotion to the cause of the Churchills but she was an intolerable woman, and grew careless in her domination over the Queen. Anne was neither clever nor strong-minded, but she was sensible, and little by little she had come to put her confidence in another friend. This was Abigail Hill, later Mrs. Masham, a very unimportant cousin of Sarah's, who was either modest, sympathetic, and devoted to the Queen or clever enough to appear so; she was also related to one of the shrewdest of the Tory politicians, Robert Harley. Harley was a persuader, a reconciler, a backstairs maneuverer, and he could maneuver public opinion as well as private individuals. The Whig party played into his hands by their foolishness in adopting the policy of *No Peace without Spain;* and by 1709 he found himself at the head of a ministry that had quietly become almost entirely Tory. He clinched his achievement by dissolving Parliament, and in the subsequent general election the Tories were everywhere successful; and the Tories wanted peace.

They got it; but the process was hardly honorable, for the French plan to end the war before their own total defeat had always been dependent upon splitting the Grand Alliance, or in other words upon inveigling one of the Allies to betray the rest, and in Harley's minstry they found what they needed. Oddly enough, the peace that followed this discreditable war—though it was not concluded in its entirety until 1714—was on the whole a just and satisfactory one, the only disgraceful act in it being the desertion by the British and Charles III of their faithful allies the Catalans, a small people who did not recognize the rule of Madrid and are still attempting to deny it. However, there were still three years before the general peace, and once the Tory ministry and the French had concluded their secret negotiations England was as often as not to be found on the side of France. In situations like this morality can only hold her reeling head and concentrate on cutting down the day-to-day casualties.

The question of the Spanish succession was materially helped in 1711 by the election of the Austrian claimant, the so-called Charles III, to the Empire. No one wanted Spain and Austria united under one ruler, so France gave a solemn undertaking—which was of no more value than other such undertakings—that France and Spain would never be united, and the Spanish succession was settled on Philip V.

Marlborough, naturally, was against the peace; he was a soldier, and he wanted to make his great march on Paris. (In this, one of his chief supporters among the Allied generals was George Elector of Hanover, who, little as the English ever comprehended it, was not profoundly excited by the fact that the Act of Settlement of 1701 had vested the succession to the English throne in his House.) Marlborough's resistance to what was plainly the will of Queen, Parliament, and a majority of the people brought about his downfall. After unhappy years of bickering, the Queen had had enough of Sarah, and the government raked up some charges of corruption against Marlborough that gave them a pretext for dismissing him from all his offices. He lived on until 1722, immensely rich, honored as the great soldier he had been, but regarded as a traitor by many: a fair comment, perhaps, on the results of having no principles whatever but naked personal ambition.

England could now attend to her home affairs: religion, the struggle between Whig and Tory, and the question of the succession. After Harley, the outstanding politician of the reign was Henry St. John, after 1712 Viscount Bolingbroke. Bolingbroke had brilliance, but even among politicians he was an evil influence, combining a total lack of scruple with a curious incapability of keeping even advantageous friends. In Harley's ministry (Harley was raised to the peerage as the Earl of Oxford) he was secretary of state, and the two men were personally antipathetic. As soon as the war was over, the Tory party started the curious process of ensuring that not for years to come would it ever be in power again.

What they did was to identify themselves with the Jacobite cause, and by now the Jacobite cause was a lost one in England. Even its strongest supporters realized that England would not be a Catholic country, and had to pin their hopes on the chance of the Old Pretender's changing his faith. The Old Pretender, the Warming-Pan Heir, gave the lie to that old story of his birth by being amazingly like his father; not for a throne would he desert his religion, and when approached directly (and treasonably) he would do no more than promise "reasonable security" for the Protestant faith in England if he were to be King. Apart from religion, the strongest feeling in Queen Anne's England was for the nation's trade, and for a multitude of reasons Francophile Jacobitism spoke to the people of everything that they thought was against the trend of English economic prosperity.

All in all, the Jacobite cause was not a healthy one; but the Whigs opposed it, and the Queen, with her guilt toward her father allied to a passionate shrinking from discussing her own death, would not commit herself to the Hanoverian succession. By 1714 the Tories were inescapably but almost accidentally committed to the Stuart succession.

It was here that the quarrel between Harley and Bolingbroke came to a head, giving the Queen an almost impossible choice between them. She was by this time very ill, but, as always, summoned the strength to do her duty. On August 7, 1714, she decided to dismiss Harley. He took his dismissal, though, with a bad grace, and in spite of her illness, Anne sat on in council for hours, attempting to reconstruct her ministry through the wrangling and squabbles that followed. Harley might have lost, but Bolingbroke had not won, for he was unpopular and strongly suspected of corrupt politics; Anne left him as secretary of state, and for the time being refused to name a new lord treasurer. Nothing else was decided, though it was two o'clock before the Queen could go to bed, and then she had to be carried.

All the next day she lay silent in bed, in what has been called a mortal lethargy. The next day, Thursday, August 9, she murmured some words, but on the Friday it was plain that she was dying. The council met without her, with the Duke of Shrewbury presiding, a supporter of Hanover who had only one talent, that of decision in emergency. Bolingbroke was undecided at this crisis; perhaps, now that it came to reality, he realized the truth about the Stuart chances of succession. Anne, still sensible and dutiful in the very arms of death, received the council at her bedside and handed the white staff of the lord treasurer to the supporter of Hanover, Shrewsbury; she had consented to the Hanoverian succession. On the morning of Sunday, August 12, 1714, the council came to their meeting and heard that the Queen had died some hours earlier. Dr. Arbuthnot wrote of this laborious death:

I believe that sleep was never more welcome to a weary traveller than death was to her.

House of

HANOVER

GEORGE I
1714–1727

✿

Born at Osnabrück in 1660.

Son of Ernst August Elector of Hanover, and Sophia,
daughter of Elizabeth Electress Palatine and briefly
Queen of Bohemia, daughter of James I of England.
Sophia's line was recognized as the line of legal succession to the throne of England by the Act of Settlement
of 1701, but she herself died in 1714, shortly before Queen
Anne.

Married in 1682 Sophia Dorothea of Celle, whom he divorced and imprisoned in 1694. By her, who died in
prison in 1726, he had a son,

George, born in 1683, later George II.

Died at Osnabrück, June 1717.

As well as the sovereignty of England, George I also held
the sovereignties of his various German territories.

GEORGE I

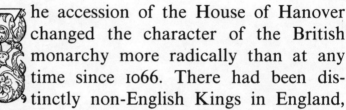he accession of the House of Hanover changed the character of the British monarchy more radically than at any time since 1066. There had been distinctly non-English Kings in England, the latest of them not so long ago, but never a line so militantly, so brutally alien as the Hanoverians. George I did not speak English, and made no effort to learn; he did not like living in England, and went back to Hanover whenever he could; he neither valued his English inheritance nor took more than the necessary interest in it, and he never hid either fact. The experience of the English had been all the other way; they had suffered from too many men who had been all too eager to be King of England.

To arrive with so much labor at a man who would very much rather have stayed away would have damped any loyalty. What entirely extinguished it, creating a gulf between monarch and people that has never since closed (it has been tenuously bridged, but that is a different matter), was the hardly credible dislikeability of the Hanoverians. In the end they became figures of fun, for there was nothing to do about such creatures but to laugh at them. They were gross, vulgar, humorless, mean, ill-tempered, and endlessly capable of combining self-importance with inelegance. The Stuarts, evasive, dishonest, and dangerous, had still known how to appeal to their people even if they meant to take away their liberties. Above all, they had style, a quality the Hanoverians hopelessly lacked.

It is said that there were fifty men living who had a better claim to the throne of England than George I. His mother, the Electress Sophia of Hanover, had a court philosopher, no less a man than the distinguished Gottfried Wilhelm Leibnitz, and she employed him, when it became clear that the inheritance of England was to fall to her line, in providing her with a distinguished family tree. Leibnitz made a remarkable job of it; he traced her pedigree back to Guelph Prince of the Scyri, a friend of Attila the Hun (only a Hanoverian could have found material for pride in that connection). She nourished the idea of herself becoming Queen of England, and even wanted the title inscribed on her tombstone. The novelist Thackeray visited her palace, and described it as a parody of the splendors of Louis XIV.

Put clumsy High Dutch statues in place of the marbles of Versailles; fancy Herrenhausen water-works in place of those of Marly; spread the table with *Shweinskopf, Specksuppe, Leberküchen,* and the like delicacies, in place of the French *cuisine;* and fancy Frau von Kielmansegge dancing with Count Kammerjunker Quirini, or singing French songs with the most awful German accent: imagine a coarse Versailles, and we have a Hanover before us.

It was a court in which horses seemed more numerous than courtiers; George kept fifty-two teams of coach-horses in his private stables alone. George himself was fifty-four at the time of his accession. He was short and stout and fair, and his face had those characteristics which were to endure throughout the whole Hanoverian succession, and emerge almost unchanged to the present day, particularly the receding forehead and the angry bulbous blue eyes. By choice he was a soldier and a huntsman. As he had shown in the French wars, he had courage, but he was essentially stupid and obstinate. His only saving grace (he is reputed to have said that he hated all poets and painters) was a love of music. His reputation had been damaged by the sinister and still obscure history of his marriage to Sophia Dorothea of Celle. George's own infidelities were numerous and indiscriminating (another of the Hanoverians' inelegancies was their choice of mistresses); Sophia, it was rumored, found him unbearable, and planned to elope with the handsome Count von Königsmarck. What happened then we do not know. Königsmarck simply disappeared; we can only guess that he was murdered. Sophia Dorothea was divorced and in 1694 imprisoned in the castle of Ahlden. She was kept there for the thirty-two years until her death, and never again saw her children or her husband.

Sophia Dorothea's place in the Elector George's bed had been taken—among many others—by two quite remarkably ugly mistresses. Charles II had once said that his brother James's mistresses were so hideous that they must have been imposed on him as a penance by his confessor; but George's mistresses were so curiously repellent as to be a continuous source of public amazement. The first was Ehrengard Melusina von Schulenberg, later the Duchess of Kendal. She was nearly sixty, very tall and thin and nicknamed the Maypole; her abiding passion was money. The other was Charlotte Sophia Kielmansegge, later Countess of Darlington, who was large and fat and known as the Elephant.

Sophia of Hanover had been preparing herself for her accession to the throne of England since the death in 1700 of Queen Anne's son Henry Duke of Gloucester. She had hoped for the succession after the flight of James II, but had taken William's accession with a good enough grace to write and congratulate him. As Anne lived on and on, Sophia realized that she would never be Queen. In a letter that deserves quotation less for its content than for its staying-power, she wrote:

If I were thirty years younger, I should have a sufficiently good opinion of my birth and my religion to believe that I should be appreciated in England. But as there is little probability of my surviving two people much younger, although more subject to ordinary dangers, than myself, it is to be feared that at my death my sons will be regarded as strangers, the eldest of whom is much more accustomed to claim a high prerogative as sovereign than the poor Prince of Wales, who is too young to profit by the King of France, and who would apparently be so glad to recover that which the King his father has so inconsiderately lost that they would be able to do with him just what they wished.

By the *Prince of Wales* she meant, oddly for one who considered herself the heir of England, the Old Pretender. It was her ill luck to die, at the age of eighty-four, at about the time that Queen Anne, nearly forty years her junior, had taken to her bed for the last time; and her son does not seem to have been greatly concerned to find himself heir-presumptive to a throne that would very soon become vacant.

At the death of the Queen the Tories seem to have been shocked into total inactivity. The Duke of Ormonde, who was Marlborough's successor as Captain-General of the Kingdom, was told by one of them, "My Lord, you have twenty-four hours' time to do our business and make yourself master of the kingdom." Ormonde, wisely, instead did nothing; the House of Hanover was proclaimed in En-

gland and messengers sent at top speed to the Elector in Herrenhausen. Another Jacobite said, "Such grand designs need a hero, and
that was what the Duke of Ormonde was not." But king makers had
never been successful in England, and it is possible that in doing
nothing Ormonde, the most outspoken and forceful of the Jacobites,
was being heroic on the grand scale.

King George I at any rate had no great anxieties about his new
kingdom; he did not set sail for England until September 5. When
he did leave, his retinue was grotesque. It included his son, thirty-
year-old George, whom (setting an unhappy pattern for all the Hanoverian Kings of England) he detested and who returned his hatred
with equal vigor; his two personal servants, Mohammed and Musta-
pha, whom he had captured in a campaign against the Turks; and,
inevitably, his two impossible mistresses. According to Thackeray:

Both of these ladies loved Hanover and at first would not quit the place.
Schulenberg, in fact, could not come on account of her debts; but finding
that the Maypole would not come the Elephant packed up her trunk and
slipped out of Hanover, unwieldy as she was. On this the Maypole straight-
way put herself in motion and followed her beloved George.

The extraordinary cavalcade disembarked at Greenwich on September 18. They were greeted by dense fog and a particularly fearful
piece of verse from the man who was to become the Poet Laureate
(the official court poet), Eusden:

> Hail, mighty GEORGE! Auspicious smiles thy Reign,
> Thee long we wish'd, Thee at last we gain.
> Thy hoary Prudence in green Years began,
> And the bold Infant stretch'd at once to Man.

The King had already found a poet worthy of him.

Of his dealings with his ministers, Bolingbroke was refused an
interview, the Earl of Mar publicly snubbed, and Harley treated with
marked coldness; Ormonde he refused to see at all. George reluctantly made a state entry into London, an event that seems to have
excited a certain amount of public derision, and held his coronation
on October 20. Of the moment in the ritual when the Archbishop
of Canterbury asked for the consent of the people, Lady Dorchester
is said to have murmured: "Does the old fool think that anybody
here will say no to his question when there are so many drawn
swords?"

Once the Whigs found themselves in power they were not disposed to be tolerant toward their opponents. Marlborough in particular (who had come back from the Continent, where he had withdrawn on his disgrace, on the day of the old Queen's death), finding himself once more in favor, joined the Whigs in a witch-hunt for Jacobite conspirators. Ormonde, Harley, and Bolingbroke were in particular under suspicion. It is possible that nothing would have happened if they had kept quiet, but this they could not do. One night in April, 1715, Bolingbroke went to the theatre at Drury Lane, quietly left his seat halfway through, and fled to the pretender's court at St. Germain in France. Harley hesitated, was arrested and sent to the Tower. Ormonde panicked, rode off at speed to the South Coast, and by July had joined Bolingbroke in Saint Germain. The remaining Jacobites planned a major rising in the west, to be supported by secondary risings in the north and in Scotland, and the country became restless. On the King's birthday the Foot Guards burned their shabby uniforms and threw dirty linen over the walls of St. James's Palace; on the Pretender's birthday there were some celebrations, while the anniversary of George's accession was marked by riots in Oxford.

It is possible now to see that George had not set out to be disagreeable to his new people; George was simply disagreeable naturally. But he was a Continental ruler, and until the rioters were at the palace doors Continental rulers did not consider their subjects' views worth consideration.

In October, 1715, the Commons were enough disturbed to order the arrest of the Jacobite lords. Their leader, the Earl of Mar, escaped to Scotland, and proclaimed the rising on the occasion of the Braemar Hunt, when most of the Scots Jacobite lords were present. He told them that

though he had been instrumental in forwarding the union of the two kingdoms in the reign of Queen Anne, yet now his eyes were opened and he could see his error, and would therefore do what lay in his power to hear their grievances and would redress their wrongs.

The standard of James III was unfurled and the rebellion, somewhat sluggishly, got under way. It was certainly too sluggishly for Mar, who wrote to one recalcitrant:

Is not this the thing we are now about, which they have been wishing these twenty-six years? And now, when it is come, and the King and country's cause is at stake, will they forever sit still and see all perish?

Louis XIV of France had died this year but his great-grandson, Louis XV, sent twelve French ships in support of the rising. The English forces were pitifully small, and their commander, Argyll, wrote:

I must end with insisting on considerable reinforcements, for without that or a miracle not only this country will be utterly destroyed but the rest of His Majesty's dominions put in the extremest danger.

Yet, when most of Scotland had declared for the Pretender and the capture of Edinburgh would have been easy for a decided man, Mar did nothing; a contemporary wrote that he was bearing himself "as if he had been another Moses, meek and spotless and without blemish." He was apparently reluctant to risk a pitched battle, and while he prevaricated, the Jacobite lords squabbled among themselves and Argyll steadily grew stronger.

In the north of England, where the old feudal and Catholic traditions had lingered longest, the Earl of Derwentwater and Thomas Forster the Member of Parliament for Northumberland raised a small revolt early in October. It was really a gesture from the past, or rather to the past, hopeless and dispirited from the first, and ended in a surrender in the streets of Preston. On the same day, Mar, despairing of the promised arrival of the Old Pretender from St. Germain, met Argyll at Sherriffmuir. He had eight thousand to the English three and a half thousand, and should have scattered them; instead he failed to give the attack, and that failure sealed the doom of the revolt. Mar's forces began to disintegrate, and it was at this point that the Old Pretender chose to land in Scotland. He had no army remaining, but appearances were kept up; he entered Dundee and Perth in state and was housed in the ancient Palace of Scone, and his coronation fixed for January 23, so long as a crown could be made in time.

He aroused little enthusiasm in his people, showing neither vigor nor cheerfulness. "If he was disappointed in us," an unknown author wrote tersely, "we were tenfold more so in him." Their judgment was sound. When Argyll, still desperately short of men, advanced from Stirling, the coronation plans were abandoned and the Pretender slipped quietly back to France. He had been in Scotland for forty-five days. He wrote to his supporters:

Convinced as I am that you would never abandon me, and that therefore my stay could only involve you in greater difficulties, I took the party to repass the seas that by that I might leave such as cannot make their mistake (towards which nothing on my side has been neglected) in full liberty to take the properest measures for avoiding at least utter ruin.

As a piece of casuistry this was worthy of Charles I, but at least Charles I never lacked courage.

The rebellion was over. Mar sailed off to join the court at St. Germain; a few Jacobite lords surrendered, the rest took refuge in the Highlands and the Orkneys. It had after all been a small affair, chiefly thanks to Argyll, who had not only commanded ably but by his influence as head as the great Clan Campbell had kept most of the Lowlands and a great part of the Highlands quiescent. In any case, the Presbyterian Lowlanders would not have risen for a Catholic King, and the towns that were beginning to share in the English prosperity were Hanoverian in feeling. On the whole the rebellion was not put down with any great severity. In England Derwentwater and his associates were executed for high treason, but one of them, Lord Nithsdale, made a famous escape from the Tower by means of the courage and ingenuity of his wife, who visited him at the last and sent him out to freedom disguised in her clothes.

George I has been called a great promoter of our constitutional liberties, because he knew and cared too little about them to deny them. He did, however, severely weaken his own position by his never-ending dispute with his eldest son, the Prince of Wales. The bitterest hatreds of Henry II and his Devil's Brood are humanly comprehensible beside the loathing between the head of the House of Hanover and his eldest son. It was like a hereditary disease, for it extended through the generations regardless of personalities or politics.

There were also serious quarrels between the rival Whig ministers (the Tories were tainted by Jacobitism and would not recover for years). Argyll should have been the great man of the time, but was suspect to some and as time went by moved more to the support of the Prince of Wales. The other two ministers, Sunderland and Townshend, had their rivalry cut short at source by an absurd circumstance: Sunderland was the only one with French fluent enough to communicate easily with the King. It was unfortunate, for Townshend was practical and capable and had the assistance of his extremely able brother-in-law Robert Walpole (who in the previous reign had spent a brief and unjustified time in the Tower after the fall of Marlborough).

By now the King was tired of England and wanted to go back to his beloved Hanover (he had had his baggage packed, possibly hopefully, throughout the 1715 rising). The trouble was that he adamantly refused to allow his detested son to act as regent during his absence. Finally he dismissed Argyll (as an associate of the prince), gave the prince the wholly meaningless and powerless title of "Guardian of the Realm and Lieutenant," which had last been used in the days of the Black Prince, and departed, confident that there would be no filial intrigues while he was away. Whatever stability he left behind him was destroyed when the ambitious Sunderland decided that it would be in his best interests to join him. The ruling of the country was left to Townshend and Walpole in London, while at Hampton Court, Argyll tried to influence the Prince of Wales against them and at Herrenhausen, Sunderland did the same to the King. Meanwhile the King, acting as Elector of Hanover, was carrying on negotiations with France and the Baltic states that did not altogether regard British trade interests, and this difficult situation was exacerbated by the fact that communication between London and Hanover often took several weeks. In desperation, Townshend wrote to the King beseeching him either to empower the Prince of Wales to summon Parliament (which sent the King into frenzies of rage) or to return to England (which plunged him into extravagant gloom). He chose to return; and once there promptly dismissed both Townshend and Walpole.

Townshend and Walpole were both, for politicians, honorable men; but they had been put into an impossible position by an impossible sovereign, and in return made all they could of the quarrel between the King and the Prince of Wales. A fresh crisis had lately arisen about the christening of the son recently born to the prince by his wife, the lively, attractive, and highly intelligent Caroline of Brandenburg-Anspach. The King insisted on naming the child's godparents, and included among them the Duke of Newcastle, whom the prince detested. At the ceremony the prince, who was never renowned for his self-control, seized Newcastle by the elbow and said, "Rascal, I find you out." So thickly German was his accent that Newcastle thought he had been challenged to a duel. This was a serious matter; he went straight to the King and asked for his help, and George at once arrested his son. His ministers had some difficulty in convincing him that under British law this meant that the prince would have to be put on trial for something; then he expelled him and his wife from court, inexcusably keeping control of their children. The foreseeable consequence of this was that the prince and his wife set up an opposition and much more attractive court, which became a focal point for all the major dissidents, including of course Townshend and Walpole. A less foreseeable and, considering the future, a very odd, consequence was the founding of the cabinet system of government in England. The Prince of Wales, who spoke bad English, had been used to act as interpreter at meetings of the King and his council. Now that he was excluded, no other person could be agreed upon to take his place, so the King quite simply stayed away. The King's council thus became an independent cabinet, which eventually needed a leader, who was to be the prime minister in our modern sense.

Townshend and Walpole only came back to power as a result of the great financial scandal known as the South Sea Bubble (a name that even now is sometimes applied warningly to optimistic schemes for making money). Of recent years ministries had contrived various schemes for raising money by loan rather by heavy taxation, and of these the largest, wildest, and most popular was a scheme meant to exploit the potential wealth of the southern hemisphere. It bore no relation at all to reality; but this did not prevent the King, his avaricious mistresses, politicians of all colors, anyone with the fancy to make money without effort, acquiring unlimited numbers of shares. Walpole alone kept his head and continued to protest that the scheme was too extravagant. Even the Bank of England felt its position undermined as fantasy bred fantasy and the nation fell victim to raging speculation-fever. Gibraltar was going to be exchanged for the gold of the Incas, the sunken treasure-ships of the Spanish Armada raised, silver extracted from lead, sea-water purified, perpetual-motion machines constructed. Assured of the prosperity of his nation, George I departed again for Hanover.

Inevitably such a bubble had to burst. Thousands found their shares worthless and themselves destitute. A contemporary wrote: "You can't suppose the number of families undone. One may say almost everybody is ruined who has traded beyond their stock." The King came grumbling back from Hanover; there was a clamor for vengeance, and Sunderland had to retire, and died two years later. Walpole alone worked steadily to restore national confidence, and in doing so protected the King, his mistresses, and the Prince of Wales from public wrath. This sensible policy proved of great value to him, for, with the King considerably in his debt and Caroline of Anspach his close friend, no rival could now stand in his way. He held first the offices of chancellor and lord of the treasury, and ultimately became prime minister, and under his capable authority England began to enjoy its strongest government since the time of the Tudors.

In June, 1727, George I set out once more for Hanover. There had been a prophecy that he would not long survive the death of his wife, the sad imprisoned Sophia Dorothea, and she had died at Ahlden in November, 1726. George died in his traveling carriage on the road to Hanover on June 11, 1727, and Lockhart of Carnwath dramatically but improbably links the two deaths:

It seems when the late Electress (Sophia Dorothea) was dangerously ill of her last sickness, she delivered to a faithful friend a letter to her husband, upon promise that it should be given into his own hand. It contained a protestation of her innocence, a reproach for her hard usage and unjust treatment, and concluded with a summons or citation to her husband to appear within the year and day at the Divine Tribunal, and there to answer for the long and many injuries she had received from him. As this letter could not with safety to the bearer be delivered in England or Hanover, it was given to him in his coach on the road. He opened it immediately, supposing it to come from Hanover. He was so struck at its unexpected contents, and his fatal citation, that his convulsions and apoplexy came fast upon him.

George I founded the system on which the government of England still rests, but more by carelessness and misjudgement than of purpose. In the same way, he gave Robert Walpole the opportunity of power, and Walpole happened to be the very man England needed at that very time. William Thackeray has perhaps said the last word in judgment of the first Hanoverian King of England:

He was not a lofty monarch, certainly: he was not a patron of the fine arts: but he was not a hypocrite, he was not revengeful, he was not extravagant. Though a despot in Hanover, he was a moderate ruler in England. His aim was to leave it to itself as much as possible, and to live out of it as much as he could. His heart was in Hanover. He was more than fifty years of age when he came amongst us: we took him because we wanted him, because he served our turn; we laughed at his uncouth German ways and sneered at him. He took our loyalty for what it was worth; laid hands on what money he could; kept us assuredly from Popery. I, for one, would have been on his side in those days. Cynical and selfish as he was, he was better than a king out of St Germain with the French King's orders in his pocket and a swarm of Jesuits in his train.

GEORGE II
1727–1760

❊

Born in Hanover in 1683.
Son of George Elector of Hanover and later King George
  I of England, and his wife Sophia Dorothea of Celle.
Married in 1705 Caroline of Brandenburg-Anspach, who
  died in 1737. Their eldest son was:

> Frederick Prince of Wales, born in Hanover in 1707
> and died in 1751. In 1736 he married Augusta of Saxe-
> Coburg, by whom he had:
> > George, born in 1738, later George III.

Died in October 1760.

GEORGE II

he early years of the reign of George II epitomize Hanoverian England: peaceful, prosperous, serene, slothful yet confident, with a strong emphasis on commercial values and material satisfaction. The common people shared little of the greater prosperity, yet even for them, in these years before the major colonial wars and the industrial revolution, there is a feeling of rural harmony, of a country free to look forward with some certainty to a happy future.

Much of this well-being is due to the odd triumvirate who governed the country: the King, the Queen, and Robert Walpole. George himself was courageous, industrious, short-tempered, domineering, and yet curiously fearful and unconfident. He suffered from the Hanoverian gracelessness, and perhaps because of it was given to those singularly undignified scenes which seem to have characterized all Hanoverian court life. He was a great sensualist, and though his particular delight was his wife Caroline of Anspach he had a series of love affairs, including, it was rumored, one with Robert Walpole's wife. His chief mistress was Henrietta Howard; she was plain and deaf, and modest, charming, and witty, and the center of a talented group of writers which included Pope and Gray. George himself had no inclination toward the arts—with one notable exception: the music of his adored George Frederick Handel.

By the time she became Queen, Caroline of Anspach had fattened and coarsened, but she still retained her creamy complexion and flaxen hair. Like her husband she was basically an honest sensualist, and like him she was capable of prodigious fits of obstinacy and ill temper; but, unlike him, she was highly intelligent, lively, cultured, and well-versed in theological and philosophical controversy. She was probably the most perceptive and intelligent of all the English consorts, and exercised a humanizing restraint on her husband. Archdeacon Coxe gives us a picture of her levées:

. . . the motley character and manners of a queen and a learned woman. She received company while she was at her toilet; prayers and sometimes a sermon were read; learned men and divines were intermixed with courtiers and ladies of the household; the conversation turned on metaphysical subjects, blended with repartees, sallies of mirth, and the tittle-tattle of the drawing-room.

It was by Caroline's influence that Robert Walpole maintained his sway over his stubborn and ill-tempered King. During the years of exile from George I's court, Caroline and Walpole had developed a close understanding and mutual respect that was to prove invaluable during Walpole's years as prime minister. Walpole himself was the very model of a Hanoverian politician. He was an impressively solid man, short, with stubby arms and legs, and weighing some three hundred pounds, but with a shrewd and lively face animated by intelligence. He was capable of great charm and considerable patience, though in manner he was blunt and vulgar. By birth he was a Norfolk squire, and was said to open his gamekeeper's letters before his official despatches. He rode to hounds, ate apples during parliamentary debates, and kept a delightfully uncomplicated mistress called Molly Skerrett in Richmond Park. His weakness was his greed; he was greedy for office, for money, for valuable paintings, and fine houses. This was outweighed by his understanding that England's security lay in trade, in peace, and in freedom from European entanglements.

The triumvirate was not established without difficulty. Because it was in the Hanoverian tradition for sons to oppose their fathers, George II loathed his father's chief minister as much as he loathed his father. When on the afternoon of June 14, 1727 Walpole galloped posthaste to Richmond to tell the Prince of Wales of his father's death, George was in bed with Caroline. Walpole, hot with his errand, thrust his way into the new King's presence, and was told curtly to go away. Walpole retired, his career seemingly in ruins. But within twenty-four hours Caroline had convinced her husband that this was no time to rid himself of the architect of his country's prosperity.

Both George and Caroline resented deeply the restraints of constitutional monarchy. George found the members of the House of Commons "King-killers or republicans," and he said he was obliged to "enrich people for being rascals and buy them not to cut his throat." Hervey wrote of Caroline:

I have heard her at different times speak with great indignation against asserters of the people's rights; have heard her call the King, not without some despite, the humble servant of Parliament, the pensioner of his people, and a puppet of sovereignty, that was forced to go to them for every shilling he wanted, that he was obliged to court those who were always abusing him, and could do nothing of himself.

Like his father, George was truly happy only in Hanover, and made no attempt to hide it.

No English or even French cook could dress a dinner; no English confectioner set out a dessert; no English player could act; no English coachman could drive, or English jockey ride, nor were any English horses fit to be drove or fit to be ridden; no Englishman knew how to come into a room, nor any Englishwoman how to dress herself, nor were there any diversions in England, public or private, nor any man or woman in England whose conversation was to be borne—the one, as he said, talked of nothing but their dull politics, and the others of nothing but their ugly clothes. Whereas at Hanover all these things were in the utmost perfection.

Dullness presided at George's court, and the King himself did little to alleviate it.

No mill-horse [wrote Hervey] ever went in a more constant track or a more unchanging circle; so that by the assistance of an almanack for the day of the week and a watch for the hour of the day you may inform yourself fully, without any other intelligence but your memory, of every transaction within the verge of the court.

Levées, meals, walks, reviews of guard all took place at a precise hour. In the evenings George would play backgammon and Caroline quadrille while the court awaited their dismissal.

Their only distraction was the protracted and farcical conflict between George and Frederick Prince of Wales, which surpassed even that between George and his own father. His extraordinary aversion for his son and heir was shared by Caroline. "If I were to see him in hell," she said, "I should feel no more for him than I should for any other rogue that went there." George would attack

Caroline for her partiality for his son, "a monster, and the greatest villain ever born," yet Caroline went out of her way to ridicule and humiliate Frederick. She was convinced that he was impotent, and made no secret of her conviction. When Frederick's wife Augusta let it be known that she was pregnant, Caroline refused to believe it, and predicted that there would be another Warming-Pan Heir. When the unfortunate Augusta's labor-pains started, Frederick took her by carriage away from St. James's, and the child was very nearly born in the streets. As George himself had done, Frederick and his wife set up their own court, and rallied round them everyone who had a grievance against the King, the Queen, or the prime minister. Walpole described Frederick as "a poor, weak, irresolute, false, lying, dishonest, contemptible wretch, that nobody loves, that nobody believes, that nobody will trust, and that will trust everybody by turns, and that everybody by turns will impose upon, betray, mislead, and plunder." Yet the prince, perhaps out of a sense of fair play, was much loved by the people. "My God," Caroline said, "popularity always makes me sick, but Frederick's popularity makes me vomit." Both she and Walpole seriously misjudged the people's regard for the prince, and this was one of the factors that contributed to Walpole's eventual downfall.

Another and more tragic factor was the death of Caroline in 1737. For considerable time she had deliberately concealed from George that she was suffering from a severe rupture of the womb, not wanting to deny him the sexual pleasure that formed such a strong bond between them. Walpole wrote:

To prevent all suspicion, Her Majesty would frequently stand some minutes in her shift talking to her ladies, and, though labouring under so dangerous a complaint, she made it so an invariable rule never to refuse a desire of the King, that every morning at Richmond she walked several miles with him.

When she finally disclosed her illness it was too late, and in November she took to her bed for the last time. Frederick was not allowed to see her, but she sent him a message of forgiveness. George was terribly affected at her death. Caroline begged him to marry again, and he sobbed *"Non, j'aurai des maîtresses."* *"Ah mon Dieu,"* she rejoined, *"cela n'empêche pas."* He hardly left her side until she died, and then locked himself up in his room with her portrait. He said he had never known a woman worthy to buckle Caroline's shoe. The sincerity of his grief astounded the court.

Yet no one was more stricken than Walpole. His own sorrow at Caroline's death was genuine, but his very career was now uncertain. How could he hope to maintain his control over George? His friends suggested that he should approach George's favorite daughter; did they expect the King to go to bed with the Princess Caroline? was Walpole's characteristic reaction. Nor would he find much hope in Countess Walmoden, who had been brought from Hanover for George's consolation; she proved totally unsympathetic to Walpole's mounting problems.

But it was not Frederick's popularity nor Caroline's death that finally finished Walpole; it was the growing wish for war with Spain. Certain traders in the West Indies had followed the old English habit of piracy in those waters, and Spain had been pushed into a policy of harrying and imprisoning English merchantmen whenever the opportunity offered. Against the mounting wish for revenge came the farcical incident of Jenkins' Ear, which was to lead to the war of that absurd name. A certain Captain Jenkins presented Parliament with his own pickled ear, which he said had been cut off by the sadistic Spanish. Walpole, always attempting to keep out of European entanglements, persuaded the Spanish to make some minor reparations, but nothing could calm the public anger. A brilliant young orator called William Pitt denounced Walpole in the Commons:

This, Sir, I think upon my soul is nothing but a stipulation of national ignominy; an illusory expedient, to baffle the resentment of the nation; a truce without a suspension of hostilities on the part of Spain; on the part of England, a surrender of the rights and trade of England to the mercy of plenipotentiaries. The complaints of your despairing merchants, the voice of England, has condemned it.

What began as a war against Spain became, on the death of the Emperor Charles VI, a major European conflict, the War of the Austrian Succession. Charles had no male heir, and strictly the empire did not admit of female succession, but he had persuaded the great powers of Europe to respect as legal the accession of his daughter Maria Teresa. This solemn promise was known as the Pragmatic Sanction, and lasted two months beyond Charles VI's death; Prussia, Bavaria, and Spain then all laid claim to various parts of the vast empire. Only England remained true to her word, and rapidly found that that had led her into the unexpected task of defending Hanover against innumerable invaders. She had envisaged a limited maritime

war, not a series of costly land battles; but for the time being the fever
for war had its way. At Temple Bar, Prince Frederick toasted the
coming struggle, and Walpole fell from office in 1742. He died three
years later. "They now ring the bells, but they will soon wring their
hands," he had said on the declaration of war with Spain; no doubt
remembering his proud words to Caroline five years earlier:
"Madam, there are fifty thousand men slain this year in Europe, and
not one Englishman."

George himself entered into the war with considerable vigor, and
actually led a combined British and Hanoverian force against the
French at the battle of Dettingen. It nearly proved his undoing, for
his horse, terrified by the storm of battle, bolted, carrying its royal
rider into the French lines. George dismounted just in time, crying,
"Now, boys, now for the honour of England! Fire and behave
bravely, and the French will soon run." The battle which ensued was
chiefly remarkable for the blunders made by both sides. Neither
could claim a clear victory, but Handel wrote a splendid *Te Deum*
for it. George II was the last English King to lead an army in battle.

He was soon to be faced by a war within his own kingdom. The
outbreak of the War of the Austrian Succession had given a new
impetus to the Jacobite cause, and the Stuarts now had in Prince
Charles Edward, the Young Pretender, a leader of conspicuously
more attraction than his father. Charles Edward, the son of the Old
Pretender and Clementina Sobieska, was handsome, mannerly, cultured (in spite of being practically illiterate), had a sense of dignity
and occasion lacking in his father, and, above all, was prepared to
take command in person of an invasion of Scotland.

I am resolved to put all to the hazard. I will erect the royal standard, and
tell the people of Britain that Charles Stuart is come over to claim the crown
of his ancestors, or perish in the attempt.

He landed secretly in Scotland in July 1745 and raised his standard
in August. His support at first was among the Highlanders, whose
patriarchal culture had led them to preserve their Stuart loyalty. In
Edinburgh the Scots authorities refused to believe the news that
reached them. The Lord President, Duncan Forbes, wrote: "I consider the report of the sailing improbable, because I am confident the
young man cannot with reason expect to be joined by any considerable force in the Highlands." The King was enoying a prolonged
summer in Hanover, and by the time Sir John Cope, the commander

of the army in Scotland, eventually convinced himself that the rising was in fact taking place, the Pretender had every advantage. By September he was holding court at the palace of his ancestors, Holyrood House in Edinburgh, and delighting the Jacobite ladies by the charm of his person and the elegance of his dancing.

Sir John Cope eventually caught up with Charles Edward at Prestonpans, and was crushingly defeated (whence comes the song "Hey Johnny Cope, are you waking yet?"). His army ignominiously fled before the charge of the Highlanders, and the whole battle was decided within ten minutes. Four hundred of Cope's men were killed, while the Highland casualties were negligible. Cope himself withdrew hastily, and was received with the remark that he must be the first general on record to carry the news of his own defeat.

Charles Edward was now eager to press on to England, but the arms and men promised by France did not arrive. He stayed on in Edinburgh, issuing splendid but empty proclamations; he dissolved the Act of Union, drilled his army, and charmed the ladies. The delay was to prove fatal. George II came hurrying back from Hanover. There was a run on the Bank of England, and to George's fury both Lords and Commons voted that the new regiments to be raised were to be placed at the charge of the crown. The command of this army was given, not to Frederick Prince of Wales (as he had hoped), but to his brother William Augustus Duke of Cumberland; he was a capable general, but a corpulent and vile-tempered youth whose nickname at the opening of the campaign was "Billy" but at the end "The Bloody Butcher."

No army came from France, and Charles Edward, realizing that none would come, decided to cross the border into England without them. He met with astoundingly little opposition, and at the beginning of December was as far south as Derby. London fell into total panic. The ladies of the royal household packed their baggage and prepared to leave for Hanover. George II alone refused to be moved or alarmed, responding, "Pooh!" when anyone suggested that disaster was imminent. Meanwhile Cumberland was steadily bottling up Charles Edward; the northwestern ports were closed to him in the west, and a vast army assembled north of London. At this point his advisers began to lose courage, for although he was everywhere received with rejoicings, no one flocked to his banners. His weary Highlanders numbered some five thousand, and Cumberland's army was said to be of thirty thousand. Charles Edward himself believed that if he could seize London the faithless French would at last send their men in and victory would be certain, but his commanders counselled only retreat. Bitter and humiliated, Charles Edward was forced to agree. The Scots army turned north; and with the retreat lost all spirit. For the first time they fell to looting and pillaging, and Charles did nothing to stop them.

Back in Scotland he rallied his forces, and even inflicted a crushing defeat on his enemies at Falkirk; but the heart had gone out of his cause. The chief officers presented the Prince with a petition begging him to retreat into the Highlands and prepare for a spring offensive. "Good God, is it come to this?" he cried; but still he acquiesced. Starving and disheartened they tramped wearily through a barren countryside. In the middle of April they confronted Cumberland's massive forces. Charles should have retreated; instead he chose to believe that his dispirited and depleted men could do again what they had done at Prestonpans and Falkirk. At Culloden, in a blinding snowstorm, the Highlanders were mown down by the English guns and cut to pieces by a series of ferocious bayonet charges. Charles Edward contemplated sharing the fate of his men in a last desperate charge, but instead he allowed himself to be led away from the field in tears. Lord Elcho, who had been one of his staunchest supporters, cried after him, "Run, you cowardly Italian!"

In London George II waited anxiously for news. When the messenger was hurried in to him at St. James's Palace, he cast aside all etiquette to demand, "What has become of my son?" Hearing that Cumberland was safe and well, he said, "Then all's well with me," and burst into tears. Salutes were fired all over London and the whole city rejoiced. In Scotland the rebellion was put down with great ferocity. As for Charles Edward, his Stuart dignity and charm maintained him through the many adventures of his flight through the Highlands, but deserted him when he reached the safety of the Continent; he lived out the rest of his life an ignominious drunkard.

Cumberland's brutality enabled the more romantic of the Scots to gloss over the shame of the flight from Culloden and keep Bonnie Prince Charlie as a bright figure of romance in their history. But it was a merely pretty romance, for even at his best Charles Edward gave no promise of being more than a charming and handsome King.

The remainder of George II's reign was wholly dominated by William Pitt. Vain, unstable, at times indeed actually insane, he was nevertheless the politician needed to take command of a war that seemed likely to drag on endlessly. He was insistent that Britain should withdraw from her European commitments:

The confidence of the people is abused by making unnecessary alliances; they are then pillaged to provide the subsidies. It is now apparent that this great, this powerful, this formidable kingdom is considered only as a province of a despicable electorate.

Pitt had spoken very differently about Captain Jenkins' pickled ear, and it is not surprising that the King loathed him and did all that he could to keep him out of office. Pitt increased George's hatred by consorting with Frederick Prince of Wales, who had virtually formed his own cabinet-in-opposition. But on March 5, 1751, Frederick caught a chill while playing tennis at Kew. It turned to pleurisy, and within ten days he was dead. The King seems to have shown a moderate degree of concern, but Cumberland sneeringly observed, "It is a great blow to the country, but I hope it will recover in time." Frederick was buried with slight honors at Westminster, and a popular rhyme sums up the popular feeling:

> Here lies Fred,
> Who was alive and is dead:
> Had it been his father,
> I had much rather;
> Had it been his brother,
> Still better than another;
> Had it been his sister,
> No one would have missed her;
> Had it been the whole generation,
> Still better for the nation;
> But since 'tis only Fred,
> Who was alive and is dead—
> There's no more to be said.

In spite of George's dislike, and the success of his rivals Newcastle and Pelham, Pitt steadily increased his domination over the cabinet and the Commons. The War of the Austrian Succession at last ended, and was followed rapidly by a complete reversion of alliances —England and Prussia against France and Austria—and a new war, the Seven Years' War. This was much more to Pitt's liking, since England's ally was Frederick the Great of Prussia, who took over the European entanglement and left England free to harass the enemy on the high seas and set up an overseas empire in the process. Wolfe in Canada and Clive in India won outstanding victories and made vast territorial acquisitions (someone told the King that Wolfe was a madman, to which George said, "Oh, he is mad, is he? Then I wish he would *bite* some other of my generals."). Pitt's squadrons secured rich spice islands in the West Indies and valuable trading posts in Africa. Admittedly there were disasters; Admiral Byng was shot for the loss of Minorca (*"Pour encourager les autres,"* as Voltaire explained); but for the first time in her history England was fighting a series of wars which, far from draining her resources, were actually increasing her prosperity.

George II himself was failing in health. He suffered from attacks of gout, and his sight and hearing were degenerating; he complained that everybody seemed to have black crepe over their faces. On October 26, 1760, he rose at his usual hour, took his customary cup of chocolate, went into his water-closet, and there died of a stroke. He was buried by the side of his beloved Caroline, and at his own request a side was removed from each coffin so that their ashes might mingle.

GEORGE III
1760–1820

❀

Born in London in 1738.

Son of Frederick Prince of Wales, son of George II, and his wife Augusta of Saxe-Coburg, who died in 1772.

Married in 1761 Charlotte of Mecklenburg-Strelitz, by whom he had thirteen children in all, including:

> George, later Prince Regent, later George IV; William Duke of Clarence, later William IV; Edward Duke of Kent, who in the absence of a legitimate heir to the throne married in 1818 Victoria of Saxe-Coburg, by whom he had one daughter,
> Alexandrina Victoria, later Queen Victoria.

George III suffered during his reign from recurring bouts of insanity due to inherited porphyria; during these bouts his eldest son George Prince of Wales acted as Regent.

Died at Windsor in January 1820 and was buried there.

During George III's reign Ireland was incorporated into the Kingdom of Great Britain and the realm titled The United Kingdom of Great Britain. The claim to the throne of France was discontinued and omitted from the Royal titles.

GEORGE III

Before his early death Frederick Prince of Wales had drawn up a political testament entitled "Instructions for my Son George," which, among some sounder advice (such as reducing the National Debt and separating England from Hanover), included the disastrous precept to "retrieve the glory of the throne."

I shall have no regret never to have wore the Crown if you but fulfil it worthily. Convince the nation that you are not only an Englishman born and bred, but that you are also this by inclination.

George III's simple but clouded mind was deeply impressed by this advice, which his mother Princess Augusta continued to reiterate. Unhappily, while he was honestly and earnestly an Englishman by inclination he was not and could not be one born and bred. He was a Hanoverian, and his ancestors had been Continental autocrats while the English were executing Charles I and calling in William of Orange. He had none of the English folk-memory, that retains its deep political instincts long after the events causing them have gone from individual memory. Yet, although his attempts to "be King" were to have a disastrous impact on the country, behind his many errors of judgment there is honesty and decency for which it is hard not to feel sympathy and pity.

His childhood was unhappy and his education abysmal. George II, who had little affection for him, said he "lacked the desire to please," and his priggish and suspicious mother was so determined to shield him from the corrupt court that he grew up a backward innocent; he was eleven before he could read, and his writing was always like a child's. He lived in fear of his vast, tetchy uncle Butcher Cumberland, who would be regent if the old King died before George reached his majority, and there were those who said that the fear was justified.

George III's loves and hates were alike strong and stubborn. He was completely dependent on the comfort and sympathy of others, and all his life was to attach himself to one man after another in the hope (for many years vain) of finding a friend both loyal and capable. His first attachment was to John Stuart Earl of Bute, an old friend of his father's and a close associate and possibly lover of his mother's. To George he was a demi-god, whose advice he sought on the least or greatest of matters. This did no good at all to the vain and unstable Bute, who told him that "the prospect of forming your young mind is exquisitely pleasing to a heart like mine."

I have often heard you say [George wrote to him] that you don't think I shall have the same friendship for you when I am married as I now have. I shall never change in that, nor will I bear to be in the least deprived of your company.

He was wrong there, for his marriage was to be the first fortunate step in detaching him from Bute. He fell desperately in love with an English girl, and wrote to him:

I submit my happiness to you who are the best of friends, and whose friendship I value if possible above my love for the most charming of her sex; if you can give me no hopes to be happy I surrender my fortune into your hands, and will keep my thoughts from the dear object of my love, and never trouble you more with this unhappy tale.

Bute replied, "Think, Sir, who you are!," and looked for a suitable German princess. He found Charlotte of Mecklenburg-Strelitz, and the couple were married in 1761. Charlotte was no beauty (in later years it was remarked of her that "the bloom of her ugliness is going off"), but George settled down to love her with dog-like devotion. They had thirteen children, of whom very few were to turn out even modestly tolerable.

The first twenty years of George III's reign were marked by his ill-starred efforts to "be King." That he succeeded as far as he did was chiefly due to the unbalanced state of Parliament. The framework of government was by now established with the executive power vested in a united cabinet, headed by the prime minister and chosen from members whose party had the majority in the Commons. But the development of Parliament itself had lagged behind. In the rapidly changing social state of England it was far from representative, the aristocrats having by various means kept membership within their own ranks. It also lacked a strong Opposition, since the Tory party had discredited itself by its self-identification with the Jacobite cause, and the working of the system is highly dependent on a fruitful tension between Government and Opposition.

On George's accession the elder Pitt was prime minister, and unfortunately George hated him. Pitt had once been a friend of George's father, and in George's view had then deserted him to become a minister; he also disliked his European policies with a stubbornness that wholly ignored the good they had brought to England. He wanted to impose Bute as prime minister, but Bute, whose attitude to high office combined ambition and terror in equal proportions, announced that he would remain "as a private person." Pitt was correct in assuming that this meant "the minister behind the curtain," for George continued to act as the mouthpiece of Bute and the Princess Augusta. At his first cabinet meeting he announced:

As I mount the throne in the midst of a bloody and expensive war, I shall endeavour to prosecute it in the manner most likely to bring about an honourable peace.

This was not happy hearing to Pitt, whose wise direction had brought England through the European wars of the time to a higher state of prosperity and worldwide esteem than at any other time in her history. He was soon to see his work destroyed. The King pushed Bute into office, and Bute brought about the Peace of Paris in 1763, forcing the measure through Parliament by such questionable means that Europe despised him and the Londoners attacked him in the streets. This experience was too much for him, and he took refuge in ill health and resigned.

It was on this issue that George had his first brush with John Wilkes, a Member of Parliament as well as of the profligates' Hell-Fire Club, and founder and editor of the satirical newspaper the *North Briton*. The *North Briton* had already compared the ascendancy of Princess Augusta and Bute over the King with that of Isabelle the She-Wolf of France and Roger Mortimer the regicide over the child Edward III (George was now twenty-five). He now added to Pitt's rage at the advantages lost in the Peace of Paris the polite hope that the King would not profane St. Paul's by attending a thanksgiving service there to celebrate so shameful a victory. He was clapped into the Tower on a charge of seditious libel, and when the warrant was pronounced illegal and he had to be freed and compensated he was the hero of the mob. The King's rage at this was intemperate; he had Wilkes expelled from the Commons and hounded out of the country. It is fair to say that Wilkes gleefully invited this treatment, but George's surrender to rage proved to be the first sign of the so-called insanity that was later to overwhelm him.

It is known now that he suffered from a rare disease called porphyria. It was hereditary, and in the royal houses of Europe intensified by the inbreeding they all practiced. Mary Queen of Scots, James I of England, and Frederick the Great of Prussia are all known to have had it, but in George III it was particularly strong, and resulted in hallucinations and mental aberration. It first showed itself in 1762, and recurred in a more acute form in 1765. The cabinet was then enough alarmed to discuss a Regency; George announced that he would appoint a regent himself if necessary, which was taken to mean Augusta and Bute, and the cabinet hastily passed a bill specifically excluding Augusta. George in a rage insisted on the measure's being canceled, but the ensuing hostility led to the formation of Rockingham's ministry.

Two years earlier Rockingham had opposed the Peace of Paris, and George was suspicious of his loyalty. But he now preferred him to Bute, whose unpopularity was becoming an embarrassment. Bute protested at being passed over in a series of anguished letters:

Is it possible that you should not see the total difference between men setting up to be leaders of a party for seditious or ambitious purposes, and *me?*

But Bute's time had passed, and doing without him proved less painful than the King had feared.

All this time, quite escaping the notice of this foolish man, there was brewing overseas the trouble that was to be the chief conflict of his reign. Pitt's wise conduct of the wars overseas had ensured that the British flag and not the French flew in North America; George III and his ministers by sheer ineptitude not only sacrificed the loyalty and friendship of the thirteen colonies that were to grow into the United States of America, but added to that war with France, war with Spain, and revolt in Ireland. Pitt (who unwisely let himself be sent to the House of Lords as the Earl of Chatham) tried to halt the foolish process. When taxing the colonies was defended on the grounds that "Great Britain protects America: America is bound to yield obedience. If not, tell me when the Americans were emancipated?," Chatham replied with all his formidable eloquence:

The gentleman asks, when were the colonies emancipated? I desire to know when they were made slaves. The gentleman tells us that America is obstinate; America is in almost open rebellion. I rejoice that America has resisted.

His passion brought down Rockingham's ministry, but it was too late for him. The ill health he had suffered from since his youth at last defeated him, and he fell into melancholia, sitting at home staring vacantly, fiercely inaccessible to anyone. He was able to rouse himself only to resign, and his ministry, deprived of his direction, embarked under Grafton on a wild program of anti-American legislation.

It was during these years that John Wilkes, tiring of boredom and his debts on the Continent, decided to come back and goad King and government into more indiscretions. He stood as candidate for Middlesex, and was elected amid wild plaudits while the reluctant authorities took him to jail on the charges he had avoided by his earlier flight. He led a splendid life there, being liberally supplied with women by his friends and glutted with gifts of wine and food and tobacco from the Americans, who interpreted his gadfly activities as support for their cause. His election was invalidated, and another held, and since he won that one, that, too, was invalidated. At the third attempt he polled eleven hundred votes in an electorate of fourteen hundred, and by the King's direction his opponent was declared elected. He had to serve his sentence, but the scandal brought down Grafton's government.

(As for Wilkes, his power to annoy was much reduced, and when later on he stood once again for Parliament he was allowed to take his seat without trouble.)

George had now found a new minister, and again a fatal one. This was Lord North, whom he had known since his childhood, a stout, lazy, endlessly charming man who was yet totally lacking in decision or moral strength. He was determined to assert British authority in the colonies, and aroused so much hostility there that even a sensible measure was interpreted as inimical. A few lone voices warned them.

Charles James Fox pointed out that England's enemies in Europe would not lose the chance of embarrassing her by helping the colonists, and Chatham stumbled dying into the House of Lords, begging Parliament to recognize the Congress recently set up in Philadelphia and raging helplessly against the men who were threatening his life's achievement:

The whole of your political conduct has been one continued series of weakness, temerity, despotism, ignorance, futility, negligence, and the most notorious servility, incapacity, and corruption.

When it came to war North wavered, but George was obdurate. The confrontation moved inexorably toward Lexington, toward war with France and Spain, toward revolt in Ireland.

Rarely can one country so totally have underestimated her opponent. By 1778, after the surrender at Saratoga, even North was crying out for peace and begging to be relieved of his post; but to George every disaster was one more reason to continue the war. When a French invasion threatened he had visions of himself as the last patriot King.

He continued against the whole feeling of the people and Parliament. In 1778 Chatham died, and was given a public funeral in Westminster Abbey, and George was so insensitive to his people's esteem for a great statesman that he complained that the funeral was "an offensive measure to me personally." The public wrath was rising against him. The Commons passed a motion that "the influence of the Crown has increased, is increasing, and ought to be diminished," and Charles James Fox, now become the leader of the opposition to the King, declared:

You must be ministers of your own deliverance, and the road to it is open. Your brethren in America and Ireland show you how to act.

Even after Cornwallis had surrendered at Yorktown George would not agree to peace. Fox said:

There was one grand domestic evil from which all our other evils foreign and domestic sprung: the influence of the Crown. To the influence of the Crown we must attribute the loss of the army in Virginia; to the influence of the Crown we must attribute the loss of the thirteen provinces in America; for it was the influence of the Crown in the two Houses of Parliament that enabled His Majesty's ministers to persevere against the voice of reason, the voice of truth, the voice of the people.

No one had spoken with this tone in England since the years before the Civil War, and at last, in February, 1782, the Commons passed a motion to end all offensive warfare in America.

It was the end of George's personal rule. He was to continue to grumble and tinker, try to corrupt with the offices still within his gift, declare that there was nothing for him to do but abdicate; but Parliament now had a firm grasp of government, and knew better than to let it slip again. But Fox, the man who chiefly fought the King's rule, was not to profit by his success. Oddly enough, at this point George found the friend he had been looking for all his life.

William Pitt the Younger was twenty-four when in 1787 a measure of Fox's was defeated in the Lords and George dismissed the cabinet and handed over power to Pitt. He was the youngest prime minister England has ever had, and had already played a valuable part, as chancellor of the exchequer, in the Treaty of Versailles that concluded the war and granted independence to the colonies. He was to build up again a great part of what George had destroyed, but he was also to be the architect of a new Tory party, freed of its old Jacobite taint and strong and responsible enough to take its place in the proper working of the parliamentary system. He was alike to put together the fragments George had left of the Empire, and reconstitute the office of prime minister responsible only to Parliament.

Pitt is a difficult man to understand. He had all the marks of the purely ambitious politician, throwing in his lot with the party that would give him the greatest personal advantage, but he was more than that. He had his father's statesmanship, and more than his father's ability to handle people. In particular, he knew how to get on with the King. He had to be patient at times, but he did not simply manage him; he had an insight into his mind that created a curious understanding that recalls that between George II and Sir Robert Walpole.

It was the saving of poor George III, as far as anything could save his last years. Pitt, whom he could wholly trust, cured him of his urge to "be King," and that cured government of its urge to thwart him. The next five years were the best of George's reign. While Pitt pursued the path of reconstruction, George spent most of his time at Windsor, improving St. George's Chapel, managing his farms, thinking about turning the castle (which was ruinous) into a royal residence. With the Queen and their many children he rode and walked in the countryside, and was enthusiastically cheered. The novelist Fanny Burney wrote of this time: "The Royal family live as the simplest country gentlefolk."

The peace of Europe was to be broken very soon, but the peace of England was broken in a fashion typically Hanoverian. Fox, out of office but set in his opposition to the King, found a weapon in the Prince of Wales.

George Prince of Wales was now twenty-one, and remarkable even in that age for his extravagance. His debts were nearly £30,000, and when Fox failed to get him voted an income of £100,000 a year it made no difference to his spending. In addition, he had the habit of falling wholeheartedly in love with entirely impossible women. Maria Fitzherbert was impossible as Queen because she was a devout Roman Catholic, and impossible as mistress because she was a woman of dignity and integrity. Like Edward IV before him, the prince cast aside all good sense, and with Fox's complicity married her.

The old King was horrified, and refused either to recognize the marriage (which had not been made public) or to pay his son's debts, which had now risen to £200,000. With an inspired theatricality, the prince shut down his London house and drove off to Brighton to live with Mrs. Fitzherbert in well-publicized penury. All this had its inevitable effect on the old King's mind. In October, 1788, he suffered a series of attacks, talking constantly and going for days without sleep. When the prince visited him he tried to strangle him (though that could have been mere Hanoverian fatherly feeling). "I am nervous," the old man kept muttering. "I am not ill but I am nervous. If you should know what is the matter with me, I am nervous." Soon he recognized no one but the Queen, tried to escape from his keepers, and had to be put into a straitjacket. Fox said that the prince should be regent, the prince was already behaving as if he was so in fact, and Pitt thought his days in power were over when at the beginning of February he was called to the palace.

There was the King, wholly recovered, dignified and clearheaded. With tears in his eyes he asked Pitt to convey his gratitude to those who had supported him in his illness. There was a five-hour service of thanksgiving in Saint Paul's for his recovery, where his sons incurred considerable public dislike for their drunken behavior.

In July of this year, 1789, came the beginning of the French Revolution, whose consequences two centuries later we have neither finished with nor fully understood. Like most such events, its greater issues were clouded at the time by the smaller and more immediate ones. Pitt welcomed it as likely to help his own efforts toward democratic reform; Fox, not dissimilarly, hoped it would bring about a republic in England. But even those in England who most honestly believed in *Liberté, Egalité, Fraternité,* drew back in horror at the excesses of the Terror. By 1791, when it was plain that all civilized restraints were breaking down in Paris, Fox was abandoning his republicanism in favor of a moderate plan of constitutional reform, and his supporter, the great orator Edmund Burke, had gone over to Pitt.

In January, 1793, news reached England that the French had executed their King Louis XVI. France was already at war with Austria (the country of the Queen Marie Antoinette) and Prussia, and, intoxicated by some early successes, offered armed assistance to all peoples wanting to overthrow their governments. The result in England was a war against France that was vigorously popular with the people. There was sympathy for the intellectual principles of the revolution, but the land of William III and Marlborough came to arms at the hint of a French hegemony in Europe. Nor was their instinct wrong; for the French people fought at first in the belief that their revolution was in danger from foreign powers (as indeed it was), but with the first successes there revived the spirit of the Sun King pursuing European domination.

The first years of the revolution increased George III's popularity. He even suffered less from the Prince of Wales, who was terrified of the "hell-begotten Jacobines," as he called them, and fled from the republican Fox. The King wrote to Pitt that this was a war

to preserve society. My natural sentiments are so strong for peace, that no event of less moment than the present could have made me decidedly of the opinion that duty as well as interest calls on us to join against that most savage as well as unprincipled nation.

His instinct, too, was sound, for the only thing the revolutionaries could have taught England then was the use of violence. England had grasped the chief political principle of the French Revolution—the rights of the subject—back in the thirteenth century, and had been going about her own revolution ever since, and if her methods were more cumbrous than the French they were nothing like so self-defeating. She was even then moving steadily toward her next step, and that was to be decided in Parliament, not on the scaffold and in the Committees of Public Safety. The philosophy of the French Revolution had an immense effect in England, but it is arguable that its political effect was altogether unfortunate. While Pitt steadily pursued defeat of France's domination in Europe, fear of the spread of Jacobinism, as the most moderate type of reformism came to be called, led to widespread repression, which was to last for many years and occasionally break out into incidents of real savagery.

As the war drew on beyond Pitt's expectations, domestic difficulties decreased the King's popularity. A shortage of bread brought the poor to starvation level, and "Farmer George" had the windows of his coach broken by a mob shouting "Peace and bread! No war! No King!" The Prince of Wales and his debts continued to be a source of scandal, and the King refused to pay them while he continued his association with Mrs. Fitzherbert. The Prince was already tiring of poor Maria, but said, "As for us Princes, the choice of wife is indeed a lottery, and one from the wheel of which I do not at present intend to draw a ticket. There are very few prizes compared to the number of blanks."

He was disastrously right. In 1795 Lady Jersey so far took his mind from Mrs. Fitzherbert that he decided to take the ticket in return for payment of his debts. It was a blank: the Princess Caroline of Brunswick, who at first sight was coarse, dowdy, garrulous, and so careless of her cleanliness that she smelled, and on further acquaintance proved even worse. The prince took one look at his bride and uttered the famous words: "Harris, I am not well; pray get me a glass of brandy." Enough brandy got him through the wedding, but Pitt refused to pay all of his debts, having a war to pay for first, and the prince was left with a repellent bride and the beggarly sum of £80,000 a year.

He did his duty to the nation as speedily as possible. His daughter Princess Charlotte was born in January of the following year, and after this the couple lived apart. "I hope," he said, "that the rest of our lives will be passed in uninterrupted tranquillity." He lamented now his treachery toward Mrs. Fitzherbert, "who is my wife in the eyes of God and who is and ever will be such in mine." The old King was delighted with his granddaughter and in no way concerned that the succession had not been secured by a male heir.

Meantime, the emergence in France, in 1795, of a young Corsican general called Napoleon Bonaparte, at the moment when France was once again ripe for autocracy, made the issues of the war even clearer. England's problem now was not what pattern revolution should follow but how to avoid the most aggressive of foreign conquests.

The threat was undeniable, and Pitt inclined toward a negotiated peace. Paradoxically, however, it was his great virtues of toleration and foresight that in the end brought him down. Once again there was the threat of a French-inspired rising in Ireland, and to Pitt the only effective solution was the courageous one of making Ireland, like Scotland, an equal partner with England. The bar to this generous and sensible idea was that it would involve ensuring toleration to the Catholic religion, and in this he met the immovable resistance of the King.

Legally, George was undoubtedly right; his very coronation oath had bound him to "maintain the Protestant Reformed religion established by law." Nowadays we regret the lost opportunity, but it is possible that neither England nor Ireland themselves would have tolerated such a radical adjustment of their relationship. George declared that he would abdicate if Pitt persisted in this policy, and in 1801 Pitt, publicly committed to Irish emancipation, had no alternative but to resign. (Eccentrically enough, George proposed this time to abdicate in favor not of the Prince of Wales but of the royal House of Savoy in the south of France. Henrietta Anne, daughter of Charles I, had married into the family.)

Pitt was succeeded by Addington, the respected Speaker of the Commons, but he had been in office only a short time before George was taken ill again. He said in despair, "I do feel myself very ill, I am much weaker than I was, and I have prayed God all night that I might die, or that He would spare my reason." Pitt and Addington, who luckily were on good terms, discussed a regency, but George improved a little. He was now a pathetically frail creature who did not recognize the face in his mirror, but his ministers preferred him to a regent. Addington, however, faithful to the necessities of his office, signed the short-lived peace treaty of 1801. George said:

Do you know what I call the peace? An experimental peace, for it is nothing else. But it was unavoidable; I was abandoned by everybody, allies and all.

The war was renewed in 1803, and England daily expected invasion. George was undeterred, and while his wife and daughters planned refuge in the Midlands he was ready to put himself at the head of his troops and "repel the usurper's forces." The invasion did not come, but the strain of expecting it was too much for George. He was walking in the grounds of Buckingham Palace when he realized that his symptoms were recurring, and burst into tears. It was not a lengthy attack, but Addington found it difficult to serve under a King who one week was ready to lead an army into battle and the next strapped into a straitjacket. He resigned, and in 1804 Pitt returned to power.

The two following years took a terrible toll of Pitt. The British forces were largely engaged in a futile struggle to save Hanover from Napoleon, and his only consolation was Nelson's victory at Trafalgar. He died in 1806, only forty-six but worn-out. He was followed only eight months later by his old enemy, and the King's, Charles James Fox. The long years left the passionate republican with only two concerns: the negotiation of an honorable peace and the abolition of the slave trade. George said to him when he took up his office: "Mr Fox, I little thought you and I should ever meet again in this place. But I have no desire to look back on old grievances, and you may rest assured I shall never remind you of them." Fox carried through the legislation against the slave trade and then died, and George said, "Little did I think I should ever live to regret Mr. Fox's death."

By now he was nearly blind, and still exhibited moments of madness; he was alienated from the Queen, and one morning tried to ride into church. Yet he could still show flashes of his old spirit, and twice forbade ministers to raise the question of Irish emancipation. Family troubles distressed him. In 1808 there was a major scandal involving his favorite son Frederick Duke of York (the Grand Old Duke of York of the nursery rhyme). His mistress Mary Ann Clark (in whom the Hanoverian talent for appalling mistresses reached its peak) had been taking bribes from officers seeking promotion, and was alleged to have shared them with the duke. In the prolonged public examination of this charge, Mrs. Clark dwelled in some detail on his sexual habits, and though he was cleared of taking bribes he had to resign his post as commander-in-chief. To add to this, the King's dearest child of all, Princess Amelia, fell ill of consumption, and this brought on him another attack of madness. When she died, in 1809, though the news of her death was broken to him with the utmost caution it made him so much worse that a Regency could no longer be put off. With great difficulty he was persuaded to affix the Great Seal to the bill ending his own reign. He had been King for fifty years.

He lingered sadly on for another ten years, quite mad, too old and weak to be dangerous, and at least safe from the great events of the world outside. He took in nothing of the retreat of Napoleon from Moscow, his return from Elba, the battle of Waterloo that at last ended his career, and the lengthy process of peacemaking in Vienna. He does not even seem to have noticed the death of the Queen in 1818. He listened to the music of Handel, laughing and crying to himself; he spent hours buttoning and unbuttoning his waistcoat. He believed that England had been covered by a great flood, and that he would have to escape to Denmark; he would often speak of himself as "the late King." He died at last in January, 1820, at the age of eighty-one.

He had not been a wise man, but he had been an honest one; he once wrote to his son George: "I cannot depart from what I have fundamentally thought right." And he had been a kindly, decent, domestic man, Britain's first bourgeois King, in whom a vast number of his subjects could see their own ideals of home life. The affection which "Farmer George" wrung from a country wholly unused to liking its King was perhaps the most remarkable of his achievements.

GEORGE IV
Regent and King

1820–1830

✿

Born at St. James's Palace, London, in August 1762.
Eldest son of George III and his wife Charlotte of Meck-
lenburg-Strelitz.
Recognized as Prince Regent from 1814.
Married (bigamously) in 1795 Caroline of Brunswick-Wol-
fenbüttel, by whom he had one daughter,

> Charlotte, born in 1796. In 1816 Princess Charlotte
> married Prince Leopold of Saxe-Coburg (later King
> of the Belgians), and died in childbirth in 1817; her
> child did not survive.

Queen Caroline died in 1821.

Died in June 1830.

GEORGE IV
Regent and King

According to the Duke of Wellington, who had good reason to know, the sons of George III were "the damnedest mill-stones about the neck of any government that can be imagined." There was the Duke of York, fallen from his post of commander-in-chief through the misdoings of his mistress Mary Ann Clark. There was the bluff, honest William Duke of Clarence, an eccentric and uncouth sailor who lived with an actress called Mrs. Jordan, who supported their ten children by going on tour. There was the Duke of Cambridge, who fortunately spent most of his time in Hanover and was distinguished only by his habit of replying in ringing tones to the rhetorical questions of preachers. The Duke of Kent was universally hated for the bestial severity of his discipline as Commander of Gibraltar, where he would order one hundred lashes as a punishment for trifling defaults in dress and 999 for desertion. The Duke of Cumberland was said to have fathered a son on his sister Sophia and to have murdered his valet. Only the Duke of Sussex seems to have been free of reproach. As for the Prince of Wales, the poet Leigh Hunt described him as:

A libertine over head and ears in debt and disgrace, a despiser of domestic ties, the companion of demireps, a man who has just closed half a century without a single claim on the gratitude of his country or the respect of posterity.

This was undoubtedly true; but no one could have done much with a domestic tie with Caroline of Brunswick, and there had been a time when the actress "Perdita" Robinson had spoken differently of the royal lover she called "Florizel," of the "grace of his person, the irresistible sweetness of his smile, the tenderness of his melodious but manly voice." In fact the prince was not sexually dissolute, for he fell in love honestly; the trouble was that he did it too many times and always with the wrong women. Maria Fitzherbert would have been —or, to put it more justly, was—an admirable wife for him if he had not been the Prince of Wales. As it was, even he knew that he had gone too far in his secret marriage to her, and at one point he even contemplated selling his jewels and sailing off with her to start a new life in the Americas. If, after this, he had attained the Regency, or the succession, within a short time he might have been spurred into capability; it was said that in 1788, with his father's first attack of madness, the prince sat up for two nights, resplendently dressed and wearing his full orders of chivalry, awaiting the summons of the ministers. But time after time the power slipped away from him with the old King's stubborn recoveries, and while he was without power he was subjected to fretting restraints—chiefly no money (though that seldom restricted his expenditure) and a terrible wife. He found his own consolations; he rebuilt Carlton House to his own taste, he listened to the arbiter of elegance, Beau Brummel (who was probably as good an influence on a future King as any, since he introduced the tolerably novel idea of cleanliness into elegance), he passed his days with his father's opponents Fox and Sheridan—and his nights with Lady Jersey or Lady Horatia Seymour (who bore him a daughter). He weathered the disaster of his marriage to Caroline of Brunswick, and once she was delivered of Princess Charlotte returned to Mrs. Fitzherbert, while Caroline took a succession of improbable lovers. Even when the Regency finally came to him, as a man of forty-one, its terms were those which had been drawn up by Pitt more than twenty years before to limit the extravagances of a young man.

Before the Regency in 1811, the Prince had given his whole-hearted support to the Whigs, and after Fox's death (which had deeply affected him) he had maintained a close association with them. Yet, they had forgotten the Hanoverian stubbornness of purpose, which had led George II to keep his enemy Walpole in office after George I's death. The best that the regent would offer the Whigs was a coalition, which they refused. He kept his father's prime minister, Spencer Perceval, in office, and even began grudgingly to revoke his antipathy toward the Duke of Wellington, whose campaigns in the Peninsula were at last beginning to turn the war in England's favor.

The Regency had come at a time of considerable public discontent. The war had been going well, but food was scarce, and the upheavals of the industrial revolution were threatening the livelihood of artisans. There were machine-smashing riots in Lancashire and Cheshire, many firms went bankrupt, and in the north, where war and blockade had removed the overseas market for textiles, there was terrible unemployment. On the May 1, 1812 a bankrupt commercial agent assassinated Spencer Perceval in the lobby of the House of Commons. There was general rejoicing in the north, and the next day a letter was received at Carlton House threatening the regent with a similar fate.

To his credit, the prince refused to panic; he calmly set about trying to form a stable government based on a coalition; in the end he had to choose Lord Liverpool, a compromise candidate, as prime minister. Liverpool was not highly thought of among his contemporaries, and even Wellington wrote to him: "You have undertaken a gigantic task and I don't know how you will get through with it." Yet, Liverpool remained prime minister for the next fifteen years, heading a highly capable government.

In contrast to this good political sense, the prince at once fulfilled his ambition for military glory by promoting himself to field marshal (he had only held the lowly rank of colonel before). He wore his splendid new uniform with pride, parading the Royal Pavilion in Brighton drinking champagne and singing very loudly. He also showed his daughter, the little Princess Charlotte, how to dance the Highland fling, but unfortunately twisted his ankle and had to take to his bed for a fortnight. His brother of Cumberland observed that what he needed was a poultice not on his ankle but on his head.

Possibly his good political sense arose from his lack of political ambition. When the business of government thrust itself upon him he dealt with it, but he had no wish to interfere unasked. He much preferred to devote his energies (though the word is too powerful for his methods) to the arts. He assembled an excellent collection of Dutch paintings, collected silver, china, and furniture, indulged in a quiet mania for orientalism, read and spoke kind words to a somewhat sceptical Lord Byron, encouraged Walter Scott, giving him every facility to use the royal library and even offering him the post of poet laureate (an honor which by then Scott was too poverty-stricken to accept). He had the good taste, too, to praise Jane Austen's novels, and accepted the dedication of *Emma*. His chief concern, however, was with architecture. He had already supervised the transformation of Carlton House and the Royal Pavilion at Brighton, and now he turned his attention to what was the single great achievement of his personal reign: the transformation of London. He had found in John Nash an architect to his own impeccable taste, and together they reconstructed London, laying out Regent Street as a triumphal path from St. James's to Regents Park; Regents Park Nash surrounded with stately villas, a project showing a remarkable feeling for urbanized landscape. To his subjects all this seemed a pointless and criminal extravagance in a time of national poverty; yet the art and architecture of Regency England are perhaps the most outstanding contribution made by an English King to the culture of his country.

Less to be commended at a time when many of his subjects were living close to starvation was the regent's passion for food and drink. Under the endlessly inventive supervision of his cook, Carême, the kitchens at Brighton produced dinners of an extravagance unequalled since the decadence of the Roman Empire. A guest would be offered a choice from over a hundred dishes served in nine courses and from wines ingeniously chosen to blend with the food: an artistic achievement, but a horrific display of self-indulgence.

After the news in 1814 that Napoleon had abdicated and gone into exile at Elba, a year of revelry followed. The newly restored King Louis XVIII of France, whose corpulence was even greater than the regent's, was escorted from Buckinghamshire (where he had been living in exile since the revolution), royally dined at Carlton House, and bidden a stately farewell at Dover; and the Tsar of Russia and the King of Prussia, with the Austrian Foreign Minister Metternich, were invited to Britain to celebrate the end of hostilities. This visit turned out to be a disaster. For reasons now wholly obscure, that shifty idealist the Tsar became a public idol, and was cheered everywhere while the regent was booed in the streets. To make matters worse, he was accompanied by his dour sister the Grand Duchess Catherine, who had a genius for casting gloom on celebrations; at a reception in Carlton House she ordered the band to stop playing because music made her feel sick, and at the Guildhall the singers from the Italian opera were forbidden to disturb her digestion at dinner. She lectured the regent on the proper education of Princess Charlotte (who was by this time becoming something of a problem to her father). The gossip Creevey wrote: "All agree that Prinny will die or go mad; he is worn out with fuss, fatigue, and rage." He was only consoled, when his royal guests had gone, by presiding at the festivities to welcome the return of the victorious Duke of Wellington.

The personal popularity of the regent was now very low, and chiefly for the usual Hanoverian reason of family quarrels. The people were not altogether just in condemning him for his prolonged estrangement from Princess Caroline, who was coarse, lustful, far from clean, and even by Hanoverian standards lacking entirely in dignity; what they saw was a lady living in confinement, excluded from all public occasions and festivities, while her husband squandered unimaginable sums on self-indulgent banquets and and useless building projects. Caroline and her daughter stepped into the place of the official opposition to the Crown, and the Whigs flocked to her support.

The quarrel with Princess Charlotte was more serious. The regent had never been close to his daughter, seeing too much of her mother in her; he preferred his illegitimate Minnie, daughter of Horatia Seymour. As Charlotte grew up their relations began to assume the familiar Hanoverian pattern of hatred between King and heir; he found her sullen and lacking in feminine grace, and she made no effort to dispel this impression. Obviously the solution was her marriage, and George asked Castlereagh to approach the heir to the throne of Holland, William of Orange, in the hope of restoring the former unity between the two countries, but Charlotte loathed the "young frog" who got disgustingly drunk at Ascot, and had no wish to live abroad; she made a melodramatic flight to take refuge with her mother and the Whig opposition. Brougham, a leading Whig not usually so sensible, advised her to reconcile herself with her father, and the regent, moved by this, sent her off to Weymouth to recover her spirits by that Hanoverian cure-all, sea-bathing. In fact, poor Charlotte's sanctuary with Caroline had not been very secure; she hated her mother's loose living, which had included efforts to provide her daughter with casual lovers, and when Caroline abruptly departed for an extravagant and scandalous tour of the Continent Charlotte felt herself deserted indeed.

However, more momentous events now intruded, with Napoleon's return from Elba and a new threat to the peace of Europe. Wellington hastily prepared to oppose him, but the regent calmly went down to Brighton to supervise Nash's work on the Royal Pavilion there.

The emergency, however, did not last long. At a ball in St. James's Square the sound of cheering in the streets drowned the violins, and Major Percy, an *aide-de-camp* of Wellington's, stumbled dusty and weary into the room and laid at the regent's feet the eagles captured from Napoleon at Waterloo. To his credit, the regent wept to see the casualty lists, but was filled with pride that the regiment over which he had somewhat distantly reigned as colonel had particularly distinguished itself against the emperor's old guard.

He was somewhat perplexed when the news of the victory was very soon followed by a letter from the emperor himself:

Pursued by the factions which divide my country, and by the hostility of the greatest European powers, I have ended my political career, and I come, as Themistocles did, to seat myself at the hearth of the British people. I put myself under the protection of its laws, which I claim from Your Royal Highness as the strongest, most consistent, and most generous of my foes.

The regent was flattered, but wisely decided not to reply, and Napoleon departed sullenly to lifelong exile on St. Helena.

The Prince now returned to the proposal that his daughter should marry the Prince of Orange. Charlotte replied:

I candidly allow that a matrimonial connection would not only be desirable but would be the most likely expedient to remove me from the unpleasant circumstances in which I am placed. But notwithstanding that, I *cannot* comply with your wishes for marrying the Prince of Orange.

The regent, perhaps reflecting on the unhappy consequences of enforced dynastic marriage, gave up the Prince of Orange and prepared to consider the man Charlotte herself preferred, Leopold of Saxe-Coburg.

Leopold arrived at Brighton in February, 1816. The occasion was a little marred by a severe attack of gout that confined the regent to a wheelchair; but Leopold and Charlotte seemed genuinely happy with each other, and Lady Liverpool wrote:

When the ceremony was over, the Princess knelt to her father for his blessing, which he gave her, and then raised her and gave her a good hearty paternal hug that delighted me.

Their happiness was tragically short-lived. In November, 1817, by medical mismanagement, the Princess gave birth to a stillborn son and died. The regent collapsed completely at this loss of a daughter to whom he had so recently been reconciled. He shut himself up at

Brighton, dismissed his musicians, and gave himself utterly to his grief and remorse, even to forsaking his corsets. "Prinny has let loose his belly," Lord Folkestone wrote without sympathy, "which now reaches to his knees." The people, who had adored the young Princess, fixed on her doctor, Sir Richard Croft, as the scapegoat for her death, and though Leopold and the regent tried to defend him, the unfortunate man was driven to suicide.

The country was now treated to a grotesque search for an heir to the throne. There was no possibility of the regent and his wife having another child, and though the royal dukes had fathered a considerable progeny between them not one of these children was legitimate. They started a race to unburden themselves of their various mistresses of long standing and marry and breed more respectable heirs. Since they were all as monstrously in debt as their eldest brother they made it quite clear that they were not going through the wearisome process without compensation. William Duke of Clarence wrote:

If the Cabinet consider the measure of my marrying one of consequence, they ought to state to me what they can and will prepare for my establishment. I have ten children totally and entirely dependent on myself; I owe forty thousand pounds of funded debts for which of course I pay interest, and I have a floating debt of sixteen thousand pounds. Thus situated, and turning fifty, it would be madness in me to marry without previously knowing what the settlement would be.

Clarence abandoned Mrs. Jordan, briefly contemplated marriage with an attractive heiress called Miss Wyckham, and finally settled for the presentable but not very wealthy Amelia Adelaide of Saxe-Meiningen. The Duke of Cambridge dashed off a proposal to Princess Augusta of Hesse-Cassel, while the Duke of Kent disposed of his French-Canadian mistress Mme St. Laurent in favor of Prince Leopold's sister the widowed Duchess of Leiningen.

In this heady matrimonial atmosphere the regent began seriously to consider how he could rid himself of the unspeakable Caroline, rumors of whose conduct on the Continent grew steadily more alarming. She had found a new and dubious companion, Bartolomeo Pergami, whom she called her private secretary, and together they travelled as far as Constantinople and Jerusalem, where she instituted the Order of St. Caroline, of which Pergami was made Grand Master. She seemed perversely set on making an exhibition of her ample charms, posing as the Magdalen (most inappropriately), dressing as an Alpine peasant and driving through the streets of Genoa in a mother-of-pearl phaeton crowned with pink feathers, her vast bosom uncovered and wearing a short white skirt and top boots. With their daughter dead, the regent no longer saw any obstacle to ending the marriage.

Yet, divorce (as other monarchs had found) was no easy matter. None of her scandalous conduct had taken place on British soil, and Pergami was an Italian. Liverpool was reluctant to let the regent risk more popular dislike, for the country was in a most unsettled state. The Corn Laws, which protected Britain against foreign imports by maintaining a prohibitively high cost of corn, had produced widespread rioting, and there was growing clamor in the new and largely unrepresented industrial cities for a reform of the electoral system. This was a time when such places as Old Sarum (which no longer existed) and Dunwich (which was under the sea) continued as of ancient tradition to send members to Parliament, while Birmingham and Manchester with their vast populations sent none.

The regent became increasingly solitary. Beau Brummel, the symbol of the great days, was living in squalid exile in Calais; he had been expelled from the court long ago for slighting Mrs. Fitzherbert, and when cut dead by the regent one day took his revenge by enquiring loudly of Lord Alvanley, "Who is your fat friend?" The regent rarely saw Mrs. Fitzherbert now, and in 1818, exhausted by the strain of her husband George III's madness, the old Queen Charlotte died at Kew. Of late the Prince had turned to her for advice and comfort, and her death brought on another collapse and period of self-imposed solitude. Now he resigned himself to his physical condition and no longer attempted to ride; he sang, he continued his artistic and architectural schemes, he ate and he drank, but the heart had gone out of him.

Meanwhile, the race for the succession continued. The Duchess of Cambridge had dutifully borne a healthy son in March, 1819, but would the elder brothers also succeed? The Duchess of Clarence gave birth to a daughter, who only lived seven hours; but the Duchess of Kent, after something of a flurry to ensure that the child should be born on British soil, was delivered, on the May 24, 1819, of a "pretty little Princess, as plump as a partridge." The christening of this child gave rise to one of the familiar Hanoverian squabbles; the Duke of Kent wanted her called Charlotte Augusta, but the regent, who ardently hated both Kent and his bride, would not allow the child to bear the names of his mother and grandmother. He presided himself at the ceremony, and the little girl was named Alexandrina (after the Tsar of Russia) and Victoria (after her mother).

In January, 1820, the Duke of Kent caught a chill which, thanks to the extraordinary exertions of his doctors, killed him. A few days later George III died at Windsor. Most Englishmen had forgotten that the poor white-bearded wild-eyed old King was still alive, and his death evoked a wave of sympathy and even affection toward the son who was now, after so many years, King of England. King George IV collapsed, as was his habit at moments of crisis, and for some time it was believed that he would not long survive his father. But he did survive, and to a pressing problem. He was King; he would not have Caroline as Queen. Some way must be found of putting an end to the wretched marriage.

At this moment, with a sense of dramatic timing worthy of John Wilkes, Caroline chose to return to England, and was received with frenzied popular rejoicing. Her defender, Brougham, had done his best to keep her in exile, but she was not to be denied her moment; in London she was received by the lord mayor, made a triumphal procession across London, and outside Carlton House cried, "Long live the King!" The King had prudently stayed away, and he urged on the reluctant government to bring in a bill to deprive her of the title of Queen and declare her marriage "for ever wholly dissolved, annulled, and made void." An investigation into the Queen's conduct was held in an annex of the House of Lords. Caroline calmly attended, playing backgammon with the lord mayor and taking an occasional short sleep; "Instead of sleeping with Pergami," said Lord Holland, "she sleeps with the Lords." The trial was inconclusive, though it gave the public much entertainment, and provided them with a new catchword: *"Non mi ricordo* (I do not remember)," from the unvarying reply of a series of Italian servants questioned on Caroline's alleged liaison with Pergami. The King did not dare show his face in London. Lord Liverpool could only sustain himself with frequent breaths of ether, and Lord Anglesey, cornered by the mob and challenged to pay tribute to their heroine, shouted, "God save the Queen, and may all your wives be like her!" The popular feeling was summed up in the rhyme:

> *Most gracious Queen, we thee implore,*
> *To go away and sin no more;*

Or, if that effort be too great,
To go away at any rate.

The Bill to deprive the Queen of her title had so small a majority on a third (and final) reading that it was withdrawn. Caroline's popularity (which had very largely consisted in her not being her husband) was already on the wane, and the King ventured into public again; he was even cheered for quarter of an hour at Drury Lane, and decided that it was safe to hold his coronation. This took place in Westminster Abbey on July 19, 1821, and was an occasion of lavish splendor. There were only two flaws in the splendor: the King made eyes at Lady Conyngham, and Caroline made a last desperate effort to take her place as Queen. She drove up to the Abbey intending to force her way in if she were denied admission. A young officer from Waterloo described how "we ran for the door and got in, the Lord Chamberlain crying out 'Close the door!,' " and how champion boxers had been placed to guard the entrances. It was the end for Caroline; as she went wildly from door to door of the Abbey and found them all barred against her, the mob booed her; it was the King's day, and she had forfeited their sympathy. Eleven days later she was seized with a stomach attack and died within a week. She was buried in Brunswick, and her coffin bore the inscription "Caroline of Brunswick, the injured Queen of England."

Like a medieval King, George determined to make a royal progress and show himself to his subjects; his ministers, eager for anything that would increase his popularity, agreed. He went first to Ireland—the first King since the time of John to do so for peaceful purposes, and was acclaimed in Dublin. Next he set off for Hanover, which had not seen its ruler since George II's last visit in 1757. From Brussels the Duke of Wellington took him round the field of Waterloo, reporting:

His Majesty took it very coolly; he never asked me a single question or said one word, until I showed him where Lord Anglesey's leg was buried, and then he burst into tears.

In Hanover he entered with great gusto into the festivities. He was forced to return to Brighton to recuperate from an attack of gout; but by June, 1822, was recovered enough to decide on a journey to Scotland, which had not seen its King since the days of Charles II. A harassed Sir Walter Scott was given a month to arrange for the royal visit, and George ordered two kilts.

Scott turned out to be an excellent stage manager, though he needed all his wits to deal with the problems of the visit. The Highland clans quarrelled over the order of precedence for the King's entry into Edinburgh, and finally, with a lack of tact that approaches the inspired, decided to form up in the battle order they had adopted at the battle of Bannockburn. The King, however, on his way to Holyrood House, the palace of the Stuarts his family had dethroned, was delighted to observe a banner reading "Descendant of the Immortal Bruce, thrice welcome!" (The descent is traceable, by way of Mary Stuart and Joan Beaufort, though probably George himself had never seen it quite in that way.) At Edinburgh Castle, in a steady downpour, he stood kilted and soaked, saying "Never mind, I must cheer the people," and admired the famous view, which was thickly shrouded in mist. He declared that he was "in every respect pleased and gratified and grateful for the devoted attention paid him," and returned to England with the souvenir, entirely appropriate to the whole occasion, of the fork and spoon used by Bonnie Prince Charlie in 1745. The very craziness of it all was in its way magnificent; time had healed these wounds at least.

Back in London he found the government in disarray; for the foreign secretary, Castlereagh, the man who had represented British interests in Europe with dignity and tact, was dead. He had poured out to Wellington a tale of blackmail after a homosexual liaison that so little agreed with the observable facts that Wellington told him that he was not in his right mind and ordered his doctor to attend him. Three days after his departure, Castlereagh cut his own throat. He may have been simply mad.

His only possible successor as foreign secretary was Canning, whose flashy brilliance George hated. The first months were very difficult. "He is a plebeian and has no manners," George said, "and as for his brilliant repartees, he dined here and said nothing but yes and no." When Canning tried to persuade him to entertain the King and Queen of the Sandwich Islands at dinner he refused to "sit at table with a pair of damned cannibals." It was generally left to Wellington (as most problems were coming to be left to the great duke, with his genius of common sense) to arbitrate between the King and his minister. A delicate diplomatic situation soon arose. The King believed that as Elector of Hanover he was entitled to treat directly, without the intervention of Parliament, with the European ambassadors; but, as the Elector of Hanover could not cease being the King of England, England could be committed to two foreign policies, George's and Canning's. In 1825 George went too far by inviting Metternich to visit him without consulting the cabinet. Canning politely warned Metternich that such an act was against the British constitution, and Metternich discreetly stayed away. George thereupon invited Canning to Windsor, and the results surprised them both. They got on famously, exchanging witticisms, and soon Canning's despatches to his King took on a note of light-hearted confidence.

In the summer of 1826 George had another visitor to Windsor. This was his little niece, Kent's daughter, to whom he had denied the names of his mother and his grandmother. Alexandrina Victoria wrote many years later:

When we arrived at the Royal Lodge, the King took me by the hand, saying "Give me your little paw." He was large and gouty but with wonderful dignity and charm of manner.

She was then seven years old, and though she had two uncles senior to her in the succession still living she was the heir of the next generation.

In 1827 the steadfast Liverpool had a stroke and resigned. George wanted Wellington as his successor, because Canning was committed to the cause of Catholic emancipation in Ireland—the cause which had brought down Pitt and accelerated George III's madness. Public pressure forced him to appoint Canning, but he died fourteen weeks later, and George evaded the issue by appointing a man he knew was not strong enough to resist him, "Goody" Goderich. Goderich's only remarkable feature was his ability to burst into tears when confronted by any problem. The King, now into his sixties, fat, perfumed, and painted, was also much inclined to tears, and most of their discussions seem to have been passed in prolonged bouts of weeping. Goderich resigned very soon, and the King sent for Wellington, crying "Arthur, the Cabinet is defunct." Wellington, whose politics were complete conservatism modified by complete good sense, agreed to form a government which would not press the matter of emancipation; but Ireland was already on the verge of rebellion, and he saw that the only solution was emancipation. George made one last effort to avoid it, summoning his ministers to Windsor and between sips of brandy and prolonged bouts of tears recalling his "revered and sainted father," and announcing his intention to retire to Hanover as the defeated defender of the Protestant faith in Europe. When it became clear that the cabinet intended to resign and George would be faced with a Whig administration, he promptly sent them home and that evening wrote to Wellington:

My dear Friend: As I find the country would be left without an administration, I have decided to yield my opinion to that which is considered by the Cabinet to be for the immediate interests of the country. Under these circumstances you have my consent to proceed as you propose with the measure. God knows what pain it causes me to write these words.—G.R.

For all his faults, George IV was, unlike his father, a political realist.

This proved to be the last important act of his reign. By the autumn he was plainly sinking, and his mind began to give way. He told a surprised Wellington that he had led the charge of the Hanoverian brigade at the battle of Salamanca and even hinted that he had led his own regiment to victory at Waterloo. Florizel in his youth, grown stout and unwieldy in the years when power always slipped through his fingers and left him nothing but banquets and *chinoiseries* to fritter his energies on—did this last dream represent what he had always known he could be, if they let him? At the beginning of 1830 he suffered a series of minor strokes. In June he clutched at his doctor's hand and said, "My boy—this is death." It was.

The *Times* wrote, "No monarch will be less generally mourned," and his contemporaries were similarly and singularly harsh; they regarded George IV as a blend of King John and Henry VIII. Undoubtedly, George had done the monarchy much harm, but when we look back on his reign now we cannot see that it was noticeably worse than that of his immediate predecessors. He was no doubt a less honest man than his father, but a more sensible one; he made no gross political errors; he had the instinct to bow to the will of the nation when he had to, and he left the powers and privileges of his office neither weakly diminished nor tyrannically augmented. He was the last of the English Kings to be conscious of the power he had, and he had the good sense to use it properly.

The *Times* of 1830 would be surprised to know in what reverence the label *Regency* or *George IV* is held by those who value the country's artistic heritage. George IV's gifts to us of later years are immense. The British Museum, the National Gallery, Windsor Castle, Brighton, Nash's London, a revival of poetry and painting that was unrivaled since the days of Elizabeth I—and, like that of Elizabeth I, that lasted beyond his reign—all these show in some measure George IV's achievement. He instigated a state of mind in which the arts could flourish with the highest approval, after years of neglect and disinterest. No King could be wholly bad who had a novel dedicated to him by Jane Austen and who had John Nash and Sir Walter Scott as his friends.

WILLIAM IV
1830–1837

❀

Born in 1765.
Son of George III and his wife Charlotte of Mecklenburg-
  Strelitz.
Married in 1818 Adelaide of Saxe-Meiningen, who died in
  1849, and by whom he had no surviving children.
Died 20 June 1837.

WILLIAM IV

illiam IV's reputation is that of an eccentric buffoon whose reign constituted a breathing-space between the end of the Georgian era and the beginning of the Victorian; yet his reign contained the most important change in the constitution for many hundred years. In addition, his personal conduct to a considerable extent rescued the monarchy from the general contempt into which it had fallen during his brother's reign.

Certainly many of his contemporaries thought that William was a fool. "Look at that idiot!" grumbled George IV. "They will remember me if ever he is in my place." His career at the Admiralty brought him into violent conflict with his fellows there and with the government, and provoked a series of rebukes from his brother:

It is with feelings of the deepest regret that I observe the embarrassing situation in which you have placed yourself. You are in error from the beginning to the end. This is not a matter of opinion but of fact.

Yet William had a great sense of political reality. In 1829, for example, he was stoutly in favor of Catholic emancipation, and declared that he had "never given a vote with so much pleasure and satisfaction."

He seems to have had no great ambition to be King. As the death of his brother grew near he was deeply grieved by his illness, and seemed attracted only by the notion that as King he would at least be freed of his debts and in a better position to support his considerable family of illegitimate children. Yet when he did at last become King he entered into the task with a buoyant enthusiasm. It is said that when the news was broken to him at six o'clock in the morning he excused himself from his ministers and went back to bed, "as he had long wished to sleep with a Queen." He brought a badly needed breath of air into the court. Princess Lieven wrote:

The King, for whom the proverb *Happy as a king* seems certainly to have been invented by anticipation, imparts to all about him this extraordinary animation. He shows by his manner, his good nature, his cordiality, a sense of gratified pleasure which is quite contagious.

On the day when he swore in his privy council, William, becoming somewhat bored by the proceedings, decided to take a stroll in Pall Mall, where he was recognized and rapidly surrounded by an enthusiastic and boisterous crowd. An Irish whore threw her arms round his neck and kissed him. "Never mind all this," he said. "When I have walked about a few times they will get used to it and take no notice."

His informality alarmed his ministers, but it had its charm. When a clergyman, a Mr. Smith, was invited in error to dinner at Brighton Pavilion William asked bluntly, "And who the devil are you, sir? I never invited you." The shaken Mr. Smith produced his invitation card, at which William welcomed him in and at dinner toasted "the health of my new friend Mr. Smith, and to our long friendship."

His marriage to Adelaide of Saxe-Meiningen was childless. They lived together in happiness and harmony, but in general she seems to have dampened his natural enthusiasm and curbed his liberal instincts. She lived in permanent fear of revolution, convinced that she would share the fate of Marie Antoinette if the least measure of reform were granted. To her great credit she accepted without demur her husband's numerous children by Mrs. Jordan and treated them as if they were her own. These FitzClarences, as they were called, proved a terrible trial to their father. The daughters he adored, but the sons plagued the life out of him with demands for money and office, threatening suicide or public disgrace if they were refused, and the *Morning Post* observed that their impudence was "un-exampled even in the annals of Versailles or Madrid."

It was William's remarkable determination to rule as a constitutional monarch and a patriot King. He wrote:

The King cannot be accused of violating the Rights of the Sovereign, as it is well known he reserves to himself no patronage, seldom interferes in the disposal of any, and that it is vested in the Minister for the time being, and is applied, as far as may be reconciled to justice and reason, to the support of the government.

At his first meeting with his ministers the proceedings opened inauspiciously when the clerk swore them in in the name of George IV. The new King, unperturbed, said only, "William, if you please." He had great confidence in the Duke of Wellington, and hoped to rule through him; he once astounded a dinner party at Apsley House by announcing that as long as he sat on the throne, the duke would continue to enjoy his confidence. Wellington's enemies chose to interpret this as a move to confer on him the post of permanent prime minister, but in fact William had no wish to undermine the constitution; he simply hoped to be able to continue with a minister he trusted.

This was not to be allowed him, for Wellington was to survive for only a few months. In July 1830 a revolution in France, largely middle-class, overthrew the bigoted Bourbon Charles X (who had said, "I would rather chop wood than reign after the fashion of the King of England"), and put in his place a democratic régime and a bourgeois citizen-king, Louis-Philippe. Reaction in England, already much troubled by demands for parliamentary reform, was swift. Wellington was alarmed by French affairs, and when Parliament reassembled in November took the occasion to state his own firm policy:

I am not only not prepared to bring forward any measure of reform, but I will at once declare that I shall always feel it my duty to resist such measures when proposed by others.

That the duke, whose good sense in other matters was so magnificent, should have refused to consider parliamentary reform, demonstrates the genuine fear of many that reform would lead to the collapse of the social system, as it had done in France.

Wellington, however, had said too much, for it was well known that some of his ministers, Brougham and Aberdeen in particular, were not of his mind and disapproved of his statement. In London the people rioted, broke Wellington's windows and threatened him with assassination (not the best way, perhaps, of convincing him that reform would be a salutary measure). Peel persuaded the duke to resign, and the King received the resignation in tears.

His next prime minister was Lord Grey, a moderate reformist, and he received him with trepidation, not knowing what desperate measures he might have to consent to—even the inclusion in the government of Brougham, who was committed to the then unthinkable universal suffrage. Yet:

The fact is [wrote Grey], he turns out to be an incomparable King, and deserves all the encomiums that are lavished upon him. All the mountebankery which signalized his conduct when he came to the throne has passed away with the excitement which caused it, and he is as dignified as the homeliness and simplicity of his character will allow him to be.

Grey and his ministers drew up a series of measures, very far from universal suffrage but designed to satisfy the popular clamor for reform. There were many constituencies which had in the course of time dwindled or disappeared; these "pocket boroughs" had become the perquisite of the landowners, who had to be paid for the election of a member ("pocket" in this sense refers not to the size of a pocket but to what is carried in it), while the great new industrial cities of the Midlands and the North were unrepresented. Grey was not confident that he could force the bill through the Commons, let alone the Lords, and if it was rejected there must be a general election. William had a mortal fear of elections, as they were traditionally the time when revolutions broke out; but, to Grey's great relief, he loyally gave the bill his full backing, only making the ominous (and quite true) comment that the power of the Commons had increased to the detriment of that of the crown and the Lords.

When the dreaded Bill reached the Commons, Lord John Russell read out a list of sixty boroughs which were to be totally abolished and forty-seven which were to lose one member each. This was asking the Tory members to abolish themselves, and they prepared for battle. But with great skill Grey piloted his bill through the Commons and got it carried by a majority of one vote. The historian Macauley wrote:

We shook hands and clapped each other on the back, and went out laughing, crying, and huzzaing into the Lobby.

There followed, however, the committee stage (in which a bill is subjected to a more minute scrutiny than is possible on the floor of the House, and, if necessary, amended in the light of objections raised in the first debate), and here the bill met with such severe opposition that Grey persuaded the King to dissolve Parliament. Wellington, who underrated Grey as a parliamentarian, wrote:

I don't believe that the King of England has taken a step so fatal to his monarchy since the day that Charles I passed the act to deprive himself of the power of proroguing the Long Parliament.

And the Queen wrote in her diary:

May God will that this step be not dangerous for the welfare of the country.

William drove down to Westminster to announce the dissolution and was greeted by the sounds of ferocious uproar: "If it please Your Majesty," said Brougham, "that is the sound of the Lords debating." Yet the election passed off without undue incident, Grey won a massive victory for the cause of reform, and William found himself a popular hero.

The government was now confident enough of William's capability to urge him to hold his long-overdue coronation. William did his best to avoid it, arguing that such an extravagance would be another incitement to revolution, but Wellington persuaded him that it must be done. It cost just one-eighth of George IV's lavish occasion. William was much loaded down by his crown and robes, and Adelaide had a fit of giggles at the sight of Brougham in his wig and coronet, but otherwise the ceremony went off in a dignified manner, and the government felt themselves a little more secure for the coming battle with the Lords.

Inevitably, when the Reform Bill went to the Lords they voted it out. The crown had the power to create peers, and indeed had always done so, though sparingly, for a number of reasons: to reward supporters as much as to refill titles left vacant (this fact, which came to mean that a peer could be an honored statesman as often as an aristocrat born, probably accounts for the survival, so far, of the House of Lords). Grey now urged the King to create enough Whig peers to get the Bill passed; but this was too much for William.

The evil cannot be met by resorting to measures for obtaining a majority in the House of Lords which no government would propose and no Sovereign consent to without losing sight of what is due to the character of that House, to the honour of the Aristocracy of the country and to the dignity of the Throne.

The King's reasons for his refusal are not such as we should give today, but in fact he was right in his instincts. The House of Lords has often held up legislation, but has been crushed by the creation of new peers exceedingly rarely; much more often the implicit threat has led to a compromise, which, whatever its intrinsic terms, has had the advantage that the English style of government has evolved toward one of compromise, and the English people instinctively feel that this is the only sensible way. Moreover the wealth, and therefore much of the power, of England was still represented largely by the House of Lords; to have stopped that House working in its own way would have been to stop the process of natural evolution in the constitution of England.

By this time the country was in an uproar for the defeat of the Reform Bill in the Lords. There were riots in the Highlands, and fires were started in Bristol that destroyed a large part of the city. The duke was seriously alarmed, and the King deeply miserable. Lady Louisa Percy wrote:

When one looks at him with his good-humoured silly countenance, it does strike one that Fate made a cruel mistake in placing him where he has to ride the whirlwind and direct the storm.

Lady Louisa was to be proved right in her feelings. Grey refused to amend his bill in the direction of compromise, and the King agreed to create enough Whig peers to get it through the Lords. The duke, the Queen, his children, his entire household urged him to retract his agreement. He attempted compromise himself by urging the anti-reform peers to abstain. He did not succeed, and Grey resigned.

To the country William was now "Perfidious Billy," and as universally hated as a few months earlier he had been universally loved. So bad was the situation that even the loyalty of the Army was in doubt. William persuaded himself that his help lay in Wellington and Peel, who might be able to carry a policy of reform that would satisfy the people yet not entail the destruction of the Lords. It was in vain; Wellington and Peel could not form a government, and the Queen told her husband that their only safety was in flight to Hanover. William did not bolt for Hanover. Instead, he did what a constitutional King was bound to do; he sent for the politicians who most plainly represented the feeling of the country and asked them to form a government. They were Grey and Brougham, and to the horror of Grey (who knew his King) Brougham tried to get William to commit himself in writing to the creation of Whig peers. "Do you doubt my word?" William exploded. In the end there arrived the solution he had been hoping for: the Tory peers abstained from voting, putting self-preservation first once they were convinced that self-preservation was involved with the bill. What is known as the First Reform Bill became law in 1832, a date English school children learn along with 1066 and 1688.

Wellington predicted disaster when the reformed Parliament assembled, and was wrong. It was quite remarkably like the old Parliament, and was at once faced with an old bogy: the problem of Ireland. Catholic emancipation in 1829, in freeing the Irish from their first preoccupation, had enabled them to move on to other grievances. They wanted the Union with England repealed, and they had found a formidable leader in Daniel O'Connell. His first demand, however, and one that the Whigs accepted, was the reasonable reform of the Anglican Church of Ireland, which took tithes to the value of £750,000 yearly from a Catholic people. Foreseeably, the Tories were violently opposed to any reform, and William found himself faced with the same situation, Brougham urging him to create Whig peers. Wisely, he solved the problem himself this time, writing to the Archbishop of Canterbury that he must warn the bishops not to interfere, and letting it be known to the Tories that he wished the bill to pass without trouble. The bill did pass; William's short cut is an example of what could be done entirely constitutionally by a sensible King.

The strain had now proved too much for Grey, who in 1834 resigned, proposing Lord Melbourne, a mild-tempered moderate Whig, as his successor. William would have liked a coalition under Melbourne, but the Tory leader Wellington would have none of it, and it had to be Melbourne at the head of another Whig ministry. William advised his new prime minister that:

the general feeling of the Nation is in favour of the more moderate and safe course, and of the Principle which advocates *letting well alone.*

Melbourne was aristocratic and lazy and in many ways a man after William's own heart, but he could not hold in check the more violent men in his ministry, such as Brougham and Lord John Russell. He was hard-pressed to make more reforms in the Irish church, which William stoutly opposed, and when it became clear that the issue could no longer be avoided William dismissed him and sent for Wellington. This was the year when the Houses of Parliament burned down; Queen Adelaide, with some satisfaction, decided that this was a sign of divine retribution.

The *Times* blamed Melbourne's dismissal on Adelaide. Wellington was reluctant for the notoriously difficult task of acting as prime minister from his own seat in the Lords, so William sent for Peel.

This was generally thought to be unconstitutional, and William's popularity suffered, though Melbourne was typically moderate about it, writing to Grey:

It is almost superfluous to state to you that towards me personally the King's conduct has been most fair, honourable, and kind; and I owe it to him to say that whether his decision be right or wrong, he has come to it conscientiously, upon his own conviction that is unbiased by any other advice or influence whatsoever.

Peel, doomed to failure, lurched on from defeat to defeat in the Commons and was pathetically eager to resign. William said, "The country shan't be disturbed in this way, to make my reign tumble about like a topsail sheet-block in a breeze." But even he had to admit that Peel could not possibly continue in office, and before Melbourne would form a government he asked for William's undertaking that he would not oppose reform in the Irish church. William grumbled about his coronation oath, but in the end gave way, and Melbourne was back in office.

In his last years William grew cantankerous of temper. He never forgave the Whigs for existing, and raged pointlessly and childishly against most of their proposals. "I am an old man," he would assert, "older than any of Your Lordships, and therefore know more than any of you." Melbourne went quietly on in his own way. It is true that he once referred to an outburst of the King's as "a mass of muddle and impropriety," but for the most part he did his best to steer clear of trouble.

William's home life grew sadder. His FitzClarence sons were by now a source of continual irritation, and he was drawn into a prolonged and bitter battle with his sister-in-law the Duchess of Kent, who was the mother of Princess Victoria, the heir to the throne. He and Adelaide had always been kindly disposed toward the little Victoria. William had been one of the few people to approve her Christian name; he asserted that sailors would believe that she had been christened after Nelson's flagship *Victory,* and would tattoo her portrait on their arms. The Duchess, however, loathed William and the Hanoverian traditions. As Controller of her household, and, it was commonly believed, as her lover, she had a clever upstart called Sir John Conroy, who foolishly encouraged her hopes of becoming regent if the King should die before Victoria came of age at eighteen. William obstinately continued to survive, cordially hating the duchess and her protégé Conroy and flatly refusing Conroy a baronetcy. The duchess decided to anticipate the pleasures of sovereignty and embarked upon a series of royal progresses around England with her daughter.

These were highly successful, and the duchess was flattered and the little princess delighted by the loyalty and affection shown to them. The princess wrote at Hastings:

Six fishermen in rough blue jackets, red caps, and coarse white aprons, preceded by a band, bore a basket, ornamented with flowers, full of fish, as a present for us.

William was outraged. He wrote to his niece:

I hope the newspapers will not inform me of your travelling *this* year. I cannot approve of your flying about the Kingdom as you have done the last three years, and this, if attempted, I *must* and *shall* prevent.

It was in vain; off went the duchess and the princess on another progress, and the worst that poor William could do was to forbid his troops to fire salutes in their honor.

The King and the duchess were at loggerheads over countless things: the upkeep of Kensington Palace (the princess's residence), Victoria's confirmation, a projected marriage between her and Albert of Saxe-Coburg. The duchess did everything she could to sever Victoria's connections with the court. In August, 1836, she ignored Adelaide's birthday, but she did not dare ignore William's; he was seventy-one this year, and had recently been thrown into an exceptional rage by the discovery that the duchess had appropriated seventeen rooms at Kensington Palace he considered his own, and at his birthday banquet at Windsor he finally had his say.

I trust in God that my life may be spared for nine months longer, in which event no Regency would take place. I should then have the satisfaction of leaving the royal authority to the personal excellence of that young lady [pointing to Princess Victoria], and not in the hands of a person now near me, who is surrounded by evil advisers and who is herself incompetent to act with propriety in the station in which she would be placed.

Victoria very properly burst into tears, but there was no doubt that she agreed with every word her uncle had spoken.

William did live on to save the country from the duchess, and his relationship with Melbourne grew warmer. He would invite his ministers to dine with him after council meetings and drink "two bottles of wine a man." (Wine bottles were smaller then.) This did not prevent disputes between King and cabinet, and in particular with Lord Palmerston on the subject of foreign policy. Here William was stubborn, conservative, violently anti-French, but, as always, governed by basic good sense. He wrote to Melbourne:

We should always be guided in Our Proceedings with respect to them by Circumstances and by a Consideration of what is best suited to our interests, always however bearing in mind that in transactions between States as between individuals Honesty is the Best Policy.

As he grew older, however, he meddled less; Melbourne had at last learned how to manage him. His domestic life in his last few months was less tranquil, for Adelaide suffered a serious illness, his favorite daughter Sophia died in childbirth, and his offer of reconciliation to his son Lord Munster was spurned. In May, 1837, he had his normal yearly attack of asthma, but this time became gravely ill. He had the deep pleasure of Princess Victoria's coming-of-age, but by June it was plain that he was dying. Adelaide was always at his bedside; "Bear up, bear up!" he said to her on one occasion when she had broken down into tears. To his doctor he said: "Doctor, I know I am dying, but I should like to see another anniversary of the battle of Waterloo. Try if you cannot tinker me up to last out that day." Wellington sent the tricolor flag to his bedside; "Unfurl it," the dying King said, "and let me feel it. Glorious day!" He died two days later.

"If William ever comes to the throne," George IV had once remarked, "he will bring about a revolution." For once George IV was right. William IV had brought about a revolution that was second only to the Glorious Revolution of 1688. This not very clever old man, who had lived as an aristocrat through the worst fears of the French Revolution, had had to deal with that ultimate terror of those in power in any country, a people clamorous for a say in their own disposal; and he had dealt with it, grumblingly, confusedly, making mistakes along the way, but always faithful to his own determination to be a constitutional monarch. His reputation has never been high; he has often even been overlooked, coming between his scandalous brother and his famous niece, but he deserves better; it could be said that he was the first English King who saw his duty as giving his people what they made plain they wanted, even if their methods of making it plain struck him as barbarous. He might also lay claim to being unique in another way, though it would need enormous research and a very fine judgment to adjudicate that: that he was the only English King both to profess and to practice (within human limits) the Best Policy of Honesty.

VICTORIA
1837–1901

✿

Born at Kensington Palace in May 1819.
Only child of Edward Duke of Kent, son of George III,
and his wife Victoria of Saxe-Coburg.
Married in February 1840 Albert of Saxe-Coburg and Go-
tha, who was born in 1819 and died at Windsor in 1861.
They had nine children in all, including:

Victoria, born 1840, who married Friedrich, later III
of Germany, and by him had a son,
Wilhelm, later Kaiser Wilhelm II of Germany;
Albert Edward, later King Edward VII;
Alice, born 1843, married Grand Duke Louis of
Hesse-Darmstadt and had two daughters:
Alix, later Alexandra Tsarina of Russia, murdered
in 1917;
Victoria, married Louis Prince of Battenburg, and
had four children:
Alice, born 1885, married Prince Andrew of
Greece, and had one son:
Philip, naturalized British as Philip Mount-
batten, now H.R.H. Prince Philip Duke of
Edinburgh and husband of Queen Elizabeth
II;
Louise, married King Gustav of Sweden;
George Marquess of Milford Haven;
Lord Louis Mountbatten, now Lord Mountbat-
ten of Burma.

In 1877 Queen Victoria assumed the style of Empress of
India.

Died in January 1901.

VICTORIA

was awoke at 6 o'clock by Mamma who told me that the Archbishop of Canterbury and Lord Conyngham were there and wished to see me. I got out of bed and went into my sitting-room (only in my dressing-gown) and *alone* and saw them. Lord Conyngham [the Lord Chamberlain] then acquainted me that my poor Uncle, the King, was no more, and had expired at 12 minutes past 2 this morning and consequently I am Queen.

This was the way, in her journal entry for June 20, 1837, in which the young Princess recounted her accession to the throne. Lady Longford in her biography of the Queen notes that when Conyngham reached that word in his official announcement the Princess shot out her small hand for him to kneel and kiss it. William's little "Victory" had emerged triumphant after a long and bitter battle.

For many years the Princess's relationship with her mother the Duchess of Kent had been severely strained by the ambitions of Sir John Conroy. Conroy had been the Duke of Kent's equerry, and on his death had stayed on to become the duchess's unofficial adviser and possibly her lover. What he and the Duchess wanted was to rule the country, either by way of a Regency, or, if William IV should survive until Victoria's coming-of-age, through a thoroughly submissive Queen. They tried to shape the child into what they wanted; but, to be fair to the distasteful couple, they also tried not to turn out another Hanoverian. If she gobbled her food they said that she would be another George IV, if she had a fit of temper that she would be another Duke of Cumberland. Part of the excessive protectiveness of the system under which Victoria lived at Kensington Palace was designed to protect her from the abominable Cumberland, who was said to have designs on the throne himself.

Victoria always had an immense hunger for affection, and the history of the years before her marriage is full of her attempts to find someone to replace the father she had never known. Recoiling from her mother and Conroy, she turned for consolation to her governess, Baroness Lehzen. This lady, a faintly absurd yet eminently sensible pastor's daughter from Coburg, contrived somehow to bring Victoria up to responsibility and independence without ever attempting to deprive her of her childhood pleasures. Together they made a vast collection of dolls, read stories, played music, and visited the ballet, which Victoria particularly loved. It was Lehzen who first showed Victoria what her mother had hidden from her, by slipping into a history book a genealogical table of the royal family. "I am nearer to the throne than I had thought," said the child, and in true Hanoverian fashion burst into tears. Recovering herself she pronounced the immortal words: "I will be good."

For her first surrogate father Victoria found Leopold of Saxe-Coburg, her mother's brother, who was now King of the newly independent Belgium. Leopold was not over-scrupulous, but he was shrewd and long-sighted, and his advice was sound. He encouraged Victoria to study history, and recommended her to read Racine and Mme de Sévigny. He warned her against following the example of Queen Anne, and at her request outlined his view of what a Queen of England should be.

I am sorry to say, with all my affection for dear old England, the very state of its Society and politics renders many in that country essentially humbugs and deceivers; the appearance of the thing is generally more considered than the reality; provided things go off well, and opinion may be gained, the real good is a matter of the most perfect indifference. Defend yourself, my dear love, against this system; let your dear character always be true and loyal; this does not exclude prudence—your concerns are now unfortunately so organized that you must be cautious or you may injure yourself and others —but it does not prevent the being sterling and true. Nothing in persons gives greater reliance, greater weight than when they are known to be true.

Leopold, in fact, had a tolerable amount of the faintly unreal complacency we now connect with the Victorian era; but he was precisely what the forlorn princess needed, and it was to him and to Lehzen that she turned when the struggle with Conroy was at its height. When the duchess and Conroy realized that the William was going to live long enough to deny them the Regency, and that Victoria showed no signs of being controlable by them, they were seized by something like panic. Their solution was to have Victoria appoint Conroy as her permanent private secretary before the old King died. Victoria refused; even when Conroy took advantage of a severe attack of typhoid to trick her into signing the appointment on her sick-bed, she remained firm. Leopold sent over his own adviser, Baron Stockmar, to assess the situation, and Stockmar gave his support to the princess. By now Conroy had the popular nickname of King John; he tried to enlist Lord Liverpool on his side by telling him that Victoria was mentally subnormal, "younger in intellect than in years" (for which he certainly deserved all that was coming to him). Liverpool refused outright to believe this, but agreed to find out whether Conroy would be acceptable to her in some humbler capacity. She received him *"alone"* (as she wrote), and resolutely refused to accept Conroy in any capacity at all. At this point Conroy seems to have gone out of his mind. "She must be coerced," he said: locked in her room, denied food, anything to force her to his will. Before he could carry out this plan the King was dead.

The new Queen entered into her duties with confidence and genuine enjoyment.

At 9 came Lord Melbourne, whom I saw in my room, and of course quite alone, as I shall always do all my Ministers.

Everyone was considerably impressed by her composure and her highly professional conduct of affairs. They had gone prepared to pity a poor girl with too weighty a burden on her young shoulders; they came away realizing that she had gifts of firmness and self-possession unseen in a British monarch since the death of William III.

The word "alone" appears constantly in the Queen's journals at this time. She took an almost savage joy in freeing herself entirely of her mother, and one of her first acts was to move her bed out of her mother's room into one of her own.

My dear Lehzen will *always* remain with me as my friend, but will take no situation about me, and I think she is right.

Yet, for all her independence Victoria needed someone other than Lehzen to turn to. Uncle Leopold prudently stayed in Belgium

("People might fancy I come to enslave you"). Half the country expected her to send for Wellington, but she chose to keep Melbourne as her prime minister, writing to Leopold:

Let me pause to tell you how fortunate I am to have at the head of the government a man like Lord Melbourne. I have seen him now every day, and the more I see him the more confidence I have in him; he is not only a clever statesman and an honest man but a good and kind-hearted man, whose aim is to do his duty for his country and not for a party.

The romance between Victoria and Melbourne—there is no other word for it—is one of the strangest in the history of the English Kings. Each fulfilled a deep need of the other: Melbourne was the father Victoria had never known, Victoria was the child Melbourne had lost in his wife Caroline Lamb's weak-minded son. Greville wrote:

I have no doubt that he is passionately fond of her as he might be of a daughter if he had one; and the more because he is a man with a capacity for loving without having anything in the world to love. It is become his province to educate, instruct and form the most interesting mind and character in the world.

Melbourne was then fifty-eight. There were many who were horrified that an aging cynic who had been cited in two divorce suits should be the person closest to a young and innocent Queen. There were others who feared that he would wholly dominate her; "Take care that Melbourne is not king," wrote the Duchess of Kent. Yet his kindliness, his wisdom, his knowledge, his balance, and above all his sophistication were precisely what the young Queen needed. He gave her the political education she lacked; he gave her poise and confidence—confidence even in her own short stature. The air of scandal which clung to him further added to his attraction for her; she was, after all, the granddaughter of George III, who in his day had loved Melbourne's mother. They passed hours together, talking, riding, doing jigsaw puzzles, and always "alone" but for the Queen's pet spaniel, Dash.

The coronation was set for June 28, 1838. It was to be a particularly splendid affair. Victoria was now nineteen, and her mother, still banished from her daughter's counsels, sent her a copy of *King Lear* as a present. She looked forward with some trepidation to her coronation, but Melbourne said "You will like it when you are there." A new crown, costing one thousand pounds, had to be made, since

St. Edward's Crown, made for the stalwart Charles II, weighed five pounds. Two hundred thousand pounds was voted for the occasion, and the whole country contracted coronation fever. Greville wrote:

There was never anything seen like the state of this town. It is as if the population had been on a sudden quintupled; the uproar, the confusion, the crowd, the noise, are indescribable; not a mob here or there, but the town all mob, thronging, bustling, gaping and gazing at everything, at anything, at nothing.

Victoria slept badly on the night before the coronation, having "a feeling that something very awful was going to happen tomorrow." She was woken by the sound of the guns firing in her honor in the Park, and the same sound awakened William IV's Queen Adelaide, who wrote to give her niece her love and blessing. The crowds were greater than Victoria, or indeed any other sovereign, had ever seen, and when she reached the Abbey

the sight was splendid; the bank of Peeresses quite beautiful all in their robes, and the Peers the other side. My young train-bearers were always near me, and helped me whenever I wanted anything.

Others were less helpful. The Bishop of Durham got hopelessly lost over details, and Victoria had to say to one of her suite, "Pray tell me what I am to do, for they don't know." The Archbishop of Canterbury rammed the ruby coronation ring onto the wrong finger, nearly making her cry out for pain, and then tried to present her with the Orb, which had already been put into her hand. When the peers came one by one to swear homage at the throne, one old man stumbled over his robes and fell to the bottom of the steps; and as he gathered himself for the second attempt, the Queen rose and came down the steps to help him—an action which evoked tears and cheers. At the moment of crowning, Melbourne could not restrain his own tears.

My excellent Lord Melbourne, who stood very close to me throughout the whole ceremony, was completely overcome at this moment and very much affected; he gave me such a kind, and I may say *fatherly,* look.

When the long and complex ceremony was over, Melbourne said quietly to her, "I must congratulate you on this most brilliant day. And you did it beautifully—every part of it, with so much taste; it's a thing you can't give a person advice upon; it must be left to a person."

The months that followed came as a considerable anticlimax.

Conroy and the Duchess were continually causing trouble, Victoria resented Uncle Leopold's efforts to involve her in the affairs of Spain and Portugal, she depended more and more on Melbourne and became fiercely jealous when he was away from her; and while she became terrified of getting fat she grew lazy and despondent. What was worse, her temper and her judgment began to suffer, as she was to show in the unhappy case of Lady Flora Hastings. Lady Flora was a lady-in-waiting to the duchess and a close friend of Conroy's, and though she was unmarried she began to grow noticeably stout. Lehzen, who was always ready to believe the worst of the Duchess's set, pointed it out to the Queen, and after a discussion with Melbourne they reached the conclusion that Lady Flora must be pregnant by "the Monster and demon incarnate" Conroy. When the scandal had spread too far to be suppressed, Lady Flora very reluctantly submitted to a medical examination by the doctor Sir James Clarke, who pronounced her virgin. Wellington advised hushing the matter up, and the Queen attempted to apologize to Lady Flora; but the Duchess and Conroy were demanding reparations and mounting a vigorous offensive against the Queen, in which they were joined by the press, and finding that apologies in no way lessened this the Queen ostracized the unfortunate lady.

In the midst of this trouble Victoria suddenly found herself more "alone" than she had bargained for, for in May, 1839 Melbourne's government was defeated and he had to resign.

The state of agony, grief, and despair into which this placed me may be easier imagined than described! *All all* my happiness gone! That happy peaceful life destroyed, that dearest kind Lord Melbourne no longer my minister. I sobbed and cried very much.

Melbourne advised her that she must accept Robert Peel as prime minister, even though she disliked him. Now, the custom of the time dictated that the Queen's ladies-in-waiting should be of the political party in power. When the Queen flatly refused to part with her ladies, Melbourne discreetly suggested that she "had better express your hope that none of Your Majesty's household except those that are engaged in politics may be removed." When the Queen saw Peel:

I said I could not give up *any* of my ladies, and never had imagined such a thing. He asked if I meant to retain *all. 'All,'* I said.

And the Bedchamber Plot was in full cry.

Peel found himself in an impossible position, and resigned. To the

Queen's inexpressible delight, back came her dear Lord Melbourne; but her action was of dubious legality and threw the country into an uproar. Greville wrote:

It is a high trial of our institutions when the caprice of a girl of nineteen can overturn a great Ministerial combination. The simple truth is this case is that the Queen cannot endure the thought of parting with Lord Melbourne, who is everything to her. Her feelings are *sexual* though she does not know it, and though probably not very well defined to herself are of a sufficient strength to bear down all prudential considerations.

(A remarkable piece of perspicacity for the time.) Undoubtedly, Victoria had forgotten Uncle Leopold's advice not to behave like Queen Anne, and a Tory joke ran: "Countries have gone to the dogs before now, but this is the first one to to go the bitches."

Stubborn and headstrong, Victoria believed that she had triumphed, particularly when Conroy at last left England for good. But she had forfeited much of her popularity, and worse was to come; for in July, Lady Flora died, and a post-mortem revealed that she had been suffering from a cancer of the liver. Victoria was universally blamed for her death, and her stock fell so low that she actually noted a day when she had ridden in Hyde Park "without one hiss."

There seemed only one solution to her problems: marriage. Melbourne and Uncle Leopold had been gently advancing the idea for some time, but Victoria considered it a "schocking [*sic*] alternative. In any case there could be no decision for two or three years at the very earliest."

But in October there arrived in England the man Uncle Leopold picked out as a suitable husband, Prince Albert of Saxe-Coburg. Victoria had met him before, and been favorably impressed but not overwhelmed. Now matters were different (she was, in fact, ready for marriage).

Albert really is quite charming and so excessively handsome, such beautiful blue eyes, an exquisite nose, and such a pretty mouth with delicate mustachios and slight but very slight whiskers; a beautiful figure, broad in the shoulders and a fine waist; my heart is quite *going*.

They rode, they danced, they talked endlessly, they played and sang at the piano. Victoria told Melbourne that she had changed her mind about marriage, and he suggested that she should take a week to make up her mind. Naturally enough, he could not feel quite so enthusiastic as she did toward Albert, and wrote to Lord John Russell:

I do not know that anything better could be done. He seems a very agreeable young man, he is certainly a good-looking one, and, as to character, that we must always take our chance of.

Victoria did not want her week. On October 15, five days after Albert's arrival in England, she proposed to him.

I said to him, that I thought he must be aware *why* I wished him to come here,—and that it would make me *too happy* if he would consent to what I wished [to marry me].

Albert, whom Uncle Leopold had been coaching for the marriage for some years, accepted her, and wrote to a friend:

I think I shall be very happy, for Victoria possesses all the qualities which make a home happy, and seems to be attached to me with her whole heart.

Albert went home to prepare for the wedding, but Victoria had to withstand much disapproval. The people were unenthusiastic about this minor German princeling, Parliament cut down his proposed allowance to thirty thousand pounds a year and refused him a peerage, and evil old Cumberland claimed precedence over him. There were ominous signs: Albert was somewhat intolerantly puritanical in outlook (what we have come to call Victorian, in fact), and suspected that Victoria's court was seething with immorality; he wanted to bring his own German courtiers with him, and even objected to two of Victoria's bridesmaids on the grounds that their mothers had been mistresses of George IV. It was a clear sign that the old easy days at court (what the Queen had called "that happy peaceful life") were coming to an end.

The wedding began badly; Albert had a bad Channel crossing, it rained without stopping, and Victoria had a cold. But it went well in the end, and the people after all cheered Victoria's princeling. She wrote to Leopold:

Really, I do not think it possible for anyone in the world to be *happier,* or as happy as I am. He is an Angel, and his kindness and affection for me is really touching. To look in those dear eyes, and that dear sunny face, is enough to make me adore him. What I can do to make him happy will be greatest delight. Independent of my great personal happiness, the reception we both met with yesterday was the most gratifying and enthusiastic I ever experienced; there was no end of the crowds in London and all along the road.

The first weeks of the marriage seem to have been truly happy, but after that, reality intervened. Victoria was still self-absorbedly intent on being a Queen "alone," and Albert became increasingly frustrated to have no better occupations than dancing, riding, and blotting his letters. Moreover, Victoria discussed matters of importance with Baroness Lehzen, but never with him, and if he objected, Victoria indulged in tantrums. Surprisingly, Melbourne took Albert's side. He had already given over to the prince his own private secretary, Anson, and was anxious to do all that he could, within the constitution, to involve Albert in the affairs of state.

Two events combine to the prince's help. Victoria became pregnant, and in June, 1840, an attempt was made on her life when she was driving up Constitution Hill. The would-be assassin, a crazy youth of eighteen, was instantly collared by a Mr. Millais, whose other claim to fame is that he was the father of the painter; but, plainly, arrangements had to be made for a Regency in case of need. Wellington declared that "it could and ought to be nobody but the Prince", and both Victoria and Albert drew strength from the dignity of his new position.

In November the Queen was safely delivered of a baby girl. "Never mind," she said, "the next will be a Prince." She did not at first show much affection toward her daughter (who was christened Victoria), for she had suffered a loss which moved her more deeply; her spaniel Dash had died. She wrote his epitaph herself:

His attachment was without selfishness, His playfulness without malice, His fidelity without deceit.

It might as well have served for Lord Melbourne. In May, 1841, his government was defeated and he had to resign in favor of Peel. He accepted it with his usual stoicism: "Nobody likes going out, but I'm not well—I am a good deal tired, and it will be a great rest for me." His fidelity was indeed without deceit, for his last piece of advice to Victoria was to trust in Albert's guidance.

The only obstacle to this was Lehzen, whom Albert called "the yellow lady" or "the house dragon spitting fire." Few of Victoria's old props had the selflessness of Melbourne, and as long as she stayed, there was no prospect of real happiness for the married couple. A violent argument flared up between them over Lehzen's control of the nursery and of the health of the infant Princess Royal. Little Victoria had recently fallen ill and been handed over to the care of Sir James Clarke of the Flora Hastings affair. Albert wrote to his wife:

Doctor Clarke has mismanaged the child and poisoned her with calomel, and you have starved her. I shall have nothing more to do with it; take the child away and do as you like, and if she dies you will have it on your conscience.

This drastic step so stunned Victoria that she turned for help to Baron Stockmar, only to find that Albert had done the same, saying to him: "She will not hear me out but flies into a rage." She saw that her only course was to give way. Lehzen left quietly in June; Albert totally reorganized the household, and saw to it that there were no more quarrels with Sir Robert Peel.

In November Victoria presented Albert and the nation with "a fine large boy," who was christened Albert Edward. (All her four sons bore their father's Christian name, and later she was to express the wish that all of her male descendants—a formidable number—should do the same.) During the years that followed she had regular pregnancies, bearing in all nine children. The household was soon full to overflowing, and Albert began to look for a place where the family could live together more privately than at court; they settled finally on Osborne House on the Isle of Wight. Pamphleteers and satirists mocked the costly fertility of the royal pair, but with the departure of Lehzen and Melbourne their domestic harmony became a reality. Albert proceeded with Victoria's education, and tried to foster in her some appreciation of the arts; he was himself an amateur musician of some skill, and Mendelssohn was a frequent visitor. Out of their carefully regulated domestic happiness grew that system of strict morality called Victorian. In fact it was a very fair system when applied with kindness and in conditions of financial ease. The Victorian ideal of the all-providing father, the all-loving mother, the dutiful sons and the innocent daughters marrying young and starting the system all over again must have been fulfilled in many happy families. Its real troubles were that it allowed nothing for the least deviation from that ideal and that its finances were based on a capitalist economy that was now entering its cruelest stage. One of its saddest flaws was demonstrated from its very beginning on the unfortunate person of little "Bertie," the Prince of Wales, who was subjected to a miserably severe and repressing upbringing. Ironically, Victoria now had a horror that the boy would grow up to be like one of her Hanoverian uncles. The mishandling of her eldest son is understandable in her, for she was not naturally maternal but a sensual Hanoverian, and all her love and attention were centred upon Albert. Albert, however, was genuinely intelligent, and far less absorbed in Victoria than she in him, and it is difficult to understand his insensitivity here. It is one of history's ironies that the era that almost succeeded in suppressing women's sexuality was inaugurated by the downright sexual absorption of its first lady.

The man who had most cause to be grateful for Albert's subjugation of the Queen was Sir Robert Peel. Thanks to the Prince's powers of persuasion, Peel, once Victoria's *bête noire,* now enjoyed her confidence almost as completely as Melbourne had done. Peel was a man of honesty and integrity, but also of tact. Whatever was Sir Robert's concern became the Queen's, whether it was the familiar bogy of the church in Ireland or the rapidly worsening controversy about the repeal of the Corn Laws.

For years it had been Tory policy to protect British produce by forbidding cheaper foreign imports; which, at times of bad harvest, put up the price of corn, and thus of bread. For years the Whigs had advocated free trade, and when, in 1845, potato blight had reduced Ireland to a state of desperate famine there was considerable pressure in England for the repeal of the Corn Laws. The conscience of that honest man Peel could not hold out against that; he became an advocate of free trade, and, because his colleagues in the Tory ministry did not agree with him, he resigned.

Victoria lamented losing him as bitterly as she had lamented losing Melbourne. She had to send for Lord John Russell; but exactly as she had spiked Peel's guns over the Bedchamber Plot, so she now spiked Russell's: she adamantly refused to have Lord Palmerston at the Foreign Office. Albert supported her in this, for Palmerston's somewhat individual attitude toward foreign affairs (and French affairs in particular) had recently aroused their antipathy. Palmerston was an exceedingly clever man, but he was the inventor of what is now called "gunboat diplomacy" in an age where the British were coming to have more and better gunboats than anyone else. Faced by the demand to exclude Palmerston from his ministry, Lord John had no alternative but to "hand back the poisoned chalice to Sir Robert." For Sir Robert's good conscience and the starving Irish and

English there was much satisfaction; he carried through the repeal of the Corn Laws and the poor could afford to eat again; but the opposition to this was so great that he was almost at once heavily defeated on a quite minor matter. In 1846 he resigned again; and this time Victoria had to acknowledge the superior weight of the constitution and accept Lord John and Palmerston.

In a very short time there was trouble, and trouble of exactly the kind Albert must have feared when he opposed Palmerston. There had been a tacit agreement between England and France that Isabel Queen of Spain, who like Victoria had succeeded in her own right and unmarried, should be allowed to marry where she pleased on condition that neither England nor France attempted to influence her. To Victoria's horror, without consulting her, Palmerston put forward the English candidate (a minor Saxe-Coburg prince). Louis-Philippe, interpreting this as an act of English treachery, at once arranged Isabel's marriage with the Duke of Cadiz, who was supposed to be impotent, while his own son married the Infanta Fernanda, the next heir to Spain. It was a bad beginning for a Foreign Secretary, and Victoria was a true Hanoverian in the quality and endurance of her hatred once it was aroused.

Not that Palmerston's meddling had any great effect, for by March, 1848, Louis-Philippe and his family were landing as fugitives in England, displaced by yet another revolution in France that set off a train of similar uprisings throughout Europe. The same month, another fugitive arrived in London in disguise: Prince Metternich, once known as the "policeman of Europe," fleeing from a Vienna that had appeared the very heart of reaction and repression. One by one in that historic year of 1848 the countries of Europe were going up in revolutionary flames, impelled by different local weaknesses but always with the same underlying cause, the determination of the people to have a say in government.

Victoria seriously feared that the discontents would spread to England; and so they did, in the English fashion. What the English were after was not the overthrow of governments but universal suffrage. The vote then was limited to men with a certain amount of property, small enough to include the bourgeois but excluding the working class, and a movement had lately sprung up, Chartism, to press for working-class suffrage. In April, 1848, Lord John Russell warned the Queen that the Chartists were planning a march on London. One hundred and fifty thousand special constables were sworn in to defend the capital, Victoria and Albert were sent for safety to Osborne, and Victoria wrote dramatically to uncle Leopold:

I never was calmer and quieter or less nervous. Great events make me quiet and calm. But I feel grown old and serious, and the future is very dark.

She was altogether out of touch. The great Chartist march ended with its massive petition being sent to Whitehall by three non-revolutionary cabs, while Chartism itself, which was a stage in the development of working-class solidarity, became part of the inexorable pressure for universal suffrage. In Europe after all the ferment, reaction came back; only in non-revolutionary England did reform still struggle forward. And after all the great men had found refuge in England, two different exiles came to settle there in 1849. They were Friedrich Engels and Karl Marx.

At the end of 1848, old and sad and almost forgotten, Lord Melbourne died. Palmerston stayed with him,

engaged in the melancholy occupation of watching the gradual extinction of the lamp of life of one who was no less distinguished by his brilliant talents, his warm affections, and his first-rate understanding, than by those sentiments of attachment to Your Majesty, which rendered him the most devoted subject who ever had the honour to serve a Sovereign.

(This is a passage to make one forgive Palmerston much.) Yet to Victoria at Osborne, Melbourne seemed very far away by now; even in her letter to Leopold telling of his death she was more interested in a bitter gibe at Palmerston.

Later in 1849 the Queen made her first visit to Ireland. She had been genuinely concerned by the desperate sufferings inflicted on the people of that unhappy country by a series of appalling famines, but her visit was also an attempt to hide the misery and discontent. Cove, where she landed, was renamed Queenstown in her honor (it is now called Cobh), and she was delighted by her reception.

The most perfect order was maintained in spite of the immense mass of people assembled, and a more good-humoured crowd I never saw, but noisy and excitable beyond belief, talking, jumping and shrieking instead of cheering. There were numbers of troops out, and it really was a wonderful scene.

For a nation where thousands had perished through starvation brought about by English greed and obstinacy and stupidity it must indeed have been a remarkable demonstration.

The months that followed were almost wholly dominated by the struggle with Palmerston. After 1848 the old balance in Europe had clearly come to an end, but it was difficult to see what could replace it. Victoria and Albert had some sympathy for the new liberalism, but their innumerable connections by birth or marriage with the royal families of Europe made any support of republican nationalism to them rather like stealing from their relations. Where Albert wished to be liberal and support the idea of an emerging Germany, Palmerston wished to break up the country by restoring Schleswig-Holstein to Denmark. Where Palmerston felt liberal and inclined to support the cause of Italian nationalism, Victoria and Albert saw him as breaking up the Austrian Empire (which still owned a sizable part of Italy). As early as 1848 the Queen was telling Lord John that she could put up with Palmerston's capricious policies no longer. Her dislike of him was personal as well as political, for in the new morality into which Albert was steering the court Palmerston represented the evil old world of Victoria's Hanoverian uncles. His nickname was "Cupid," and it had been well-earned: even, Victoria had good reason to suspect, among her ladies-in-waiting.

At the beginning of 1849 Palmerston financed a group of Sicilian rebels an an effort to dethrone King "Bomba" of Naples (who certainly deserved it); the Queen was outraged and tried, but failed, to get Palmerston removed. The next year he really excelled himself. A Portuguese Jew, born in Gibraltar, Don Pacifico, had been roughly handled in Greece, and since the man was technically a British subject, Palmerston demanded compensation. When it was refused, he sent a squadron of gunboats to seize the Greek fleet. The Queen declared: "The levity of the man is inconceivable!"; but when Palmerston defended himself in the Commons his speech made him a public hero.

It was in fact one of the most memorable speeches of the time; he reminded the House that while Europe had been deluged with the blood of civil war, England alone had survived in peace. "We have shown that liberty is compatible with order; that individual freedom is reconcilable with obedience to the law." England was a land in which "every individual of each class is constantly striving to raise himself in the social scale—not by injustice and wrong, not by violence and illegality, but by persevering good conduct." Given such a consitutional country, he asked the House to consider whether it were not right that "as the Roman, in days of old, held himself free from indignity when he could say *Civis Romanus sum,* so also a

British subject, in whatever land he may be, shall feel confident that the watchful eye and the strong arm of England will protect him against injustice and wrong."

At this defeat Albert decided it was time to consult Baron Stockmar, and together they drafted a memorandum for Victoria to send to Lord John. It was one of the last attempts to define the relationship between Sovereign and Minister. The Queen required from her Foreign Secretary:

One, that he will distinctly state what he proposes in a given case, in order that the Queen may know as distinctly to what she has given her Royal sanction; two, having once given her sanction, that it be not arbitrarily altered or modified by the Minister; such an act she must consider as failing in sincerity towards the Crown, and justly to be visited by her exercise of her constitutional right of dismissing that Minister.

Palmerston went to Albert and obtained forgiveness by a masterly impression of a man seized by remorse and humility. In 1851 the Hungarian patriot Louis Kossuth fled to Turkey, and Austria (Hungary was part of the Austrian empire) demanded his extradition. Palmerston was determined to save Kossuth, and sent his famous gunboats to the Dardanelles to support Turkey. The grateful Kossuth came to England, where the Queen forbade Palmerston to receive him. Palmerston replied that he would not be dictated to about whom he received in his own house, but the harassed Lord John had to write that he could not "separate the private from the public man in this instance," and Palmerston yielded.

But a few weeks later he found himself in a corner from which not even he could escape. In France in 1857, a nephew of Napoleon Bonaparte had contrived to get himself elected as president of the Republic that had followed the ejection of Louis Philippe. In 1852, he staged a *coup d'état* and declared himself to be the Emperor Napoleon III. Palmerston, without consulting anyone at all, sent his congratulations and promises of support. He was summoned to account for himself in the Commons, and this time Lord John, who by now was as anxious as the Queen to be rid of him, prevented a repetition of the Don Pacifico defense by first reading to the House the Queen's memorandum, which Palmerston had accepted. According to Disraeli, Palmerston sat with his head in his hands "like a beaten fox." Dismissed by Lord John, he could see only one thing to do: to change parties.

Much of the strain of this long conflict with Palmerston had fallen upon Albert, but Albert had loftier preoccupations. Since the beginning of 1850 he had been presiding over a committee for the inauguration of a Great Exhibition to be held in the following year. It was to be a union of art and industry, in which, under the vast glass domes, soon to be called the Crystal Palace, designed by Joseph Paxton, the world's marvels were to be displayed. It was to be the supreme projection of Victorian optimism, power, and wealth, allied to a high-minded insistence on the humanizing influence of great art. The project aroused fierce opposition. Paxton's vast conservatory was denounced as a new Tower of Babel, and was widely expected to share the fate of its predecessor; riders objected to its intrusion upon Rotten Row in Hyde Park; the champions of law and order and public health were alarmed at the prospect of the great crowds of drunken and unwashed hooligans who would be attracted there; Lord John was frightened that the glass would be shattered by the salvos of cannon that were to salute the exhibition's opening.

At very nearly the last moment disaster took a more real form: the London birds took to the Crystal Palace with pleasure, and the precious exhibits were in great danger from their droppings. As always at moments of national crisis the Duke of Wellington was sent for. He came and surveyed the problem and said: "Sparrow-hawks." It was very nearly his last service to the sovereign he had supported since her earliest days.

All went well in the end, and the Great Exhibition was a personal triumph for Albert. Victoria wrote to Leopold:

I wish you could have witnessed the First May 1851, the greatest day in our history [sic], the most beautiful and imposing and touching spectacle ever seen, and the triumph of my beloved Albert. It was the happiest, proudest day in my life and I can think of nothing else. Albert's dearest name is immortalized with this great conception, his own, and my own dear country showed she was worthy of it.

These were the happiest days of the Queen's life. With Albert she had found remarkable peace and tranquility; at Osborne, and at their new retreat in the Highlands of Scotland, Balmoral (whence the telling word soon coined of Balmorality), they were able to live a life unburdened by court formality. Albert wore the kilt, and dried his socks in front of the fire, they went for long walks in the mountains, picnicked, drank whiskey, took tea with the local gentry, talked with engaging crofters, read, made music.

Every year [wrote Victoria of Balmoral] my heart becomes more fixed in this dear Paradise, and so much more so now, that all has become my dear Albert's own creation, own work, own building, own laying out, as at Osborne; and his great taste and the impress of his dear hand have stamped everywhere.

Not everyone agreed with her; ministers who had to undertake the then extremely uncomfortable journey to Balmoral when papers required the Queen's signature shied from it, and some have left on record their loathing of the draughty Highland life.

The Queen's ninth and last child, Princess Beatrice, was born in 1858.

Children, though often a source of anxiety and difficulty, are a great blessing and cheer and brighten up life.

They were determined—far too determined—that their children should not grow up like those of George III, and the Prince of Wales was the subject of special concern and attention. Stockmar drew up a plan for his education, which unfortunately did not work out in practice, the prince proving disappointingly slow and reluctant as a student. New tutors were engaged, new systems of discipline discussed, and soon the usual rumors began. Greville wrote:

The hereditary and unfailing antipathy of our Sovereigns to their Heirs apparent seems thus early to be taking root, and the Queen does not much like the child.

In 1852 the Duke of Wellington died, and was given a magnificent funeral. In the same year Palmerston had his revenge on Lord John, bringing down his government by representing as inadequate England's defenses against that upstart Napoleon III of France whom Palmerston himself had been so quick to congratulate. The Opposition to Lord John now included those supporters of Palmerston who had "crossed the floor" of the House with him when he left the Tory party, as well as the Peelites, who were the Tories who had broken with Peel over the reform of the Corn Laws. The party now called themselves Liberals instead of Whigs, but because the Queen would not have Palmerston as prime minister he had to take the comparatively harmless post of home secretary under Lord Aberdeen.

Meantime Europe was drifting toward a pointless war in the East. The Turkish Empire, known as the "sick man of Europe," had for many years been so weak that it was ready for dismemberment by any country hoping for loot. The Russians in particular were known to covet not only Constantinople, which would give her control of the Dardanelles, her only ice-free sea-passage to the west, but various Turkish possessions on the road to British India. The war party in England, naturally led by Palmerston, was determined to prevent a Russian presence in Constantinople, and was joined in its hostility to Russia by France, where Napoleon III had no such specific interests but needed to strengthen his own position by becoming a conqueror like his uncle the first Emperor. England was carried away by war fever, in spite of Aberdeen's wish to negotiate with the Russians, and in 1854 the Crimean War was under way.

An absurd rumor started at this point that Albert had been intriguing with the Tsar of Russia and that the Queen was going to send him to the Tower for it. Unhappily this came at a time when for once he was not on the best of terms with Victoria, and he was deeply wounded by it. Aberdeen said:

The Prince has now been so long before the eyes of the whole country, his conduct so invariably devoted to the public good, and his life so perfectly inattackable, that Lord Aberdeen has not the slightest apprehension of any serious consequences arising from these contemptible exhibitions of malevolence and faction.

The Crimean War was chiefly remarkable for the inept way in which it was conducted by everyone concerned. The English commander, Lord Raglan, proved to be wholly inadequate, and the one event by which the war was to be remembered in England, the Charge of the Light Brigade—"into the jaws of death, into the mouth of hell"—was a massacre caused by a command blunder. However, one good thing came out of it, and that was Florence Nightingale. Contrary to her legend, she was no beautiful Lady with the Lamp; she was one of the most formidable personalities in English history, and thanks to her not only the military but eventually the civilian nursing services of the country were thoroughly reorganized.

In January, 1855, Aberdeen was defeated. The Queen approached Derby, she approached Russell, but neither of them could form a government. Palmerston was now old and deaf—Disraeli described him as "an old painted pantaloon, with false teeth which would fall out of his mouth when speaking"—but it was he the country wanted, and Victoria had to accept the inevitable. It was suggested to her that she might ease the tension between allies by inviting Napoleon III for a State visit. The occasion proved astonishingly successful, and

Victoria found herself charmed by the flashy little man she had once disapproved of. She and Albert made a return visit to see the Paris Exhibition—the first British sovereign to set foot in that city since Henry VI.

I am delighted, enchanted, amused, and interested, and think I never saw anything more beautiful and gay than Paris—or more splendid than all the palaces.

She was particularly charmed to have a street named after her, and Napoleon flirted with her discreetly while Albert went through agonies of indigestion from French cooking.

By March, 1856, all sides in the war were exhausted, and a grudging peace was concluded. The following year, in spite of Palmerston's opposition, the Queen at last created Albert Prince Consort, which gave him precedence even over Uncle Leopold. The same year saw the engagement of her daughter Vicky, now seventeen, to Prince Frederick William of Prussia, the first of a series of dynastic marriages which were finally to make the Queen the head of a royal European family. Victoria bitterly regretted the departure of her eldest child for Prussia, for she had had a close relationship with her, and she was now left very much alone with Albert and the problem of Bertie. Albert's chief concern was to protect his son from the temptations and wickedness of the outside world; he was soon to learn that he would have done better to equip him for dealing capably with it.

In March, 1861, the Duchess of Kent died, and in a typically Hanoverian style Victoria collapsed completely. Albert, too, was in poor health, and in fact was incubating typhoid, though no one realized it. In November there came horrifying news from Ireland, where Bertie had been sent for a strengthening spell of army life: he had had an affair with an actress. Albert's reaction to this hardly surprising news was out of all proportion; he became frantic; the whole plan of his son's upbringing was in ruins; he wrote page after hysterical page to him. He was convinced that the girl must be pregnant; she would, he wrote, be able to

give before a greedy multitude disgusting details of your profligacy for the sake of convincing the Jury, yourself cross-examined by a railing indecent attorney and hooted and yelled at by a Lawless mob! Oh horrible prospect which this person has in her power, any day to realize! to break your poor parents' hearts!

Albert already had a severe chill caught on an official inspection at Sandhurst, but still insisted on going to Cambridge to administer yet more admonishment to poor Bertie (we can only hope that the actress had been nice to the boy), and on his return was confronted by a full-scale diplomatic crisis.

In America the Civil War had recently broken out, and two Confederate envoys, Mason and Slidell, had boarded a British ship, the *Trent,* to plead the Confederate cause in England. The *Trent* had been attacked by a Federalist vessel, and Mason and Slidell (among others) seized. With the approval of Lord John, Palmerston had prepared an ultimatum for the Federalists: they were to release the Confederate envoys or Britain would declare war. Albert had the good sense to see that all that was needed was to redraft the document to leave room for negotiation, saying, in the time-honored way, that the British Government believed that the captain of the Federalist ship had misinterpreted his instructions. Although he was now so ill that he could hardly hold the pen, he redrafted the document and averted the pointless ultimatum.

But the effort had exhausted a strength already drained by the chill and the advancing typhoid. Albert fell into a fever, but Jenner, his doctor, assured the Queen that there was no reason for alarm. She sat by his bedside, reading to him George Eliot's *Silas Marner* and trying to make him eat. The other doctor attending upon Albert was the long-surviving Sir James Clarke; he insisted that Albert should not know the true nature of his illness, so that Jenner could not give any treatment adequate to typhoid, and Albert took every emergence from delirium as a sign of complete recovery and wasted his energy in playing with the children. It was only when he was moved into the Blue Room at Windsor, the room in which George IV and William IV had died, that he realized the truth, but for some time the doctors contrived to deceive Victoria. Eventually even she knew that there was no more hope. "Oh, this is death," she said; "I know it; I have seen this before." Albert died on December 14.

Two or three long but perfectly gentle breaths were drawn, the hand clasping mine, and (oh! it turns me sick to write it) *all all* was over. I stood up, kissing his dear heavenly forehead and called out in a bitter, agonizing cry: 'Oh! my dear Darling!' and then dropped on my knees in mute, distracted despair, unable to utter a word, or shed a tear!

The room in which the Prince had died was cleaned, but not a thing in it was moved, and so, by the Queen's order, it remained. She slept each night with Albert's nightshirt in her arms—*"All Alone!"* A mausoleum was built for him at Windsor, and a National Memorial planned for Kensington. In her wilder moments (moments which shed unexpected light on her) Victoria felt that Albert had deliberately deserted her; he had died, she said, for want of *pluck*. A photograph taken at this time of the Queen with Princess Alice (her second daughter) shows her in an appalling depth of mourning clothes, her face turned away from the camera and gazing bleakly at Albert's bust. This was her chosen attitude, and she was to maintain it for so long and with such purely Hanoverian determination that she very nearly ruined the monarchy.

In effect, the Queen retired. A poster appeared outside Buckingham Palace:

These commanding premises to be let or sold, in consequence of the late occupant's declining business,

and the wording was just. The Hanoverians had always needed close personal support, and Victoria, for all her pride, had never attempted to rule unsupported; first from Melbourne, then from Albert, she had demanded full-time devotion and help. For years now, Albert had supplied her political and moral education and guided her on every matter. Bereft of him, left entirely to her own resources, she could only retreat into her grief and "decline business," asking herself at every point, "What would Albert have done?" Poor Bertie was married in 1863 to Princess Alexandra of Denmark, and Victoria blighted the celebrations by spending the time in Albert's mausoleum. A European crisis arose when Prussia invaded the Danish provinces of Schleswig-Holstein, and Palmerston was prevented from sending out his gunboats, and Victoria only remarked to her daughter, "I am glad darling Papa is spared this worry and annoyance." Palmerston died in 1865, just before his eighty-first birthday, and Leopold of Belgium in the same year; Lord John was defeated on the question of further reform of the suffrage and Lord Derby took up the cause, though thinking it "a leap in the dark"; the Queen remained withdrawn.

Most of the time she passed at Balmoral, with her chief companions: her equerry Henry Ponsonby (whom she had to caution sternly "not to be too funny"), and Albert's former Highland servant, John Brown.

John Brown was thirty-nine, handsome in his way, shrewd and abrupt in manner; his presence gave her a sense of security, but chiefly he supplied the masculine presence she always needed. His familiarity with her, which plainly he did not adopt without thought, was to be source of continual scandal, and the popular press was soon satirizing her as Mrs. John Brown. Even in court circles his presence aroused resentment, but she told Ponsonby:

The Queen will not be dictated to or made to alter what she has found to answer for her comfort.

It is most unlikely that they were in fact lovers, but there can be no doubt that she was as infatuated by him as she had been as a girl by Melbourne. She would not allow him to marry, or to leave her; he tramped round the Highlands with her, drank whiskey with her in private, stood behind her at functions of state. The Prince of Wales loathed him, but he was the man the Queen had chosen for her support, and undeniably his blunt common sense (even if it were a pose) preserved her balance at a time when many feared that her terror of being alone might drive her into seclusion and madness.

And presently there appeared a more suitable figure to be the support of a fifty-year-old Queen with nine children. In 1868 Derby made way for a younger man and Benjamin Disraeli became prime minister. He was a man very different from the rich aristocrats who had so far formed the governing parties of England; in his own words, he had climbed to the top of the greasy pole by nothing but his own efforts. His father was a Jewish writer, and he himself had had to battle against the prejudice aroused by his origin; he was charming, intelligent, extravagant, in English terms more than a little flashy, and to Victoria he seemed almost one of the unknown working class. He had fashionable mistresses, who adored him, and a rich, plain wife whom he adored, and he knew very well how to deal with the Queen. Where Brown was blunt and bullying, Disraeli was all flattery, and Victoria was delighted and fascinated by him.

This glimpse of a new pleasure in accepting business was short-lived, for Disraeli's first government lasted only a brief time and was succeeded by that of a far less welcome character: William Ewart Gladstone.

Gladstone was nearly sixty then, frock-coated, rock-jawed, with the expression of a morally outraged bird of prey. Where Disraeli had spoken of climbing greasy poles, Gladstone spoke of a "steepening path, with a burden of ever-gathering weight." He knew that the Queen did not like him, in spite of the fact—an interesting fact in considering Victoria—that he was the very embodiment of Albert's high moral sense, and he is some ways an ambiguous character, spending his spare time in trying to reform "fallen women" (as prostitutes were then called). To us today, much of Victorian morality is ambiguous, and in no way better symbolized than by the dislike of the Queen for Gladstone and her undisguised liking for the unashamed though veiled erotic support of John Brown and Disraeli. Gladstone's wife urged him to "pet" the Queen, his friends warned him not to try to argue her into submission, but few men could have been less capable of such behavior. Since the first problem of his ministry was that of the Protestant Church in Ireland, an alien growth in a Catholic country which Gladstone proposed to resolve by demoting it from the position of the governmentally established church, Victoria was outraged, refused even to appear at the opening of Parliament, and withdrew again from public life.

Gladstone, an honest man by his own lights, deeply resented her lofty withdrawal, and was incapable of seeing that she disliked his interminable monologues ("Mr Gladstone, We are not a public meeting") and could not understand his labyrinthine memoranda. He complained that "The Queen is invisible and the Prince of Wales not respected," and his sensible attempts to make the Prince more respect-worthy were scorned. He was not allowed to send him to Ireland as viceroy, since the Queen said the climate would not suit his health, and although there was no overt hostility between Queen and heir (the Queen notes complacently, "I am sure no heir apparent was ever so nice and unpretending as Bertie is") she declined to do anything to help him prepare for the position he must eventually assume.

She had never in fact entirely forgiven him for what she thought to be his part in Albert's death. She regarded him as shiftless and irresponsible, and, quite naturally, the prince and his young wife, like all Hanoverian heirs, formed their own court and society. They associated with three classes that horrified the Queen: Jews, bankers, and Americans. They raced, they gambled, they smoked, they gave smart parties. The Queen took refuge in Scotland and in literature, combining the two in her *Leaves from the Journal of Our Life in the Highlands*. This was published, in spite of the prince's objections, in 1868, and Victoria thus became the first author in the royal family since James I. It was of course dedicated to Albert—"To the dear memory of him who made the life of the writer bright and happy," and in its own way has great charm. It enabled Disraeli at a later date to produce one his most famous flatteries—since he had written several sophisticated novels of his own—"We authors, Ma'am. . . ."

In February the Queen's worst fears of her son were realized when he was cited in a divorce suit. He was adjudged innocent in court, but there were a few hisses at the theatre. What the Queen did not understand was that it was her behavior rather than that of her son which brought the monarchy into disrepute. Gladstone was desperate to demonstrate "the Royal family in the *visible* discharge of public duty," and could find no opportunity. In 1870, when Prussia attacked France and exposed the flimsy foundation of Napoleon III's imperial pretensions, the Queen was only interested in her daughter Vicky's welfare. She had become intensely puritanical after her son's involvement in a divorce case, and regarded the Prussian bombardment of Paris as "a great moral." Gladstone was almost reduced to taking his wife's advice to pet her; he invented reasons for her leaving Balmoral a little earlier, he persuaded her to open a bridge, he failed to get her to prorogue Parliament in person. The Queen informed him that overwork had killed her husband and was not going to kill her, and, when all other excuses failed, accused him of trying to use her for his own political purposes. He described this as "the most sickening experience I have had in forty years of public life." All she would do was open the Albert Hall, the great concert hall built in memory of her husband (which, characteristically of the times, proved to have an echo from its imposing dome which has only just been stifled). By 1870, feeling against the Queen had risen far enough for the historian Charles Dilke to say that the time had come to set up a republic in England.

At last, fate was kind toward Gladstone; in 1871, on the tenth anniversary of his father's death, the prince nearly died of typhoid, and immediately afterward an attempt was made on the Queen's life (the sixth she had endured). John Brown was given a gold medal for apprehending the attacker, whose pistol turned out not to have been loaded; but the wave of sympathy for her rapidly reduced the strength of the republican feeling. Gladstone varied his attack; since the Queen refused to fulfill public engagements, would she allow the Prince of Wales to deputize for her in purely ceremonial duties? He was promptly told that this was "a question which more properly concerns the Queen herself to settle." He suggested again that the prince should go to Ireland as viceroy, and again was refused, leaving Queen and minister on such bad terms that his summer visit to Balmoral was abandoned. Ponsonby noted that the Queen was putting the monarchy in grave danger:

Ministers are getting rapidly reconciled to keeping her well away and in point of fact enjoy the appearance of having all the power in their own hands.

The next year the Queen did consent to entertain the Shah of Persia, in spite of his three wives and an entourage that shocked Gladstone. Her temporary good humor was then dampened by the marriage of her son Alfred to the Grand Duchess Maria, the daughter of the Emperor of Russia. She deeply resented being outranked, and was offended by the Tsarina's suggestion that they should meet in Germany to discuss the wedding. Princess Alice tried to plead her brother's cause, and was answered:

I do not think, dear Child, that you should tell me who have been nearly twenty years longer on the throne than the Emperor of Russia and am the *Doyenne* of Sovereigns and who am a Reigning Sovereign, which the Empress is not,—what I ought to do. How could I who am not like any little Princess ready to run to the slightest call of the mighty Russians—have been able in twenty-four hours to be able to travel!

But the Queen's tantrums were drawing to an end, for in 1874 the Liberal Government fell and Gladstone retired to his estate to cut down trees and endeavor to reconcile Homer with Christianity. Disraeli came to kiss hands on his appointment as prime minister, and noted that she was "wreathed in smiles" and "glided about the room like a bird." The only men Victoria ever fully warmed to were those who acted like lovers to her, and Disraeli, with his rouged face and his curls, exerted to the full (by his own admission) his immense powers of flattery. "Gladstone," he said, "treats the Queen like a public department; I treat her like a woman." It was cynical, but politically justified; the Queen at last began to act again like a Queen.

Perhaps his most brilliant stroke was to proclaim her Empress of India. She now had a son and a daughter (Alfred in Russia, Vicky in the newly united Germany) married into Imperial families, and declared to Ponsonby: "I am an Empress, and in common conversation am sometimes called Empress of India." Politically, the move was of value to Disraeli, who needed to forestall Russian ambitions in India, and though the bill had a difficult passage through Parliament, Victoria was deeply satisfied with her new title. Bertie had secured an Indian tour for himself and was happy, too; the only one who was not pleased was Princess Alexandra, to whom the Queen refused permission to accompany him. When the prince left in October, 1875, Disraeli said that the princess looked as if she were preparing to commit suttee.

Disraeli's whole Eastern policy seemed to be going well. He acquired control of the Suez Canal by buying shares from the bankrupt Khedive of Egypt, and this secured the vital trade route to India. But Turkey at this time was taking a harsh line with her Christian subjects, and Germany, Austria, and Russia formed a league to persuade her into religious tolerance. The move was of course aimed at getting a share of the loot if their opposition should break up the Turkish empire, and Disraeli tried to counter it by sending the British fleet to the Dardanelles. Unfortunately he had chosen the wrong moment to declare himself a defender of the sultan (who was insane anyway), since in 1876 a revolt in Bulgaria, which was then part of Turkey, was put down with fearful severity and twelve thousand Christians were massacred. Gladstone could now safely denounce Disraeli for putting ambition before morality and political expediency before the rule of law and religion. In a pamphlet on the "Bulgarian Horrors," Gladstone wrote characteristically:

There is not a criminal in a European gaol; there is not a cannibal in the South Sea Islands whose indignation would not arise and overboil at the recital of that which has been done, which has too late been examined, but which remains unavenged. No government ever has so sinned; none has proved itself so incorrigible in sin or, which is the same, so impotent in reformation.

He called upon the Russians to drive the Turks out of Bulgaria.

The Queen was shaken, but soon found a satisfactory answer: the Bulgarian rising had been contrived by the Russians to give them an excuse to invade Turkey, and the Russians had been instigated by Mr. Gladstone. She stood defiantly by Disraeli, dined with him at his house, and even consented to open Parliament for him. In April, 1877, the Russians very obligingly took up Gladstone's invitation and declared war on Turkey. Disraeli was in considerable difficulties, struggling to avoid a war on Turkey's behalf, with his cabinet in danger of splitting, and the Queen threatening to abdicate if Russia seized Egypt, and Gladstone daily thundering denunciations on him. However, he struggled on, and steadily the tide of popular feeling turned against Gladstone. The ambitions of Russia were restrained, and in the process England quietly acquired Cyprus. Gladstone denounced the agreement as "an act of duplicity not surpassed and rarely equalled in the history of nations," but Victoria gave her hero the Garter.

Under Disraeli's influence a new Queen was emerging: industrious, politically prejudiced, more tolerant, more confident, a woman who could smoke a cigarette in the presence of her ladies-in-waiting and permit herself to laugh at a dubious joke. Her tolerance was beginning to extend itself toward the Prince of Wales, who in any case had come back from his Indian tour with enhanced prestige, and she drew closer also to Vicky, who herself was having her own troubles with her son, the arrogant young Prince Wilhelm. The Queen even learned to bear sorrow with fortitude, when in November, 1878, her second daughter, Alice, died of diphtheria on the anniversary of Albert's death.

The empire which Disraeli's policies had called into being was presenting its problems, involving wars with the Zulus, the Afghans, and the Ashanti and giving Gladstone a new field for denunciation.

Remember the rights of the savage, as we call him. Remember that the happiness of his humble home, remember that the sanctity of human life in the hill villages of Afghanistan, among the winter snows, is as inviolable in the eyes of Almighty God as can be your own.

If anyone but Gladstone had put forward this argument it is possible that Victoria would have been won over, but from him she dismissed it as politically motivated bombast. In February, 1880, Disraeli decided on an election. Gladstone embarked on a formidable campaign, and, when he won, rejoiced in his victory in words that might well have come from the mouth of Oliver Cromwell: "It seemed as if the Arm of the Lord had bared itself for work that He has made His own." The Queen, who was in Baden Baden, was deeply shocked by the old man's arrogance, and declared:

The Queen will sooner abdicate than send for or have any communication with that half-mad fire-brand who would ruin everything and be a dictator.

But the "fire-brand" had to be sent for, an interview neither of them relished. Gladstone told his wife to pray for him, and was lectured on his past conduct and his lack of respect in public speeches. Disraeli did not long survive his defeat, for his health had been taxed by the Bulgarian crisis, and he died in April, 1881. To Gladstone's astonishment he chose to be buried at his home rather than in Westminster Abbey. Victoria bore his death calmly, and Gladstone did his best to deliver an appropriate parliamentary eulogy. He confessed later that the effort of composing it had brought on an attack of diarrhea.

Little by little, Gladstone contrived to reverse Disraeli's foreign policy. Afghanistan was abandoned, to the Queen's annoyance, and the Transvaal given its independence; with surprising shrewdness Victoria lamented giving the Boers power over the natives: "a most merciless and cruel neighbor and a cruel oppressor." There was even a rumor that Gladstone was going to withdraw from Cyprus, but even he decided that this would be going too far.

He was, in fact, in trouble at home, and the cause was, as always, Ireland. The country was largely controlled by English absentee landlords, against whose greed the only Irish weapon was either sporadic attacks of violence or a system of refusing support, contact, or service to the landlords or their agents. This system was known as boycotting, after its first victim, a Captain Boycott. The Irish now had a brilliant and determined parliamentary leader in Charles Stewart Parnell, who used his small party of Irish Nationalists in the Commons with a skill that played havoc with Gladstone's policies. Gladstone's honest attempts to improve the position of the Irish, in which the Queen was wise enough to join, did not satisfy Parnell, who denounced him as "this masquerading Knight Errant, the pretending champion of the rights of every nation except the Irish nation." A rent strike was declared in Ireland, and Parnell for supporting it was arrested. Recognizing that this would solve nothing, Gladstone secretly negotiated with Parnell, through a certain Captain O'Shea, an agreement by which Parnell would support his Land Act if Gladstone added certain extra concessions to tenants. Parnell was released on May 4, 1882, but on May 5, the lord lieutenant and his under-secretary were assassinated in Dublin, and in the ensuing uproar Gladstone was denounced in the Commons for the secret treaty with Parnell. Ireland was still a luckless country.

Discontent was rife, it seemed, throughout the world. In 1881 Tsar Alexander II was assassinated and in 1882 yet another attempt was made on Victoria's life. The would-be assassin was collared by two boys from Eton, and this time the pistol was loaded; "It is worth being shot at," said the Queen, "to see how much one is loved." The next year John Brown died. Victoria was with difficulty dissuaded from publishing a "little memoir" about him, and had to content herself with dedicating *More Leaves from a Journal of Our Life in the Highlands* to him. Gladstone went on a European tour, and infuriated the Queen by allowing himself to be fêted by the crowned heads of Denmark and Russia.

The Prime Minister, and especially one not gifted with prudence, is not a person who can go about where he likes with impunity.

Constitutionally the Queen was correct, and Gladstone sent a grudging apology and talked of retirement. "The Queen," he said, "is enough to kill any man."

In 1882, to safeguard the Suez Canal and the short route to India, he had reluctantly embarked on an invasion of Egypt, which was disliked by both the Government and the Opposition. More trouble was added to this when a religious fanatic in the Sudan, the Mahdi, slaughtered an army of ten thousand Egyptians under a British commander, and to survey the possibility of a complete withdrawal Gladstone with great unwisdom sent out General Gordon. Gordon was fanatically religious, sexually eccentric, and apt to retire for days into an alcoholic stupor, but because of his courage was a public hero and a great favorite of the Queen. Once in Khartoum he disregarded his orders in playing with ideas of reoccupying the Sudan, got himself cut off by the Mahdi, and telegraphed to Gladstone for reinforcements.

Gladstone was too preoccupied to think of him. He was attempting to extend the suffrage still further with the Third Reform Bill, which the Tories in the Upper House refused to pass. The Queen, whose new good sense was now allied to nearly fifty years of experience, was reluctant to force it through by the creation of Liberal peers, and wrote to Gladstone:

The monarchy would be utterly untenable were there no balance of power left, no restraining power! The Queen will yield to no one in TRUE LIBERAL FEELING, but not to destructive, and she calls upon Mr Gladstone to restrain, as he can, some of his wild colleagues and followers.

With her new industry she set about reconciling the two parties. Gladstone ungratefully embarked on a tub-thumping tour of Scotland to undermine her efforts (his oratory had a magnetic effect in Scotland particularly, where the rhythms of the Old Testament were held to be a sure sign of godliness). He got a stinging rebuke from Balmoral:

The Queen is utterly disgusted with Mr Gladstone's stump oratory—so unworthy of his position—almost under her very nose.

Her efforts prevailed in the end and the bill was passed, Gladstone even expressing his gratitude for her efforts. But their moment of harmony was brief, for Gordon was still beleaguered in Khartoum, and the fact that he had got there in disregard of his orders made no difference to the feelings of Queen or country. When Gladstone did send a relieving force it arrived too late, and the Mahdi took Khartoum and Gordon was killed on January 26, 1885. The Queen sent Gladstone an open telegram, the nearest she could come to a public rebuke:

The news from Khartoum are frightful, and to think that all this might have been prevented and precious lives saved by earlier action is too fearful.

Gladstone's government fell in June.

The Queen was for the time being preoccupied with the deliveries and demands of her by now great brood of grandchildren, but when Lord Salisbury's Tory government was defeated, in January, 1886, on the Irish question, she at first refused to accept his resignation. She wished it to be known, she said that she had "the greatest possible disinclination to take this half-crazy and really in many ways ridiculous old man." She had to take him, but ignored her constitutional duty by corresponding with Salisbury and keeping him informed of all Gladstone's moves. This ministry lasted only a few months, for Gladstone was now convinced that it was his divine mission to settle the Irish question, and the Irish, thus encouraged, made it clear that they would accept nothing short of Home Rule. The Liberals crumbled under the strain, and when the question went to the country the Tories were returned with a decisive majority, and the Queen had Salisbury back in Downing Street.

The next year, 1887, was the fiftieth anniversary of the Queen's accession, and after some reluctance she entered into the celebrations with great energy and bustle. There were medals and presentations, concerts, state openings of everything conceivable, royal visits, services of thanksgiving. The Thanksgiving service in June reminded her of the splendors of the Great Exhibition of 1851, but then she had been a mere Queen; now she was empress of a great and prosperous empire.

Above all she enjoyed the family reunions. The one shadow on these reunions was her anxiety about the health of Vicky's husband, the Crown Prince Friedrich Wilhelm of Germany. In 1888 his father Wilhelm I died and he became emperor, and Victoria wrote:

My OWN dear Empress Victoria it does seem an impossible dream, may God bless her!

It was an impossible dream, for Friedrich was suffering from cancer of the throat. Victoria was on holiday in Florence when she heard that he was ill, and to the outrage of the German chancellor, Bismarck, made straight for Berlin. Bismarck thought she had come to force a political marriage for her granddaughter, and when he discovered that she had no such idea was relieved and surprisingly charmed. He paid her his ultimate compliment, saying, "That was a woman! One could do business with her!" The Emperor Friedrich died on June 15, after a reign of ninety-nine days, and Vicky's arrogant son Wilhelm (whom Victoria loathed) became Kaiser of Germany.

Gladstone, with a tactlessness astounding even in him, declared that it was time for the Queen to abdicate in favor of the Prince of Wales. He was not taken seriously, for no one imagined that the old man would ever hold office again. The only cause that now mattered to him, Home Rule for Ireland, had been shattered by the disgrace of Parnell, whom Captain O'Shea, who had once negotiated with Gladstone on his behalf, cited in his divorce suit against his wife Kitty. Parnell never recovered his influence in politics, and the Liberals, who were largely supported by the nonconformist vote, withdrew their support from him. But in 1892 the Liberals won the general election, and to her profound consternation the Queen had to face Gladstone's fourth ministry. When she first received him they were both leaning on sticks, and "You and I, Mr Gladstone," she said, "are lamer than we used to be." Gladstone said later that the interview was as dismal as that between Marie Antoinette and her executioner. The foreign secretary was Lord Rosebery, and his first act was probably treasonous and certainly sensible; he sent the Prince of Wales the key that unlocked the Foreign Office despatch boxes.

Relations between Queen and prime minister were unimproved.

He listens to no one and won't bear any contradiction or discussion. He is really half crazy, half silly, and it is better not to provoke discussion.

In fact he was so obsessed by Irish Home Rule, which he decisively failed to get Parliament to accept, that he did not notice the opposition that was building against him in his refusal to re-equip the navy. He made a move toward discussing his successor with the Queen (he was now eighty-five), and in reply received a letter accepting his resignation. He could not go back, and the Queen gave him a farewell dinner at Windsor. Mrs. Gladstone was much affected and spoke to the Queen of William's devotion to the crown. It may only have been in relief, but to her credit the Queen kissed her.

Since the Liberals had not been defeated in the House, they continued in office under Lord Rosebery, and the Queen was able to turn her attention to holidays abroad and family affairs. Bertie's eldest son had been betrothed to Princess Mary of Teck, who was a great-granddaughter of George III by way of the Duke of Cambridge, but in 1892 he died, and Princess Mary married his brother George (who was to become King George V). In June, 1894, a son and heir was born to them who was to become Edward VIII. In the same year the Queen heard (to her consternation) that her granddaughter Princess Alix of Hesse, daughter of the dead Princess Alice, was to marry the Crown Prince Nicholas of Russia. Within the year Nicholas had succeeded his father and the rechristened Alexandra was Tsarina; they and their children were all to be murdered at Ekaterinburg in 1917. In 1895 the Liberals, worn out by Gladstone and Irish Home Rule, were defeated in a general election, and Salisbury returned to power with a useful Tory majority. He was to be the Queen's last prime minister.

In September, 1896, Victoria noted with satisfaction that she had now reigned longer than any other British monarch, and in the next year the government decided to make imperial capital out of her Diamond Jubilee.

For Victoria this was her point of greatest achievement. She had shown that, while royal houses throughout Europe were toppling or moribund, the British monarchy could survive with honor and affection from its subjects. She wrote of the state progress to Saint Paul's:

No one ever, I believe, has met with such an ovation as was given to me, passing through those six miles of streets. The cheering was quite deafening, and every face seemed to be filled with real joy.

The next year Gladstone died, nearly ninety. The Queen was indignant that the Prince of Wales and his son George should act as pallbearers at his funeral in the Abbey, but the Prince told her that "at the age of fifty-seven he was old enough to know his own mind." She did at least send a long and gracious telegram to Mrs. Gladstone.

She complained spiritedly about the conduct of the Boer War, which broke out in 1899, and even made a state visit to Ireland, where the cheering marginally drowned the booing. She was now over eighty and very frail; her eyesight had almost gone and she walked only with great difficulty. In January, 1901, she gave up the journal she had kept for all of her life, and with this her vital energy gave out. By the nineteenth of that month it was plain that the seemingly impossible was happening: Queen Victoria was dying. The Prince of Wales was sent for, and her last word was for him. On the twenty-second of January, calmly and peacefully, she died, whispering not "Albert" but "Bertie."

Her massive and elaborate funeral recalled the splendors of the Great Exhibition and the two Jubilees. Most of the thousands who watched it had never known another monarch, and the England in which she died was hardly recognizable as the country to which she had succeeded. She had not been a great Queen nor yet a great woman, allowing her personal preferences to rule her and, in her withdrawal after Albert's death, very nearly bringing the monarchy down. She was no Elizabeth Tudor, but then the nineteenth century was no time for Elizabeth Tudors. The Victorian age had instead had the Queen it deserved.

EDWARD VII
1901–1910

⚘

Born in November 1841.

Eldest son of Queen Victoria and her husband Albert of Saxe-Coburg and Gotha.

Married in 1863 Alexandra of Schleswig-Holstein-Sonderburg-Glückburg (Denmark), who was born in 1844 and died in 1925. Their children were:

Albert Victor Duke of Clarence, born 1864 and died in 1892;

George Duke of York, later King George V;

Louise Victoria, born 1867, married the Duke of Fife;

Victoria, born 1868

Maud, born 1869, married King Haakon VI of Norway;

Died in May 1910.

EDWARD VII

n his nine years on the throne Edward VII left his mark as emphatically as his mother had done in sixty-four years. In a sense the Edwardian Age had begun many years before the sixty-year-old Prince ascended the throne. It was an opulent, self-indulgent, dignified age, confident, slow-moving: an age of brandy and cigars, of long garden parties, of racing at Cowes or Ascot, of strict obedience to a morality that permitted laxity if it were covered by discretion. Above all it was an age of material prosperity and ceremonial pageantry that masked the fact that beneath it all was the abyss. Edward's world was a sunset world for European monarchies, and he was the last of our Kings to live out his reign in the vast aristocratic entanglement of that royal house of Europe whose head had been Queen Victoria.

Edward had been largely shaped by his disastrous upbringing. His education had been a failure, for none of it was made interesting to him. When he went to Oxford he was warned that "the only use of Oxford is that it is a place for study, a refuge from the world and its claims." As for the world and its pleasures, so closely was Edward protected from them that as soon as he could, he fled to them as a refuge from his upbringing. It was said that he would have been a very good boy if he had only been left to himself.

All these faults were compounded by his mother's conduct after Albert's death. Blaming her son for the death, and believing him to be unfit for responsibility, she deliberately deprived him of any political activity that would have prepared him for the business of kingship. When Gladstone mooted the idea of the Queen's abdication at the time of the Jubilee, he was trying to find some way of preparing the Prince for his role before it was too late. When Edward had the temerity to call on Garibaldi, the hero of the Italian fight for unity and independence, the Queen told his comptroller that the prince must take "no step of the slightest political importance" without consulting her.

The style of living the prince devised for himself had certain strong characteristics. The first was the prince's dependence on women. He loved and respected his wife Alexandra, but she could not satisfy his roving appetite. There was a long series of mistresses from wildly varying social positions, yet he insisted upon secrecy and discretion, partly from a genuine sense of dignity and partly because his ingrained fear of his mother had made him secretive. In his world anything was permissible so long as it did not lead to public scandal. (Within this context it was of course not scandalous for the cancan dancer La Goulue to greet him from the stage of the Moulin Rouge with a shout of " 'Ullo, Wales! Are you paying for the champagne?")

The second characteristic was his choice of diversions. He adored the theatre, he enjoyed hunting, he gambled constantly, he smoked heavily and drank and ate with fortitude; horseracing gave him great pleasure, and so did yachting, especially at Cowes, and he was fascinated by military ceremony and splendid uniforms.

His sense of dignity, however, did little to keep him out of trouble, or indeed out of the courts. He had been as early as 1870 involved as a witness in a divorce case, and in 1890 there had been a gambling scandal at Tranby Croft leading to a lengthy trial in which he appeared as witness for the plaintiff. His whole way of life came in for considerable condemnation in court and out of it, and the Queen was quite distraught.

This horrible trial drags on, and it is a fearful humiliation to see the future king of this country dragged (and for the second time) through the dirt, just like anyone else, in a Court of Justice. It is very painful and must do his prestige great harm.

The Kaiser (the son of Edward's eldest sister Vicky) took the opportunity to inform her that it was a disgrace for anyone holding the honorary rank of colonel in the Prussian Hussars to be involved in a scandal of this nature.

Of greater potential danger was the quarrel in the following year with Lord Charles Beresford. Beresford had had an affair with Lady

Brooke, but had been reconciled with his wife; Lady Charles, who had come by a compromising letter from Lady Brooke, instructed her solicitor to warn her that his discretion about the letter depended on her good behavior. Lady Brooke—"Darling Daisy" as she came to be known—was now the mistress of the Prince of Wales, and he chivalrously attempted to help her. When the solicitor refused to destroy the letter, he called upon Lady Charles and was firmly told not to interfere. He cut her out of his society. So powerful was his influence that she had to go abroad. Her husband threatened to expose the prince in the newspapers; the letter was shown to Salisbury (who was then prime minister) before being passed to the prince. Salisbury did his best to mediate, and at length a grudging and formal apology was wrung from the prince, and Darling Daisy's letter was restored to her and burned. The prince wrote in deep grief to Beresford's brother:

I can never forget and shall never forgive the conduct of your brother and his wife towards me. His base ingratitude, after a friendship of about twenty years, has hurt me more than words can say.

The note of naïve innocence is astonishing in a man of fifty. It is as if the prince had never made up the early knowledge denied him by his education.

In 1892 Gladstone succeeded in finding him a job. It was only as a member of the Royal Commission on the Aged Poor, and it did not achieve very much; but he threw himself into it with vigor, attending thirty-five sittings and even canceling his annual trip to the South of France. But most of his public life was still passed in purely formal gatherings. He entertained the Tsarevitch Nicholas at Sandringham, and horrified him by the company he kept and the topics of conversation they preferred; Nicholas wrote in disgust to his mother that the guests were Jews and bankers and horse-dealers. A visit of the Kaiser to Cowes was even less successful. The prince's delight in yachting had enhanced his popularity with the people, but Wilhelm decided to make the annual meeting an opportunity to demonstrate German naval superiority; he sought out the designer of Edward's yacht *Britannia* and persuaded him to build a bigger and better one.

Steadily, however, as inevitably he drew nearer to the throne, the prince did gain prestige. On the death of the tsar he visited St. Petersburg (then the Russian capital); this was the kind of thing he did very well, and he did his best to be kind to the new young Tsar Nicholas and to offset some of the consternation he had caused at Sandringham. He did not, however, share his nephew's lofty and impractical views on world peace and disarmament, writing to Darling Daisy:

It is the greatest rubbish and nonsense I ever heard of. The thing is simply impossible!

He could by no means charm his other Imperial nephew, Kaiser Wilhelm. The arrogant young man was continually turning up at Cowes and goading his uncle into silent but ill-concealed fury. He boasted of German military prowess and made fun of the prince for his lack of experience in battle. Edward (with surprising prescience) referred to him as "the most brilliant failure in history."

On the advice (or command) of his mother he kept a diary. It was a terse and laconic affair, quite devoid of Victoria's underlinings and exclamation points.

16 April 1855 [when he was fourteen]. Arrival of Emperor and Empress of the French. The Emperor is a short person. He has very long moustachios but short fair hair. The Empress is very pretty.

And as a man:

30 June 1897. Drive to Mrs Chamberlain's evening party at Piccadilly, 11.15. Owing to dense crowd, unable to enter house and drive home.

He failed to mention that he had had to get out of his carriage to rescue his daughter, Princess Maud, from an overenthusiastic mob. Nothing seems to have fired him into literary extravagance:

4 April 1900. Arrive at Brussels, 4.50. Walk about station. Just as train is leaving, a man fires a pistol at P of W through open window of carriage. (No harm done.)

When at long last he ascended the throne, he announced that he would style himself Edward VII. Before this he had been known as "Bertie" (apart from some less reverent names such as "Tumtum") after his father, and there was some feeling that he was casting a slur on the memory of the prince consort. However, he assured his council that there could be only one Albert—"who, by universal consent is, I think deservedly, known by the name of Albert the Good." We must admire the ingenuity of this reply. The nation was in some doubt about the kind of monarch it had acquired; the *Times* took it upon itself to remind its readers that their new King had been "importuned by temptation in its most seductive form," and grudgingly admitted that he had "never failed in his duty to the throne and to the nation." Edward showed no sign at all that he was about to change his way of life, and the first London season of his reign was markedly Edwardian in tone.

Salisbury saw no reason to educate this elderly sovereign, and at first ministers appeared to inform the King of their actions rather than of their intentions. A separation of powers had inevitably taken place during Victoria's long reign, since with the growth of the empire, the European entanglements, the rise in population, the expansion of industry, and the great changes in the electoral and administrative systems, government had become a profession. Deference to the monarch could in sheer practicality only be made on major issues of the constitution or critical points of foreign policy; for the rest, the crown had graciously to consent to be a rubber stamp.

Because of his almost total ignorance of affairs of state, the King formed a kind of private council to advise him. Its members between them mustered a good array of talents, and guided the King successfully through affairs that otherwise he would probably have handled as he had handled Darling Daisy's letter. He thoroughly alarmed Salisbury in the first weeks of the reign by informing him that he was going to persuade Rosebery to come back to lead the Liberals, and to rebuke Sir Henry Campbell Bannerman (who was then leading the party) for his criticism of the barbarity of the British army in the Boer War. Salisbury had to explain to his sovereign that such acts were constitutionally impossible.

In June, 1902, the King had a severe attack of appendicitis which led to peritonitis, and to his annoyance the coronation had to be postponed. An operation was successful, and his popularity increased enormously with his recovery. The coronation was held in August and went off in great style and to thunderous applause. Edward paraded himself in front of his delighted grandchildren in his coronation robes, saying, "Good morning, children; am I not a funny-looking old man?" and there was a novel feature of the ceremony in the Abbey in the form of a special stall for the various ladies of the King's entourage; it was most happily christened "the King's Loose Box," and contained, among others, the actress Sarah Bernhardt.

Salisbury had resigned just before the coronation, and Arthur Balfour had taken over the government. The foreign secretary was Lord Lansdowne, whose relations with the King were immediately strained almost to breaking-point by the riotous affair of the state visit of the Shah of Persia. The shah had been reluctant to come, and Lansdowne had only brought him by making him a Knight of the Garter. Edward in a rage told Lansdowne that the Garter was a Christian order and could not be bestowed on a heathen. (The fact that Victoria had given it to the shah's father made no difference to him.) Lansdowne desperately proposed a special order for non-Christians, and the shah, who by now had arrived and discovered what was happening, angrily returned a miniature of the King in gold and diamonds Edward had sent him. Edward was so angry that when Lansdowne sent him the designs for the new order he pitched them through the porthole of the royal yacht, and wrote to Lansdowne:

If the Shah leaves the country in the sulks, like a spoilt child, because he cannot get what he wants, it cannot be helped.

The shah did precisely that, and it was only when Balfour represented to the King that "We have a very difficult game to play in Persia and Russia has most of the cards" that Edward gave way and the shah got his order, unpaganized.

The King had two meetings with his detested nephew the kaiser, one in Berlin and one at Sandringham in 1902; neither was successful, and the kaiser's plans for an Anglo-German alliance were abandoned. "Thank God he's gone," said Edward when Wilhelm left England. He himself then left on a European tour that was to be a constant nightmare for poor Lansdowne. He refused to take a cabinet minister with him, seeing no reason why he should be told whom he could or could not see. In Rome he proposed to visit the Pope, and in spite of objections (Lansdowne was afraid of the effect in Ireland) persisted and made a great success of the visit. He was delighted to have scored over the kaiser, who had twice visited Rome without being granted an audience with the Pope. He was invited to visit Paris on his way home, and again Lansdowne had misgivings and again had to stifle them. The French were cool on the King's arrival, for England was violently unpopular, but by his steady calm, courtesy, and charm Edward broke down their resistance, and by the end of his visit he was greeted at the Paris Opera with cheering and cries of "Good old Teddy!" It seemed as if, single-handed, he had brought about a new understanding with France—the *Entente Cordiale*, as it was called—and the agreement signed with France in April, 1904, would not have been possible without the King's initial courting of French public opinion.

His way of doing things on his own did not always have such happy results. His attempts to remain incognito often ended in disaster, since while he enjoyed pretending to be an ordinary citizen he was not prepared to put up with the attendant disadvantages; he would force his way first into a lift, and once his impatience at the service in a German restaurant made him so conspicuous that the band turned out and played *God Save the King*.

The subjects he concerned himself in were chosen for his own reasons. Abstract problems bored him, but he responded at once to any human situation. One matter he did enter into with great effect was the reform of the War Office. His only regret as the work steadily progressed was the sacrifice of the traditional scarlet uniforms to the more practical khaki.

His preoccupation with military affairs was fully justified, for in Europe every month brought the kaiser nearer to a European war and the tsar nearer to revolution. King and kaiser clashed wherever the kaiser chose to make a show of power, and the Anglo-Japanese alliance (sanctioned by the award of the Garter to the Shinto emperor of Japan) did nothing to increase England's accord with Russia, who was soon to enter into the Russo-Japanese War.

Balfour's Tory ministry fell in December, 1905, and Edward had to send for the Liberal Campbell Bannerman, though he considered him too old and too ineffectual. Edward's real fear was that the reform that must inevitably follow a Liberal revival would revive also the old trouble about the House of Lords. It did; the Education Bill, designed to set up a system of state education, was rejected in the Upper House. No more action was taken at the time, but Campbell Bannerman's words were ominous:

A way must be found by which the will of the people, expressed through their elected representatives in this House, will be made to prevail.

The arms race in Europe continued, led by the kaiser's passion to build up the German navy to an unopposable strength. Against stiff opposition Edward encouraged a major program of naval expansion.

In January of 1907, the King and Queen together visited Paris.

Under the somewhat unlikely incognito of the Duke and Duchess of Lancaster, they stayed in the British Embassy, and the Queen greatly enjoyed her husband's now habitual way of dining out in public restaurants. They walked arm in arm along the boulevards and rejoiced in their freedom. They did, however, find time for more formal business, strengthening the *entente* with the French president and advancing English popularity in France.

For a man whose preoccupations were generally supposed to be those of the bed and the field, Edward showed a surprising enthusiasm for the arts. His pleasure in the theatre was not confined to dancers and chorus girls; during the season he was continually in his box at Covent Garden, and was a particular admirer of Wagner's operas. When his ministers were much concerned with the project of the Nile barrage, the King was the single person to be worried that this would drown "that beautiful relic of Egyptian history," the temple of Philae.

Having at their disposal a monarch who, unlike Victoria, took a positive pleasure in public appearances and travel, the government began to make that diplomatic use of the royal presence which has in our time become an accepted part of the monarch's life. Where a disaffected province needed appeasing, a foreign entanglement sorting out, a foreign ruler soothed and cajoled, the King was inevitably sent and generally went with a good grace. His remarkable outward affability and charm maintained accord in Europe throughout years when most of his fellow sovereigns seemed concerned only to exploit savagely their petty differences. As the French alliance grew more assured, an anti-British campaign, inspired by the kaiser, was mounted in the German press. Edward patiently did what little he could to keep his nephew calm, inviting him to Windsor and expressly refusing to discuss politics. He visited the aged and formidable Emperor Franz Josef of Austria, and to everyone's relief got on famously with him.

Yet, as always in this delicately balanced Europe, when relations with one power had been strengthened there was another to be appeased. In pursuit of this, the kaiser was invited on yet another state visit to England. At first he petulantly pleaded ill health, but was finally persuaded to come, and, to outward view, the visit was a conspicuous triumph. Possibly to spare himself the tedium of actually having to talk to his nephew, the King had planned for Wilhelm a succession of magnificent banquets, hunting parties, visits to the theatre, reviews, concerts, and displays. The kaiser disconcerted his hosts only once, when he boasted of the way in which he had personally planned Lord Roberts's strategy in the Boer War. But it was all in vain; by the next year, when he had seen that the Anglo-Russian alliance was growing in strength, the kaiser had relapsed into his usual anglophobia. He gave an interview to an American journalist in which he denounced Edward's personal corruption and England's general perfidy, and announced that a war between the two countries was inevitable. The German foreign office was horrified and hastily prevailed upon the kaiser to issue a denial; but Edward was not deceived.

I know the Emperor hates me, and never loses an opportunity of saying so (behind my back), whilst I have always been nice and civil to him. As regards my visit to Berlin, there is no hurry to settle anything at present. The Foreign Office, to gain their own object, will not care a pin what humiliation I have to put up with.

(The language is still that of the schoolboy.)

In October, 1908, there occurred an incident which in its complexity was an evil portent for the future. Without warning Austria announced that she was annexing to her empire the two Turkish provinces of Bosnia and Herzegovina. Turkey was in no position to object, but these provinces had been coveted by the Slav kingdom of Serbia, and, in this Serbia was supported by Russia, who as the greatest Slav power disliked Germanic domination in Slav lands. The situation was further complicated by an extraordinary mistake of the Russian ambassador to Britain, who thought it was all part of a secret bargain between Russia and Austria leading to Russia's old aim, control of the Dardanelles. Edward felt a personal obligation to protect the ambassador, and patiently pursued compromise until Tsar Nicholas had agreed neither to dismiss the ambassador nor to pursue the Bosnian issue. European war was averted, but the ambiguous situation of the Balkan provinces, Germanic by domination but Slav by preference, still remained; and in this crisis the neurotically aggressive kaiser had not been concerned. It was Edward's view that the European powers were afraid of war; but their fears made them involve themselves in ever more complex webs of alliances offensive and defensive.

In February, 1909, Edward reluctantly visited Berlin. He did his best to put his charm and tact to good use, but he was tired and unwell and could not miss the plain signs that the kaiser meant to push Austria into a war with Serbia. He wrote:

Unless the military party at Vienna is too strong, I hope that war with Serbia may yet be avoided, for Austria will gain nothing by attacking Serbia. We may safely look on Germany as our bitterest foe, as she hardly attempts to conceal it.

He returned from trouble abroad to trouble at home. In 1908 Campbell Bannerman had died and been succeeded (with no change of party) by Asquith, who had resolved to attack the power of the House of Lords. The chancellor, Lloyd George, had proposed a land tax, because money was badly needed for defense, and (as he observed) "A fully-equipped duke costs as much as two dreadnoughts." Like Victoria and William IV before him, Edward tried to preserve the Lords by persuading them to pass the measure. He failed; the Lords rejected it by a massive majority, and Parliament was dissolved. In the following general election the Liberals were returned, but with a weakened majority. Edward was still searching for a viable compromise when the state of his health led his doctors to advise a recuperative spell in Biarritz. Asquith assured him that no crisis would take place while he was away, and he consented to go. In his absence Asquith formulated a measure forbidding the Lords to reject any finance bill and restricting their right to reject any measure passed by the Commons in three successive sessions. It was a combative measure, and in April, 1910, the King came back from Biarritz ready to play his own peacemaking part in the struggle. He did not have to; he had a series of heart attacks and on May 6 fell into a coma. The last entry he ever made in his diary was "The King dines alone," and his last conscious words were in answer to the news that one of his race-horses had won: "I am very glad." He died late that night, and his son George wrote:

I have lost my best friend and the best of fathers. I never had a cross word with him in my life. I am heart-broken and over whelmed with grief.

It was a good end, brought about by a man who had had every excuse to let his own good-heartedness be soured, to the Hanoverian hostility between King and heir. Edward VII was the only British monarch of the House of Saxe-Coburg and Gotha. His descendants were to call themselves the House of Windsor.

House of

WINDSOR

GEORGE V 1910–1936.

Born in 1865.
Second son of King Edward VII and his wife Alexandra
of Denmark.
Married in 1893 Princess Mary (May) of Teck, great-
granddaughter of George III by his own Adolphus
Duke of Cambridge.
Among their children were:

EDWARD VIII January–December 1936.

Born in 1894.
Abdicated December 1936, and on June 3, 1937 married Mrs. Wallis Warfield, formerly Simpson;

GEORGE VI 1936–1952.

Born in 1895.
Succeeded upon the abdication of his brother Edward
VIII.
Married in 1923 Lady Elizabeth Bowes-Lyon, daugh-
ter of the Earl of Strathmore, who was born in 1900.
Their children were:

ELIZABETH II 1952–

Born in 1926.
Married in 1947 Philip Mountbatten Duke of
Edinburgh, formerly Prince Philip of Greece, son
of Prince and Princess Andrew of Greece and
great-great-grandson of Queen Victoria by her second daughter Alice.

Their children are:

Charles Prince of Wales, born in 1948, Heir Apparent, Anne, born in 1950, married in 1973 Mark Phillips,
Andrew, born in 1960, and
Edward, born in 1964;

Margaret, born in 1930, who in 1960 married Antony Armstrong Jones Earl of Snowden, and had two children:

Viscount Linley, born in 1961, and Lady Sarah Armstrong Jones, born in 1964.

As a result of the First World War King George V dropped the German surname (inherited from Albert, Prince Consort of Queen Victoria) of Saxe-Coburg-Gotha, and took that of Windsor, after the royal castle of that name in Berkshire.

HOUSE OF
WINDSOR

At the funeral of King Edward VII there were gathered the Kaiser of Germany, the King of Belgium, the Archduke Franz Ferdinand of the Austrian Empire, the Dowager Empress of Russia, President Theodore Roosevelt of the United States of America, and the Foreign Minister of the French Republic. Four years later the First World War broke out, and when it ended very little indeed was to remain of the spirit of those first years of the twentieth century, and very few of the royal and imperial guests were to survive unharmed.

Anyone familiar with the history of Europe in the reign of Edward VII will find great gaps in the last chapter. Where was Lord Grey, whose patience as foreign secretary removed so many causes of friction between England and Germany? The Agadir crisis, where once again Europe was on the brink of war, this time between Germany and France? The Anglo-French and Anglo-Russian alliance, which English public opinion would not permit as firm treaties of mutual defense?

In those great matters Edward VII took no personal part. He used his influence where he could, but in anything else he had no power; government had at last slipped out of the hands of the British monarchs into the hands of ministers and Parliament. This is why, when Europe emerged from the satanic darkness of the First World War nine years after Edward's death, of the royalty who had attended his funeral only his son survived with his royalty, and his hold on his subjects' loyalty, unscathed.

George V looked remarkably like his father, though on a smaller scale. He was forty-five at the time of his accession, and inevitably had not his father's influence; nor had he Good Old Teddy's common touch, being stiffer, shyer, and very much less fond of the gay life. He let the life of smart society continue under its own impetus, for his interests were those of the country gentleman. His favorite home was Sandringham in Norfolk, which was a typical and not markedly royal country house of the time, but he preferred it for the shooting, not for frivolous diversions with which his father had so shocked Tsar Nicholas of Russia; he was a very fine marksman, for many years the finest in England. By his wife, Princess Mary of Teck, he had six children, born between 1894 and 1905: the Prince of Wales, who had been christened with a string of names including Albert and all four patron saints of England, Wales, Scotland and Ireland but was known in the family as David, a gay and handsome boy; the Duke of York, another Albert, a shy boy because he had a difficult stammer; the Princess Royal, Mary, who was to mark the difference in royalty by marrying an English peer, the Earl of Harewood, and living a quiet life with her family; and three more boys, Henry Duke of Gloucester, Edward Duke of Kent, and little Prince John who was to die in 1919.

There was little that the King could do during the war; which is not to say that he was idle, for by now the crown was an integral part of the administrative machine, and the monarch was as necessary as ministers for the day-to-day running of the country—a kind of labor that would surely have damped even the ambitions of a Charles I. England at last had a thoroughly constitutional King. The ceremonial took on a less splendid and more personal note; the Queen's energies went—again personally—into nursing and war charities, and the Princess Royal trained as a volunteer nurse. The Prince of Wales, who was twenty in 1914, joined the Grenadier Guards, and made a considerable nuisance of himself to be allowed to fight. It did not matter, he said, if he were killed, since he had four brothers, but it would have mattered if he had been captured, and he was kept away from the front; but his spirit made him, and the monarchy, more popular.

By the end of the war the Kaiser of Germany was in shameful refuge in Holland, the Austrian empire was broken up into small states and the Hapsburgs exiled, the revolution had come to Russia and the Romanovs were dead. All three rulers had jealously kept power in their own hands, suppressing or disrgarding the signs that their people were tired of them. Only in Great Britain had the monarchy become one part of the immensely complex system of representative government.

In the years after the war George V proved himself an inconspicuous monarch, carrying out his constitutional and ceremonial duties punctiliously but otherwise living the quiet life he preferred. The principle was now accepted that the crown was "above politics," and the King, as nominal head of the government, was "advised" by his ministers and had very little actual power. His influence on ministers, however, could still be felt, and because of the continuity of his position and experience it tended to be exercised on the side of moderation and compromise.

The love of society shown by Edward VII had been inherited by the Prince of Wales, but not his sense of discretion. The discretion was exhibited more by the British press, though in America there was often criticism of his taste for "unsuitable" companions. In 1928 the King had a serious illness, and the prince had to give up some of his amusements to deputize for his father. There was even a mild word of criticism in a London paper that he would "rightly interpret the wishes of the nation" if he settled to a little work. All that he had done so far was to undertake some overseas tours and interest himself in the unemployed. This made him popular in some quarters, but his interest had no material result, genuine though it was.

In 1935 there fell George V's Jubilee, and it brought a spontaneous surge of popular affection for him and the Queen that seems to have surprised him more than anyone. It was the first sign of that steady esteem the people were ready to develop for their monarchs as soon as they had rendered them harmless. It was George V who started the habit of making a royal broadcast on Christmas Day (a habit his granddaughter still keeps up, though she uses television); his style was that of a distant but affectionate grandfather, responding a little rustily to an affection he had not expected.

This affection was soon to be shaken; though what then seemed a constitutional crisis now appears unimportant, except that it brought to the throne a King more suitable than the Prince of Wales. In January, 1936, George V died at the age of seventy, much lamented; he was called "a squire rather than a King," and was said to have left the monarchy at a higher standard of respectability and popularity than ever before.

When the Prince of Wales succeeded George V he announced his resolve to "follow in the way my father has set before me"; yet among court and government many people already suspected that abdication was in his mind.

In London society some years before he had met a Mr. and Mrs. Ernest Simpson. Both had previously been divorced, and divorced persons were not received at court. This was not a moral but a constitutional matter, since the King was head of the Church, and the Church did not sanction divorce. Both Mr. and Mrs. Simpson were Edward's guests during the following years, and though many people knew the position, there were no comments in the British press. On May 27, 1936, the names of Mr. and Mrs. Simpson appeared in the Court Circular as guests of the King at dinner; in July that of Mrs. Simpson appeared alone. In the intervening months she had brought a divorce action against her husband on the ground of adultery. It was heard in an out-of-the-way court and not fully reported, and at the end the judge made the unenthusiastic remark "Well, I suppose I must come to the conclusion that there was adultery," and granted the decree (which would not be absolute for six months).

For the next few months there was pleasurable speculation in the country at large about which eligible princess would be the next Queen; the youngest royal brother, the Duke of Kent, had not long since married the charming and elegant Princess Marina of Greece, and there was a taste for royal weddings. Edward, however, spent most of his time around the Mediterranean, with Mrs. Simpson and a party of their own set; if he was preparing to do battle for what he wanted he was not much troubling to find himself supporters.

In October, 1936, Prime Minister Stanley Baldwin at last spoke to the King; he was a man of strict morals, himself married for forty years, but not unsympathetic. He warned the King of the danger of gossip, and the King said, "You and I must settle this matter together." A week later he sent for him and said, "I am going to marry Mrs. Simpson and I am prepared to go."

He was not as prepared as he said; a few days later he again sent for Baldwin and asked if it would be possible for him to marry Mrs. Simpson morganatically (a Continental custom of marriage whereby the lady became wife but not queen, and her children had no rights of succession). This at once changed the situation between Edward and Baldwin; they were no longer consulting privately but raising a constitutional question, which was a matter for Parliament and would also have to go to the dominion prime ministers. On December 2, Baldwin told the King that after consultations he was of the opinion that no such legislation would be acceptable. It was open to the King then to dismiss Baldwin, dissolve Parliament, and take his chance that a general election would return a House less concerned with religious and constitutional traditions. He chose not to, leaving at once for his private home and bearing his defeat—if it was a defeat —with dignity. Baldwin said, "I honor and respect him for the way he behaved at that time."

The matter was thus quite briefly settled, though press and public comment went on for a long time, a great deal of it not very relevant. Two London newspapers, both enemies of Baldwin, pronounced abdication to be "out of the question because of the mischief that would ensue." The Abdication Bill was passed without opposition. This is the document on which it is based:

I, Edward the Eighth, of Great Britain, Ireland, and the British Dominions beyond the seas, King, Emperor of India, do hereby announce My irrevocable determination to renounce the Throne for Myself and for My descendants, and My desire that effect should be given to this Instrument of Abdication immediately. In token whereof I have hereunto set My hand this tenth day of December, nineteen hundred and thirty-six, in the presence of the witnesses whose signatures are subscribed.

Edward R. I.

The witnesses signed *Albert, Henry, George;* they were the King's three brothers, the Dukes respectively of York, Gloucester, and Kent. In his last public act in Great Britain, Edward said in a broadcast to his people:

This decision has been made less difficult for me by the knowledge that my brother, with his long training in the public affairs of this country, and with his fine qualities, will be able to take my place forthwith. And he has one matchless blessing, enjoyed by so many of you and not bestowed on me, a happy home with his wife and children. During these hard days I have been comforted by Her Majesty my mother and by my family. The Ministers of the Crown, and in particular Mr Baldwin, the Prime Minister, have always treated me with full consideration. There has never been any constitutional difference between me and them and between me and Parliament.

It was a generous farewell to a life he had most likely never wanted. A sourer note, which its author would no doubt have described as Christian, was struck by Cosmo Lang, the Archbishop of Canterbury:

From God he had received a sacred trust. Yet by his own will he had surrendered the trust for private happiness. Even more strange and sad it is that he should have sought his happiness in a manner inconsistent with the Christian principles of marriage and within a social circle whose standards and ways of life are alien to all the best instincts and traditions of his people. Let those who belong to this circle know that today they stand rebuked by the judgement of the nation.

This was a shocking piece of uncharitable arrogance; but there was a tiny grain of truth at the end of it, though it did not become apparent for many years, and under the unconscious influence of Edward's brother and his matchless blessings. As anyone who lived through those years will remember, the majority of the people ignored the constitutional and religious aspects of the problem. Quite simply, they did not like Mrs. Simpson. They objected to the number of her divorces far less than to the hole-and-corner fashion of the second; and while they tolerated a King who enjoyed himself expensively so long as he did his duty as King, they had a stubborn distrust of a lady whose whole life had been expensive enjoyment. The years of the Depression were not forgotten; the great majority of the people earned every penny they spent, and by now they were used to royal ladies who carried out their public duties, worked for charities, and brought up their children.

And, of course, once Edward Duke of Windsor—as his brother King George VI at once created him—had slipped quietly out of England, there was no life possible for him but the self-indulgent way that was to be so very unsuited to the coming years. He married Mrs. Simpson when her divorce decree was made absolute, and the two of them behaved with perfect dignity and propriety; but they were useless members of a society that was soon to see uselessness as a moral evil.

The former Duke of York, with his Duchess and his two pretty little girls, was just the man to fulfil what the people now wanted of the royal family. He was a small man, with the Hanoverian features grouped pleasantly; he looked ill-at-ease on formal occasions, and it was known that he suffered from a stammer that made him shy;

when he had to make his first Christmas broadcast his obvious efforts to conquer this stammer brought him immense sympathy. His Queen, a sweet-faced plump little woman, had been born Lady Betty Bowes-Lyon, of a Scottish family of immense antiquity but unassuming ways; gossip said that she had at first been reluctant to marry the Duke of York because she did not want a great position. Their two daughters, Elizabeth, born in 1926, and Margaret Rose, four years younger, were what every English mother wanted her daughters to be. Best of all, apart from the usual royal ceremonial duties they had lived the life of a modest country family. The sympathy of the country was entirely with them.

It was to become even more so. Three years after the abdication came the Second World War, when for the first time in history the whole of the people were involved as one. For the monarchy it was a time of triumph, though, with its insistence that the King and Queen, like everyone else, had no more than five inches of hot water in their baths, it was wholly unlike any other triumph. After the fall of France in 1940 the King stayed in England (the few remaining European royalties had had to escape the German invasions). They did not even do what a few wealthy people were doing and send their children to America. It was said that the Queen had remarked in astonishment at this proposal, "But they couldn't go without me, and of course I couldn't leave the King." They stayed in London during the air-raids, they ate the meager rations of the people, they bought their new clothes with the sparse clothing-coupons issued by the government. (You could see clearly the marks where the little girls had had the hems of their dresses let down.) When universal conscription came in for men and women, Princess Elizabeth joined the women's branch of the army at the proper age. (It is said that she can still take down the engine of a car.)

When the war ended, public affection for the King and Queen was deep, but interest began to shift to the two princesses. There is something endearing still about the photographs taken of them in those gray years; clothes were still rationed, and they wear plain skimpy dresses and blossom out into gay flowered hats. Two years after the end of the war, when Princess Elizabeth was twenty-one, it was announced that she was to marry Philip, son of Prince and Princess Andrew of Greece. The times were long past when politically-suitable princes were picked out years in advance; this couple met socially and settled the marriage themselves, with the bride's parents insisting on some months' delay to be sure she knew her own mind.

Her choice was still politically suitable, for Prince Philip, while a descendant of Queen Victoria, was of a family distinguished by more than birth and had himself served with capability in the Royal Navy. Queen Victoria's second daughter Princess Alice Grand Duchess of Hesse-Darmstadt (mother of the murdered Tsarina of Russia) had another daughter, Victoria, who married Prince Louis of Battenburg. Of their four children, Alice married Prince Andrew of Greece, Louise King Gustav of Sweden, and George and Louis settled in England, taking the Anglicized version of their family name, Mountbatten. When, just before his marriage, Prince Philip adopted British nationality, it was under the sponsorship and name of his youngest uncle, then Lord Mountbatten of Burma. He was a tall, spare young man, three years older than the princess, personable, agreeable, with a confidence that suggested the naval officer rather than the prince. The wedding, on November 20, 1947, was on a scale suiting the times, and Lieutenant Philip Mountbatten, R.N., was raised to the peerage as the Duke of Edinburgh. On November 14, 1948 their first child, Charles, was born, and two years later their only daughter, Anne.

This was the great period of the royal gossip writers, and for a time the effect was a little sickening. It is curious to contrast the occasion of the birth of Prince Charles, all sentiment and details about christening-robes, with the passions surrounding the births of other heirs in other centuries. No one in 1948 had to thank God that the succession was secured.

In 1951 there was a celebration of the anniversary of the Great Exhibition of 1851. It was not quite "the greatest day in our history, the most beautiful and imposing and touching spectacle ever seen," as Queen Victoria had written of the 1851 Exhibition, but it was a brave attempt to deny the pessimism of those days. Photographs of the King opening the exhibition show him as haggard in spite of his smiles, and it was at this time that he experienced the symptoms of his final illness, but concealed them to allow the exhibition to proceed undimmed. On February 6, 1952, he died with great suddenness. It was a curious day in England, the more so because the B.B.C. closed down and for some hours the news was passed round by word of mouth. The event was of no public importance, and yet people behaved as if something valuable had been lost. As indeed it had; this shy stammering man, not very clever, devoted to his quite ordinary family, conscientiously taking up a duty he did not want, had given his people something of great value.

And so we come to the present Queen Elizabeth II. She was twenty-six on her accession, and had been Heiress Presumptive for sixteen years and educated to the throne. As a girl she once said that she would like to be "a lady living in the country with dogs and horses"; like her father and grandfather, her tastes are for country sports (she is said to have a good eye for a steeplechaser), and her way of life outside London is that of any well-to-do busy mother. With the memory of Queen Victoria still fresh, the people retain a gratitude to her that she has stayed handsome and lively, with her still athletic husband who is occasionally too outspoken in his public utterances, and her children following the usual course of British education. Ten years after Princess Anne, Prince Andrew was born, and four years later Prince Edward. The Prince of Wales went to public school, to university, and then into the armed forces. Princess Anne, after a normal schooling, followed her talent for horsemanship, and in 1973 married a commoner, Captain Mark Philips, a professional soldier and a rider of international standard. He remains a commoner, which increases the liking of the people for Princess Anne, who is a strong-minded young woman who can do something that is dependent not on her royalty but on her own capabilities. The people have long since tired of Princess Margaret, the Queen's sister, who was once a favorite of theirs; they see her now as an expensive lady who married a commoner but let him be ennobled by an absurd title. In contrast, the son of George V's daughter, Lord Harewood, who has had a thoroughly professional career as a musical impresario, is hardly thought of as a member of the royal family. Some years ago the courtesy titles of Prince and Princess were restricted to the descendants of the monarch alone, so that, while the children increase in the royal family, the titles decrease, and unobtrusively the younger ones are going out to earn their own livings. Royal blood will soon be doing the cooking and driving the children to school in the suburbs. But the monarchy itself?

It has been part of the political, spiritual, social, and legal system of England for over nine hundred years: if we count those Anglo-Saxon Kings who determined the spirit William I could not suppress and the laws he was glad to preserve, for long past a thousand years. For it to fall there would have to be a change so violent that the laws and constitution of the country would be torn apart to be rid of it. You do not tear apart the work of a thousand years without wrecking it, and the English have never taken kindly to wholesale wrecking. Nor, now, do they need to. They have deprived their Kings of all power to harm them, they have taught them manners, and in return allowed themselves to be taught too. If the Kings do their job, the people will allow them the perquisites of royalty; if they are immoral, arrogant, or lazy, the people will withdraw their affection and support. But there is more than this businesslike arrangement to the relationship between the Kings and the people of England.

In the time of Harold Godwinson, who died where the high altar of the Abbey of Battle now stands, the King was made different from his fellows at the moment when he was crowned; at that moment, they believed, God hallowed him as King. When it became plain that God's choice of Kings was too poor to tolerate, the English people still retained their instinct that a King was a King only by reason of his hallowing by the consent of his people. While he retains that consent, he has the right to a loyalty too deep to be withdrawn for any but the most fundamental of reasons.

The King reigns but does not rule. He represents to the people of England the continuing presence of their own power in the constitution; by his very permanence he is the symbol of the impermanence of politicians, and by his stability the reminder to them that their business is not their own power but the well-being of his people.

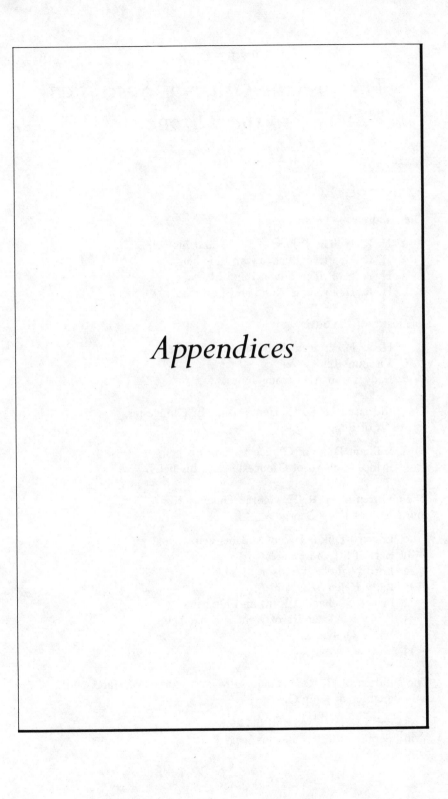

Appendices

The Present Order of Succession to the Throne

❁

The children of the Sovereign:

   1. H. R. H. The Prince of Wales and his heirs.
   2. H. R. H. Prince Andrew and his heirs.
   3. H. R. H. Prince Edward and his heirs.
   4. H. R. H. Princess Anne and her heirs.

The sister of the Sovereign:

   5. H. R. H. Princess Margaret and her heirs,
   6. Viscount Linley, &
   7. Lady Sarah Armstrong Jones.

The children of H. R. H. Henry Duke of Gloucester, third son of King George V:

   8. William Duke of Gloucester and his heirs.
   9. Prince Richard of Gloucester and his heirs.

The children of H. R. H. George Duke of Kent, fourth son of King George V:

   10. Edward Duke of Kent and his heirs,
   11. Earl of St Andrews, &
   12. Lord Nicholas Windsor, &
   13. Lady Helen Windsor.
   14. Prince Michael of Kent and his heirs.
   15. Princess Alexandra of Kent and her heirs,
   16. James Ogilvie &
   17. Marina Ogilvie.

The children of H. R. H. Princess Mary Countess of Harewood, only daughter of King George V:

   18. Earl of Harewood and his heirs.
   19. Gerald Lascelles and his heirs.

British Ministries
1770–1914

☉

1770	North (Tory)	1852	Derby (Conservative)
1782	Rockingham (Whig)	1852	Aberdeen (Liberal)
1782	Shelburne (Whig)	1855	Palmerston (Whig)
1783	North and Charles James Fox (Coalition)	1858	Derby (Conservative)
		1859	Palmerston (Liberal)
1783	Pitt (Tory)	1865	Russell (Liberal)
1801	Addington (Tory)	1866	Derby (Conservative)
1804	Pitt (Tory)	1868	Gladstone (Liberal)
1806	Ministry of All the Talents (Coalition)	1874	Disraeli (Conservative)
		1880	Gladstone (Liberal)
1807	Portland (Tory)	1885	Salisbury (Conservative)
1809	Spencer Perceval (Tory)	1886	Gladstone (Liberal)
1812	Liverpool (Tory)	1886	Salisbury (Conservative)
1827	Canning (Tory)	1892	Gladstone (Liberal)
1828	Wellington (Tory)	1894	Rosebery (Liberal)
1830	Grey (Whig)	1895	Salisbury (Unionist)
1834	Melbourne (Whig)	1902	Balfour (Unionist)
1834	Peel (Conservative)	1905	Campbell Bannerman (Liberal)
1835	Melbourne (Whig)		
1841	Peel (Conservative)	1908	Asquith (Liberal)
1846	Lord John Russell (Whig)		

Party groupings, particularly in earlier years, are only approximately indicated.

The Tory Party, turning to more liberal policies during the Ministry of Liverpool, was officially the Conservative Party by the time of Peel's first Ministry.

The Whig Party was joined after 1846 by the Peelites, who had left the Tory Party to follow Peel, and the two amalgamated to form the Liberals.

Reading List

❁

This list is meant as a first help for anyone who would like to read in more detail about any one monarch and his times. To be even reasonably full on such a stretch of time as that covered by this book is plainly impossible, but I have tried to name at least one authoritative book on each monarch, and anyone who wants more information will find it in the specialized bibliographies there.

As a matter of interest, I have mentioned also the chief of the contemporary or near-contemporary documents I have consulted. In the earlier reigns these are sometimes not easily available to the general reader, being untranslated, out-of-print, or contained in the papers of historical societies, and in the later reigns there is too much material to list it all. In both cases the documents need a fair amount of knowledge of the period to yield their full interest, and are often unreliable or overly partisan.

For the sake of brevity I have omitted the constant references to State papers. They are of the greatest importance, but anyone consulting them is already too much of a specialist to need guidance from me.

Finally, I have omitted also, since they do not bear directly on the subject of this book, any references to the literature of the periods. Contemporary references to reigning monarchs are notoriously unreliable, but *The Canterbury Tales* (translated from Middle English), *The Paston Letters,* the literature of the Elizabethan age, and the novels of Thackeray and Dickens tell more about their times than many merely adequate histories.

For the background, G. M. Trevelyan's *History of England* gives a full account with much economic and social information, and can usefully be supplemented by the same author's *Illustrated English Social History.* H. A. L. Fisher's *History of Europe* (which includes England) gives the necessary European background.

The history of the real Arthur (if there ever was such a king) is still in the hands of the archaeologists. An early version of the legend is in Geoffrey of Monmouth's *Historia Regum Britanniae,* but the greatest early work, as well as the accepted form of the complete legend, is Sir Thomas Malory's *Morte d'Arthur.* Richard Barber, in *King Arthur in Legend and History,* has an interesting account of other versions. There is a history of King Alfred by his contemporary, Bishop Asser, and the standard modern account will be found in F. M. Stenton's *Anglo-Saxon England.*

The outstanding modern authority on the Normans is David C. Douglas *(William the Conqueror, The Norman Heritage)*. Duncan Grinnell-Milnes has written an interesting investigation of William II's death *(The Killing of William Rufus)*, and Hope Muntz's remarkably vivid novel of the Conquest, *The Golden Warrior*, deserves mention here because it is vouched for by G. M. Trevelyan. Of the contemporary evidence, the non-specialist reader will find great interest in the Bayeux Tapestry, which is graphic even without translation of the captions. The most valuable chronicle is the *Anglo-Saxon Chronicle*, a collection of annals kept by monks in several centers; the first part may have been inspired or even written by Alfred the Great. It continues to the year 1154 (in the Peterborough Ms). William of Malmesbury *(Gesta Regum Anglorum* and its sequel *Historia Novella)* is the most reliable of the chroniclers of his own time, as well as most readable, and the other standard chronicler is Ordericus Vitalis *(Historia Ecclesiastica)*. Henry of Huntingdon's *Historia Anglorum* is not altogether reliable, and the *Gesta Stephani,* an anonymous chronicle of Stephen's life, breaks off dispiritedly in the middle of a sentence in 1147.

Shortly after this book was written, W. L. Warren published his monumental *Henry II,* which must remain the standard biography for many years to come. There is a shorter biography by Richard Barber *(Henry Plantagenet)*. The contemporary authorities are Giraldus Cambrensis, Walter Map, William of Malmesbury again, and (the best of them) William of Newburgh *(Historia Rerum Anglicarum)*. Many modern writers have been attracted to Henry II, among them T. S. Eliot, Christopher Fry, and Jean Anouilh, but the results have been more literary than historical.

Since Richard I's short reign was so largely taken up by his Crusade and its aftermath, Steven Runciman's *History of the Crusades* is useful; the contemporary sources here are the *Itinerarum Regis Ricardi* of unknown authorship and Ambroise's *Estoire de la Gloire Sainte.* The most reliable English chronicle is by Richard of Devizes. The standard modern biography is by Kate Norgate *(Richard the Lion Heart),* though there is a more recent account in John Gillingham's *Richard I.*

Kate Norgate has also written *John Lackland* and *England under the Angevin Kings.* The best modern life of John is that by W. L. Warren, a valuable corrective to centuries of virulent dislike by historians, beginning with Walter Map and Matthew Paris *(Chronica Maiora* and *Historia Minor)*.

The best account of Henry III is F. M. Powicke's *King Henry III and the Lord Edward.* There is a history of Edward I by Tout, but the most authoritative accounts of his reign are naturally from the constitutional and legal historians, of whom the greatest is Maitland *(English Constitutional History)*. For the whole of this period Sir Charles Oman covers the military history in his *Art of War in the Middle Ages.*

Tout has also written *The Place of Edward II in English History.* There is an anonymous *Vita Edwardi Secundi* that is contemporary, but a remarkably vivid account may be found in Christopher Marlowe's *Edward II* (produced in 1593).

By 1325 we can go to Froissart's *Chronicles* (in Lord Berners' 1525 translation). He based the work on his own travels and inquiries up to the year 1400. They are splendid reading for the period, but, being based much on oral testimony, not always reliable. Joshua Barnes wrote a *History of Edward III* that is reliable in spite of its late date (1685).

There is a biography of Richard II by A. Steel, and more specialized book by Gervase Matthew, *The Court of Richard II,* that is full of fascinating detail about the King. The contemporary chronicler is Adam of Usk, with the *St. Albans Chronicle* (1376–1422 with one break) and the *Chronicles of London.*

There is no reliable contemporary account of Henry IV: certainly not Holinshed's *Chronicles,* a compilation which was not published until 1577. A word of warning may be inserted here about Shakespeare. His sources for his historical plays were popular works of his own time which were far from accurate, and he interpreted them according to his own ends. For an extreme example, see the opening of the chapter on Henry V. There is a modern biography of Henry IV by John Lavan Kirby.

The standard biography of Henry V is that of J. H. Wylie, but there are shorter and more recent lives by Harold F. Hutchinson and Peter Earle. The contemporary writers are Thomas Walsingham *(Historia Anglicana)* and Titus Livius Forojuliensis, an Italian in the service of Duke Humphrey of Gloucester. There is an eye-witness report of the Battle of Agincourt in the anonymous manuscript *Henrici Quinti Angliae Regis Gesta* in the British Museum.

The four reigns of Henry VI, Edward IV, Edward V, and Richard III are so closely involved that any work on one is bound to impinge on others. There is no adequate modern work on Henry VI. Eric N. Simmons has written *The Reign of Edward IV,* and Paul Murray Kendall and Anthony Cheetham have both written on the rehabilitation of Richard III. Kendall's *Warwick the Kingmaker and the Wars of the Roses* is also interesting for the time. There is a fascinating version of the rehabilitation of Richard III in Josephine Tey's *The Daughter of Time,* where the death of Edward V is treated as a problem of detective fiction. The chroniclers here are notoriously unreliable, as we are now coming to the age of the early Tudors, who saw to it that the historians supported their cause. The Croyland Chronicle is moderately good on Edward IV, but Hall *(The Union of the two Noble and Illustre Famelies of Lancastre and Yorke),* Holinshed, Polydore Vergil *(Anglica Historia),* Rous *(Historia Regum Angliae),* and Thomas More (The History of Richard III), are all tainted by Tudor propaganda. There is a not very enlightening account of Edward V in the Italian

APPENDIX III

Dominic Mancini's *De Occupatione Regni Angliae per Ricardum Tertium Libellus.*

The best modern account of Henry VII is by S. B. Chrimes. The contemporary authorities are many, and useful information can be found in Pollard's *Reign of Henry VII from Contemporary Sources.* Philippe de Commines' *Mémoires* contain much interesting material about relations with France and Burgundy; he served the dukes of Burgundy and then Louis XI of France, and was one of the earliest of modern historians to consider his material in a critical fashion. The later parts of Robert Fabyan's *Concordance of Histories* is interesting (he was sheriff of London in 1493), and so are John Stowe's many works.

The standard modern biography of Henry VIII is Scarisbricke's, but the great authority on Tudor times remains A. F. Pollard, who has written extensively. The first half of Henry VIII's reign is more than adequately covered by Garrett Mattingley's biography of Catherine of Aragon, a book that combines scholarship with great narrative pleasure (see below on Elizabeth I). There is a useful book by Elton, *England under the Tudors.*

There is a biography of Edward VI by Hester Chapman *(The Last Tudor King),* and a sympathetic one of Mary Tudor by H. F. M. Prescott (a novelist whose *Man on a Donkey* may be recommended as a work of imagination, set in the 1530s, remarkable for its deep knowledge of Tudor times). A glance at Foxe's *Actes and Monuments,* better known as his *Book of Martyrs,* though it was published in translation from the Latin only in 1563, is immensely enlightening on the religious feeling in England for more than a century after Mary I's death.

For the reign of Elizabeth I there is no better guide than the works of J. E. Neale. For the few years around 1588, the date of the Spanish Armada, there is a splendid book by Garrett Mattingley, a distinguished historian who here has allowed himself to write with the narrative gusto of a novelist. After the present book was written Paul Johnson published a biography with much personal material about the Queen.

The best modern account of James I—a King who has not attracted biographers—is in G. M. Trevelyan's *England under the Stuarts.* For the scandal, some of it unsavory, Sir Walter Scott edited a *Secret History of the Court of James I.*

The undisputed authority on Charles I is C. V. Wedgwood, whose three books, *The King's Peace, The King's War,* and *The Trial of Charles I,* combine the history of the great men with the history of the little men in a way few other historians have achieved. Where she has stated that "the material for the seventeenth century is limitless" (*King's Peace,* bibliographical notes), there is little more that I can say; except that Edward Hyde Lord Clarendon, who was grandfather to two reigning Queens, Mary II and Anne, and one of the chief supporters of the Royal cause from 1641 until his fall from favor in 1667, wrote his *True Historical Narrative of the Rebellion and Civil Wars in England* from his personal knowledge.

The Interregnum does not enter into this book, but the most recent biography of Cromwell is by Antonia Fraser, and there is a useful earlier one by John Buchan. At the Restoration, Clarendon is still an authority, Evelyn's diary covers the period until his death in 1706, and Pepys' diary opens on January 1, 1660. There is also Bishop Burnet's *History of my Own Times;* he was chaplain to Charles II and dismissed in 1674 for disapproving of his monarch's morals, and did not die until 1715. Maurice Ashley has written a biography of Charles II, and Ogg's *Reign of Charles II* is the fullest account and continues into the next reign.

Although it was written more than a century ago, Macauley's *History of England from the Reign of James II* is still a great book; it extends into the reign of William III, but in that reign is incomplete. David Ogg has written *England in the Reigns of James II and William III,* and Maurice Ashley on *The Glorious Revolution* (of 1688). There is a biography of James II by F. C. Turner.

Hester Chapman has written a biography of Mary II, and Stephen B. Baxter one of William III, and there is a more recent one of both husband and wife that is excellent on the personal side by Henri and Barbara van der Zee.

Abel Boyer's *Annals* are interesting for Anne's reign, and her own letters have been published. Winston Churchill's biography, *Marlborough,* covers the period, but the best general history is Trevelyan's *England under Queen Anne.*

Entertaining accounts of the period of the four Georges are contained in Thackeray's *Four Georges,* and in J. H. Plumb's more recent *The First Four Georges.* Single biographies are by Joyce Marlowe (George I), Charles Chenevix Trench (George II), Stanley Ayling (George III), and Christopher Hibbert (George IV). Useful contemporary works are Lord Hervey's *Some Materials for the Memoirs of the Reign of George II,* Horace Walpole's *Memoirs of the Reign of George II* and *Memoirs of the Reign of George III* (he was Sir Robert Walpole's son), the Creevey papers, and the Grenville memoirs.

The most recent life of William IV is by Philip Ziegler, and contemporary material can be found in Watkins, *Life and Reign of William the Fourth,* and A. J. Muley, *Historical Recollections of the Reign of William IV.*

The most outstanding modern biography of Queen Victoria is that of Elizabeth Longford. Cecil Woodham-Smith has so far published only the first volume of hers. There are hundreds of contemporary memoirs, but none more useful than the journals and letters of the Queen herself.

The standard life of Edward VII is by Philip Magnus, and the most entertaining contemporary account Sir Frederick Ponsonby's *Memoirs of Three Reigns.*

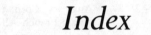

Index

Index

INDEX

ABOUT THE AUTHOR

Jean Morris was born in 1924 in Kent. Her parents came from the Welsh Marches, but she has lived all her life in the South of England. She is a graduate of London University, and has been a professional writer for all of her working life. Her interests include music, English architecture, prehistory, and every aspect of wild life from gardening to ecology. She lives now in Richmond, Surrey, which was the second of the many Richmonds of the English-speaking world, having been renamed by Henry VII after his former Earldom in Yorkshire; she has a daughter, Mercy, born in 1966.